Praise for *The Case Against the Supreme Court*

"Chemerinsky is a superb litigator, a prominent scholar, and a beloved teacher, and all three sets of skills are on display here. *The Case Against the Supreme Court* is unfailingly lucid and, among other things, a good primer on the history of constitutional law."   —Jedediah Purdy, *BookForum*

"Erwin Chemerisnsky has a lot of nerve. Thank goodness. If more scholars had his intellectual power, passion, and pluck, the country would be better off. . . . He has become that most dangerous of fellows—the brilliant, disillusioned idealist who knows what he's talking about; a man committed to change and not incrementally. . . . What I admire most about the book is that Chemerinsky wrote it at all. Reformation of rotten institutions is often a brutal, even bloody business. Yet it often begins with the publishing of a document."
Jonathan Shapiro, *Los Angeles Review of Books*

"He expresses thoughtful criticism where too few others do . . . [with] a thoughtful analysis of a failing institution that deeply affects our way of life. *The Case Against the Supreme Court* is no partisan screed, rather a warning to thinking persons (lawyers or non-lawyers). In reading this book, everyone will hear the canary in the mineshaft. We ignore it at our peril."
—John W. Dean, author of the bestselling *The Nixon Defense: What He Knew and When He Knew It*, in *Verdict*

"This bold work enables us to think more clearly about the Court's decisions which have protected business and state's rights. He shares his evaluations of the Warren Court and the rulings of the John Roberts Court. Best of all, Chemerinsky identifies some changes which might help these nine justices to do a better job in the future."   —*Spirituality and Practice*

"An accessible, refreshingly candid, and no-holds-barred indictment of the Supreme Court."   —*Publishers Weekly*

"Thoroughly researched, well articulated, and incredibly thought provoking . . . An important contribution."   —*Choice*

PENGUIN BOOKS

THE CASE AGAINST THE SUPREME COURT

Erwin Chemerinsky is the founding dean and Distinguished Professor of Law and Raymond Pryke Professor of First Amendment Law at the University of California, Irvine School of Law, with a joint appointment in political science. He is the author of seven other books about constitutional law and he has argued several cases at the Supreme Court. Chemerinsky holds a law degree from Harvard Law School and a bachelor's degree from Northwestern University. He has written for the *New York Times*, the *Los Angeles Times*, and the *Boston Globe*, among many other places. In January 2014, *National Jurist* magazine named him the most influential person in legal education in the United States.

ALSO BY ERWIN CHEMERINSKY

THE
CASE AGAINST
THE
SUPREME COURT

ERWIN CHEMERINSKY

PENGUIN BOOKS

PENGUIN BOOKS
An imprint of Penguin Random House LLC
375 Hudson Street
New York, New York 10014
penguin.com

First published in the United States of America by Viking Penguin,
a member of Penguin Group (USA) LLC, 2014
Published in Penguin Books 2015

THE LIBRARY OF CONGRESS HAS CATALOGED THE
HARDCOVER EDITION AS FOLLOWS:
Chemerinsky, Erwin, author.
The case against the Supreme Court / Erwin Chemerinsky.
p. cm.
Includes bibliographical references and index.
ISBN 978-0-670-02642-5 (hc.)
ISBN 978-0-14-312800-7 (pbk.)
1. United States. Supreme Court.   2. Judicial review—United States.   I. Title.
KF8742.C46 2014
347.73'26—dc23   2014004507

Printed in the United States of America

For my family—

Catherine, Jeff, Kim, Adam, Alex, and Mara

Contents

Contents

THE
CASE AGAINST
THE
SUPREME COURT

Introduction: Assessing
the Supreme Court

arrie Buck was born in 1906 in Charlottesville, Virginia. She was the first of three children born to Emma Buck. Frederick Buck was Carrie's father, but he left Emma soon after their wedding. Unable to afford to care for Carrie, Emma placed her with foster parents, J. T. and Alice Dobbs. Carrie went through the sixth grade at the local public school and by all accounts was a normal child. At age seventeen, while Carrie was still living with her foster parents and helping out with chores around their house, she was raped by a nephew of her foster parents and became pregnant.

The Dobbs blamed Carrie for the pregnancy and were shamed by it. On January 23, 1924, they involuntarily committed Carrie to the Virginia State Colony for Epileptics and Feeble-Minded. A few months later, on March 28, Carrie gave birth there to a daughter, Vivian. The State of Virginia immediately took Vivian away from Carrie and put her in the care of Carrie's foster parents, who ultimately adopted Vivian. As if this story were not tragic enough, the state then sought to have Carrie surgically sterilized by tubal ligation.

Virginia had a new eugenics law that authorized the involuntary surgical sterilization of those deemed to be of low intelligence. Virginia was not alone. By the 1930s, more than thirty states had laws that allowed for the involuntary sterilization of criminals, those of low intelligence, and those with so-called hereditary defects, including alcoholism and drug addiction in some states and even blindness and deafness in others.

A hearing was held before Carrie Buck's sterilization. Harry Laughlin, the drafter of many of these eugenics laws, provided a deposition in Carrie's case. He began his "family history" of the Bucks by writing, "These people belong to the shiftless, ignorant and worthless class of anti-social whites of the South." Laughlin stated that Carrie and Emma were "feeble-minded," as determined by the Stanford-Binet intelligence test, which had recently been created. Carrie, he said, scored a mental age of nine years; Emma, her mother, seven years and eleven months.

Laughlin said that most feeblemindedness is inherited, and Carrie Buck fit this pattern. "Generally feeble-mindedness is caused by the inheritance of degenerate qualities; but sometimes it might be caused by environmental factors which are not hereditary," he said. "In the case given, the evidence points strongly toward the feeble-mindedness and moral delinquency of Carrie Buck being due, primarily, to inheritance and not to environment."

A social worker, Caroline Wilhelm, testified that Carrie's daughter, Vivian, was mentally retarded. At the time of the hearing, Vivian was seven months old. Wilhelm said that "there is a look about it that is not quite normal, but just what it is, I can't tell." She said that the baby seemed "apathetic." She then urged Carrie Buck's sterilization: "I think," she said, "it would at least prevent the propagation of her kind."

We now know that neither Carrie nor Vivian Buck was mentally retarded. Many years later, professor Paul Lombardo found Carrie Buck and wrote: "As for Carrie, when I met her she was reading newspapers daily and joining a more literate friend to assist at regular bouts with the crossword puzzles. She was not a sophisticated woman, and lacked social graces, but mental health professionals who examined her in later life confirmed my impressions that she was neither mentally ill nor retarded."

Vivian Buck died at the age of eight, from enteric colitis. Harvard professor Stephen Jay Gould tracked down her records and found that at the Venable Public Elementary School of Charlottesville, which she attended for four terms—from September 1930 to May 1932, a month before her death—she received passing grades in every subject.

Carrie Buck's sister, Doris, also was surgically sterilized without her consent. Doris was told that she was having an appendectomy, but instead a tubal ligation was performed on her. It was not until 1980 that Doris learned what had been done to her. She, too, was of normal intelligence.

The United States, of course, was not alone in performing surgical sterilizations—vasectomies for men and tubal ligations for women—on those who were deemed "unfit." Before World War II, Nazi Germany subjected 375,000 people to forced sterilization—most for "congenital feebleness," but at least four thousand for being deaf or blind.

But isn't the United States different, because we have a Constitution that protects individual liberties and we have a Supreme Court to enforce it? Carrie Buck's case made it all the way to the Supreme Court in a lawsuit with the doctor who performed the operation, John Bell. A guardian for Buck, R. G. Shelton, filed the case on her behalf and challenged the constitutionality of the Virginia law that authorized involuntary sterilizations. Buck's attorney, Irving Whitehead, argued that her fundamental rights had been violated by surgically sterilizing her without her consent and that forced sterilization was "cruel and unusual punishment." After all, Carrie Buck had committed no crime and had done nothing wrong. She was involuntarily institutionalized by her foster parents after she was raped. Buck's case was the vehicle for challenging state eugenics laws that were being used to surgically sterilize the "unfit" all across the country.

But the Supreme Court, in *Buck v. Bell*, in 1927, ruled against her by an 8–1 margin. None other than the eminent Justice Oliver Wendell Holmes Jr. regarded as one of the greatest jurists in American history, wrote the opinion for the Court against her. Before being appointed to the Supreme Court in 1902, Holmes had fought in the Civil War, been a professor at Harvard Law School, and served as a justice and chief justice of the Massachusetts Supreme Judicial Court. He served for thirty years on the United States Supreme Court before retiring at age ninety. His opinions in many areas, such as those arguing in favor of protection of freedom of speech, are among the most revered in American history.

In *Buck v. Bell,* Holmes began his opinion by stating that "Carrie Buck is a feeble-minded white woman who was committed to the State Colony. . . . She is the daughter of a feeble-minded mother in the same institution, and the mother of an illegitimate feeble-minded child." Justice Holmes, writing for the almost unanimous Court, then upheld the Virginia law and the constitutionality of the sterilization of Carrie Buck. The Court said that sterilizing her could not be deemed cruel and unusual "punishment" because she had not been convicted of any crime. The Court then went further, not only upholding the Virginia law that Buck was challenging, but defending the desirability of eugenics laws. Justice Holmes said that such eugenics laws are desirable because they keep the country from being "swamped with incompetence." In some of the most offensive and insensitive language to be found in the *United States Reports,* Holmes declared, "It is better for all the world, if instead of waiting to execute degenerate offspring for crime, or to let them starve for their imbecility, society can prevent those who are manifestly unfit from continuing their kind. The principle that sustains compulsory vaccination is broad enough to cover cutting the Fallopian tubes. Three generations of imbeciles are enough."

Thousands more were surgically sterilized as a result of this decision. In the United States, by 1935, more than twenty thousand forced sterilizations had occurred, nearly half in California. In fact, at the Lynchburg Hospital, where Buck was sterilized, four thousand individuals were involuntarily surgically sterilized, some as late as 1972. Altogether, according to attorney John G. Browning, "over 60,000 Americans nationwide were subjected to salpingectomies [the removal of one or both of a woman's fallopian tubes], vasectomies, or castrations."

How can this be? How could the Supreme Court have failed so miserably? It is not that her case was poorly briefed or argued. It is not that the justices could not perceive the inhumanity and injustice in surgically sterilizing a young woman without her consent. In fact, most lower courts to consider the issue prior to *Buck v. Bell* had declared involuntary sterilization unconstitutional. It is simply that the Court sided with the government and failed to protect an individual from a horrific abuse of power.

Evaluating the Supreme Court

Throughout this book, I tell stories of instances in which the Supreme Court sanctioned terrible injustices. The examples are drawn from throughout American history and from every area of constitutional law.

For more than thirty years I have taught these cases and been outraged by them. I have wanted to believe that they are the exceptions to the Supreme Court's overall successful enforcement of the Constitution. But as the years went by, as the cases that seem misguided—even tragically so—filled my casebook and my syllabus, I came to realize that it is time for me to reexamine the Supreme Court. It is important to ask directly the question, Has the Supreme Court been a success or a failure?

My conclusion is the thesis of this book: The Court has frequently failed, throughout American history, at its most important tasks, at its most important moments. This is not easy for me to conclude or to say. Almost forty years ago, I decided to go to law school because I believed that law was the most powerful tool for social change and that the Supreme Court was the primary institution in society that existed to stop discrimination and to protect people's rights. In a society filled with inequalities and injustices, the civil rights lawyers of the 1950s and '60s were the model for what I wanted to be.

I have been teaching, writing, and litigating about constitutional law for more than thirty years now. I have argued cases before the Supreme Court. I am the author of the leading law school textbook about constitutional law. Through it all, I have uncritically assumed that despite obvious missteps the Supreme Court has done far more good than harm. But now, as I try to assess the performance of the Court, all of my years of studying, teaching, and practicing constitutional law have convinced me that the Supreme Court is not the institution that I once revered. It has rarely lived up to these lofty expectations and far more often has upheld discrimination and even egregious violations of basic liberties.

My disappointment in the Court is both historical and contemporary. One need only look at the Court's decisions from the past few years—preventing employment discrimination suits and class actions against the largest corporations, keeping those injured by misconduct of generic drugmakers from having any recovery, denying remedies to those unjustly convicted and detained—to see what has historically been true: the Supreme Court usually sides with big business and government power and fails to protect people's rights. Now, and throughout American history, the Court has been far more likely to rule in favor of corporations than workers or consumers; it has been far more likely to uphold government abuses of power than to stop them.

I realize, of course, that there needs to be a rubric for assessing whether the Court is succeeding or failing. One measure is the decisions of the Court, like *Buck v. Bell,* that are uniformly condemned by subsequent generations of scholars and judges. Can anyone seriously contend that the Court was not mistaken, terribly so, in its ruling against Carrie Buck? To make the case against the Supreme Court, I will focus especially on examples like this, where virtually everyone today—liberal and conservative alike—can agree that the Court was wrong.

Why Have a Constitution?

Before we can judge the Court, we have to know why it exists. This in turn requires thinking about what the Constitution is meant to accomplish. I begin every constitutional law class, whether for law students or undergraduates, by asking them a basic question: Why have a Constitution? Why, in 1787, was it desired, and why have it today?

It is easy to describe what the Constitution does. The Constitution both empowers and limits government; it creates a framework for American government, but it also limits the exercise of governing authority by protecting individual rights. It creates the institutions of American government—Congress, the president, the Supreme Court and federal judiciary—defines how they are chosen, delineates key aspects of how they operate, and grants powers to each. It also specifies, especially in the Bill of Rights, the liberties that people possess upon which the government cannot infringe.

But that does not address the question I pose to my students: Why accomplish these things through a constitution? Great Britain, for example, has no written constitution. In the Netherlands, no court has the power to declare any law unconstitutional; in fact, its judiciary is prohibited from doing so. The governments in these countries are not totalitarian.

If no constitution existed in the United States, there likely would have been some initial informal agreement creating the institutions of government, and those institutions would have determined both the procedures of government and its substantive enactments. For example, the framers at the Constitutional Convention, in Philadelphia in 1787, could have served as the initial legislature and, in that capacity, devised a structure of government embodied in a statute that could have been altered by subsequent legislatures.

The key difference between this approach and the Constitution is that the latter is far more difficult to change. Whereas legislative enactments can be modified by another statute, the Constitution can be amended only by a much more elaborate and difficult procedure. Article V of the Constitution prescribes two ways of amending the Constitution. One is for both houses of Congress, by a two-thirds vote, to propose an amendment that becomes effective when ratified by three-fourths of the states. All twenty-seven amendments to the Constitution have been adopted through this procedure. The other mechanism outlined in Article V, though never used, is for two-thirds of the states to call for Congress to convene a constitutional convention that would propose amendments for the states to consider. These amendments, too, would require approval of three-fourths of the states in order to be ratified.

Therefore, a defining characteristic—indeed, *the* defining characteristic—of the American Constitution is that it is very difficult to alter. It has been amended only seventeen times in the more than 220 years since the first ten amendments were ratified in 1791 in the form of the Bill of Rights. (And two of those seventeen amendments enacted and then repealed Prohibition.) Thus, in focusing on the question "Why have a Constitution?" the real issue is: Why should a society generally committed to majority rule choose to be governed by a document that is very difficult to change? Harvard law professor Laurence Tribe puts the question succinctly: "[W]hy would a nation that rests legality on the consent of the governed choose to constitute its political life in terms of commitments to an original agreement—made by the people, binding on their children, and deliberately structured so as to be difficult to change?"

It is hardly original or profound to answer this question by observing that the framers chose to create their government in a constitution deliberately made difficult to change as a way of preventing tyranny of the majority, of protecting the rights of the minority from oppression by social majorities. They did not place the structure of government in a statute that could be easily changed; history shows that there is often an overwhelming tendency to create dictatorial powers in times of crisis. If protections of individual liberties were placed only in statutes, a tyrannical government could overrule them. If terms of office were specified in a statute rather than in the Constitution, those in power could alter the rules to remain in office.

Thus, a constitution represents an attempt by society to limit itself in order to protect the values it most cherishes. A powerful analogy can be drawn to the famous mythological story of Ulysses and the Sirens, from Homer's *Odyssey*. Ulysses, fearing the Sirens' song, which seduced sailors to their death, had himself bound to the ship's mast to protect himself from temptation. Ulysses's sailors plugged their ears with wax so they would be immune to the Sirens' call, whereas Ulysses, tied to the mast, heard the Sirens' song but was not harmed by it. Despite Ulysses's pleas for release, his sailors followed his earlier instructions and kept him bound and safe from the Sirens' song. His life was saved because he recognized his weakness and protected himself from it.

A constitution is society's attempt to tie its own hands, to limit its ability to fall prey to weaknesses that might harm or undermine cherished values. History teaches that the passions of the moment can cause people to sacrifice even the most basic principles of liberty and justice. The Constitution is society's attempt to protect itself from itself. The Constitution enumerates basic values—regular elections, separation of powers, individual rights, equality—and makes change or departure very difficult.

Although the analogy between the Constitution and Ulysses is appealing, there is a problem: Ulysses tied only his own hands; a constitution binds future generations. No one alive today had the chance to participate in deciding whether to be governed by the American Constitution, and few of us even had ancestors who were part of approving the document. The survival of the Constitution likely is a reflection of the widespread belief, throughout American history, that it is desirable to be governed under it. Indeed, one enormous benefit of the Constitution is that it is written in terms sufficiently general and abstract that almost everyone in society can agree to them. For example, people disagree about which speech should be protected and under which circumstances—there is great disagreement over whether the First Amendment should protect pornography or hate speech—but there is almost universal agreement that there should be protection for freedom of speech. The Constitution thus serves as a unifying device, increasing the legitimacy of government and government actions. Stanford professor Thomas Grey observed that the Constitution "has been, virtually from the moment of its ratification, a sacred symbol, the potent emblem . . . of the nation itself."

Why the Supreme Court?

The primary reason for having a Supreme Court, then, is to enforce the Constitution against the will of the majority. In a democracy, the majority can protect itself through the political process; it is minorities—political, racial, social, economic—that need protection that democracy often cannot and will not provide.

Therefore, I believe that the two preeminent purposes of the Court are to protect the rights of minorities who cannot rely on the political process and to uphold the Constitution in the face of any repressive desires of political majorities. This is why the justices of the Supreme Court, and of the lower federal courts, are granted life tenure and can be removed from office only by the very difficult method of impeachment by the House of Representatives and conviction by two-thirds of the Senate. Judges with these protections, it always has been hoped, will be more likely to safeguard minorities and enforce the Constitution against repressive desires than government officials who are elected and are accountable to the voters.

These purposes, then, provide the criteria for all of us to use to evaluate the Court: How has it done in protecting the rights of minorities of all types? How has it done in upholding the Constitution in the face of the repressive desires of political majorities?

My thesis, developed in the chapters of this book, is that the Court has largely failed at both of these tasks. Throughout American history, the Court usually has been on the side of the powerful—government and business—at the expense of individuals whom the Constitution is designed to protect. In times of crisis, when the passions of the moment have led to laws that compromise basic rights, the Court has failed to enforce the Constitution.

This reality is often overlooked because we all share the perception that the Court is "objective" and decides questions based on the law, separate from the ideologies of the justices. There is thus a sense that it is the "law," not the justices, that is responsible for the Court's decisions. This is nonsense and always has been. The Court is made up of men, and now finally women, who inevitably base their decisions on their own values, views, and prejudices.

The Court's choice in 1857 to hold that slaves are property and not citizens, which paved the way for the Civil War, reflected the fact that a majority of the justices had been slave owners. The Court's choice in 2011 to deny any recovery to a man who spent eighteen years on death row for a crime that he did not commit reflects a Court composed of conservatives who favor government power over individual freedom. The broad, open-ended language in the Constitution means that decisions in important cases are products of who is on the Court and their personal views. What is "cruel and unusual punishment," and whether a life sentence for shoplifting violates this, depends entirely on the ideology of the justices on the bench at the time the case comes before them. What is "equal protection," and whether that is violated by a system that executes more African Americans than whites for the same crimes, likewise is a function of the values of the nine justices. Whether pornography and hate speech are entitled to protection under the First Amendment depends on who is on the Court, and their values.

To be clear, I am not saying that the Supreme Court has failed at these crucial tasks every time. Making a case against the Supreme Court does not require taking such an extreme position. I also will talk about areas where the Court has succeeded in protecting minorities and enforcing the limits of the Constitution. My claim is that the Court often has failed where and when it has been most needed. That is the case against the Supreme Court that this book presents.

There have been thousands and thousands of Supreme Court decisions, and I, of course, can discuss only a fraction of these. I realize that it is possible to respond to my criticisms by arguing that I have focused on the atypical mistakes. All branches of government, all institutions, err; a case could be made against any of them by pointing to their worst mistakes. But I believe that the case against the Supreme Court is more than that. I focus on the Court's most important responsibilities and argue that the justices have failed especially at the times when they were needed most. I believe that by looking at the Court over the sweep of its history and by considering many different areas of law, a convincing case can be made for the Court's failure that answers the charge that I am cherry-picking the unrepresentative mistakes.

I am sensitive, too, to the criticism that this is no more than a liberal's critique of a Court that through American history has been largely conservative. To answer this, I focus especially on Supreme Court decisions that both liberals and conservatives today would consider grave mistakes. My goal is to show why both liberals and conservatives should see the Court as failing relative to its core missions under the Constitution. I recognize, of course, that there is no way to exclude ideology when evaluating the Court, any more than there is a way for the justices to decide cases divorced from their own ideologies. My goal, though, is to show why those of all political views should be deeply troubled by the Supreme Court's performance throughout American history.

So What Should We Do About It?

What should we do about the Court, and how should we think about it in light of its historic and contemporary failure? Do we really need, or even want, a Supreme Court and lower courts with the power to strike down laws and executive actions?

If looked at over the entire course of American history, given that the case against the Supreme Court is such a strong one, should judicial review—the power of the federal courts and the Supreme Court to invalidate executive and legislative acts—be kept? And if it is to be kept, what changes can be made to better ensure that it will fulfill the purposes intended by the framers of the Constitution? It is these questions, too, that this book seeks to answer.

The book is divided into three parts, looking roughly at the past, the present, and the future. Part I considers the Court's performance over the course of American history. First, I look at the Court's overall record with regard to protecting racial minorities. Second, I focus on the Court's performance in upholding the Constitution in times of crisis. Third, I discuss the Court's decisions that have protected business and states' rights. In each chapter, I seek to answer this question: Has the Court, overall, made society better off than it would have been without it? In addressing these questions, I look at both the Court's historical and contemporary performance in these areas.

The fourth chapter then addresses a question that is raised by my students and that I've always pointed to in defending the Court: What about the Warren Court? Wasn't it a great success in enforcing the Constitution? After all, it ordered an end to segregation, expanded the rights of criminal defendants, enforced a separation of church and state, and ordered the reapportionment of state legislatures. I applaud the Warren Court and in many ways see it as a model for what the Court can be. But even here, if I force myself to be honest, as I explain in chapter 4, it was much less of a success than I have always assumed.

Part II of the book examines the Court today, the John Roberts Court. Roberts became chief justice in 2005, and there is now an ample record by which we can assess the Court under his leadership. Chapter 5 examines the failure of the Roberts Court to protect people—employees, consumers, and all of us—from abuses by business. It thus has continued the disturbing pattern that has been present throughout American history. Chapter 6 focuses on the Roberts Court's failure to protect people from abuses of government power. Chapter 7 addresses the question that was in the back of my mind as I was writing this book: Is the current Court really so bad? In answering this question, I focus especially on its decisions regarding the political process: *Bush v. Gore* (decided by the Rehnquist Court in 2000); *Citizens United v. Federal Election Commission,* which in 2010 gave corporations the right to spend unlimited amounts of money in elections; and *Shelby County, Alabama v. Holder,* in 2013, which struck down crucial provisions of the Voting Rights Act of 1965. As I argue, these decisions have caused great harm to the political process in the United States and made the country much worse off than it would have been without the Supreme Court.

Part III considers whether, in light of this record, the Supreme Court—and, more specifically, the power of judicial review—should be kept, and if so, what might be changed so that the Court is more likely to succeed in its role of upholding the Constitution. Chapter 8 asks whether it is worth keeping the Court and judicial review. Some prominent scholars have called for the elimination of the power of judicial review, and, after recounting the Supreme Court's failures, it is a tempting solution. But I conclude that the Court's failures were not inevitable, and that despite its failings the Court is essential as a check on the democratic process. My conclusion is that we should look for ways to change the Court and its processes to make it better.

In chapter 9, I consider why the Court has so often failed and how the Court might be reformed to make success more likely. I propose a host of reforms—some simple to implement, others more difficult—that together could make a difference and improve the chances that the Court in the future will succeed at its core missions of protecting minorities and enforcing the Constitution.

I conclude with a short chapter about how we should think and talk about the Supreme Court. We should realize that this is an emperor that truly has no clothes. For too long, we have treated the Court as if they are the high priests of the law, or at least as if they are the smartest and best lawyers in society. We have pretended that the Court is a neutral body, discovering the law and then mechanically applying it. But none of these perceptions are correct. The Court consists of nine human beings who decide hard questions about the meaning of the Constitution. Their decisions are the product of their life experiences, their views, and their values. Antonin Scalia and Ruth Bader Ginsburg so often disagree—in about half of the cases decided each year—not because one of them is smarter or knows the Constitution better. They diverge because of their ideologies. Now, and throughout American history, the Supreme Court's decisions have been the product of the justices and their values and views. Only after we've recognized this reality will we be able to discuss and appraise the Court in a useful way.

The book is thus an attempt to carefully examine one of the major institutions of American government, one that affects each of us, often in the most important and intimate aspects of our lives. I am sure that all will agree that some of the mistakes I identify are serious errors by the Court; others are more controversial; and in some cases, readers might not share my conclusions. But I seek to challenge all of us to think more critically about the Court and to confront the reality that, by any measure, it has too often failed at its most important responsibilities under the Constitution.

The Fate of Carrie Buck

Soon after her sterilization, Carrie Buck was released from the Lynchburg Hospital. She married Charles Detamore, and they remained together until her death. She and her sister, Doris, both expressed great regrets that they were not able to have additional children. Carrie Buck died in 1983, at age seventy-six.

Of the thousands who were surgically sterilized by the government without their consent, Carrie Buck's story can most easily be told, because her case made it all the way to the Supreme Court and has been researched and documented. It was Carrie Buck whom Oliver Wendell Holmes wrote about in such cruel and degrading language.

In 1942, fifteen years after *Buck v. Bell,* the Court declared in *Skinner v. Oklahoma* that the right to procreate is a fundamental right protected under the liberty of the Due Process Clause. *Skinner,* like *Buck v. Bell,* involved a state law adopted as part of the eugenics movement. The Oklahoma Habitual Criminal Sterilization Act allowed courts to order the sterilization of those convicted two or more times for crimes involving "moral turpitude."

The Court, in an opinion by Justice William O. Douglas, declared the Oklahoma law unconstitutional and spoke broadly of the right to procreate as a fundamental right:

> We are dealing here with legislation which involves one of the
> basic civil rights of man. Marriage and procreation are

fundamental to the very existence and survival of the race. The power to sterilize, if exercised, may have subtle, far-reaching and devastating effects. In evil or reckless hands it can cause races or types which are inimical to the dominant group to whither and disappear. There is no redemption for the individual whom the law touches. . . . He is forever deprived of a basic liberty.

Perhaps *Skinner* reflects the waning of the eugenics movement that had inspired the laws challenged in both cases. Surely, fighting in World War II against the Nazis, with their attempt to create a master race, also helped make these laws unpalatable. What is clear is that in *Skinner,* the Court said what it should have declared in *Buck v. Bell.* Astoundingly, though, *Skinner* did not overrule *Buck v. Bell* or try to distinguish it. In fact, to this day, *Buck v. Bell* never has been expressly overruled by the Supreme Court. Twenty-two states still have laws on the books that allow the government to impose surgical sterilization on those deemed mentally retarded.

Buck v. Bell is not the only or the last case in which the Court failed when a person was surgically sterilized without consent. In July 1971, Ora Spitler McFarlin went to see a judge in his chambers in DeKalb County, Indiana. She said that she was concerned about her fifteen-year-old daughter, Linda. The mother said that the girl was "somewhat retarded" (although Linda attended public school and was promoted each year with her class), and Ora was concerned that Linda was staying out overnight with older men. The mother asked the judge to issue an order to have the girl surgically sterilized. Ora said that sterilizing Linda would "prevent unfortunate circumstances."

Although the judge lacked authority under Indiana law to issue such an order, he did so. Linda was told that her appendix was being taken out, when actually she was being surgically sterilized. She learned the true nature of the operation later, when she was married and unable to conceive a child. She then sued, among others, the judge who had approved the operation.

A compelling case can be made that the judge was acting totally without jurisdiction. There was no authority under Indiana law for the judge to hear such a case or issue such an order. No case was filed with the court; there were no pleadings, and no docket number was assigned. Neither the girl nor any representative for her was present or allowed to respond. No semblance of due process was provided to Linda before her ability to have children was permanently ended. But the Supreme Court, in a 5–4 decision in *Stump v. Sparkman,* in 1978, ruled against Linda and said that a judge could not be sued under such circumstances, even for an order that lacked any legal basis and inflicted a terrible permanent injury. As Justice Potter Stewart said in a dissent joined by two other justices, "what Judge Stump did on July 9, 1971, was in no way an act 'normally performed by a judge.' Indeed, there is no reason to believe that such an act has ever been performed by any other Indiana judge, either before or since."

Carrie Buck and Linda Sparkman lived a half-century apart, but they both suffered a great loss and a violation of a basic constitutional right: the government took away from them the ability ever to have a child. It did so without a good reason. The Supreme Court could have ruled in their favor, and in doing so it would have protected so many others from a similar fate. But the Court failed to do so, ruling against both of them without expressing the slightest bit of compassion for what they suffered.

PART I

THE PAST:
THE SUPREME COURT
IN HISTORY

CHAPTER 1

Protecting Minorities

The word *slavery* is not mentioned in the Constitution. Nor is *race*. Nor is "equal protection" found in the document drafted in Philadelphia in 1787. The latter is not surprising, because the Constitution explicitly protects the institution of slavery and the rights of slave owners. If the failures of the Supreme Court are to be chronicled, the place to begin must be race. And to be fair, that failure begins with the Constitution itself.

Slavery, though not mentioned, was clearly written into the Constitution. Delegates from southern states never would have agreed to a constitution, and southern states never would have ratified one, if it did not protect the rights of slave owners. For example, Article I, Section 2 of the Constitution allocates representation in the House of Representatives based on the number of free persons and "three fifths of all other persons," a reference to slaves.

Article I, Section 9 of the Constitution declared that, until 1808, Congress could not ban the importation "of such persons as any of the states now existing shall think proper to admit." That is, Congress could not limit the slave trade or keep states from importing more slaves for at least twenty years after the adoption of the Constitution. Article V of the Constitution, which delineates the process for constitutional amendments, identifies only two provisions in the document that cannot be amended: the restriction on Congress limiting the importing of slaves and the requirement that every state have equal representation in the Senate.

Article IV, Section 2 of the Constitution says that "[n]o person held in service or labor in one state . . . escaping to another shall . . . therein be discharged from such service or labor, but shall be delivered up on claim of the party to whom such service or labor may be due." Known as the Fugitive Slave Clause, this provision decreed that if a slave managed to escape to a non-slave state, he or she was not free and had to be returned to his or her owner. The Constitution was thus explicit in protecting the rights of slave owners and in treating slaves as pieces of property.

I always ask my students whether, if they had been at the Constitutional Convention in Philadelphia in 1787, they would have voted to ratify a constitution that so clearly and expressly protected the institution of slavery. I ask them to imagine that they were from a northern state and that they believed that slavery was abhorrent and incompatible with everything they held dear. It was clear at the time that southern states would not have approved a constitution that lacked these provisions and failed to protect the institution of slavery. Would it have been better to allow the country to be split into two (or maybe more) separate nations rather than accept a document that enslaved so many for so long?

Interestingly, one of the most common answers I receive from my students is that they would have voted for the Constitution and then expected the Supreme Court, over time, to interpret the document to protect the rights of slaves and to gradually eliminate the institution of slavery. Their hope was that the Court, whose members have life tenure and never have to face election, would have had the courage to stand up for basic human decency and worked to eliminate a practice that was inconsistent with the most elemental notions of humanity.

But it didn't work out that way at all. Quite to the contrary, at every opportunity until the Civil War, the Supreme Court acted to protect the rights of slave owners and denied all rights to those who were enslaved. Consider, for example, a case from 1842, *Prigg v. Pennsylvania*. Pennsylvania adopted a law that prevented the use of force or violence to remove any person from the state in order to return the individual to slavery. Notice that the Pennsylvania law did not give freedom to slaves who had escaped to the state. Nor did it prevent the removal of slaves from Pennsylvania in order to return them to their owners. All Pennsylvania did was prevent "force or violence" to remove and return slaves. Every state has an interest—indeed, a duty—to preserve order and prevent violence.

The Fugitive Slave Act of 1793, adopted by the second Congress, required that judges return escaped slaves to their owners. The Pennsylvania law did not say otherwise. In *Prigg*, though, the Supreme Court relied on this act and the Fugitive Slave Clause in Article IV of the Constitution to invalidate the Pennsylvania law. Justice Joseph Story wrote the opinion for the Court. Story was one of the most revered justices in American history and the youngest person ever appointed to the Supreme Court, having taken his seat on that bench at age thirty-two. He was a justice for thirty-four years, from 1811 to 1845, and in 1833 published the highly influential *Commentaries on the Constitution of the United States,* which are still cited to this day. There is a dormitory named for him at Harvard Law School and even a town in Iowa named Story in his memory.

Surprisingly, Justice Story's place in history does not appear to have been significantly tarnished by what he wrote in striking down the Pennsylvania law preventing force or violence to remove slaves who had escaped into the state. Writing for the Court, Story said that the "object of this clause was to secure to the citizens of the slaveholding states the complete right and title of ownership in their slaves, as property, in every state in the Union into which they might escape from the state where they were held in servitude." The Court said that the Fugitive Slave Clause "was so vital . . . that it cannot be doubted that it constituted a fundamental article, without the adoption of which the Union could not have been formed." Thus, the Court concluded that "we have not the slightest hesitation in holding that under and in virtue of the Constitution, the owner of a slave is clothed with entire authority, in every state in the Union, to seize and recapture his slave." The Court also emphasized that the government could punish those who harbored fugitive slaves.

Prigg v. Pennsylvania is typical of the Supreme Court's attitude toward slavery for the first seventy years of American history. At no point prior to the Civil War did the Supreme Court significantly limit slavery or even raise serious questions about its constitutionality or legitimacy. The importance of slavery as a social and political issue during this period cannot be overstated. It was, as it had to be, the central dispute of the time and affected the debate of almost all other matters. The Supreme Court certainly could have influenced that debate in a positive way to hasten the elimination of slavery, but it did just the opposite.

The Court's failure with regard to slavery was most evident in one of the most infamous and universally condemned decisions of all time: *Dred Scott v. Sandford,* in 1857.

In 1819, a major national controversy surrounded the admission of Missouri as a state. The question was whether Missouri and other areas covered by the Louisiana Purchase would be free states or slave states. In a compromise that was intended to resolve the issue, known as the Missouri Compromise, Congress admitted Missouri as a slave state but prohibited slavery in the territories north of latitude 36°30'. Territories below this line could decide whether to allow slavery and could make that choice when admitted as states.

In *Dred Scott v. Sandford,* the Supreme Court declared the Missouri Compromise unconstitutional and broadly held that slaves were property, not citizens. Dred Scott was a slave in Missouri, owned by John Emerson. He was taken by Emerson into Illinois, a free state. After Emerson died, his estate was administered by John Sandford, a resident of New York. Scott sued Sandford in federal court and claimed that his residence in Illinois made him a free person. Scott asked the court to hear his case under a constitutional provision and a federal statute that allow a citizen of one state to sue a citizen of another state in federal court. This authority of federal courts to hear cases when there is "diversity of citizenship" continues to this day. An automobile accident between someone from California and someone from New York can be litigated in federal court solely because they are from different states, so long as there is a claim for more than $75,000 (the current "amount in controversy" requirement for such suits to be heard in a federal court).

The United States Supreme Court ruled against Scott in a decision that fills more than two hundred pages in the *United States Reports*. Chief Justice Roger Taney wrote the opinion for the Court. Taney was the fifth chief justice of the United States and served in that role from 1836 until his death, in 1864. Unlike Joseph Story, whose reputation does not seem sullied by his rulings in favor of slavery, Taney will forever be most remembered for his reviled opinion in *Dred Scott*.

The Court held that slaves, including Dred Scott, were not U.S. citizens; they were just property. Therefore, they could not sue under the law that allowed a citizen of one state to sue a citizen of another state. The Court explained that when the Constitution was ratified, slaves had been considered "as a subordinate and inferior class of beings, who had been subjugated to the dominant race." The Court reviewed the laws that existed in 1787 and concluded that a "perpetual and impassable barrier was intended to be erected between the white race and the one which they had reduced to slavery." Even a slave born in the United States was not a citizen of this country. Nothing in the Constitution required this conclusion; the Court could have defined "citizens" to include slaves.

If this had been all the Court did, its opinion would deserve universal reprobation for deeming an entire group of human beings to be chattels, merely property of their owners. But the Court went far beyond this. Even though the Court concluded that it lacked jurisdiction to hear Scott's suit, it went on and declared the Missouri Compromise unconstitutional. This was only the second time in American history that the Supreme Court had declared a federal law unconstitutional. The first was *Marbury v. Madison*, in 1803, which established the power of the federal judiciary to declare laws unconstitutional and invalidated a minor provision concerning Supreme Court jurisdiction.

In *Dred Scott*, the Supreme Court ruled that Congress could not grant citizenship to slaves or their descendants; this would be a taking of property from slave owners without due process or just compensation.

Congress's eliminating slavery in territories north of the specified line in the Missouri Compromise was deemed an impermissible taking of property from slave owners. The Court concluded: "[T]he right of property in a slave is distinctly and expressly affirmed in the Constitution. . . . [I]t is the opinion of the court that the act of Congress which prohibited a citizen from holding and owning property of this kind in the territory of the United States north of the line therein mentioned, is not warranted by the Constitution, and is therefore void." Hence, any federal law that sought to limit slavery was unconstitutional if it had the effect of freeing a single slave, because it was taking property away from its owner.

For Scott, the Court's decision meant that he was not made free by being taken into Illinois; he was forever and permanently the property of his owner. But on May 26, 1857, the sons of Peter Blow, Scott's first owner, purchased emancipation for Scott and his family. Their gaining freedom was national news and celebrated in northern cities. Scott went to work in a hotel in St. Louis, where he was considered a local celebrity, but he died of tuberculosis just eighteen months after being granted his freedom.

Although the Supreme Court undoubtedly thought that it was resolving the national controversy over slavery in *Dred Scott v. Sandford*, the decision had exactly the opposite effect. The ruling became the focal point in the debate over slavery, and, by striking down the Missouri Compromise, the decision helped to precipitate the Civil War.

It is certainly fair to ask whether the fault was with the Supreme Court or really with the Constitution, which protected the institution of slavery. Several years ago, Harvard Law School professor Charles Ogletree had an event at which he asked a group of lawyers, law professors, and judges to debate the question of whether *Dred Scott* was inevitable. Was slavery so written into the fabric of the Constitution that there would inevitably come a point at which protecting it would lead to a decision like *Dred Scott*? Is it fair to expect better from a Court on which a majority of the justices had been slave owners and several still owned slaves?

I raise these questions for my students to consider, too. My own sense is that the Court could have and should have done far better. The Court could have held that slaves were U.S. citizens—especially those who were born in this country. No matter what, it did not need to even reach the question of whether the Missouri Compromise was constitutional. Once it held that it lacked jurisdiction to hear the case, the matter should have been dismissed. That is a basic rule of law that is learned by every first-year law student.

The Court took upon itself trying to resolve the issue of slavery for the nation. That, in itself, reflected enormous hubris. The country had been debating slavery, directly and indirectly, for seventy years. It is hard to imagine that the justices really thought that their ruling could put the issue to rest. But if it was going to try to do so, it is inexcusable that it put all of its chips on the side of slave owners and the institution of slavery. England, by act of Parliament, had abolished slavery throughout its empire in 1833. To say that *Dred Scott* was inevitable is to fail to recognize that justices always have tremendous discretion in their decisions. It is unrealistic to think that the Court could have eliminated slavery all at once, but it could have, in a series of decisions, including *Dred Scott*, slowly chipped away at the repugnant institution. It could have ruled that Scott was a citizen of the United States. It could have said that he was made free by being taken to Illinois. But it did exactly the opposite.

The Post–Civil War Amendments

The Court's record on race did not improve after the Civil War. The Constitution was amended to overturn the *Dred Scott* decision and to eliminate slavery. Three crucial amendments were adopted between 1865 and 1870.

In 1865, the Thirteenth Amendment was passed by Congress and ratified. It prohibits slavery and involuntary servitude and gives Congress the authority to adopt laws to enforce this. The adoption of the Thirteenth Amendment was the focus of Steven Spielberg's recent movie *Lincoln*.

President Lincoln knew that the Emancipation Proclamation, declaring the slaves to be free, was not enough and had no real legal effect; the president lacked the authority under the Constitution to prohibit slavery or to free slaves from their owners. The Supreme Court's decision in *Dred Scott* was still the law: slaves were property of their owners, and to decree otherwise, under that decision, would be an unconstitutional taking of property. Lincoln thought it essential that the Constitution be amended before the end of the Civil War to eliminate slavery and thus to overrule *Dred Scott*. The Thirteenth Amendment was passed by the Senate on April 8, 1864, and after having been initially rejected by the House of Representatives, it was passed by that chamber on January 31, 1865. President Lincoln was assassinated less than three months later, on Friday, April 14, 1865. It wasn't until December 8, seven months after his death, that the Thirteenth Amendment was ratified by the required three-fourths of the states.

After the Civil War, the overwhelming majority of Congress—which was still almost exclusively those from the North—realized that abolishing slavery was not sufficient. There was a need to overturn *Dred Scott* and make clear that slaves were citizens of the United States. There was a need to make sure that states, especially in the former Confederacy, protected the rights of former slaves and that state governments could not violate the rights of their citizens. The Fourteenth Amendment was proposed to do just this. In its first section, it directly overrules *Dred Scott* by declaring that all persons born or naturalized in the United States are citizens of this country. Section 1 also says that no state can deprive any person of life, liberty, or property without due process or deprive any citizen of the privileges or immunities of United States citizenship or deny any person "equal protection" of the laws. This was the first mention of equality in the Constitution.

The Fourteenth Amendment was a major limit on what state governments could do to those within their borders. Indeed, of all the amendments since the Bill of Rights, the Fourteenth Amendment is the most important. It bestowed citizenship on the former slaves, prohibited states from denying any person equal protection, ensured that no person could be deprived of life, liberty, or property without due process of law, and empowered Congress to adopt legislation to implement it. It is through the Fourteenth Amendment that the Bill of Rights has been applied to the states.

Yet of all the amendments, the Fourteenth is the most questionable in terms of the procedures followed for its ratification. It raises the issue— one that I put to my students—of whether its legitimacy is questionable because of how it was adopted.

Soon after the Fourteenth Amendment was proposed, the legislatures of Georgia, North Carolina, and South Carolina rejected it. Congress was furious and saw this as an attempt by Southern states to undermine the North's victory in the Civil War. Therefore, in Section 5 of the Reconstruction Act, Congress specified that no rebel state would be readmitted to the Union and entitled to representation in Congress until it ratified the Fourteenth Amendment. The Reconstruction Act, adopted over President Andrew Johnson's veto just days before his scheduled impeachment trial, also created military rule over the states of the Confederacy. Johnson was a native of Tennessee, and his sympathies in many ways were with the Southern states, such as in his opposition to the terms and manner of Reconstruction.

New governments were created in these states, and the three states that had rejected it, along with most of the other Southern states, then ratified the Fourteenth Amendment. They had no choice and they knew it. However, Ohio and New Jersey, which had ratified the amendment, subsequently passed resolutions withdrawing their ratification.

Nonetheless, on July 20, 1868, the secretary of state issued a proclamation that the required three-fourths of the states (twenty-eight of the thirty-seven states) had ratified the amendment. His list included the Southern states that had initially rejected the amendment but had later approved it because of coercion from Congress, and Ohio and New Jersey, even though they had rescinded their ratification. The following day, Congress passed a concurrent resolution declaring that the Fourteenth

Amendment was a part of the Constitution because it had been ratified by three-fourths of the states. The list of ratifying states included Ohio and New Jersey. Many years later, the Supreme Court recited this history and said that nonetheless the Fourteenth Amendment was properly ratified.

One more constitutional amendment was ratified, not long after the Civil War, to create racial equality. This was the Fifteenth Amendment, in 1870, which provides that the right to vote cannot be denied on account of race or previous condition of servitude. It, too, authorizes Congress to adopt laws to enforce it.

The Thirteenth, Fourteenth, and Fifteenth Amendments were adopted to transform government, especially with regard to race. They were a major shift in power from the state governments to the national government. I am always bemused, if not outraged, by discussions of "states' rights" under the Constitution that focus on what the framers intended in 1787 and totally disregard how the post–Civil War amendments completely changed the Constitution in this regard.

But the promise of these amendments went largely unrealized for almost a century, until the Warren Court in the mid-1950s, and especially *Brown v. Board of Education,* in 1954. The failure was clearly the Supreme Court's; its very cramped view of the post–Civil War amendments began almost immediately after their ratification. To be fair, there is plenty of blame to go around, and racism was deeply embedded in the country, limiting what any court could do. Yet an important part of the story is that the Court did nothing to advance racial equality for almost ninety years after the Civil War and instead used its power and influence to limit the protections of the post–Civil War amendments. There can be a debate over how far the Court could have gone, but there can be no dispute that for nearly a century it did nothing helpful in the area of race.

The first Supreme Court case to interpret the Thirteen and Fourteenth Amendments came soon after they were ratified, in the Slaughter-House Cases of 1873. Seeing a huge surplus of cattle in Texas, the Louisiana legislature gave a monopoly in the slaughterhouse business for the City of New Orleans to the Crescent City Live-Stock Landing and Slaughter-

House Company. The law required that the company allow any person to slaughter animals in the slaughterhouse for a fixed fee. The monopoly was created to give enormous profits to a small group of people in Louisiana. They could cheaply buy Texas cattle and then sell them for monopoly profits.

Several butchers brought suits challenging the grant of the monopoly. They argued that the state law impermissibly violated their right to practice their trade. The butchers invoked many of the provisions of the recently adopted constitutional amendments. They argued that the restriction created involuntary servitude, deprived them of their property without due process of law, denied them equal protection of the laws, and abridged their privileges and immunities as citizens.

The Supreme Court narrowly construed all of these provisions and rejected the plaintiffs' challenge to the legislature's grant of a monopoly. At the outset, the Court said that it recognized the importance of the case before it as the first to construe the post–Civil War amendments. Justice Samuel Freeman Miller, writing for the Court, said, "No questions so far reaching and pervading in their consequences, so profoundly interesting to the people of this country, and so important in their bearing upon the relations of the United States, and of the several States … have been before this court during the official life of any of its present members." Having recognized the significance of the case, the justices then proceeded to write a broad opinion negating much of what the post–Civil War amendments were meant to accomplish.

The Court said that the purpose of the Thirteenth and Fourteenth Amendments was solely to protect former slaves. Justice Miller wrote that "[t]he most cursory glance at these articles discloses a unity of purpose, when taken in connection with the history of the times … [that there was] one pervading purpose found in them all," namely, "the freedom of the slave race, the security and firm establishment of that freedom, and the protection of the newly-made freeman and citizen from the oppression of those who had formerly exercised unlimited dominion over him."

The Court then interpreted each of the provisions of the Fourteenth Amendment very narrowly, as if they were written solely to achieve this limited goal. For example, the Court said that the Equal Protection Clause was meant to protect only blacks and offered this prediction: "We doubt very much whether any action of a State not directed by way of discrimination against the negroes as a class, or on account of their race, will ever be held to come within the purview of this provision." That, of course, is not what the Constitution says. The Fourteenth Amendment could have been written so that it was limited to guaranteeing equal protection to former slaves or to those of African descent. But instead it says that "no person" shall be denied equal protection of the laws.

For almost a century after the Slaughter-House Cases, the Court followed this narrow reading of the Equal Protection Clause and refused to use it to stop other types of discrimination. For example, in 1875, two years after the Slaughter-House Cases, the Supreme Court held that it was constitutional to deny women the right to vote. Virginia Minor, a leader of the women's suffrage movement in Missouri, attempted to register to vote on October 15, 1872, in St. Louis County. Missouri refused to allow this, because she was a woman. Her husband, Francis Minor, who was a lawyer, filed a lawsuit against Reese Happersett, the registrar who had rejected her application to register to vote. Minor argued that the denial of the right to vote to women violated equal protection and infringed on the "privileges or immunities" of citizenship guaranteed by the Fourteenth Amendment. In *Minor v. Happersett,* in 1875, the Court flatly rejected these contentions and held it constitutional for a state to deny women the right to vote.

It took another forty-five years, until the Nineteenth Amendment was adopted in 1920, for women to be granted the right to vote. It was not until ninety-six years after that, in 1971, that the Supreme Court for the first time found that sex discrimination violated equal protection. The Court's prophecy in the Slaughter-House Cases that equal protection would never be used except to stop race discrimination turned out to be wrong, but it took a century for the Court to abandon that view, which so blatantly ignored the Fourteenth Amendment's assurance that no person may be denied equal protection of the laws.

There are other aspects of the Court's decision in the Slaughter-House Cases that never have been abandoned, despite their very restrictive view of a constitutional amendment that was intended to broadly protect people from state and local government power. Section 1 of the Fourteenth Amendment says that no state "shall make or enforce any law which shall abridge the privileges or immunities of citizens of the United States." Earlier justices had ruled that the phrase "privileges or immunities" referred to fundamental rights that people possess. This provision of the Fourteenth Amendment clearly was meant to ensure that state governments could not infringe on the basic liberties that individuals possess by virtue of being U.S. citizens.

But in the Slaughter-House Cases, the Supreme Court essentially read this provision out of the Constitution. The Court held that the Privileges or Immunities Clause was not meant to protect individuals from state government actions and was not meant to be a basis for federal courts to invalidate state laws. Justice Miller wrote that "such a construction . . . would constitute this court a perpetual censor upon all legislation of the States, on the civil rights of their own citizens, with authority to nullify such as it did not approve as consistent with those rights, as they existed at the time of the adoption of this amendment. . . . We are convinced that no such results were intended by the Congress which proposed these amendments, nor by the legislatures of the States which ratified them." The Court was explicit that "privileges and immunities . . . are left to the State governments for security and protection, and not by this article placed under the special care of the federal government."

It is astounding that five years after the Constitution was amended to prevent states from denying citizens their basic rights, their privileges or immunities of citizenship, the Court said that the federal judiciary could not use that provision to strike down state and local laws. This was immediately evident and was noted by the dissenting justices. Justice Stephen Johnson Field, in dissent, lamented that under the majority's view, the

Privileges or Immunities Clause "was a vain and idle enactment, which accomplished nothing, and most unnecessarily excited Congress and the people on its passage." The entire point of the Fourteenth Amendment, including the Privileges or Immunities Clause, was to limit state and local governments; the Supreme Court in the Slaughter-House Cases ignored this and rendered the Privileges or Immunities Clause a nullity.

In fact, such has been the case: The Privileges or Immunities Clause was rendered meaningless by the Slaughter-House Cases, and it has been ever since. Professor Edward Corwin remarked that "[u]nique among constitutional provisions, the Privileges or Immunities Clause of the Fourteenth Amendment enjoys the distinction of having been rendered a practical nullity by a single decision of the Supreme Court rendered within five years after its ratification." In fact, in the entire history of the Privileges or Immunities Clause, only twice has the Court found anything to violate it, and one of those decisions has been overruled.

If the Court wanted to uphold the Louisiana law, it could have decided the case narrowly by holding that being a butcher, practicing one's trade, is not a "privilege or immunity" of citizenship. Instead, as in *Dred Scott,* the Court decided to rule very broadly and did so in a clearly mistaken and unfortunate way.

Separate but Equal

The Privileges or Immunities Clause might have been used to protect the fundamental rights of African Americans from infringement by state and local governments. But even without it, the Court could have done so under the Equal Protection Clause. In fact, the Slaughter-House Cases even said that this was the basic purpose of the assurance of the provision: protecting those of African descent from discrimination.

But for almost a century, the Court refused to do so. An institution that exists especially to protect minorities did exactly the opposite, consistently upholding laws that harmed minority races. The Court did not create the racist attitudes that led to the laws that required segregation of the races. The Court did not adopt those laws. But the Court could have declared them unconstitutional and held that laws mandating segregation are based on the assumption of the superiority of one race and the inferiority of another and that such a distinction would be inconsistent with a guarantee of equal protection of the laws. Or the Court could have ruled narrowly by finding that the facilities were not equal and that separate and unequal facilities violate the Constitution. Either way, the Court could have prevented and ended the apartheid that lasted for decades.

The most important such case was *Plessy v. Ferguson,* in 1896. It, too, is widely regarded as one of the Supreme Court's worst decisions. In *Plessy v. Ferguson,* the Court upheld laws that mandated that blacks and whites use "separate, but equal facilities."

A Louisiana law adopted in 1890 required railroad companies to provide separate but equal accommodations for whites and blacks; the law required there to be separate coaches, divided by a partition, for each race.

In 1892, Louisiana prosecuted Homer Adolph Plessy, a man who was seven-eighths Caucasian, for refusing to leave the railroad car assigned to whites. This was a test case deliberately brought by those who opposed government-mandated segregation. Plessy—an "octoroon" by virtue of his having one of eight great-grandparents being of African descent—was regarded as the ideal plaintiff to challenge laws like Louisiana's, which had become so common in the South after the end of Reconstruction.

In a 7–1 decision, the Supreme Court ruled against Plessy and upheld the Louisiana law. The opinion was written by Justice Henry Billings Brown, who had been appointed to the Court in 1890 by President Benjamin Harrison. Brown had grown up in Massachusetts and practiced law in Detroit before becoming a federal judge. Although a northerner, Justice Brown concluded that laws requiring "separate, but equal" facilities are constitutional and declared, "[W]e cannot say that a law which authorizes or even requires the separation of the two races in public conveyances is unreasonable, or more obnoxious to the Fourteenth Amendment than the acts of Congress requiring separate schools for colored children in the District of Columbia, the constitutionality of which does not seem to have been questioned, or the corresponding acts of state legislatures." The same Congress that ratified the Fourteenth Amendment also had voted to segregate the District of Columbia public schools, indicating that it did not see government-mandated segregation as a denial of equal protection.

Plessy argued to the Supreme Court that laws requiring segregation were based on an assumption of the inferiority of blacks and thus stigmatize them with a second-class status. Such actions by a state government, deeming one race superior and the other inferior, should be regarded as inimical to the Constitution's guarantee of equal protection of the laws. The Supreme Court rejected this argument: "We consider the underlying fallacy of the plaintiff's argument to consist in the assumption that the enforced separation of the two races stamps the colored race with a badge of inferiority. If this be so, it is not by reason of anything found in the act, but solely because the colored race chooses to put that construction upon it." Stunningly, then, the Court said that it was the fault of the "colored race" that it saw laws segregating the races as being based on a belief in white superiority, even though that notion was often expressed in legislatures and by elected officials, especially in southern states.

Justice John Marshall Harlan was the sole dissenter and wrote that "[e]very one knows that the statute in question had its origin in the purpose, not so much to exclude white persons from railroad cars occupied by blacks, as to exclude colored people from coaches occupied by or assigned to white persons." Of course, he is right: laws requiring segregation were all about proclaiming the superiority of one race and the inferiority of the other. Justice Harlan concluded eloquently that "in view of the Constitution, in the eye of the law, there is in this country no superior, dominant, ruling class of citizens. There is no caste here. Our Constitution is color-blind, and neither knows nor tolerates classes among citizens. In respect of civil rights, all citizens are equal before the law. The humblest is the peer of the most powerful."

Harlan saw the obvious parallel with the Court's decision a

half-century earlier in *Dred Scott v. Sandford*. He wrote: "In my opinion, the judgment this day rendered will, in time, prove to be quite as pernicious as the decision made by this tribunal in the Dred Scott case. . . . The destinies of the two races, in this country, are indissolubly linked together, and the interests of both require that the common government of all shall not permit the seeds of race hate to be planted under the sanction of law."

Justice Harlan, of course, was correct: *Plessy v. Ferguson* is remembered together with *Dred Scott* as being among the most tragically misguided Supreme Court decisions in American history. But it took more than a half-century for the Supreme Court to repudiate its racist holding. After *Plessy*, "separate but equal" became the law of the land, even though separate was anything but equal. Southern states, border states, and even parts of some northern states had laws that segregated the races in every aspect of life. Whites and blacks were born in separate hospitals, played in separate parks and on separate beaches, drank from separate water fountains and used separate bathrooms, attended separate schools, ate at separate restaurants and stayed at separate hotels, served in separate Army units, and were buried in separate cemeteries. By every measure and standard, separate was never equal, as the facilities for blacks were never nearly the same as those for whites.

It is often forgotten today that *Plessy v. Ferguson* was not an isolated Supreme Court decision. In case after case, the Court reaffirmed and upheld the ability of states to enforce apartheid.

For example, "separate but equal" was expressly approved in the realm of education. In *Cumming v. Board of Education*, in 1899, the Court upheld the government's operation of a high school open only to white students while none was available for blacks. The Court emphasized that local authorities were to be allowed great discretion in allocating funds between blacks and whites and that "any interference on the part of Federal authority with the management of such schools cannot be justified except in the case of a clear and unmistakable disregard of rights secured by the supreme law of the land."

In *Berea College v. Kentucky,* in 1908, the Supreme Court affirmed the conviction of a private college that had violated a Kentucky law that required the separation of the races in education. In *Gong Lum v. Rice,* in 1927, the Supreme Court concluded that Mississippi could exclude a child of Chinese ancestry from attending schools reserved for whites. The Court said that the law was settled when it came to racial segregation being permissible and that it did not "think that the question is any different, or that any different result can be reached . . . where the issue is as between white pupils and the pupils of the yellow races."

Is it reasonable to have expected the Supreme Court to have ruled differently? Absolutely. There is no reason that a majority of the justices could not have accepted Justice Harlan's reasoning in *Plessy.* The Court certainly could have decided that laws mandating segregation were inconsistent with a Constitution guaranteeing equal protection of the laws. The Court could have explained that such government-required segregation is based on the premise of the superiority of one race and the inferiority of another, which is inherently a denial of equal protection. The Court's reasoning in *Plessy v. Ferguson* was fundamentally flawed because it ignored the Fourteenth Amendment's mandate of "equal protection" and how government-mandated segregation is inherently at odds with this constitutional requirement.

There is no way around the conclusion that the Court tragically failed in the area of race for the first century and a half of American history.

The End of Separate but Equal

In 1954, this changed when, in *Brown v. Board of Education,* the Court unanimously held that laws requiring segregation of the races violated equal protection. It is often forgotten how close the Court came to an opposite conclusion.

In October Term 1952, the Supreme Court granted review in five cases that challenged the doctrine of separate but equal in the context of elementary and high school education. At the time, seventeen states and the District of Columbia required segregation of their public schools. The school systems challenged in the five cases before the Supreme Court involved schools that were totally unequal. For example, one of the cases was a challenge to South Carolina's educational system. The white schools had one teacher for every twenty-eight pupils; the black schools had one teacher for every forty-seven students. The white schools were brick and stucco; the black schools were made of rotting wood. The white schools had indoor plumbing; the black schools had outhouses.

The five cases were argued together during October Term 1952. The justices could not agree on a decision, and the cases were set for new arguments in the following year. According to Justice William O. Douglas's autobiography, had the Supreme Court ruled then, the decision would have been 5–4 to affirm *Plessy v. Ferguson* and the separate-but-equal doctrine:

> When the cases had been argued in December of 1952, only four of us—Minton, Burton, Black, and myself—felt that segregation was unconstitutional. . . . It was clear that if a decision had been reached in the 1952 Term, we would have had five saying that separate but equal schools were constitutional, that separate but unequal schools were not constitutional, and that the remedy was to give the states time to make the two systems of schools equal.

The Supreme Court asked the parties to brief several questions that focused primarily on the intent of the framers of the Fourteenth Amendment. This did not bode well for those opposing segregation. After all, the same Congress that had ratified the Fourteenth Amendment also passed a law that required segregation of the District of Columbia public schools. Never, though—not before *Brown* and not since—has a majority of the Court taken the "originalist" position that the meaning of a constitutional provision is limited to what its framers intended. The vast majority of justices have realized that even if the original meaning of a constitutional provision could be determined, there is no reason for that interpretation to be controlling. In the words of Chief Justice John Marshall, it is a document that was meant to be adapted and endure for ages to come.

In the summer between the two Supreme Court terms, Chief Justice Fred Vinson died of a heart attack, and President Dwight Eisenhower made a recess appointment of California governor Earl Warren to be the new chief justice. The cases were argued on October 13, 1953, and Chief Justice Warren persuaded all of the justices to join a unanimous decision holding that separate but equal was impermissible in the realm of public education. *Brown* vividly illustrates, as much as any case in American history, the importance of judicial appointments. It is impossible to know what the Court would have done had Fred Vinson still been chief justice, but it is unlikely that the Court would have been unanimous or gone nearly so far as it did in *Brown*. Earl Warren, who had spent decades as an elected official, understood the importance of unanimity and had the personal political skills to make it happen.

Brown and the cases that followed it, ending racial segregation, are the most powerful evidence against my thesis about the failures of the Supreme Court. The Court used its authority and influence to help transform society and to perform its core mission of protecting the constitutional rights of minorities. In chapter 4, I return to *Brown* and the decisions that followed it and argue that the Court did less than it is remembered for and much less than it should have done.

But even conceding the importance and success of these decisions, it must be remembered that it took the Court until 1954—eighty-six years after the ratification of the Fourteenth Amendment and fifty-eight years after *Plessy v. Ferguson*—to get there. Furthermore, the Court's use of the Equal Protection Clause to protect racial minorities was relatively short-lived. Earl Warren was chief justice from 1954 to 1969. After being elected president, in 1968, Richard Nixon quickly had four vacancies to fill on the Supreme Court and picked four justices—Warren Burger, Harry

Blackmun, Lewis Powell, and William Rehnquist—who were far more conservative than the individuals they replaced. Blackmun, over time, became quite liberal, but in his initial years on the Court he so consistently voted together with Burger in a conservative direction that they came to be referred to as the "Minnesota Twins," a reference to their home state's baseball team.

The Modern Court and Racial Equality

The Nixon appointees and the conservative justices who subsequently came onto the Court over the next thirty five years—including Antonin Scalia, Clarence Thomas, John Roberts, and Samuel Alito—have greatly limited the use of the Constitution, and even of government, to achieve racial equality. Two important examples of this are the Court's refusal to allow equal protection challenges based on a law's discriminatory effect against racial minorities and the Court's significantly limiting the ability of the government to use race to benefit racial minorities.

Before explaining this, I should pause to acknowledge that while virtually everyone agrees that decisions such as *Prigg, Dred Scott,* and *Plessy* were tragically wrong, there is no consensus that the Court's race decisions since 1971 have often been misguided. Here, liberals and conservatives disagree. But I would argue that the Court's view of equal protection—simultaneously cramped when racial minorities attempt to use it to challenge discrimination and expansive when whites use it to object to affirmative action—has been a serious obstacle to achieving greater racial equality.

Some laws that are facially race neutral—that is, laws that don't mention race—are administered in a manner that discriminates against minorities or has a disproportionate impact upon them. The Supreme Court has made it almost impossible to challenge such laws as violating equal protection and has held that there must be proof of a discriminatory purpose in order for such laws to be declared unconstitutional. This often makes it impossible to challenge government actions that have the clear effect of disadvantaging racial minorities. Especially now that legislators rarely openly express racism, it is very difficult—and often impossible—to challenge government actions that greatly disadvantage racial minorities.

Washington v. Davis, in 1976, was a key case articulating this limit on the ability to use the Equal Protection Clause to challenge race discrimination. Applicants for the police force in Washington, D.C., were required to pass a test, and statistics revealed that blacks failed the examination much more often than whites. Because of the long history of disparities in education, standardized tests often have a discriminatory impact on racial minorities. Frequently they have no relationship to the job tasks involved in the position for which they are used to screen applicants. The effect is to significantly disadvantage minorities in hiring.

The Supreme Court, however, held that proof of this discriminatory impact was insufficient, by itself, to show the existence of race discrimination or to provide a basis for a challenge under equal protection. Justice Byron White, writing for the majority, said that discriminatory impact "[s]tanding alone . . . does not trigger the rule that racial classifications are to be subjected to the strictest scrutiny and are justifiable only by the weightiest of considerations."

Many times the Court has reaffirmed this principle that discriminatory impact is not sufficient to prove a racial classification, and the clear effect has been to uphold laws that greatly harm racial minorities. For example, in *Mobile v. Bolden,* in 1980, the Supreme Court held that an election system that had the impact of disadvantaging minorities was not to be deemed to violate equal protection unless there was proof of a discriminatory purpose. The case involved a challenge to Mobile, Alabama's use of an at-large election for its city council. Mobile had a three-person city council. It might have, but didn't, divide the city into three election districts. Instead it had an at-large election, in which every voter cast three votes for the three-person city council.

The city was predominantly white but had a sizable African American population. The long history of racially polarized voting in Mobile meant that only whites were elected in the at-large system. In fact, not one African American was elected to the Mobile city council in the twentieth century. Mobile, of course, like the state in which it is located, has a long history of race discrimination. Nonetheless, the Supreme Court found no equal protection violation because there was not sufficient evidence of a discriminatory purpose. The Court declared: "[O]nly if there is purposeful discrimination can there be a violation of the Equal Protection Clause.... [T]his principle applies to claims of racial discrimination affecting voting just as it does to other claims of racial discrimination." Election systems like Mobile's, which significantly disadvantage minority voters, are thus rendered immune from constitutional challenge.

Similarly, in *McCleskey v. Kemp,* in 1987, the Supreme Court held that proof of discriminatory impact in the administration of the death penalty was insufficient to show an equal protection violation. Warren McCleskey, an African American man, was convicted of murder and sentenced to death in Georgia. Statistics powerfully demonstrated racial inequality in the imposition of capital punishment in that state. A study conducted by University of Iowa law professor David Baldus found that the death penalty was imposed in 22 percent of the cases involving black defendants and white victims; in 8 percent of the cases involving white defendants and white victims; in 1 percent of the cases involving black defendants and black victims; and in 3 percent of the cases involving white defendants and black victims. Baldus found that "prosecutors sought the death penalty in 70 percent of the cases involving black defendants and white victims; 15 percent of the cases involving black defendants and black victims; and 19 percent of the cases involving white defendants and black victims." After adjusting for many other variables, Baldus concluded that "defendants charged with killing white victims were 4.3 times as likely to receive a death sentence as defendants charged with killing blacks."

Studies across the country constantly show that the death penalty is administered in a racially discriminatory manner. Prosecutors are more likely to seek the death penalty and juries are more likely to impose it when the defendant is African American or Latino.

The Supreme Court, however, said that for the defendant to demonstrate an equal protection violation, he "must prove that the decisionmakers in his case acted with discriminatory purpose." Because the defendant could not prove that the prosecutor or jury in his case was biased, no equal protection violation existed. Moreover, the Court said that to challenge the law authorizing capital punishment, the defendant "would have to prove that the Georgia Legislature enacted or maintained the death penalty statute because of an anticipated racially discriminatory effect." This is an obviously impossible burden—juries and legislators do not express their racism—and closed the door on constitutional challenges to racial discrimination in administering the death penalty. After the Court rejected his challenge, McCleskey was executed by the State of Georgia.

Cases such as *Washington v. Davis, Mobile v. Bolden,* and *McCleskey v. Kemp* establish that proof of a racially discriminatory impact is not sufficient by itself to prove an equal protection violation; there also must be proof of a discriminatory purpose. This has a huge effect on the law and on people's lives. To pick a single example, federal law imposed punishments for crack cocaine that were as much as a hundred times greater than those for powder cocaine. More than 90 percent of those convicted of crack cocaine offenses were racial minorities, while more than 90 percent of those convicted of powder cocaine offenses were white. The result was an enormous discriminatory effect against African Americans and Latinos, even though evidence showed that both forms of the drug were equally harmful and addictive. Although this disparity was narrowed recently, for years it existed, and a successful constitutional challenge could not be brought because it could not be proven that the purpose of the disparity was to harm racial minorities. There has been a tragic human cost in the greatly disproportionate incarceration of men of color.

It would not have been difficult for the Court to have permitted proof of a racially discriminatory impact to be the basis for an equal protection claim or at least to shift the burden to the government by requiring it to show that its action was based on other than race discrimination. It should be noted that civil rights statutes can, and often do, allow violations to be proved based on discriminatory impact without evidence of a discriminatory purpose. For example, Title VII of the Civil Rights Act of 1964 allows employment discrimination to be established by proof of discriminatory impact, and the Voting Rights Amendments of 1982 permit proof of discriminatory impact to establish a violation of that law. North Carolina had a racial justice law that allowed challenges to death sentences based on proof of a racially discriminatory impact, though it has since been repealed. So the Court could have found proof of a discriminatory effect to be enough to show race discrimination under equal protection. But instead the Court has said that under the Constitution, proof of discriminatory effect is, by itself, insufficient to establish a denial of equal protection.

Proving discriminatory purpose is very difficult; legislators and government officials will rarely say that they are taking an action to harm racial minorities, and even if that is their goal, they usually can articulate some benign purpose for their action. Therefore, many laws with both a discriminatory purpose and a discriminatory effect often will be upheld just because of evidentiary problems inherent in requiring proof of such a purpose. Scholars such as professor Charles Lawrence observe that this is especially true because racism is often unconscious, and such "unconscious racism . . . underlies much of the disproportionate impact of governmental policy." In a society with a long history of discrimination, there should be a presumption that many laws with a discriminatory impact likely were motivated by a discriminatory purpose.

More important, the Court has failed to realize that equal protection should be concerned with the results of government actions and not just their underlying motivations. Professor Laurence Tribe explains: "The goal of the equal protection clause is not to stamp out impure thoughts, but to guarantee a full measure of human dignity for all. . . . Minorities can also be injured when the government is 'only' indifferent to their suffering or 'merely' blind to how prior official discrimination contributed to it and how current official acts will perpetuate it."

Limiting Government Actions to Benefit Minorities

The Court's decisions requiring proof of discriminatory purpose have made it extremely difficult to challenge government actions, even ones with enormous discriminatory impact. At the same time as the Court has adopted this restrictive view of equal protection, it has taken an expansive approach with this constitutional protection when the cases involve whites challenging government affirmative action plans.

The Court repeatedly has held that affirmative action plans to benefit minorities should be treated the same, under equal protection, as government racial discrimination against minorities. All must meet what is called "strict scrutiny," that is, to be upheld it must be shown that they are necessary for achieving a compelling government interest. Put another way, for the government to engage in affirmative action, it must show that it has a truly vital purpose and there is no other way to achieve it. The Court has thus declared that "all racial classifications imposed by government must be analyzed by a reviewing court under strict scrutiny."

But the Court has failed to realize that there is a great difference between the government using racial classifications to benefit minorities and the government using racial classifications to disadvantage minorities. There is a long history of racism and discrimination against minorities, but no similar history of persecution of whites. Professor Richard Lempert forcefully explains the significance of this difference:

> Why does racial discrimination excite us when so many other kinds of discrimination do not? It is because of the way we interpret history, associating racial discrimination with practices that now appear self-evidently evil: forcing blacks from their homeland, enslaving blacks, lynching blacks for actions

that among whites would not be criminal, intimidating blacks who sought to exercise their rights, in sum, systematically disadvantaging a people in almost every way that mattered because of the color of their skin.

But whites, of course, did not suffer this fate. Lempert concludes, "A claim made by a white person as a member of the dominant majority draws its moral force from our collective horror at centuries of oppressing black people. It would be ironic indeed if evils visited on blacks had lent enough force to the moral claims of whites to prevent what appears to many at this point to be the most effective means of eliminating the legacy of those evils."

Achieving social equality requires affirmative action at this point in American history. The tremendous continuing disparities between blacks and whites in areas such as education, employment, and public contracting necessitate remedial action. Applying strict scrutiny greatly impedes such remedial efforts, because relatively little has ever survived this rigorous review.

There is a major difference between a majority discriminating against a minority and the majority discriminating against itself. Professor John Hart Ely explained, "A White majority is unlikely to disadvantage itself for reasons of racial prejudice; nor is it likely to be tempted either to underestimate the needs and deserts of Whites relative to those of others, or to overestimate the cost of devising an alternative classification that would extend to certain Whites the disadvantages generally extended to Blacks."

The significance of the Court's failure to realize this difference is evident in a recent decision, *Parents Involved in Community Schools v. Seattle School District No. 1*, which greatly limits the ability of school boards to remedy racial separation. The case involved public school systems in Louisville, Kentucky, and Seattle, Washington, that had adopted plans that used race as one factor in assigning students to schools to achieve greater racial diversity. Louisville had a program that included all students from kindergarten through twelfth grade. The Louisville school system had previously been segregated by law and had been subject to a judicial desegregation order that had been lifted not long before it adopted its own desegregation plan. Seattle never had been segregated by law and had a plan that used race as one of several factors in assigning students to high schools to achieve greater racial diversity.

The Court, in a 5–4 decision, found both plans to be unconstitutional. All five justices in the majority—Roberts, Scalia, Thomas, Alito, and Anthony Kennedy—agreed that the government must meet strict scrutiny even if it is using race to achieve school desegregation.

Chief Justice Roberts, writing for a plurality of four, found that Seattle and Louisville lacked a compelling interest for their desegregation efforts. Chief Justice Roberts flatly rejected the notion that providing racial diversity in the classroom is a compelling government purpose. All five justices in the majority held that race can be used in assigning students only if there is no other way of achieving desegregation. This will make such desegregation efforts enormously difficult and often impossible.

Justice Stephen Breyer wrote a lengthy dissent joined by Justices Ginsburg, John Paul Stevens, and David Souter that showed the terrible effects of the Court's decision. Justice Breyer described how American public schools are increasingly racially segregated and lamented that the Court's decision will have the effect of placing many effective desegregation plans in jeopardy. Justice Breyer attached an appendix to his dissent that listed the many voluntary desegregation plans that will be in jeopardy in light of the invalidation of the Louisville and Seattle programs. Many have since been struck down or ended because of the Court's decision.

The majority and the dissent have dramatically different views about the importance of diversity in public schools and the meaning of *Brown v. Board of Education*. Chief Justice Roberts sees in the Constitution a command for color blindness. He sees no difference between racial discrimination against minorities and efforts to achieve racial diversity.

By contrast, Justice Breyer and the dissent express the need for deference to school boards in desegregating schools and see the majority as abandoning the promise of *Brown v. Board of Education*. Justice Breyer concluded his dissent by stating, "The last half century has witnessed great strides toward racial equality, but we have not yet realized the promise of *Brown*. To invalidate the plans under review is to threaten the promise of *Brown*. The plurality's position, I fear, would break that promise. This is a decision that the Court and the Nation will come to regret."

In other cases as well, the Court has limited the ability of the government to engage in affirmative action to benefit minorities. In *J. A. Croson v. City of Richmond*, in 1989, the Court said that Richmond, Virginia—the capital of the Confederacy—could not set aside a percentage of public works contracts for minority-owned businesses. The Court came to this conclusion even though minority-owned businesses received less than 1 percent of public works contracts in a city that was more than 50 percent African American. In *Wygant v. Jackson Board of Education*, the Court struck down a school district's plan to retain minority teachers when layoffs were required, even though the result would be very few teachers of color in a school largely composed of minority students. These cases, too, are based on the premise that there is no difference between a program to benefit minorities and a law that discriminates against them.

One area where the Court has allowed affirmative action is higher education. In *Grutter v. Bollinger*, in 2003, the Court held, 5–4, that colleges and universities have a compelling interest in having a diverse student body and that they may use race as one factor in admissions decisions to benefit minorities. In a companion case, decided the same day, *Gratz v. Bollinger*, the Court concluded that colleges and universities may not add points to applicants' admissions scores based on race.

The Court returned to the issue of affirmative action in 2013, in *Fisher v. University of Texas at Austin*. In 2004, the Regents of the University of Texas realized that they had a less diverse student body than they had in 1996. A new admissions plan was adopted. Under it, about 75 percent of the entering class was taken from the top 10 percent of every Texas high school's graduating class. Texas is sufficiently racially segregated that this would produce some racial diversity. The other 25 percent of the class was to be taken by calculating an admissions score for each student. The score would be the sum of two numbers: an academic achievement index, made up of the applicant's grades and test scores, and a personal achievement index, arrived at by grading two essays and looking at six factors, one of which was what the student would add to diversity.

Abigail Fisher, a white high school graduate, applied to the University of Texas in 2008 and was rejected. She enrolled at Louisiana State University, from which she graduated in 2012. After being rejected, she brought a lawsuit against the University of Texas, challenging its use of race as being a denial of equal protection. The federal district court and the United States Court of Appeals for the Fifth Circuit ruled in favor of the University of Texas, saying that it had followed *Grutter* and had permissibly used race as one factor among many in its admissions decisions.

In a 7–1 decision, the Court reversed the Fifth Circuit's decision and remanded the case for reconsideration. Justice Kennedy wrote for the Court. Only Justice Ginsburg dissented, and Justice Kagan was recused.

The Court said that it was not reconsidering *Grutter v. Bollinger* and its holding that colleges and universities have a compelling interest in having a diverse student body. The Court said, though, that *Grutter* had established that any use of race in admissions must meet strict scrutiny and thus must be shown to be necessary for achieving a compelling interest. The Court also said that it is not enough to have a compelling interest in achieving diversity; a college or university also must show that the use of race is necessary for achieving it.

Justice Kennedy wrote that there must be a "careful judicial inquiry into whether a university could achieve sufficient diversity without using racial classifications." In crucial language, the Court said, "The reviewing Court must ultimately be satisfied that no workable race-neutral alternatives would produce the educational benefits of diversity. If a nonracial approach . . . could promote the substantial interest about as well and at tolerable administrative expense, then the university may not consider race."

In one sense, this did not change the law concerning affirmative action. The Court reaffirmed *Grutter*: colleges and universities have a compelling interest in having a diverse student body, but they must meet strict scrutiny if using race as a factor in admissions decisions.

In another sense, though, *Fisher* adopts a tougher, much less sympathetic tone when it comes to affirmative action programs. For example, in *Grutter*, the Court spoke of the need to defer to the judgment of colleges and universities. In *Fisher*, the Court said that such deference was appropriate only with regard to the importance of diversity; there is no deference given as to whether race is necessary for achieving it. Justice Kennedy declared, "The University must prove that the means chosen by the University to attain diversity are narrowly tailored to that goal. On this point, the University receives no deference."

Fisher leaves open many crucial questions, which will need to be decided in this case and in challenges to other affirmative action plans. Colleges and universities use race to gain diversity precisely because other alternatives don't achieve racial diversity. But what kind of evidence is required to show that race-neutral alternatives are insufficient for achieving diversity? Must each institution compile its own evidence, and how much evidence is required? In fact, it is even unclear what qualifies as a "race-neutral" alternative. For example, is a top 10 percent plan—a state university taking the top 10 percent of graduates from around the state—really to be regarded as race neutral? Justice Ginsburg made the point in her dissent that top 10 percent plans are adopted with the intent of creating racial diversity and have that effect. A government action taken with the intent of using race and that has a racially disparate impact is treated as a racial classification under equal protection. In fact, any proxy for race that is done with the purpose and effect of using race is a racial classification.

Nor does the Court offer any guidance about what "diversity" means. In *Grutter*, the Court recognized that there must be a "critical mass" of minority students to attract them to attend and to provide the benefits of diversity. One of the key issues raised in the briefs and oral arguments in *Fisher* was how to determine what is sufficient for a "critical mass." The Court did not address that issue.

Fisher and the other affirmative action cases are significant examples of how much the Court is limiting the ability of government to take action to remedy past discrimination and enhance diversity.

Conclusion: The Court and Race

Having traced the Court's history with regard to race from its earliest days through 2013, the key question is whether, overall, the Supreme Court has made the country better or worse off in the area of racial equality. On one side of the ledger are the ways in which the Court has been an impediment to progressive government efforts regarding race by striking down laws. These include the Court's invalidating state laws to protect fugitive slaves, its declaring the Missouri Compromise unconstitutional, and, in the contemporary era, its limits on affirmative action and, most recently, its striking down a key provision of the Voting Rights Act. In all of these instances, society would have been better off without a Supreme Court; in each area, the Court kept legislatures from doing more to advance racial equality.

Another category of cases is those in which the Court upheld race-related government actions that were undesirable, such as its allowing "separate but equal" and its refusal to allow equal protection challenges based on the racially discriminatory effects of a law. In these cases, the Court did not directly make things worse; if the Court had not existed, governments would have been able to do the same things. But the Court's rulings certainly had indirect undesirable consequences. The Court's express approval of laws mandating racial segregation encouraged them and gave them support from on high. So it is not accurate to say about this category of cases that the Court's effect was neutral; its rulings made racial equality more difficult.

Finally, there is the category of cases in which the Court has been a positive force in moving the country toward racial equality. *Brown v. Board of Education* and the cases that followed it are very important in this regard. The Court struck down Jim Crow laws that segregated every aspect of southern life. It is unlikely that the political process would have done this for many, many years. The Court's desegregation decisions helped spur the civil rights movement and the adoption of landmark civil rights laws in the 1960s, which prohibited discrimination in employment, public accommodations, voting, and housing.

What's the bottom line? The Court, overall, has done much more harm than good with regard to race. The beneficial decisions during the seventeen years of the Warren Court cannot outweigh the horrendous ones in the century and a half before that or the troubling ones since. There is a strong case against the Supreme Court in the area of race. These decisions should weigh heavily in any overall evaluation of the Supreme Court. Race has been a central issue in American society since the Constitution was written. It is a preeminent role of the Court to protect minorities who cannot rely on the political process. The Court, at each moment, realistically could have done so much more.

CHAPTER 2

Enforcing the Constitution
in Times of Crisis

During World War II, 110,000 Japanese Americans—forty thousand aliens and seventy thousand citizens—were uprooted from their longtime homes and placed in what President Franklin Roosevelt called "concentration camps." Many, if not most, of them had their property seized and taken without due process or compensation. They were incarcerated behind barbed wire in the relocation camps and unable to leave. Ethnicity alone was used to determine who was free and who was confined.

Professor William Manchester explains that under Executive Order 9066,

> the people of Japanese descent were given 48 hours to dispose of their homes, businesses, and furniture. During their period of resettlement, they were permitted to carry only personal belongings and hand luggage. All razors and liquor were confiscated. Investments and bank accounts were forfeited. Denied any right to appeal or even protest, Japanese Americans lost $70 million in farm acreage and equipment, $35 million in fruits and vegetables, nearly a half billion in annual income, and savings, stocks, and bonds beyond reckoning. . . .

Beginning at dawn on Monday, March 30th, copies of General DeWitt's Civilian Exclusion Order No. 20, affecting persons of Japanese ancestry, were nailed to doors like quarantine notices. It was a brisk army operation. Toddlers too young to speak were issued tags like luggage, and presently truck convoys drew up. From the sidewalks soldiers shouted, "Out Japs," an order chillingly like what Anne Frank was hearing from German soldiers on Dutch pavements. The trucks took the internees to 15 assembly areas, including a brewery, Pasadena's Rose Bowl and racetracks, at Tanforan and Santa Anita. The tracks were the worst. There, families were housed in horse stalls. The President never visited these bleak garrisons, but he once referred to them as concentration camps. That is precisely what they were. The average family of six or seven members was allowed an apartment measured 20 by 25 feet. None had a stove or running water, each block of barracks shared a community laundry, mess halls, latrines, and open shower stalls where women had to bathe in full view of the sentries.

The human impact of the actions of the U.S. government toward Japanese Americans during World War II cannot be overstated. It is almost beyond comprehension that our government imprisoned 110,000 people—most of them American citizens—solely because of their ethnicity. It is a cruel irony that it occurred at the same time that the United States was fighting Nazi racism and that many of those interned had family members who were serving in the military in Europe.

The constitutionality of the evacuation of Japanese Americans came before the Supreme Court in 1944. By then, any fear of a Japanese invasion of the West Coast was over (not that this fear ever justified imprisoning 110,000 people solely on the basis of their ethnicity). The Court should have emphatically declared the government's action unconstitutional as a denial of equal protection. If equal protection means anything, it surely is that people should never be incarcerated solely because of their race or ethnicity.

But in *Korematsu v. United States*, the Court, in a 6–3 decision, ruled in favor of the federal government and upheld the evacuation of Japanese Americans. The case involved Fred Korematsu, who was appealing his conviction for violating the evacuation order. At the time of his arrest, Korematsu was twenty-two years old. He was born in the United States and an American citizen. He was a welder in a Bay Area shipyard and strongly objected to being ordered to leave his home and his girlfriend (who was Italian American) and to being incarcerated.

Korematsu did everything he could think of to avoid being evacuated and interned. He altered his draft registration card to claim Spanish-Hawaiian ancestry and said his name was Clyde Sarah. Nonetheless, he was arrested in 1942 for violating the exclusion order. He was prosecuted and convicted. He was sentenced to five months probation and sent to Topaz, an overcrowded internment camp in Utah.

Justice Hugo Black, regarded as a great civil libertarian, wrote for the Supreme Court against Korematsu. Black's opinion was joined, by among others, Justice William O. Douglas, remembered as one of the most liberal justices in American history. The Court accepted the government's claim that there was a serious risk to national security from Japanese Americans who were disloyal to the United States and that there was no way of screening to identify such individuals. Justice Black stated:

> Like curfew, exclusion of those of Japanese origin was deemed necessary because of the presence of an unascertained number of disloyal members of the group, most of whom we have no doubt were loyal to this country. It was because we could not reject the finding of the military authorities that it was impossible to bring about an immediate segregation of the disloyal from the loyal that we sustained the validity of the curfew order as applying to the whole group. In the instant case,

temporary exclusion of the entire group was rested by the military on the same ground.

The Court emphasized that it was upholding the order because it was wartime, and "hardships are part of war."

Korematsu is deeply objectionable because the government used ethnicity alone as the basis for predicting who was a threat to national security and who would remain free. The racial classification was vastly over-inclusive: All Japanese Americans were evacuated and interned because a few might be disloyal. In fact, there was no evidence of a threat from any Japanese Americans, and subsequent research by professor Peter Irons has shown that the government's attorneys intentionally exaggerated the risk to persuade the Court to accept the evacuation order. The racial classification also was greatly under-inclusive: Those of other races who, by the same logic, might have posed a threat of disloyalty were rarely interned and evacuated. A much smaller number of individuals of German and Italian descent were detained during World War II. As Justice Frank Murphy lamented in dissent, the evacuation of Japanese Americans was "one of the most sweeping and complete deprivations of constitutional rights in the history of this nation."

Justice Black erred in focusing almost entirely on the ends that the government was seeking to achieve and not nearly enough on the means it was using. It long has been established that the constitutionality of a government action has to be examined both with regard to the ends desired and the means employed. Justice Black said that it was wartime, and, of course, protecting national security is always a compelling government interest. But the mistake that Justice Black made was that he too quickly assumed that incarceration without any form of hearing or due process was necessary for achieving the goal. Why couldn't there have been some form of individual screening to determine whether or not particular individuals were in any way a threat to national security?

In England, over a very short period, there was screening of those who were of German descent. Very few were then evacuated or interned. If

England, facing a much greater danger of invasion, was able to do this, there was no reason the United States could not have engaged in similar screening, rather than mass incarceration.

In the United States, about 40 percent of those incarcerated were children or senior citizens. Many had family members who were serving in the U.S. military. By no means could it be said that the government's actions were necessary for achieving its objective, or even a reasonable way to accomplish it.

This is not just hindsight. Justice Robert Jackson, a Roosevelt appointee to the Supreme Court and before that an attorney general for President Roosevelt, dissented, writing that Korematsu's "crime would result, not from anything he did, said, or thought, different than they, but only in that he was born of different racial stock. Now, if any fundamental assumption underlies our system, it is that guilt is personal and not inheritable."

Justice Frank Murphy, another Roosevelt appointee to the Supreme Court, also dissented. He wrote, "This exclusion of 'all persons of Japanese ancestry, both alien and non-alien,' from the Pacific Coast area on a plea of military necessity in the absence of martial law ought not to be approved. Such exclusion goes over 'the very brink of constitutional power' and falls into the ugly abyss of racism. . . . Justification for the exclusion is sought, instead, mainly upon questionable racial and sociological grounds not ordinarily within the realm of expert military judgment." Justice Murphy powerfully concluded, "I dissent, therefore, from this legalization of racism. Racial discrimination in any form and in any degree has no justifiable part whatever in our democratic way of life. It is unattractive in any setting but it is utterly revolting among a free people who have embraced the principles set forth in the Constitution of the United States."

History has validated the views of Justices Jackson and Murphy; the Court's decision in *Korematsu* is regarded as one of its greatest embarrassments. In 1983, a federal district court judge in San Francisco, Marilyn Patel, overturned Korematsu's conviction on the grounds that the government had knowingly submitted false information to the Supreme Court that adversely affected its appraisal of him. Professor Irons did extensive research, uncovering the lies and false information that had been presented to the courts in Korematsu's case. He persuaded Judge Patel, almost forty years later, to reverse Korematsu's conviction.

In 1998, President Bill Clinton awarded Fred Korematsu the Presidential Medal of Freedom. Korematsu died in 2005, at age eighty-six.

Korematsu upheld the government's infringing the most basic liberties of Japanese Americans solely on the basis of ethnicity, without in any way making the nation safer. During World War II, not one Japanese American was ever accused, indicted, or convicted of espionage or any crime against national security.

Congress recognized the tragedy of what occurred and tried to prevent it from happening again by adopting the Non-Detention Act of 1971, which states, "No citizen shall be imprisoned or otherwise detained except pursuant to an Act of Congress." The legislative history makes it clear that its goal is to prevent a situation like the Japanese internment from reoccurring.

But *Korematsu* has never actually been overruled by the Supreme Court. Although it is widely regarded as a tragic mistake, prominent jurists—such as former chief justice William Rehnquist and federal appeals court judge Richard Posner—have written books defending it and the need for judicial deference to the executive in wartime. Justice Jackson, in his dissent in *Korematsu,* expressed the great danger of this view and of what the Court did: "[T]he Court for all time has validated the principle of racial discrimination in criminal procedure and of transplanting American citizens. The principle then lies about like a loaded weapon, ready for the hand of any authority that can bring forward a plausible claim of an urgent need."

A Pattern

Unfortunately, *Korematsu* fits a pattern that has repeated itself throughout American history. Whenever there has been a crisis, especially a foreign-based crisis, the response has been repression. Fundamental liberties have been denied. The Supreme Court's role is to stop the violation of rights and to enforce the Constitution, but this has not happened. As in *Korematsu,* the Court has upheld the government's actions.

Is it realistic to expect more from the Supreme Court? The justices, of course, live in society and are susceptible to the same pressures and, at times, hysteria that cause the other branches of government to become repressive.

I do believe that we can and should expect the Supreme Court to be the branch to stand up to these pressures and to enforce the Constitution, even when it is unpopular to do so. Supreme Court justices—and all federal judges—are given life tenure and protection from any decrease in salary precisely so that they can be more independent and stand up to majoritarian pressures. Also, a preeminent purpose of the Constitution is to restrain majoritarian passions and make sure that our short-term impulses do not cause us to abandon our long-term values. The justices must see it as their role to accomplish this even when there is great pressure to abandon constitutional protections. If not the Court, then who will protect our most basic liberties and prevent people from suffering greatly from their infringements?

In hindsight, time after time, it is clear that the country was not made any safer by the government's actions or by the Court's upholding them. In this way, *Korematsu* reflects the pattern, not the exception. But the Constitution should not be like a deck chair put out in nice weather and then removed during a crisis. We can and should expect more from the Court than what it has historically done to enforce the Constitution in the face of repressive government actions during crises.

There are many examples of this pattern, including the Supreme Court's decisions during World War I, during the McCarthy era, and since September 11.

World War I and the Punishment of Dissent

It is often forgotten that there was significant dissent within the country to the United States' participation in World War I. There was much opposition to the draft, and it is estimated that there were more than 350,000 draft evaders or delinquents during the war. At about the same time, the success of the Bolshevik Revolution in Russia led to fears of a leftist uprising in this country.

In response to all of this, two months after America's entry into World War I, Congress enacted the Espionage Act of 1917. Among other things, the law made it a crime, when the nation was at war, for any person willfully to "make or convey false reports or false statements with intent to interfere" with the military success or "to promote the success of its enemies." The law also made it a crime to willfully "obstruct the recruiting or enlistment service of the United States." Convictions could be punished by sentences of up to twenty years imprisonment and fines of up to $10,000. The law even gave the postmaster general the authority to block delivery of publications that he deemed to be illegal.

The law thus punished speech, allowing imprisonment for speech that was seen as promoting the success of "enemies" and/or "obstructing recruitment or enlistment in the military." It gave the postmaster the authority to censor speech by refusing to deliver material that he deemed to be subversive. As professor Thomas Healy explains, "The postmaster at the time was perhaps the worst person that power could have been given to. He was Albert Burleson, a reactionary racist from Texas who despised labor unions and the people who supported them. As soon as the new law went into effect, Burleson began a campaign to root out magazines and newspapers that promoted socialist or radical causes."

In 1918, Congress adopted a law even more restrictive of speech than the one enacted the year before. The Sedition Act of 1918 prohibited individuals from saying anything with the intent to obstruct the sale of war bonds; to "utter, print, write, or publish any disloyal, profane, scurrilous, or abusive language" intended to cause contempt or scorn for the form of the government of the United States, the Constitution, or the flag; to urge the curtailment of production of war materials with the intent of hindering the war effort; or to utter any words supporting the cause of any country at war with the United States or opposing the cause of the United States.

The purpose of this law was to punish speech critical of the United States. It was inimical to the very core of the First Amendment's protection of freedom of speech. Freedom of speech is crucial in a democracy. Open discussion of candidates is essential for voters to make informed selections in elections. It is through speech that people can influence their government's choice of policies. Public officials are held accountable through criticisms that can pave the way for their replacement. Alexander Meiklejohn wrote that freedom of speech "is a deduction from the basic American agreement that public issues shall be decided by universal suffrage." He argued that "[s]elf-government can exist only insofar as the voters acquire the intelligence, integrity, sensitivity, and generous devotion to the general welfare that, in theory, casting a ballot is assumed to express." Indeed, the Supreme Court has spoken of the ability to criticize government and government officers as "the central meaning of the First Amendment."

Nonetheless, the 1917 and 1918 laws were not the first attempts by the government to silence its critics. Early in American history, Congress passed the Alien and Sedition Acts of 1798. The law prohibited the publication of

> false, scandalous, and malicious writing or writings against the government of the United States, or either house of the Congress of the United States, or the President of the United States, with intent to defame . . . or to bring them . . . into contempt or disrepute; or to excite against them . . . hatred of the good people of the United States, or to stir up sedition within the United States, or to excite any unlawful combinations therein, for opposing or resisting any law of the United States, or any act of the President of the United States.

The Federalists under President John Adams aggressively used the laws against their rivals, the Republicans. People were imprisoned for speech tamer than what David Letterman and Jon Stewart say on a daily basis. The Alien and Sedition Acts were a major political issue in the election of 1800, and after he was elected president, Thomas Jefferson pardoned those who had been convicted under the laws. The Alien and Sedition Acts were repealed at Jefferson's urging, and the Supreme Court never had to rule on their constitutionality. It took almost a century and a half for the Supreme Court to finally declare, in *New York Times v. Sullivan,* in 1964, "Although the Sedition Act was never tested in this Court, the attack upon its validity has carried the day in the court of history."

The Alien and Sedition Acts and the Espionage and Sedition Acts of 1917–18 fit the pattern described above: in times of crisis, the response is repression. Although the Supreme Court did not have the opportunity to rule on the constitutionality of the Alien and Sedition Acts, it did have the chance to safeguard speech and declare unconstitutional provisions of the 1917 and 1918 acts and their restrictions on expression. Instead, in a series of cases, the Supreme Court upheld the constitutionality of both the laws and their application to speech that, in hindsight, was mild and ineffectual.

In *Schenck v. United States,* in 1919, the Court considered the convictions of two individuals—Charles Schenck and Elizabeth Baer—who had been prosecuted for circulating a leaflet arguing that military conscription violated the Thirteenth Amendment as a form of involuntary servitude. The leaflet was titled "Long Live the Constitution of the United States." It read, "Do not submit to intimidation" and "Assert Your Rights," but it did not expressly urge violation of any law; it only advocated repealing the draft law and encouraged people to write to their representatives in Congress to do so. As professor Thomas Healy pointed out, neither Schenck nor Baer was known as a radical, and neither had ever been arrested. Baer was a physician who had previously run for Congress, and her "most radical proposal was the creation of community kitchens to relieve the drudgery of housework."

There was no evidence that their leaflet had caused a single person to resist the draft. Nonetheless, they were prosecuted, convicted, and sentenced to jail for violating the 1917 Espionage Act. The Supreme Court, in an opinion by Justice Oliver Wendell Holmes, upheld their convictions and sentences; he dismissed as irrelevant that the leaflet had had no effect. He said, "Of course the document would not have been sent unless it had been intended to have some effect, and we do not see what effect it could be expected to have upon persons subject to the draft except to influence them to obstruct the carrying of it out."

The Court said that, although in "many places and in ordinary times" the speech would have been protected by the First Amendment, wartime circumstances made the situation different. In some of the most famous words in the *United States Reports,* Justice Holmes said, "But the character of every act depends upon the circumstances in which it is done. The most stringent protection of free speech would not protect a man in falsely shouting fire in a theatre, and causing a panic. . . . The question in every case is whether the words are used in such circumstances and are of such a nature as to create a clear and present danger that they will bring about the substantive evils that Congress has a right to prevent."

With relatively little elaboration, the Court found that this test was met and upheld Schenck's and Baer's convictions. Yet their speech was the antithesis of falsely shouting "Fire" in a crowded theater or posing a "clear and present danger." The problem is not with the phrase "clear and present danger"; it conveys what should be required to justify punishing speech. The difficulty with the Court's reasoning in *Schenck* is that none of the elements of a clear and present danger were present. The phrase "clear and present danger" connotes a (1) likelihood of (2) imminent, (3) significant harm. Yet the speech of Schenck and Baer arguing that the draft was unconstitutional posed neither a *likely* nor an *imminent* harm to the war effort. The famous analogy to falsely shouting "Fire" in a crowded theater, first articulated by Justice Holmes in *Schenck,* is about a situation in which speech poses a great likelihood of imminent substantial harm. It is about circumstances that don't allow the chance for more speech to respond or prevent the harm. That obviously was not true for the speech of Schenck and Baer.

A week after *Schenck* was announced, the Court upheld convictions under the 1917 act in two other cases: *Frohwerk v. United States* and *Debs v. United States*. Both were part of the same effort by the federal government to punish antiwar speech during World War I.

Jacob Frohwerk was the publisher of a German-language newspaper, *Missouri Staats-Zeitung*. He was tried in federal district court for publishing a dozen articles between June and December 1917. Professor Healy notes that "[f]or the most part, and compared with much antiwar rhetoric, the articles were tame. Several of them criticized England, claiming that it had instigated the conflict to shore up its empire and had manipulated the United States into joining the cause. A few repeated the stock socialist line that the country had gone to war to appease the bankers on Wall Street."

Again, the speech was the antithesis of shouting "Fire" in a crowded theater or any other expression that would pose a clear and present danger. Without doubt, any court today would regard it as expression protected by the very core of the First Amendment. It took the jury only three minutes of deliberation to convict Frohwerk of violating the 1917 Espionage Act, and the judge sentenced him to ten years in prison for his writings.

The Supreme Court had the chance to find that the conviction was a violation of the First Amendment, given that it pertained to speech that posed no danger. Once more, though, the Court failed to enforce the Constitution and upheld the convictions and sentences. Justice Holmes, writing for the Court, acknowledged that there was no evidence that the articles had had any adverse effect on the war effort. But he said that "on the record it is impossible to say that it might not have been found that the circulation of the paper was in quarters where a little breath would be enough to kindle a flame and that the fact was known and relied upon by those who sent the paper out." The Court thus said that Frohwerk could be sentenced to ten years in prison without violating the First Amendment because there was a *possibility* that his speech might have some influence. What is left of freedom of speech if that is all that it takes to punish dissenters?

In *Debs v. United States,* decided on the same day as *Frohwerk* in 1919, the Court affirmed the conviction of Socialist Party leader Eugene Debs, who had been sentenced to jail for ten years for violating the 1917 act. Debs was a national political figure, having run for president in 1900, 1904, 1908, and 1912. Although he never got more than 6 percent of the vote, "he was known, admired, feared, and talked about across the country." Debs opposed American participation in World War I from the time war broke out in Europe in 1914.

Debs was convicted for delivering a speech that was primarily advocacy of socialism but included some mild criticism of the draft. At one point in the long speech, Debs remarked that he had to be "prudent" and not say all that he thought, but that "you need to know that you are fit for something better than slavery and cannon fodder." For this mild statement, Debs was convicted of attempting to incite disloyalty in the military and obstruct the draft.

The Court found it irrelevant that this language was a small part of Debs's speech. Justice Holmes said that the speech was not protected if "one purpose of the speech, whether incidental or not does not matter, was to oppose . . . this war, and if, in all the circumstances, that would be its probable effect." The Court thus said that the speech could be punished if its intent was "to oppose the war." But in a democracy, shouldn't people be able to speak out against any government policy, including whether to go to war? In fact, isn't allowing free speech particularly important when the stakes are the greatest, such as whether the nation will go to war?

In 1921, President Warren G. Harding commuted the remainder of Debs's sentence. Debs died five years later.

These three cases, taken together, are a powerful example of the Supreme Court's failure in a time of crisis. Merely criticizing the United States, even obliquely, was enough to justify being put in prison for a decade. Yet the Supreme Court abandoned the First Amendment and upheld the convictions and sentences.

In the term following *Schenck, Frohwerk,* and *Debs,* in *Abrams v.*

United States, the Supreme Court affirmed the convictions of a group of Russian immigrants who had circulated leaflets, in English and in Yiddish, objecting to America sending troops to Eastern Europe after the Russian Revolution. The defendants' speech had nothing to do with World War I or the draft. Nonetheless, they were convicted of encouraging resistance and conspiracy to urge curtailment of the production of war materials and sentenced to twenty years in prison. The Supreme Court, relying on *Schenck* and *Frohwerk,* upheld the convictions.

Here, though, Justice Holmes, who had written for the Court in *Schenck, Frohwerk,* and *Debs,* dissented, along with Justice Louis Brandeis. This seems a rare instance of a justice changing his mind, and doing so within months. In his dissent, Holmes eloquently articulated a theory of freedom of speech that remains at the core of First Amendment jurisprudence to this day. Holmes invoked the powerful metaphor of the "marketplace of ideas" and wrote that "the best test of truth is the power of the thought to get itself accepted in the competition of the market, and that truth is the only ground upon which their wishes safely can be carried out." Professor Healy observed that Holmes's "metaphor of the marketplace of ideas and his concept of clear and present danger have worked their way into our collective consciousness, becoming part of our language, our view of the world, and our identity as a nation."

Unlike in *Schenck, Frohwerk,* and *Debs,* Holmes believed that the clear-and-present-danger test was not met in *Abrams.* He said, "Now nobody can suppose that the surreptitious publishing of a silly leaflet by an unknown man, without more, would present any immediate danger that its opinions would hinder the success of the government arms or have any appreciable tendency to do so." It can be asked, however, whether the same description might not have been used in *Schenck:* a silly leaflet, circulated by an unknown man, without more.

Justice Holmes claimed that he saw no contradiction between his dissent in *Abrams* and his majority opinions in *Schenck, Debs,* and *Frohwerk.* In *Abrams,* he said that he "never [had] seen any reason to doubt that . . . *Schenck, Frohwerk,* and *Debs* were rightly decided." But in a recent book,

Professor Thomas Healy persuasively shows that Justice Holmes changed his mind and that he had been persuaded by friends such as Harold Laski, Learned Hand, Felix Frankfurter, and Zechariah Chaffee that he had made a mistake in the earlier cases. Holmes and Brandeis could not convince their colleagues of this, though. In *Abrams*, like the decisions from a year earlier, the Court failed miserably to stand up for freedom of speech and the First Amendment.

The McCarthy Era

During the late 1940s and early '50s, Senator Joseph McCarthy led a crusade to identify and exclude Communists in government. It was the age of suspicion—a time when merely being suspected of being a part of a Communist or radical group was enough to cause a person to lose a job or appear on an employment blacklist.

There are many theories to account for the rise of McCarthyism. Following World War II, America's economy was booming, but Europe's remained in shambles. There was great concern that unless Europe's economy quickly rebounded, it could not be a market for U.S. goods, and this could drag the American economy back into a recession. President Harry Truman proposed economic aid to Greece and Turkey. Congressional reaction was lukewarm at best. Truman's advisers told him that he had to "scare the hell out of Congress."

Truman then changed his appeal. He said that the world was in the midst of a battle between democracy and Communism, that Communism bred in poverty, and that fighting Communism required economic prosperity in Europe. This appeal won over Congress, and Truman followed it with the Marshall Plan, which provided economic assistance to Western Europe. It, too, was sold as a way of fighting Communism.

Joseph McCarthy, a senator from Wisconsin, took the lead in the fight against Communists in government. He stood on the floor of the Senate with a bulging briefcase that he said contained the names of

individuals with Communist ties who worked for the federal government. People lost their jobs for being suspected of having Communist
ties. Blacklists developed, in the entertainment industry and other places.
Sometimes people found their names listed because of groups they had
belonged to years or decades before. Sometimes people were there by
mistake. Loyalty oaths became the norm in many professions.

Amid this hysteria, in 1951, *Dennis v. United States* came to the
Supreme Court. This was the Court's chance to enforce the First Amendment in a time of crisis and to stand up to the hysteria of McCarthyism,
which punished people because of their speech and the groups they
joined. Once more, the Court failed.

Dennis involved individuals who had been convicted and sentenced
to prison for organizing people to study four books written by Stalin,
Marx and Engels, and Lenin. Although there was no accusation that they
had done anything other than teach these works, they were convicted of
violating the Smith Act. Section 2 of the Smith Act made it unlawful for
any person "to knowingly or willfully advocate, abet, advise, or teach the
duty, necessity, desirability, or propriety of overthrowing or destroying
any government in the United States by force or violence, or by the assas-
sination of any officer of such government." Section 3 made it "unlawful
for any person to attempt to commit, or to conspire to commit, any of the
acts" prohibited in Section 2.

The defendants were convicted in New York of conspiring to organize
the Communist Party of the United States, which was described as a
group that taught and advocated the overthrow of the U.S. government.
Specifically, their crime was conspiracy to advocate the overthrow of the
U.S. government. Notice that the defendants were not convicted of conspiring to overthrow the government or even of advocating its overthrow;
they were convicted of "conspiracy to advocate."

The Court, in a plurality opinion written by Chief Justice Vinson,
said that the appropriate test was the clear-and-present-danger approach
articulated in *Schenck*. Chief Justice Vinson said that the measure of the
clear-and-present-danger test was a formula articulated by federal appeals

court judge Learned Hand: "In each case [courts] must ask whether the gravity of the 'evil,' discounted by its improbability, justifies such invasion of free speech as is necessary to avoid the danger."

Chief Justice Vinson concluded that the harms of an overthrow of the government are so enormous that the government need not show that the danger is imminent or probable in order to punish speech. He wrote: "Obviously, the words cannot mean that before the Government may act, it must wait until the putsch is about to be executed, the plans have been laid and the signal is awaited. . . . The damage which such attempts create both physically and politically to a nation makes it impossible to measure the validity in terms of the probability of success, or the immediacy of a successful attempt."

In other words, the approach taken by Chief Justice Vinson in *Dennis* makes probability and imminence—two seeming requirements of a clear-and-present-danger test—irrelevant. If the potential harm, such as the overthrow of the government, is great enough, then speech advocating it can be punished without *any* showing of likelihood or imminence. In this case, the individuals were convicted merely for studying the works with others; there was no charge that they were "advocating." Chief Justice Vinson acknowledged that his approach was inconsistent with the position of Justices Holmes and Brandeis, but he said that those justices "were not confronted with any situation comparable to the instant one— the development of an apparatus designed and dedicated to the overthrow of the Government, in the context of world crisis after crisis."

Justice Frankfurter wrote a separate opinion upholding the convictions and urging even more deference to Congress. He said that "[p]rimary responsibility for adjusting the interests which compete in the situation before us of necessity belongs to the Congress." He further said that "[f]ree speech cases are not an exception to the principle that we are not legislators, that direct policy-making is not our province. . . . It is not for us to decide how we would adjust the clash of interests which this case presents were the primary responsibility for reconciling it ours. Congress has determined that the danger created by advocacy of overthrow justifies the ensuing restriction on freedom of speech." It is stunning that Justice Frankfurter gave the Court no role in enforcing the First Amendment.

Not all of the justices were blinded by the Communist threat or accepted the majority's position that speech could be punished without any showing that it posed a serious, or even a minor, threat. Justices Black and Douglas each wrote impassioned dissenting opinions. Each emphasized that the convictions were handed down for nothing more than engaging in speech. Justice Black lamented that the defendants were "not charged with an attempt to overthrow the Government. They were not charged with overt acts of any kind designed to overthrow the Government. They were not even charged with saying anything or writing anything designed to overthrow the Government. The charge was that they agreed to assemble and to talk and publish certain ideas at a later date." Justice Douglas said that, to punish expression, "[t]here must be some immediate injury to society that is likely if speech is allowed." He wrote, "How it can be said that there is a clear and present danger that this advocacy will succeed is . . . a mystery. . . . In America, [the Communists] are miserable merchants of unwanted ideas; their wares remain unsold."

But the majority of the Court gave in to the pressures of the times and abandoned freedom of speech and the First Amendment.

Enforcing the Constitution After 9/11

The next major episode of government repression in the face of a threat did not occur for almost a half-century. But since September 11, 2001, one of the worst aspects of American history has repeated itself. The response to the attack has been to take away rights without any evidence that the exercise of those rights posed a serious danger and without any indication that the country was made safer. Some of what has been done, such as torture, has not made it to the Supreme Court. As for what has come before the Court, once more it has largely failed to check the abuses of power and the violation of rights. There are three areas where the Court has considered civil liberties in the context of the war on terrorism: freedom of speech, electronic eavesdropping, and detentions.

Freedom of Speech. *Holder v. Humanitarian Law Project,* decided in 2010, shares much in common with the World War I speech cases: the Court interpreted a federal law broadly to allow punishment of speech that posed no risk. Federal law prohibits providing "material assistance" to a "foreign terrorist organization." Material assistance is defined as including such activities as "training," "personnel," and "expert advice or assistance." The Humanitarian Law Project brought the suit on behalf of two groups of Americans seeking to establish First Amendment protection for their assistance to groups that had been designated by the Department of State as foreign terrorist organizations.

One group of Americans sought to help a Kurdish group use international law and the United Nations to peacefully work to create a separate country. The other group of Americans sought to help a group in Sri Lanka, which also sought to form a separate nation, apply for humanitarian assistance. It is notable that neither group was aiding terrorist activities in any way, and no one in the litigation claimed otherwise. Both groups just wanted to engage in speech, advising those in foreign countries about how to use the law to achieve their ends.

Nonetheless, the Supreme Court, in a 6–3 decision, ruled that the speech of these two groups of Americans could be punished without violating the Constitution, so long as they had spoken in coordination with a foreign terrorist organization, without any need to prove that they actually assisted terrorism in any way. Chief Justice Roberts, writing for the Court, stressed that the plaintiffs could speak out on any topic they wished, but if the speech was done in concert with a foreign terrorist organization, it was not protected by the First Amendment. He wrote, "Under the material-support statute, plaintiffs may say anything they wish on any topic. They may speak and write freely about the PKK and LTTE, the governments of Turkey and Sri Lanka, human rights, and international law. They may advocate before the United Nations. . . . [T]he statute is carefully drawn to cover only a narrow category of speech to, under the direction of, or in coordination with foreign groups that the speaker knows to be terrorist organizations." Chief Justice Roberts stressed the need for great judicial deference to the judgment of the president and Congress.

Justice Breyer's dissenting opinion, joined by Justices Ginsburg and Sonia Sotomayor, criticized the majority for allowing the punishment of speech without any proof that it was likely to cause harms. Justice Breyer reviewed the Supreme Court's decisions concerning incitement of illegal activities and said that they do not justify allowing punishment of the speech of the sort the plaintiffs sought to engage in. He explained that prior cases had permitted "pure advocacy of even the most unlawful activity—as long as that advocacy is not 'directed to inciting or producing imminent lawless action and . . . likely to incite or produce such action.'"

As in *Schenck, Debs, Frohwerk,* and *Abrams,* from the World War I era, the Court allowed individuals to be punished for their speech without the slightest showing that the speech was likely to cause harm. The Court's opinion in *Humanitarian Law Project* did not even mention the need for a clear and present danger to justify restricting speech.

Electronic Eavesdropping. We likely know only a fraction of what the government has done in the area of illegal surveillance since 9/11. In June 2013, Edward Snowden disclosed classified documents showing that the National Security Agency was obtaining "metadata" from service providers, such as Verizon, containing the telephone numbers people called. Other surveillance was revealed through aggressive investigative reporting. In December 2005, the *New York Times* revealed that the NSA was intercepting and listening to telephone calls and reading e-mails, without a warrant or probable cause, between individuals in the United States and others in foreign countries. The NSA traditionally had never intercepted calls in the United States; its doing so with communications by those lawfully in the country was a major change in policy.

New York Times reporter Eric Lichtblau, who broke the story with his colleague James Risen, explained that "the idea that the NSA was running the operation was a seismic shift in how domestic surveillance was carried out." He quoted a former government official who said that it "is almost a mainstay of this country that the NSA only does foreign searches."

The *New York Times* had the story of the NSA surveillance for a year before the paper published it. Top Bush administration officials, including the president himself, implored the *Times* not to reveal the wiretapping. The president told the publisher and editors of the paper that "blood would be on their hands" if they disclosed the secret spying.

There is no doubt that this program was illegal. The Fourth Amendment says that searches, including government wiretapping and electronic surveillance, require a judicially approved warrant. The law has long been clear that when the government listens to a person's calls or reads his or her e-mail communications, this constitutes a "search" within the meaning of the Fourth Amendment. The Foreign Intelligence Surveillance Act (FISA) of 1978 explicitly states that the government may engage in electronic eavesdropping only with a warrant, either from a federal district court or from the Foreign Intelligence Surveillance Court. The Bush program violated this law. No challenge ever was heard by the Supreme Court—the Court denied review in the primary case that would have given it an opportunity to review the constitutionality of this program.

After this program was revealed, in 2008, Congress amended FISA to allow the government to intercept electronic communications with persons in foreign countries. Under the amended version of FISA, the government is not required to show that the target of the electronic interception is an agent of a foreign power or to specify the nature and location of each place at which electronic surveillance will occur. Upon the issuance of an order from the Foreign Intelligence Surveillance Court, "the Attorney General and the Director of National Intelligence may authorize jointly, for a period of up to 1 year . . . the targeting of persons reasonably believed to be located outside the United States to acquire foreign intelligence information." Interceptions—listening to phone calls and reading e-mails—include communications between these persons in foreign countries and those in the United States.

On the day that the 2008 amendments were enacted, a lawsuit was brought on behalf of attorneys and human rights, labor, legal, and media organizations who alleged that their work required them to engage in sensitive and sometimes privileged telephone and e-mail communications with colleagues, clients, sources, and other individuals located abroad. The plaintiffs said they believed that some of the people with whom they exchanged foreign intelligence information were likely targets of surveillance. They claimed that their communications were chilled because of fear that the government was listening, and thus that their First Amendment rights were violated.

For example, plaintiff lawyers said that the concern over the interception and monitoring of attorney-client discussions required that they refrain from electronic communications altogether with those in foreign countries who might be targets of surveillance. The lawyers said that the only way to ensure secure communications with their clients would be to travel to the foreign countries at great cost and inconvenience.

The Supreme Court, in an opinion by Justice Alito, ordered the case dismissed and held that the plaintiffs lacked standing because they could not show that it was likely that their communications would be intercepted. The Court declared: "[I]t is speculative whether the Government will imminently target communications to which respondents are parties." Because the government does not reveal which communications it intercepts under FISA, the Court said that the plaintiffs "merely speculate and make assumptions about whether their communications with their foreign contacts will be acquired."

The Court rejected the argument that the chilling of the plaintiffs' speech was sufficient to allow standing and said that "[a]llegations of a subjective 'chill' are not an adequate substitute for a claim of specific present objective harm or a threat of specific future harm."

The result is that likely no one will have standing to challenge the constitutionality of the secret interception of communications between those in the United States and those in foreign countries. If these plaintiffs do not have standing, it is impossible to imagine who could sue. The National Security Agency does not tell people when it is intercepting their calls. An allegedly unconstitutional government practice is rendered unreviewable in the courts. The Court said that this does not matter. Quoting earlier decisions, the Court stated, "The assumption that if respondents have no standing to sue, no one would have standing, is not a reason to find standing."

The plaintiffs argued that the government's interception chills their communication and that this violates the First Amendment. The Court's error was in failing to recognize that the loss of these communications is itself a harm within the meaning of the First Amendment. The plaintiffs' injury does not depend on whether their communications were actually intercepted, but instead on whether they had a reasonable fear that this would occur, such that they refrained from electronic communications with these clients. The reasonable fear of communications being intercepted, and the resultant chilling of speech, should have been sufficient for standing to bring a challenge and have the Court rule on the constitutionality of the law.

The Court required far more certainty of harm than it did in prior cases. Justice Breyer, writing for the dissent, explained, "As our case law demonstrates, what the Constitution requires is something more akin to 'reasonable probability' or 'high probability.' The use of some such standard is all that is necessary here to ensure the actual concrete injury that the Constitution demands. . . . [T]hat standard is readily met in this case."

The Court did not deny that—or even address whether—the secret interception of the plaintiffs' communication violated the rights of American citizens. The Court's opinion focused entirely on whether the plaintiffs had standing to bring the lawsuit. In other words, even assuming, as the Court was required to do, a serious violation of the First

Amendment, no one would have standing to challenge it. This just cannot be right.

Detentions. Since 9/11, the federal government has engaged in preventive detention—holding people without due process for long periods—on a scale, and for lengths of time, unlike any in American history. In the summer of 2013, there were still 166 prisoners at Guantánamo Bay, Cuba, and some of them have been there since 2002 without having had a trial or even a meaningful factual hearing.

At first glance, the Supreme Court's record with regard to these detentions seems mixed. On closer examination, though, it becomes clear that the Court has largely failed to enforce the Constitution and to protect human beings from arbitrary imprisonment.

The Court thus far has considered detentions in three contexts: American citizens apprehended in the United States and held as enemy combatants; American citizens apprehended in a foreign country and then held in the United States as enemy combatants; and non–United States citizens held in Guantánamo. Each raises somewhat different constitutional and legal issues.

First, the most clearly unconstitutional government action has been the detention of a U.S. citizen apprehended in the United States and then held as an enemy combatant. José Padilla is an American citizen who was apprehended at Chicago's O'Hare Airport in May 2002. He was accused of planning to build and detonate a "dirty bomb" in the United States. For almost four years—from May 2002 to January 2006—Padilla was held as an enemy combatant and was not indicted or tried for any crime. Padilla says that during this time he was tortured by means that included extreme sleep deprivation, shackling, stress positions, long periods of solitary confinement, and the involuntary administration of psychotropic drugs.

The Bush administration claimed that Padilla could be held indefinitely as an enemy combatant without being indicted or tried for any crime, even though he was arrested in the United States for actions occurring in the United States. That is clearly wrong. The Bush administration was claiming no less than the ability of the president to suspend the Fourth Amendment, which requires a judge-issued warrant for an arrest; the Fifth Amendment, which requires a grand jury indictment before a person is held for trial; and the Sixth Amendment, which says that a person can be imprisoned only after conviction by a jury based on proof beyond a reasonable doubt.

Under the Bush administration position, why could Timothy McVeigh and Terry Nichols not have been held as enemy combatants for bombing the Federal Building in Oklahoma City? There never would have been a need to try them. Why couldn't any drug dealer be held as an enemy combatant as part of the "war on drugs"? Indeed, what is to stop the government from unilaterally designating anyone, such as a liberal (or conservative) critic, an enemy combatant and imprisoning the person indefinitely without trial?

The Supreme Court twice had the opportunity to declare such detentions unconstitutional but failed to do so. After his arrest, Padilla was taken to New York. A lawsuit challenging his confinement, a petition for a writ of habeas corpus, was filed on his behalf in federal court in New York. Shortly thereafter, Padilla was transferred to a military prison in South Carolina. But the litigation over his detention and rights remained in New York and ultimately in the federal court of appeals there.

In June 2004, the Supreme Court, in a 5–4 decision, with the majority opinion written by Chief Justice Rehnquist, concluded that the federal court in New York lacked the authority to hear Padilla's habeas corpus petition. The Court said that a person must bring a habeas petition in the jurisdiction where he or she is being detained, against the person immediately responsible for the detention. Padilla needed to file his habeas petition in South Carolina, against the head of the military prison there.

Justice Stevens wrote for the four dissenters and lamented that Padilla, who already had been held for more than two years at that point, had to start all over again. There was no dispute that the New York courts had jurisdiction to hear Padilla's suit under the Constitution and federal statutes. Nonetheless, the Court said that Padilla had to bring his petition for habeas corpus in federal court in South Carolina. But this makes little sense; the same lawyers would be defending the United States and the detention of Padilla whether he was at the time being held in New York or South Carolina.

Ironically, it appeared clear that Padilla had five votes on the Supreme Court that it was illegal to hold him as an enemy combatant. In a footnote near the end of his dissenting opinion, which was joined by three other justices, Justice Stevens expressly stated that he agreed with the court of appeals that there was no legal authority to detain Padilla as an enemy combatant. Justice Scalia, who voted with the majority, nevertheless was emphatic in his dissent in another case—*Hamdi v. Rumsfeld*, decided the same day and discussed below—that an American citizen cannot be held without trial as an enemy combatant unless Congress suspends the writ of habeas corpus. And yet he was unwilling to join the four more liberal justices in allowing Padilla to challenge the constitutionality of his confinement.

After Padilla's case was dismissed by the Supreme Court, he filed a new habeas petition in federal court in South Carolina. The federal district court ruled in Padilla's favor and held that the government either had to criminally charge Padilla or release him from custody. However, the United States Court of Appeals for the Fourth Circuit reversed and found presidential power to detain Padilla, an American citizen, as an enemy combatant.

At this point, Padilla again sought Supreme Court review. The U.S. government knew that it almost certainly would lose in the Supreme Court, because there were five justices already on record as saying that it was unconstitutional for the government to detain an American citizen as an enemy combatant.

After Padilla filed his petition for Supreme Court review, in November 2005, the United States issued an indictment of Padilla, so he was now charged with a crime and no longer would be held as an enemy combatant. The United States then asked the Supreme Court to dismiss Padilla's case as moot. The United States Court of Appeals for the Fourth Circuit, which had ruled in favor of the government at every opportunity, was outraged. It expressed its belief that the government was gaming the system, holding Padilla as an enemy combatant as long as it could but knowing all along that it would charge him with a crime before the matter got back to the Supreme Court.

In January 2006, the Supreme Court agreed with the government and dismissed the matter as moot; Padilla was objecting to his being held as an enemy combatant, and he was no longer being detained on that basis. The Court could have heard the case regardless, under a long-standing principle that allows courts to decide cases when they become moot because of the actions of one of the parties, but it declined to do so. Padilla was tried, and in 2007 he was convicted of materially assisting a foreign terrorist organization and sentenced to seventeen years and four months in prison.

The Court had two opportunities to hold that the government cannot detain American citizens as enemy combatants for actions occurring in the United States. Such authority is inconsistent with the most basic rights and the most elemental concepts of checks and balances. The Supreme Court never did so.

The Court also considered the detention of American citizens apprehended in a foreign country and held in the United States. Yaser Hamdi was captured in Afghanistan, among a group of surrendering Taliban fighters, and brought to Guantánamo Bay. There it was discovered that he was an American citizen, and he was taken to a military prison in South Carolina. He was held as an enemy combatant and not charged with any crime. His situation was identical to that of John Walker Lindh, except that Walker was indicted and pled guilty to crimes, while Hamdi was never indicted or tried.

The United States Court of Appeals for the Fourth Circuit agreed with the government that an American citizen apprehended in a foreign country and held as an enemy combatant is not entitled to any form of due process or judicial review. A person in this situation could be imprisoned indefinitely without trial.

On June 28, 2004, the Supreme Court held, 5–4, that it was permissible for the government to detain Hamdi as an enemy combatant, though it also said that he had to be given some form of due process. Hamdi contended that his detention violated the Non-Detention Act, the law adopted by Congress in 1971 to prevent another situation like the Japanese internment. The Non-Detention Act states that "[n]o citizen shall be imprisoned or otherwise detained by the United States except pursuant to an Act of Congress."

A plurality of four justices—Justice Sandra Day O'Connor, joined by Chief Justice Rehnquist and Justices Kennedy and Breyer—concluded that Hamdi's detention was authorized pursuant to an act of Congress: the Authorization for Use of Military Force, passed after September 11. Justice O'Connor stated that this constituted sufficient congressional authorization to meet the requirements of the Non-Detention Act and to permit detaining an American citizen apprehended in a foreign country as an enemy combatant. Justice Thomas, the fifth vote for the government on this issue, concluded in a separate opinion that the president had inherent authority, pursuant to Article II of the Constitution, to hold Hamdi as an enemy combatant.

The other four justices vehemently disagreed. In a powerful dissenting opinion, Justice Scalia, joined by Justice Stevens, argued that there is no authority to hold an American citizen in the United States as an enemy combatant without charges or trial, unless Congress expressly suspends the writ of habeas corpus. Justice Souter, in an opinion joined by Justice Ginsburg, contended that it violates the Non-Detention Act to hold an American citizen as an enemy combatant. Souter argued that Congress must expressly authorize such detentions and that it had not done so.

The Court thus said that Hamdi could be detained indefinitely as an enemy combatant and that he did not need to be charged with any crime. The Court did say that Hamdi had to be given due process, though it did not specify the procedures that had to be followed. The justices said that

Hamdi had to be given a meaningful factual hearing. At a minimum, this included notice of the charges, the right to respond, and the right to be represented by an attorney. The Court, however, suggested that hearsay evidence might be admissible and that the burden of proof even could be placed on Hamdi to show that he was not an enemy combatant. It is unclear how any of us could prove a negative—that we are not an enemy combatant. The Court sent the case back to the lower court for the determination of what due process requires when an American citizen apprehended in a foreign country is detained as an enemy combatant.

In the fall of 2004, following the Supreme Court's decision, the government and Hamdi reached an agreement. In exchange for Hamdi being released from custody, he agreed to plead guilty, leave the country, renounce his citizenship, and never take up arms against the United States. Thus, Hamdi's case would not be the occasion for the Court to spell out the procedures required. I often have wondered whether the government wanted this guilty plea, in part, to make sure that the matter never got back to the Supreme Court, where the justices might have imposed more procedural protections for detainees.

Guantánamo

Since January 2002, the United States government has held, at one time or another, more than six hundred individuals as prisoners at a military facility in Guantánamo Bay, Cuba. These are individuals who were apprehended in foreign countries and then brought to the bleak prisons on an American military base in Cuba. The government has claimed the ability to hold these individuals indefinitely without trial, and many have been tortured. Senators Dianne Feinstein and Dick Durbin declared in 2013 that "Guantánamo has devastated our reputation as a champion of human rights, weakened our international partnerships and remains a powerful recruiting tool for terrorists." Upon being elected, President

Obama pledged to close Guantánamo within a year, but it didn't happen. Five years into the Obama presidency, prisoners remain in Guantánamo.

There have been two Supreme Court cases concerning the ability of Guantánamo detainees to bring habeas corpus petitions in federal court to challenge their confinement. *Rasul v. Bush,* in 2004, was the first case. It was brought by the father of an Australian detainee, the father of a British detainee, and the mother of another British detainee.

The government moved to dismiss, contending that the federal courts lacked authority to hear habeas corpus petitions by those being held in Guantánamo. In March 2003, the United States Court of Appeals for the District of Columbia Circuit affirmed the dismissal of the case for lack of jurisdiction and ruled that no court in the country could hear the petitions brought by the Guantánamo detainees. The court of appeals based this conclusion on the Supreme Court's decision in *Johnson v. Eisentrager* (1950). In that case, twenty-one German nationals sought habeas corpus after they were arrested in China for working in Japan on behalf of the German government before Germany surrendered. They were taken into custody by the U.S. Army and convicted by a U.S. military commission of violating laws of war by engaging in continued military activity for Japan after Germany's surrender. The defendants were convicted and repatriated to Germany to serve their sentences in a prison whose custodian was a U.S. Army officer. The prisoners sought habeas corpus in federal court, and the Supreme Court found that there was not jurisdiction in a federal district to hear the petition. In *Rasul,* the United States Court of Appeals found that the Guantánamo detainees were like the petitioners in *Johnson* and thus held that the petition in the case had to be dismissed.

The Supreme Court, in a 6–3 decision, reversed the court of appeals and held that a federal court could hear the habeas corpus petitions of those being held in Guantánamo. Justice John Paul Stevens wrote the opinion for the Court. He emphasized that *Johnson v. Eisentrager* was distinguishable in many important respects. In *Johnson,* those detained had been accorded a trial in a military tribunal, but those being held in Guantánamo had never had any form of trial or due process. Also, the Court stressed that, in contrast to the situation in *Johnson,* Guantánamo was functionally under the control and sovereignty of the U.S. government.

The Court in *Rasul v. Bush* did not address what type of hearing ultimately must be accorded to those in Guantánamo or anything about the rights of those held in Guantánamo. Rather, the case was limited to the issue of whether a federal court could hear their habeas corpus petition.

Immediately after the Court's decision in *Rasul,* Congress adopted the Detainee Treatment Act, which provided that federal courts could not hear writs of habeas corpus by "enemy combatants." In 2006, in *Hamdan v. Rumsfeld,* the Supreme Court ruled that the Detainee Treatment Act does not apply retroactively to those held prior to its enactment. The Court found that the military tribunals created by President Bush's executive order failed to comply with the Geneva Accords or federal law. Congress then responded to *Hamdan* by enacting the Military Commissions Act of 2006, which provides that no one held at Guantánamo, whenever they arrived, could seek relief in the federal courts via a writ of habeas corpus. This act provides that a noncitizen held as an enemy combatant shall not have access to federal courts via a writ of habeas corpus or otherwise, unless there is a military proceeding, in which case the detainee may seek review of its decision in the United States Court of Appeals for the District of Columbia Circuit.

In *Boumediene v. Bush,* in 2008, in a 5–4 decision, with Justice Kennedy writing an opinion joined by Justices Stevens, Souter, Ginsburg, and Breyer, the Court held that this preclusion of habeas corpus jurisdiction was unconstitutional. Justice Kennedy explained that Article I, Section 9 of the Constitution allows Congress to suspend habeas corpus only in times of rebellion or invasion. The government did not claim that either of these situations was present.

The Court concluded that Congress had impermissibly suspended the writ of habeas corpus. Moreover, the Court decided that the remedy provided—review in the D.C. Circuit—did not substitute for habeas corpus. The Court thus declared, "We hold that petitioners may invoke the fundamental procedural protections of habeas corpus. The laws and Constitution are designed to survive, and remain in force, in extraordinary times. Liberty and security can be reconciled; and in our system they are reconciled within the framework of the law. The Framers decided that habeas corpus, a right of first importance, must be a part of that framework, a part of that law."

Chief Justice Roberts dissented, joined by Justices Scalia, Thomas, and Alito, saying that the Court should have deferred to the choices made by Congress and the president. He wrote, "Today the Court strikes down as inadequate the most generous set of procedural protections ever afforded aliens detained by this country as enemy combatants. The political branches crafted these procedures amidst an ongoing military conflict, after much careful investigation and thorough debate."

Justice Scalia wrote an even more vehement dissent, joined by the other dissenting justices, in which he argued that the judiciary has no business being involved in the matter at all. He wrote, "What competence does the Court have to second-guess the judgment of Congress and the President on such a point? None whatever. But the Court blunders in nonetheless. Henceforth, as today's opinion makes unnervingly clear, how to handle enemy prisoners in this war will ultimately lie with the branch that knows least about the national security concerns that the subject entails."

Boumediene is a strong example refuting my thesis that the Court fails to enforce the Constitution in times of crisis. The Court held that those detained in Guantánamo have the ability to bring a habeas corpus petition asserting their rights. A federal law preventing this was declared unconstitutional. It took six years after the detainees were brought to Guantánamo for the Court to do this, but it was an important vindication of the Constitution.

Unfortunately, the Court's decision has turned out to be a hollow victory, because the Supreme Court then lost interest in the detention of prisoners at Guantánamo Bay. It has denied review in every case involving a Guantánamo detainee since 2008. In fact, the judicial events since *Boumediene* are very disturbing. The United States Court of Appeals for the District of Columbia Circuit has openly defied the Supreme Court's ruling, denying relief in every case, and the Supreme Court has denied review in all of these cases.

For example, on June 11, 2012, the Supreme Court denied review in seven cases posing unresolved questions presented by Guantánamo detainees seeking redress. At that time, there were 169 prisoners in Guantánamo, some of whom had been there for more than ten years without a trial, and they were left with no apparent legal recourse.

Following the Supreme Court's decision, federal district court judges in the District of Columbia granted relief to a number of Guantánamo detainees. But in each instance, a conservative panel of the D.C. Circuit reversed and then the Supreme Court denied review.

In *Kiyemba v. Obama,* a federal district court ordered the release of five Chinese Muslim (Uighur) detainees who had been cleared for release from Guantánamo. But the D.C. Circuit reversed and held that a federal judge lacks the power to order the transfer of Guantánamo detainees to the United States. Subsequently, in the same case, the D.C. Circuit denied federal judges the power to regulate transfers of Guantánamo detainees to elsewhere in the world. What is the meaning of habeas corpus, which the Supreme Court so carefully preserved for Guantánamo detainees in *Rasul* and *Boumediene,* if the federal courts cannot order the release of prisoners who are being held without legal justification? Yet the Supreme Court denied review, and the prisoners were left in Guantánamo.

In *Latif v. Obama,* the D.C. Circuit ruled that federal district judges must "presume" that government intelligence reports used to justify detention are reliable and accurate. Adnan Farhan Abdul Latif, a Yemeni man, was picked up near the border between Afghanistan and Pakistan in December 2001. The government has relied on an intelligence report prepared at the time to justify holding him ever since. The district court ordered his release, saying that the report was not sufficiently reliable to warrant keeping him imprisoned. But the D.C. Circuit, while acknowledging problems with the report, said that it was entitled to "a presumption of regularity."

This likely will create an insurmountable obstacle to relief for many detainees. The government does not need to justify detaining a person; it can invoke a presumption in its favor and put the burden on those seeking release to prove a negative: that they are impermissibly detained and not a threat. The usual burden of proof that is on the government is turned on its head. In dissent, D.C. Circuit judge David Tatel said that the effect is that the government would win virtually every case and that "it is hard to see what is left of the Supreme Court's command in *Boumediene*." The Supreme Court denied review.

Some of the conservative judges on the D.C. Circuit have been openly disdainful of the Supreme Court's decisions in *Rasul* and *Boumediene*. Judge A. Raymond Randolph compared the justices in the majority in *Boumediene* to fictional characters in *The Great Gatsby*, "careless people" making messes for other people to clean up. In the *Latif* case, Judge Janice Rogers Brown said that "*Boumediene*'s airy suppositions have caused great difficulty for the executive and the courts."

The open disdain for and defiance of the Supreme Court by judges on a federal court of appeals—in their words and their decisions—is rare, if not unprecedented. Yet the Supreme Court has done nothing to enforce its earlier rulings, and the result has been that the conservative judges on the D.C. Circuit have been able to deny any relief for Guantánamo detainees. Why the Supreme Court has made this choice—and why not a single justice dissented from the denial of review in the seven Guantánamo cases on June 11, 2012—is inexplicable.

By appearances, it seems as if the Court has simply lost interest in the Guantánamo detainees and the difficult legal issues raised by indefinite imprisonment of individuals without trial. Sadly, this seems to reflect the attitude of the Obama administration and the country.

During the Bush administration, liberals were outspoken in their criticism of Guantánamo, which had become a symbol of the government's disobedience of international law and basic notions of human rights. But with a Democratic president, these critics' voices have been muted. It seems that the country has simply gotten used to the idea that the government can hold these individuals indefinitely.

In February 2002, I argued the first habeas corpus case in the country on behalf of Guantánamo detainees in federal district court. The court denied relief on the ground that it could not hear such a challenge. I could not possibly have imagined that more than twelve years later—longer than any war in American history—the government would still be holding these individuals as prisoners. When the Supreme Court finally ruled, in *Rasul v. Bush* and *Boumediene v. Bush,* that Guantánamo detainees had a right to seek habeas corpus relief in federal courts, I never could have believed that this would be a Pyrrhic victory and that the Court would allow the D.C. Circuit to nullify the availability of habeas corpus.

If a foreign nation had imprisoned 169 Americans without trial, some for longer than a decade, the reaction would be outrage. But how can the United States expect foreign nations to follow international law and adhere to the rule of law if this country does not do so? It is time for outrage at the government and the courts for abandoning relief for the Guantánamo detainees, but unfortunately there is mostly just silence.

Conclusion

In assessing the Supreme Court's performance over the course of American history, its failure to enforce the Constitution in times of crisis should weigh heavily. History shows that in times of war, elected officials all too often follow pressures that lead to the compromising of constitutional values. A preeminent purpose of the Constitution—and therefore of the Court—is to restrain majorities in times of crisis. This is when it is crucial for the Court, whose justices have life tenure so that they can be immune from political pressures, to enforce the limits of the Constitution. Indeed, in such circumstances, the Court really is the last defense for important constitutional protections.

The Court's failure to uphold protections during such periods of American history has caused great harm to basic constitutional values, and many people, often innocent individuals, have suffered as a result. Men and women have been imprisoned, interned, and detained in violation of the Constitution. The Court failed to halt these actions, and quite to the contrary, repeatedly legitimated them in opinions siding with government power and ruling against individual rights.

There is also a long-term consequence to the Court's failure: its written decisions upholding repression remain on the books and can be used by the government in the future. This was precisely Justice Jackson's point in dissent in *Korematsu,* where he lamented that the Court's ruling for the government "lies about like a loaded weapon, ready for the hand of any authority that can bring forward a plausible claim of an urgent need."

The suppression of speech during World War I, the internment of Japanese Americans in World War II, the repression of the McCarthy era, and the abuses since 9/11 all should have been halted by the Supreme Court. None were. In each instance, the Court failed the people whose rights had been violated, the country, and the Constitution. It is too easy to make excuses for the justices and say that it is unrealistic to have expected them to do better. On the contrary, the Court could have stood up to pressure, and the powerful dissents could have been the positions of the majority. And it is important to remember that these are not isolated failures: over and again, throughout American history, the Supreme Court has failed to enforce the Constitution in times of crisis.

CHAPTER 3

Protecting Property and States' Rights

ndustrialization in the late nineteenth century caused a great increase in the use of child labor in the United States. Factory owners, for example, used child labor wherever possible, because children were seen as more manageable, less expensive, and less likely to strike. By 1900, "children worked in large numbers in mines, glass factories, textiles, agriculture, canneries, home industries, and as newsboys, messengers, bootblacks, and peddlers." It is estimated that in the early years of the twentieth century, approximately two million children aged sixteen and under worked in the fields, mines, mills, and factories of the United States. Unhealthy and dangerous working conditions were common; many children were injured or killed, while many left school, still illiterate, to take jobs.

Some states enacted laws limiting child labor, but others did not. States that restricted the use of child labor found themselves at a competitive disadvantage with states that did not impose limits. Some factories relocated to states where child labor was unregulated. Goods produced in states that permitted child labor cost less and had an advantage in the marketplace, since children there could be paid significantly lower wages than adult workers.

Constant exposés by journalists, labor, and progressives showed the great harms to children and created pressure for federal action. In 1916, Congress adopted the Keating-Owen Child Labor Act of 1916, which prohibited interstate commerce of any merchandise that had been made by children under the age of fourteen or merchandise that had been made in factories where children between fourteen and sixteen worked more than eight hours a day, worked overnight, or worked more than six days a week. Article I, Section 8 gives Congress the power to regulate commerce among the states, and that was exactly what Congress did with this law, forbidding the shipment in interstate commerce of goods made by child labor. The law did not even eliminate all child labor; it just prohibited shipment in interstate commerce from factories that employed children below a certain age. From the perspective of social policy, it is impossible to imagine opposing such a law.

David Clark, publisher of the *Southern Textile Bulletin,* organized southern mill owners into the Southern Cotton Manufacturers. Clark recruited Roland Dagenhart, who worked with his two sons in a cotton mill in Charlotte, North Carolina, to challenge the constitutionality of this law. In *Hammer v. Dagenhart,* in 1918, the Court declared the federal law limiting the use of child labor unconstitutional because it violated the Tenth Amendment.

The Tenth Amendment states, "The powers not delegated to the United States by the Constitution, nor prohibited by it to the States, are reserved to the States respectively, or to the people." By its terms, the Tenth Amendment is an important reminder and embodiment of a basic principle of American government: Congress can act only if it is granted power to do so by the Constitution, but state and local governments can do anything except what is prohibited by the Constitution. But that is all the Tenth Amendment says, and for the first century of American history, that was how the Supreme Court interpreted it.

But in *Hammer v. Dagenhart,* the Supreme Court said that the Tenth Amendment meant much more than this. The Court held that Congress's attempt to control the production of goods, even though it was exercising its constitutional power to regulate commerce among the states, violated the Tenth Amendment. The Court held that the Tenth Amendment gives exclusive control of production to the states. It did not question Congress's authority to regulate shipments in interstate commerce, but it said that this power could not be used to control production and to ban child labor. It is a highly dubious conclusion, because there is nothing in the text of the Tenth Amendment or anything about its history that implies this. The Court said that regulating hours of labor by children was entrusted "purely [to] state authority." Thus, the federal effort to limit child labor—surely an important, even essential, government action—was deemed unconstitutional.

The practical problem with the Court's approach of leaving this to "state authority" was that economic pressure from states that did not prohibit child labor would keep other states from being able to do so. States that wanted to outlaw it would find it difficult to keep their businesses competitive as long as other states allowed cheap child labor. Over time, the pressures would be great enough to induce all states to allow it. Economic pressures realistically limited state choices as much as any federal regulation.

This argument was made to the Supreme Court and expressly rejected. The Court said that Congress could not act to prevent unfair competition among the states. The Court spoke in apocalyptic terms about the consequences if Congress was accorded such regulatory power: "The far reaching result of upholding the act cannot be more plainly indicated than by pointing out that if Congress can thus regulate matters entrusted to local authority by prohibition of the movement of commodities in interstate commerce, all freedom of commerce will be at an end, and the power of the States over local matters may be eliminated, and thus our system of government be practically destroyed." It is hard to believe that a majority of the justices really believed that allowing Congress to ban the interstate shipment of goods made by child labor would practically destroy the entire system of government.

The decision cannot be understood as anything other than a reflection of the ideologies of the justices at the time and their hostility to regulation of business, even when it was a law to protect children. This becomes apparent when the Child Labor Case is contrasted with another decision from that era, the Lottery Case (*Champion v. Ames*), in 1903, where the Court upheld a federal law prohibiting the interstate shipment of lottery tickets. In both the Child Labor Case and the Lottery Case, the law prohibited the shipment of a specified class of item—goods made by child labor or lottery tickets—in interstate commerce. In both, Congress obviously was seeking to stop specific intrastate activities—the use of child labor and gambling in lotteries—by blocking distribution. Yet in the former the Court declared the federal law unconstitutional, whereas in the latter the Court upheld the federal law.

In the Lottery Case, the Court made it clear that the power to regulate interstate commerce includes the ability to prohibit items from being shipped in interstate commerce. The Court concluded that it was within Congress's commerce-clause power to stop lottery tickets from being a part of interstate commerce. The Court explicitly rejected the argument that the federal law violated the Tenth Amendment and intruded on state government prerogatives. It also rejected the argument that according Congress such power would give Congress seemingly limitless authority and would endanger the constitutional structure. The Court simply said, "[T]he possible abuse of a power is not an argument against its existence." Of course, this is exactly the opposite of what the Court held in the Child Labor Case.

There is no way to reconcile these decisions, even though they were decided just fifteen years apart and by a Court with the same ideological views. They simply reflect a conservative Court much more willing to defer to laws regulating conduct deemed immoral than to economic regulations. In the Lottery Case, the Court spoke of the "pestilence of lotteries" and of Congress's power to legislate to eradicate them. In the Child Labor Case, the Court never spoke of or even acknowledged the "pestilence" of child labor and denied Congress any power to act to limit it.

In 1941, the Supreme Court, in *United States v. Darby*, overruled the Child Labor Case, *Hammer v. Dagenhart*. It also overruled the idea that the Tenth Amendment reserves to the states a zone for their exclusive control. The Court said that the Tenth Amendment stated a "truism" that for Congress to act it must have constitutional authority, while state and local governments can do anything that is not prohibited by the Constitution. This is a simple notion that has been understood since the founding of the Constitution: the federal government has limited powers and must point to a power in the Constitution in order to act, but state governments have broad authority and can act unless they are violating the Constitution. As explained below, in recent years, the Court has abandoned this literal reading of the Tenth Amendment and returned to the idea that the Tenth Amendment does more than this, most recently and notably in striking down a key provision of the federal Affordable Care Act.

Of course, today there are federal laws limiting child labor. But from 1918 until 1941, a not insignificant stretch of time—including the Depression, when such laws were especially needed—the Supreme Court denied Congress this authority. How many lives were ruined as children were forced by economic circumstances into labor? It is a compelling example where the country would have been much better off without a Supreme Court.

The Court from the 1890s to 1937

In making the case against the Supreme Court, its decisions in the late nineteenth and the first third of the twentieth century are among the worst and most widely criticized of any in American history. For approximately forty years, from the mid-1890s to 1937, the Court regularly declared unconstitutional federal, state, and local laws protecting employees, consumers, and the public. A very conservative Court struck down more than two hundred laws, most regulating business in various ways. Federal statutes were invalidated on the ground that they invaded states' rights, while state and local laws were declared unconstitutional for interfering with freedom of contract. Both liberals and conservatives—later Supreme Court justices and academics alike—agree that these decisions were terribly misguided.

How did this happen? By the late nineteenth century, scholars and judges increasingly espoused a belief in a laissez-faire, unregulated economy. In part, this was based on a philosophy of social Darwinism that asserted that society would thrive most with the least government regulation, so as not to interfere with allowing the "best" to advance and prosper. In part, it was based on a belief that government regulations unduly interfered with the natural rights of people to own and use their property and with a basic liberty interest in freedom of contract. And, in part, support for a laissez-faire philosophy simply reflected hostility by businesses toward the increased government regulation—designed to protect workers, unions, consumers, and competitors—that had accompanied the Industrial Revolution.

The Court's decisions in this time period also were very inconsistent. The Court was conservative both economically and morally, so laws regulating corporations were routinely struck down, but laws based on moral judgments—regulating gambling, obscenity, prostitution—were always upheld. The justices read their conservative values into the Constitution, and ultimately the results kept Congress and the states from dealing with the economic and social crisis of the Depression.

Freedom of Contract and the *Lochner* Era

During this period of constitutional history, from the mid-1890s until 1937, the Court used two doctrines to limit government economic regulation. First, the Court said that freedom of contract was a fundamental right protected under the due process clauses—the constitutional provisions that say that neither the federal nor the state governments can deprive a person of life, liberty, or property without due process of law. Laws that interfered with freedom of contract, such as those regulating employment to protect workers, were repeatedly declared unconstitutional.

The most famous case during this period was *Lochner v. New York*, in 1905. In fact, this entire phase of constitutional history, from the mid-1890s through 1936, is often referred to as the "*Lochner* era."

In *Lochner v. New York*, the Supreme Court declared unconstitutional a New York state law that set the maximum hours that bakers could work. The New York law provided that no employee shall "work in a biscuit, bread or cake bakery or confectionery establishment more than sixty hours in any one week, or more than ten hours in any one day." The Supreme Court declared the law unconstitutional as violating the Due Process

Clause of the Fourteenth Amendment because it interfered with freedom of contract and the ability of bakers and bakeries to agree to whatever employment terms they wished. In *Lochner,* the Court articulated three major principles that were followed in numerous cases until 1937.

First, the Court, in *Lochner* and throughout this era, stated that freedom of contract is a basic right protected as liberty and property under the Due Process Clause of the Fourteenth Amendment. The Court in *Lochner* expressly declared, "The general right to make a contract in relation to his business is part of the liberty of the individual protected by the Fourteenth Amendment. . . . The right to purchase or sell labor is part of the liberty protected by this amendment."

This was not the Court's first declaration that freedom of contract is a fundamental right that overwhelms other considerations. In *Allgeyer v. Louisiana,* in 1897, the Supreme Court declared unconstitutional a state law that limited the ability of people to buy insurance from out-of-state companies that were not licensed or approved to do business in the state. The Court found that the Louisiana law interfered with freedom of contract and thus violated the Due Process Clause of the Fourteenth Amendment. The state's goal of protecting consumers from unscrupulous insurance companies did not, in the Court's eyes, justify limiting the ability of people to contract with whatever insurance companies they wished.

Second, the Court said in *Lochner* that the government could interfere with freedom of contract only to serve a valid police purpose—that is, to protect the public safety, public health, or public morals. But wasn't the purpose of the New York law, which limited the hours worked by bakers, to protect their health? Justice John Marshall Harlan in his dissenting opinion stressed that the legislation was a reasonable way to protect the health of bakers who suffered serious medical problems because of exposure to flour dust and intense heat. He quoted one study that found that the "average age of a baker is below that of other workmen; they seldom live over their fiftieth year, most of them dying between the ages of forty and fifty."

But the Court's majority said that the law was not sufficiently clear about protecting public health. The Court said, "Clean and wholesome bread does not depend upon whether the baker works but ten hours per day or only sixty hours a week. . . . [The law provides] for the inspection of premises where the bakery is being carried on, with regard to furnishing proper wash-rooms and water-closets, [with] regard to providing proper drainage, plumbing, and painting." As for the health of bakers, the Court declared, "There is no contention that bakers as a class are not equal in intelligence and capacity to men in other trades or manual occupations, or that they are not able to assert their rights and care for themselves without the protecting arm of the State, interfering with their independence of judgment and of action." The Court thus adopted a very narrow view of when the government could act to protect the health of workers.

Third, the Court said that it was the judicial role to carefully scrutinize legislation interfering with freedom of contract to make sure that it was necessary for achieving the police purpose. The Court believed that many laws that purported to be exercises of the police power in reality were intended to redistribute wealth or to help a particular group at the expense of others. The Court in *Lochner* said, "It is impossible for us to shut our eyes to the fact that many laws of this character, while passed under what is claimed to be the police power for the purpose of protecting the public health or welfare, are, in reality, passed for other motives." The majority of the justices who were committed to laissez-faire economics and social Darwinism strongly opposed allowing the government, through regulation, to shift wealth from employers to employees.

The *Lochner* Court applied these three principles to declare the New York law unconstitutional. The Court saw the maximum-hours law as interfering with freedom of contract, because it prevented bakery owners and bakers from contracting for as many hours of work as they wished. Of course, the economic reality was that bakers had no choice. Bakery owners could dictate the hours of employment, and anyone wanting to be employed as a baker had no choice but to go along or be out of work. Freedom of contract—the premise of the Court's decision—was illusory for those wanting to work as bakers.

Nonetheless, for more than thirty years, the Court followed the principles of *Lochner* and protected businesses by striking down laws designed to safeguard employees and consumers as impermissibly interfering with freedom of contract. As I mentioned above, it is estimated that between the 1890s and 1937 almost two hundred state laws were declared unconstitutional as violating the Due Process Clause of the Fourteenth Amendment. These decisions were emphatically pro-business, as the Court struck down laws protecting unions, helping workers, and safeguarding consumers. During this time, many states were adopting progressive legislation; as the Depression deepened, the federal government increasingly did so as well. It was these laws that were struck down by the Supreme Court.

With regard to laws protecting unions, in *Adair v. United States* and *Coppage v. Kansas,* the Court declared unconstitutional federal and state laws that prohibited employers from requiring that employees not join a union. Again, given the inequality of bargaining power, employers could insist on this as a term of work, and those wanting employment had no choice but to turn in their union cards or not get one in the first place. In the early part of the century, as workers attempted to unionize, many states and the federal government tried to help workers, adopting laws to facilitate unionization by prohibiting employers from insisting, as a condition of employment, that employees agree not to join a union. But the Supreme Court invalidated these laws as impermissibly infringing on freedom of contract. In *Adair,* the Court said that "it is not within the functions of government, at least in the absence of contract between the parties, to compel any person in the course of his business and against his will to accept or retain the personal services of another." In *Coppage,* the Court said that it was not a legitimate exercise of the police power for the government to attempt to equalize bargaining power between employer and employee. The Court said that an individual "has no inherent right to [join a union] . . . and still remain in the employ of one who is unwilling to employ a union man." The Court put its weight strongly on the side of business and kept legislatures from helping workers unionize.

The Court also repeatedly declared unconstitutional minimum-wage laws. In *Adkins v. Children's Hospital,* the Court declared unconstitutional a law that set a minimum wage for women. States knew that they could not adopt laws that required that all employees be paid a minimum wage; such statutes unquestionably would have been found to infringe on freedom of contract. But states saw a possible way to have a minimum wage for some workers—women—based on a Supreme Court decision during this era that upheld a state law limiting the number of hours that women could work.

Three years after *Lochner,* in *Muller v. Oregon,* the Court upheld a state law prescribing the maximum hours that women could work. *Muller* is especially famous because the attorney Louis Brandeis—later a Supreme Court justice—wrote a detailed 113-page brief for it, purporting to document that women's reproductive health required limiting nondomestic work. After *Lochner* held that there had to be proof that a law was closely related to advancing public health, public safety, or public morals, attorneys began filing detailed briefs, filled with social science data, seeking to show the need for the law. Often termed "Brandeis briefs" after the type that Louis Brandeis filed in *Muller,* these documents used social science data to demonstrate the need for a particular law.

In *Muller,* the Court upheld the maximum-hours law for women because there was "widespread belief that women's physical structure, and the functions she performs in consequence thereof, justify special legislation restricting or qualifying the conditions under which she should be permitted to toil." The Court said that regulating the hours worked by women was justified because of "women's physical structure and the performance of maternal functions." Today, my students are justifiably horrified by the sexism of the arguments made and by the Court's decision. But I point out that at the time, the Court's upholding a maximum-hours law, even if just for women, was seen as a significant progressive victory.

Progressives thought then that the Court might be willing to allow a minimum-wage law for women, even if in general it would strike down minimum-wage statutes as unduly interfering with freedom of contract.

The Court, though, said that a minimum-wage law, even one for women, was unconstitutional and was different from a maximum-hours law: it interfered with freedom of contract but did not serve any valid police purpose. The Court rejected the claim that without a minimum wage, women would be forced to earn money in an immoral manner. In fact, the Court stressed the growing equality of women, as reflected in the recent adoption of the Nineteenth Amendment, which guaranteed women the right to vote. The Court said, "But the ancient inequality of the sexes, otherwise than physical, has continued with diminishing intensity. In view of the great changes which have taken place ... in the contractual, political, and civil status of women, culminating in the Nineteenth Amendment, it is not unreasonable to say that these differences have now come almost, if not quite, to the vanishing point."

The Court reaffirmed *Adkins* in 1936, when it declared unconstitutional a New York law that required that female employees be paid a minimum wage. The Court saw minimum-wage laws as impermissibly intruding on the right of employees and employers to decide the amount of pay; if workers wanted to be employed for less than a minimum wage, and that was what employers wanted to pay, the Court held that the legislature could not interfere. Minimum-wage laws were perceived as blatant attempts by legislatures to redistribute money from businesses to workers.

Another type of legislation that was invalidated was consumer protection laws, such as price regulations. Laws setting the maximum prices for theater tickets, employment agencies, and gasoline were declared unconstitutional as interfering with freedom of contract.

Other types of consumer protection laws were invalidated as well. In *Weaver v. Palmer Bros. Co.*, the Court declared unconstitutional a state law prohibiting the use of "shoddy" (rags and other debris) in making bedding. Such materials often were filthy, and the concern was that they were germ-ridden. But the Court rejected the claim that the ban was needed to protect public health, finding that the law interfered with freedom of contract for those who wished to buy and sell pillows and mattresses made with shoddy. The Court said that the public interest in health could be served adequately by mandating sterilization of the material rather than prohibiting the sale or purchase of bedding made with shoddy. Later, after this decision was overruled, Congress adopted a law regulating the content of bedding—this is what accounts for the tags on our pillows and mattresses. The law is so clearly constitutional under post-1937 law that no one would even seriously consider challenging it.

Many different types of laws to protect workers and consumers were invalidated by the Supreme Court in the first third of the twentieth century. What was wrong with these decisions? The Court was wrong to protect freedom of contract as a fundamental right. It was absurd to talk of bakers having freedom to bargain to work fewer hours or of workers being able to bargain to have the ability to join a union. The Court's commitment to laissez-faire economics was misguided and ultimately greatly favored some, such as employers and corporations, over others, such as workers and consumers.

Moreover, the Court erred in concluding that the government could interfere with this freedom of contract only in order to enhance public health, public safety, or public morals. The government should be able to regulate to achieve many other goals, including protecting workers, consumers, and the public in general. In areas of grossly unequal bargaining power, legislatures should be able to act to safeguard those who cannot protect themselves in a free market economy. Nothing in the Constitution—or, for that matter, good social policy—justifies so circumscribing the power of legislatures to act for the welfare of society.

By the mid-1930s, enormous pressures were mounting for the Court to abandon the laissez-faire philosophy of the *Lochner* era. The Depression created a widespread perception that government economic regulations were essential. With millions unemployed and with wages very low for those with jobs, employees had no realistic chance of bargaining in the workplace. As Laurence Tribe remarked, "In large measure . . . it was the economic realities of the Depression that graphically undermined Lochner's premises. . . . The legal 'freedom' of contract and property came increasingly to be seen as an illusion, subject as it was to impersonal economic forces. Positive government intervention came to be more widely accepted as essential to economic survival, and legal doctrines would henceforth have to operate from that premise."

At the same time, there were strong political pressures for changes in the Court's composition. Four of the justices—Pierce Butler and George Sutherland (both appointed by President Harding), James Clark McReynolds (appointed by Wilson), and Willis Van Devanter (appointed by Taft)—were very conservative and virtually always voted to invalidate New Deal programs and progressive state laws. They were referred to in the press as "the Four Horsemen," after the allegorical figures of the Apocalypse, associated with death and destruction. They often found a fifth vote in Owen Roberts, who had been appointed by President Hoover and in 1936 was the youngest justice on the Court, at age sixty-one.

After Franklin Roosevelt was elected to a second term as president, in 1936, he proposed a "Court-packing plan," by which the president could appoint one additional justice for every justice on the Court who was over age seventy, up to a maximum of six additional justices. This would have allowed Roosevelt to quickly appoint enough justices to create a sympathetic majority on the Court to uphold New Deal programs.

Roosevelt's plan met with substantial opposition in Congress—even a Congress that was controlled by Democrats. But even without that failed scheme, the Court in 1937 dramatically reversed course and rejected forty years of Lochnerism. That year, in two cases—one involving freedom of contract and one involving the scope of Congress's commerce power (discussed below)—Justice Owen Roberts switched sides and cast the fifth vote to uphold the laws. Perhaps this was a reaction to the Court-packing plan, or perhaps he had made up his mind in these cases before even learning about that threat. We will never know why Roberts changed his mind so dramatically, but regardless, in these two decisions, the Court signaled the end of the laissez-faire jurisprudence that had dominated constitutional law for several decades.

In *West Coast Hotel Co. v. Parrish*, in 1937, the Supreme Court upheld a state law that required a minimum wage for women, and in doing so it overruled the earlier decisions. Chief Justice Charles Evans Hughes, writing for the Court, made it clear that the Court was abandoning the principles of *Lochner v. New York*. Noting that the minimum-wage law had been challenged as interfering with freedom of contract, he commented, "What is this freedom of contract? The Constitution does not speak of freedom of contract. It speaks of liberty and prohibits the deprivation of liberty without due process of law. . . . [R]egulation which is reasonable in relation to its subject and is adopted in the interests of the community is due process." In this single sentence, the Court brushed aside four decades of cases protecting freedom of contract as a fundamental right.

Moreover, the Court was emphatic that the government was not limited to regulating only to advance the public safety, public health, or public morals. The Court said, "There is an additional and compelling consideration which recent economic experience has brought into a strong light. The exploitation of a class of workers who are in an unequal position with respect to bargaining power and are thus relatively defenseless against the denial of a living wage is not only detrimental to their health and well being but casts a direct burden for their support upon the community." For forty years, the Court had refused to allow the government to regulate to equalize bargaining power; now it would be permitted.

In these paragraphs, the Court unequivocally declared that it no longer would protect freedom of contract as a fundamental right, that government could regulate to serve any legitimate purpose, and that the judiciary would defer to the legislatures' choices, so long as they were reasonable. This has been the law ever since 1937. Between 1937 and 1941, the composition of the Court changed dramatically, and there was no longer doubt about the fate of the jurisprudence of the *Lochner* era. The conservative justices—Van Devanter, McReynolds, Butler, and Sutherland—left the Court and were replaced by Roosevelt appointees. In fact, between 1937 and 1941, Roosevelt made eight appointments to the Supreme Court, and this created an overwhelming majority committed to repudiating *Lochner*-era jurisprudence and to deferring to government economic regulations.

Since 1937, not one state or federal economic regulation has been found unconstitutional on the ground of infringing on liberty of contract as protected by the due process clauses of the Fifth and Fourteenth Amendments. The Court has made it clear that economic regulations—laws regulating business and employment practices—will be upheld when challenged under the due process clauses, so long as they are rationally related to serving a legitimate government purpose. The Court often has been explicit in its rejection of this earlier era of jurisprudence. It has stressed that it has long since repudiated the "Allgeyer-Lochner-Adair-Coppage constitutional doctrine" and has said that the "day is gone when the Court uses the Due Process Clause to strike down state laws regulatory of business and industrial conditions, because they may be unwise, improvident, or out of harmony with a particular school of thought."

But for forty years, the Court made people's lives much worse than they would have been without a Supreme Court. For four decades, the Court kept legislatures from protecting workers and consumers, and many suffered greatly as a result.

Limiting Federal Power from the 1890s to 1937

At the same time that the Court was striking down state and local economic regulations as interfering with freedom of contract, it also was invalidating federal laws regulating business as impermissibly intruding on the prerogatives of state governments. Many federal laws were invalidated as exceeding the scope of Congress's commerce power or as violating the Tenth Amendment and the zone of activities reserved to the states. So, for example, where a *state* law requiring a minimum wage during this period would be invalidated as unconstitutionally interfering with freedom of contract, a *federal* law requiring a minimum wage would be declared unconstitutional as exceeding the scope of Congress's power and as impermissibly usurping states' prerogatives.

Between the late nineteenth century and 1937, the Court espoused a philosophy often termed "dual federalism." Dual federalism was the view that the federal and state governments were separate sovereigns, that each had separate zones of authority, and that it was the judicial role to protect the states by interpreting and enforcing the Constitution to protect the zone of activities reserved to the states.

Dual federalism was embodied in three important doctrines that the Court developed and followed during this period. Individually and together, they kept Congress from adopting laws to protect employees and consumers. In order for Congress to enact a federal law, it must have authority under the Constitution to do so. The Supreme Court restricted this authority in a way that struck down many highly desirable federal laws. First, the Court restricted the scope of congressional authority to regulate commerce among the states and narrowly defined the meaning of "commerce" so as to leave a zone of power to the states. Specifically, the Court held that commerce was one stage of business, distinct from earlier phases, such as mining, manufacturing, and production. Under this view, only commerce itself could be regulated by Congress; the other areas were left for state regulation.

In *United States v. E.C. Knight Co.,* in 1895, the Court held that the Sherman Antitrust Act could not be used to stop a monopoly in the sugar-refining industry, because the Constitution did not allow Congress to regulate manufacturing. The Sherman Act, adopted in 1890, is a major federal law designed to break up monopolies and cartels and other actions in restraint of trade. The U.S. government attempted to use the Sherman Act to block the American Sugar Refining Company from acquiring four competing refineries. The acquisition would have given the company control of more than 98 percent of the sugar-refining industry. Without competition, monopolies can charge far higher prices and get windfall profits.

Nonetheless, the Court held that federal law could not be applied, because the monopoly was in the production of sugar, not in its commerce. The Court flatly declared, "Commerce succeeds to manufacture, and is not a part of it." The Court was clear that this rigid distinction was based on a need for reserving a zone of activities to the states. The Court explained that although the commerce power was the "strongest bond of the union ... the preservation of the autonomy of the States [w]as required by our dual form of government."

This distinction between manufacturing and commerce was arbitrary; a company would desire a monopoly in production because it would benefit from monopoly profits in sales. The Court acknowledged this but said that the relationship was too indirect to allow federal regulation under the commerce power.

This very limited definition of commerce continued throughout this era, until 1937. For example, in *Carter v. Carter Coal Co.,* the Court declared unconstitutional the Bituminous Coal Conservation Act of 1935. The law contained detailed findings on the relationship between coal and the national economy and declared that the production of coal directly affected interstate commerce. The law provided for local coal boards to be established to determine prices for coal and also to determine, after collective bargaining by unions and employers, wages and hours for employees. A shareholder in the Carter Coal Company sued the company to stop it from complying with the law.

The Supreme Court declared the law unconstitutional. The Court focused on the unconstitutionality of federal regulation of wages and hours. The Court said, "The employment of men, the fixing of their wages, hours of labor and working conditions, the bargaining in respect of these things—whether carried on separately or collectively," are all aspects of production and could not be regulated by Congress.

The Court again emphasized that this narrow definition of commerce was essential for protecting the states. The Court lamented, "Every journey to a forbidden end begins with the first step; and the danger of such a step by the federal government in the direction of taking over the powers of the states is that the end of the journey may find the states so despoiled of their powers, or—what may amount to the same thing—so relieved of responsibilities ... as to reduce them to little more than geographic subdivisions of the national domain."

Decisions such as *E.C. Knight* and *Carter* rested on many highly questionable assumptions: that it makes sense to distinguish commerce from other stages of business; that the Constitution requires that a rigid zone of activities be left to the states; and that it is the judicial role to protect this zone. From the late nineteenth century until 1937, these premises were fervently accepted by the Supreme Court and greatly limited Congress's ability to regulate the economy. For the first time in American history, there was ongoing tension between Congress, which sought to regulate the economy to protect consumers and workers, and a Court that was hostile to such federal regulation. For the first century of American history, the Supreme Court rarely had struck down any law—none were invalidated from 1803 to 1857. Now, for the first time in history, many federal laws were declared unconstitutional.

Second, the Court restrictively defined "among the states" as allowing Congress to regulate only when there was a direct, substantial effect on interstate commerce. Congress could not exercise its commerce-clause authority if the effects were only indirect. Unless Congress was regulating to deal with direct effects, the matter was left to the states. But a distinction between direct and indirect effects is inherently elusive and difficult to draw.

In *A.L.A. Schechter Poultry Corp. v. United States,* often referred to as the Sick Chickens Case, the Court declared a federal law unconstitutional based on an insufficient direct effect on interstate commerce. The National Industrial Recovery Act, a key piece of New Deal legislation, authorized the president to approve "codes of fair competition" developed by boards of various industries. Pursuant to this law, the president approved a Live Poultry Code for New York City. In part, the code was designed to ensure quality poultry by preventing sellers from requiring buyers to purchase the entire coop of chickens, including sick ones. The code also regulated employment by requiring collective bargaining, prohibiting child labor, and establishing a forty-hour workweek and a minimum wage.

The Supreme Court declared the entire code unconstitutional, because there was not a sufficiently "direct" relationship to interstate commerce. Although the Court acknowledged that virtually all of the poultry in New York was shipped from other states, it said that the code was not regulating the interstate transactions; rather, the code concerned the operation of businesses within New York. The Court emphasized that Congress could regulate only when there was a direct effect on interstate commerce.

The Court once again explained that this distinction was essential in order to protect state governments and ultimately the American system of government. The Court declared that enforcing the distinction between direct and indirect effects on commerce "must be recognized as . . . essential to the maintenance of our constitutional system."

As with any arbitrary distinction, the Court used it to achieve the results it wanted. For instance, regulation of railroads to protect railroad workers was unconstitutional, but when a regulation was intended to protect the railroads, it was upheld. In *Railroad Retirement Board v. Alton R. Co.*, the Court declared unconstitutional the Railroad Retirement Act of 1934, which provided a pension system for railroad workers.

But railroads obviously were part of the stream of interstate commerce, and the Court had upheld other federal regulations of railroads. Earlier in this era, in the Shreveport Rate Cases, the Court upheld the ability of the Interstate Commerce Commission to set intrastate railroad rates. Specifically, a railroad was required by a federal regulation to charge the same rates for shipments to Marshall, Texas, whether they came from Shreveport, Louisiana, or from Dallas. The Court upheld the federal regulation and held that "Congress in the exercise of its paramount power may prevent the common instrumentalities of interstate and intrastate commercial intercourse from being used in their intrastate operations to the injury of interstate commerce."

What explains the difference between these two cases? In the Shreveport Rate Cases, the national railroads wanted federal regulation to control intrastate railroad rates, so as to assure that intrastate railroads did not charge less and undercut their prices and profits. But in *Alton R.*, the Court said that Congress could not use its commerce power to require a pension program for railroad employees, because the law was designed only to help "the social welfare of the worker, and therefore [was] remote from any regulation of commerce." The Court's strong pro-business bias could not have been clearer: regulations to protect railroad profits were upheld, while regulations to protect railroad workers were declared unconstitutional.

Third, the Court held that the Tenth Amendment reserved a zone of activities to the states and that even federal laws within the scope of the congressional power were unconstitutional if they invaded that zone. For example, as explained above, the Court held that regulation of production was left to the states, and therefore a federal law that prohibited shipment in interstate commerce of goods made by child labor was unconstitutional— even though it was limited to interstate commerce—because it violated the Tenth Amendment.

Similarly, in 1936, the Court struck down another key piece of New Deal legislation: the Agricultural Adjustment Act of 1933, which sought to stabilize production in agriculture by offering subsidies to farmers to limit their crops. By restricting the supply of agricultural products, Congress sought to ensure a fair price and thus to encourage agricultural production. If the supply of a product was too great, prices would plummet, no profit could be gained, and future production would then be curtailed. In *United States v. Butler*, the Court declared the Agricultural Adjustment Act unconstitutional on the ground that it violated the Tenth Amendment because it regulated production; the regulation of production, according to the Court, was left to the states.

But the Court during this era was not at all consistent in applying these principles. It was most likely to follow them when considering federal economic regulations; it was least likely to adhere to them, and most willing to uphold federal laws, when the federal laws regulated aspects of morality. Thus, the Court invalidated federal antitrust laws and employment-regulation statutes but upheld federal laws prohibiting lotteries and obscene materials and making it a crime to take a woman across state lines "for immoral purposes." The decisions were simply products of the Court's particular brand of conservatism: economically conservative and thus aggressive in striking down economic regulations; morally conservative and thus deferential to laws directed at what was perceived as sin.

The result of these doctrines was that for forty years, including during the first years of the Depression, Congress was greatly limited in its ability to regulate business by a Court that narrowly construed the scope of congressional powers. As explained above, economic and political pressures mounted for these decisions to be overruled, and in 1937 the Court dramatically changed course, just as it had with regard to the earlier rulings concerning freedom of contract. In a series of decisions between 1937 and 1942, the Court held that commerce included all stages of business, that Congress could regulate based on both direct and indirect effects, and that the Tenth Amendment did not reserve a zone of activities to the states. But for four decades, the Court's strong pro-business bias meant that laws intended to protect workers, including children, and to safeguard consumers were invalidated.

States' Rights in the Contemporary Era

From 1937 until 1995, not one federal law was declared unconstitutional on the ground of exceeding the scope of Congress's powers. The Supreme Court broadly defined the scope of federal authority to deal with national problems and rejected the idea that the Tenth Amendment reserved a zone of activities to the states.

But in the 1990s, the new conservative majority of the Court, in a series of 5–4 rulings, returned to the repudiated states' rights jurisprudence of the earlier era. The appointments of Richard Nixon, Ronald Reagan, and George H. W. Bush created a conservative five-justice majority that returned to the federalism principles of the earlier era: William Rehnquist (appointed associate justice by Richard Nixon and chief justice by Ronald Reagan), Sandra Day O'Connor, Antonin Scalia, Anthony Kennedy (all Reagan appointees), and Clarence Thomas (a Bush appointee). What is most striking about these states' rights decisions is that they have all declared unconstitutional federal laws that are unquestionably socially desirable: preventing guns near schools, allowing victims of rape and domestic violence to sue, requiring states to clean up nuclear waste, mandating state and local governments to do background checks before issuing permits for firearms, and expanding Medicaid coverage for the poor.

Unlike the decisions from the 1890s to 1936, which have few defenders today, the contemporary rulings are favored by political conservatives. But I believe that the Court's return to its pre-1937 federalism jurisprudence has repeated the mistake of the past: the Court has struck down highly desirable and important laws for little identifiable benefit. The Court, in its rulings, has made society worse by invalidating these federal laws.

First, as in the earlier era, the Court has narrowed the scope of Congress's power to regulate commerce among the states. In *United States v. Lopez*, in 1995, by a 5–4 margin, the Supreme Court declared unconstitutional the Gun-Free School Zones Act of 1990, which made it a federal crime to have a gun within one thousand feet of a school.

Alfonso Lopez was a twelfth-grade student at Edison High School, in San Antonio, Texas, in 1992 when he was arrested for carrying at the school a concealed .38-caliber handgun and five bullets. He was charged with violating the Gun-Free School Zones Act, which made it a federal offense "for any individual knowingly to possess a firearm at a place that the individual knows, or has reasonable cause to believe, is a school zone." The law defines a school zone as "in, or on the grounds of, a public, parochial, or private school" or "within a distance of 1,000 feet from the grounds of a public, parochial, or private school." Lopez was convicted of violating this law and sentenced to six months imprisonment and two years of supervised release.

The Court reversed Lopez's conviction and concluded that the presence of a gun near a school did not substantially affect interstate commerce and that therefore the federal law was unconstitutional. Splitting along ideological lines, the Court ruled that the relationship to interstate commerce was too tangential to uphold the law as a valid exercise of

Congress's commerce power. Chief Justice Rehnquist wrote the opinion of the Court and was joined by Justices O'Connor, Kennedy, Scalia, and Thomas. Justices Stevens, Souter, Ginsburg, and Breyer dissented.

The decision is disturbing on many levels. For the first time in almost sixty years, the Court declared a federal law unconstitutional on the ground that it exceeded the scope of Congress's commerce power. As the government argued to the Supreme Court, looked at cumulatively across the country, guns near schools have an effect on the economy, such as in the location of businesses. Guns near schools are inherently a bad thing. It is hard to identify what is gained by declaring this law unconstitutional. The Supreme Court frequently has said that states' rights are protected as a way to prevent tyranny, to safeguard individual liberties, and to allow states to serve as laboratories for experimentation. But prohibiting guns near schools is hardly tyrannical, and even staunch advocates of gun rights must pause when it comes to guns near schools. Nor does it make sense to allow states to experiment with this.

Five years later, in *United States v. Morrison,* the Court followed *Lopez* and declared unconstitutional a federal law intended to help women who were victims of violence. The federal Violence Against Women Act allowed victims of gender-motivated violence to sue for money damages. Congress had authorized the act in 1994, based on detailed findings of the inadequacy of state laws in protecting women who are victims of domestic violence and sexual assault. Congress found that gender-motivated violence costs the American economy billions of dollars a year and is a substantial constraint on freedom of travel by women throughout the country. Congress also found that state courts were not receptive to claims by women who were victims of gender-motivated violence.

The case was brought by Christy Brzonkala, who was raped by football players while a freshman at Virginia Polytechnic Institute. The players were not criminally prosecuted and ultimately avoided even sanctions by their university. Brzonkala filed suit against her assailants and the university under the civil-damages provision of the Violence Against Women Act.

In a 5–4 decision again split along ideological lines, the Court held that

Congress lacked the authority to adopt the provision. The Supreme Court expressly rejected the argument that Congress could act based on its finding that violence against women costs the American economy billions of dollars a year. Chief Justice Rehnquist emphasized that Congress was regulating noneconomic activity that has traditionally been dealt with by state laws and thus exceeded the scope of its commerce-clause power.

Again, it is unquestionably desirable to allow women who are raped or are victims of domestic violence to be able to sue where they have a realistic chance of success. Yet the Court struck this down.

In its most recent decision concerning the scope of Congress's commerce power, the five most conservative justices again took a very restrictive view. The case, *National Federation of Independent Business v. Sebelius*, involved the constitutionality of the Patient Protection and Affordable Care Act.

There are fifty million Americans without health insurance, and the Affordable Care Act seeks to remedy that. Insurance companies are required to provide coverage to all and no longer can deny policies based on preexisting conditions, charge higher premiums based on health conditions, or impose yearly or lifetime caps on payments. But Congress knew that simply imposing these restrictions on insurance companies would be self-defeating: if people could wait until they were very sick to obtain insurance and could do so without any additional cost, fewer healthy people would pay into the system. The costs of health insurance would dramatically increase. The individual mandate seeks to remedy this by expanding the risk pool as much as possible. Subject to some exceptions, such as those with income below a specified level and those who have religious objections to receiving medical care, all the rest of us have to buy insurance or pay a penalty. The idea actually originated with a conservative think tank, the Heritage Foundation—which developed it as an alternative to a single-payer plan favored by liberals. Massachusetts became the first state to adopt an individual mandate when its Republican governor, Mitt Romney, signed it into law.

Five justices—Chief Justice Roberts and Justices Scalia, Kennedy,

Thomas, and Alito—said that the individual mandate was not a constitutional exercise of Congress's commerce-clause power. They said that Congress under the commerce clause can regulate economic activity that, taken cumulatively, has a substantial effect on interstate commerce. They saw the individual mandate as regulating inactivity, regulating those not engaged in commerce, and thus exceeding the scope of Congress's power.

This is conclusion misguided, because all of us are engaged in economic activity with regard to health care. As Justice Ginsburg pointed out in her dissent, more than 99 percent of people will receive medical care in their lifetimes, and 60 percent of the uninsured do so each year. Everyone is engaged in economic activity, in that they are either purchasing insurance or self-insuring. Congress is regulating the latter economic behavior because of its ill effects on the economy and society.

The five justices created a new distinction limiting Congress's commerce power: it can regulate activity, but not inactivity. How much will this matter? Some suggest that it won't matter much, because Congress rarely is going to compel economic transactions. On the other hand, any distinctions like "activity/inactivity" or "direct/indirect" are an open invitation to litigation where a great deal turns on labels and characterizations. It is reminiscent of the distinction between "direct" and "indirect" effects on commerce from the earlier era that proved impossible to draw or implement.

Consider an example: Title II of the Civil Rights Act of 1964, which was adopted under Congress's commerce-clause power, prohibits hotels and restaurants from discriminating on the basis of race. Does that law regulate the "inactivity" of hotels and restaurants that refuse to serve African Americans, or was it regulating "activity"? I am not suggesting that the Court will strike down Title II, but it does illustrate how much can turn on a label. A federal law, adopted by Congress under its commerce power, makes it a crime for a person to cross state lines if his or her child support payments are not up to date. Does that law regulate activity or inactivity? Another federal statute makes it a crime for a person to cross state lines if he or she is a sex offender who failed to register as required by his or her state law. Does this regulate activity or inactivity? The constitutionality of such laws will depend on the characterization given by the courts.

However, it should be noted that the Court upheld the individual mandate based on a different congressional power: Congress's authority to tax and spend for the general welfare. Chief Justice Roberts, joined by Justices Ginsburg, Breyer, Sotomayor, and Kagan, said that the individual mandate is a tax and within the scope of Congress's taxing power. He explained that the mandate is calculated like a tax; for example, in 2014, it is 1 percent of income or $95 (whichever is larger) for those who do not purchase insurance. It is collected by the Internal Revenue Service, and the funds go to the federal treasury; it will generate about $4 billion in 2014. The Court said that it was irrelevant that the Obama administration never called it a tax—the labels used by the government are not determinative.

This does not change the law in any way in terms of the scope of Congress's taxing and spending power or how it is determined whether something is a tax. Congress always has had the power to tax behavior it wants to discourage. As Chief Justice Roberts noted, if Congress wants to encourage installation of energy-efficient windows, it could tax those who don't have them. But it does make all the more puzzling why Roberts went on to discuss how the individual mandate did not fit within the scope of the commerce power; it was completely unnecessary to his conclusion.

Second, since the early 1990s, the Court has returned to the view that the Tenth Amendment leaves a zone of activities to the states. In *New York v. United States,* in 1992, the Court invalidated the 1985 Low-Level Radioactive Waste Policy Amendments Act, which created a statutory duty for states to provide for the safe disposal of radioactive waste generated within their borders. The act provided monetary incentives for states to comply with the law and allowed states to impose a surcharge on radioactive waste received from other states. Additionally, and most controversially, to ensure effective state government action, the law provided that states would "take title" to any waste within their borders that was not properly disposed of by January 1, 1996, and then would "be liable for all damages directly or indirectly incurred."

The Supreme Court ruled that forcing states to accept ownership of radioactive waste would impermissibly "commandeer" state governments, and that requiring state compliance with federal regulatory statutes would impermissibly impose on states a requirement to implement federal legislation. The Court concluded that it was "clear" that because of the Tenth Amendment and limits on the scope of Congress's powers under Article I, "[t]he Federal Government may not compel the States to enact or administer a federal regulatory program."

The Court explained that allowing Congress to commandeer state governments would undermine government accountability, because Congress could make a decision, but the states would take the political heat and be held responsible for a decision that was not theirs. Why, though, couldn't voters understand when states were acting pursuant to a federal mandate? We all do things, such as paying taxes, because the federal government requires it. Besides, where in the Constitution does it say that Congress cannot compel state legislative or regulatory activity? Most important, isn't it a really good thing to make sure that highly toxic nuclear waste is cleaned up? There is an obvious national interest in making sure that this occurs. The Court struck down an important federal law designed to safeguard the environment. The Court did so in the name of states' rights, even though the initial proposal had come from the National Governors Association, which realized that states on their own could not solve the problem of toxic nuclear waste.

The Court followed this decision in *Printz v. United States.* The issue was whether the Brady Handgun Violence Prevention Act violated the Tenth Amendment in requiring that state and local law enforcement officers conduct background checks on prospective handgun purchasers. In a 5–4 decision, with Justice Scalia writing for the Court, the Court found the provision unconstitutional.

Justice Scalia's majority opinion emphasized that Congress was impermissibly commandeering state executive officials to implement a federal mandate. He observed that historically—and particularly in the early years of the United States—Congress had not exercised such a power.

Making an explicitly "originalist" argument, Justice Scalia said that the original meaning of the Constitution would not allow such commandeering. Reaffirming *New York v. United States,* the Court held that Congress violates the Tenth Amendment when it coerces state governments.

The decision is troubling, because background checks for those purchasing guns are regarded by most as a very good thing. Congress adopted the requirement overwhelmingly. Conservative justices who object to the Court protecting rights not stated in the text of the Constitution nevertheless found a right of states to be free from federal regulation that is found nowhere in the document or its history. Justice Stevens, in a dissenting opinion, stressed the need for the Brady Act. He wrote:

> The Act's legislative history notes that 15,377 Americans were murdered with firearms in 1992, and that 12,489 of these deaths were caused by handguns. . . . The partial solution contained in the Brady Act, a mandatory background check before a handgun may be purchased, has met with remarkable success. Between 1994 and 1996, approximately 6,600 firearm sales each month to potentially dangerous persons were prevented by Brady Act checks; over 70% of the rejected purchasers were convicted or indicted felons.

Except for the most ardent gun-rights activists, there is a widespread belief that gun registration and background checks are desirable.

The Court's most recent decision using the Tenth Amendment to limit federal power was in the Affordable Care Act case, *National Federation of Independent Business v. Sebelius,* mentioned above. Although the Court upheld the individual mandate and rejected the call by four justices to strike down the entire 2,700-page law, it did strike down a key part of the act that was meant to increase medical care coverage for the poorest in society.

The Court, in a 7–2 ruling, held that the act's denial of all Medicaid funding to states that do not comply with the new conditions for Medicaid exceeded the scope of Congress's spending power and violated the Tenth

Amendment. The act requires that states cover within their Medicaid programs those at or below 133 percent of the federal poverty level. The federal government pays 100 percent of these costs until 2019 and 90 percent thereafter. Any state that fails to comply would lose all of its Medicaid funds.

The Court said that it was unduly coercive to tie existing Medicaid funds to a failure to comply with the new requirement. The Court saw Medicaid as being two programs—the old one and the new requirements—and said that it was impermissible to tie existing funds to the failure to comply with new requirements. But why see this as two programs rather than one? Moreover, why see this as Congress coercing or, to use Chief Justice Roberts's word, "dragooning" the states? Admittedly, given the huge amount of money involved, any state would face a hard choice to turn it down. But there is a basic difference between being forced to do something and facing a very difficult choice. No state is required to take federal Medicaid money. It would be a hard choice to turn it down, but that is not the same as being forced to take part. Why shouldn't Congress, in giving federal dollars, be able to condition them on complying with its terms, especially when the conditions are entirely about fulfilling the purpose of the Medicaid program in ensuring health care for those who cannot afford it?

It is this part of the opinion that is likely to have the broadest implications. This was the first time in history that the Court had ever found conditions on federal funds to be so coercive as to be unconstitutional. Countless federal statutes provide funds to state and local governments on the condition that they comply with requirements. There likely will be challenges to many of these laws on the ground that the requirements are too coercive.

Conclusion

My goal throughout this book is to determine whether the Supreme Court made American society better or worse. Did the Supreme Court make the country better off with its rulings during the *Lochner* era, protecting business by declaring laws that protected workers and consumers unconstitutional? The overwhelming consensus of Supreme Court justices and scholars is that these decisions were terribly misguided and did great harm. I also believe that the Court's contemporary application of these doctrines—its protection of states' rights over the past couple of decades—will be regarded in hindsight as just as misguided. The Court has struck down laws that are unquestionably desirable and kept injured people from being able to get any recovery.

The decisions protecting freedom of contract and limiting the scope of Congress's powers are important to our thinking about the Supreme Court in another way. For decades, conservatives have railed against so-called liberal judicial activism. Although the term "judicial activism" is never defined, it is invoked especially when the Supreme Court strikes down laws to protect individual rights. Conservatives have urged deference to the political process and legislatures. The cases discussed in this chapter are all examples in which it was the conservatives who were engaged in activism, showing no deference to the legislature and invalidating laws—both in the earlier era and today—of great importance in protecting people from harm.

It is impossible to escape the conclusion that in protecting freedom of contract and in safeguarding states' rights, the Supreme Court has done far more harm than good.

CHAPTER 4

What About the Warren Court?

In January 1942, in the earliest days of America's involvement in World War II, the West Virginia Board of Education adopted a resolution ordering that the salute to the American flag become "a regular part of the program of activities in the public schools," that all teachers and pupils "shall be required to participate in the salute honoring the Nation represented by the Flag; provided, however, that refusal to salute the Flag be regarded as an Act of insubordination, and shall be dealt with accordingly." What was required was a "stiff-arm salute" to the flag; students and teachers had to raise their right hand with their palm turned up while they said the Pledge of Allegiance. Oddly enough, the salute was remarkably like that used in Nazi Germany, where it was accompanied by "*Heil* Hitler"—an objection to the law made without effect by the American Red Cross and the National Parent Teacher Association.

A student who failed to comply with this statute would be expelled from school and could not be readmitted until he or she complied with the law and saluted the flag each day. The parents of the student faced criminal prosecution, because the expelled child was deemed "unlawfully absent," and the parents could be jailed for up to thirty days. A teacher who failed to comply in leading the class in a flag salute would be fired.

Jehovah's Witnesses believe that such a salute to a "graven image" violates the Bible and their religion. The Barnette family, who had daughters in the public schools, brought a lawsuit to challenge the requirement of saluting the flag. The case came to the Supreme Court in 1943, during a time of war and intense patriotism. Even worse for the plaintiffs, just three years earlier, in *Minersville School District v. Gobitis,* the Court had ruled that public schools could compel students to salute the flag and recite the Pledge of Allegiance even if it violated their religion to do so.

Nonetheless, in *West Virginia State Board of Education v. Barnette,* the Court declared the West Virginia law unconstitutional and overruled *Gobitis.* Justice Robert Jackson, writing for the Court, eloquently said, "[T]he compulsory flag salute and pledge requires affirmation of a belief and an attitude of mind. . . . If there is any fixed star in our constitutional constellation, it is that no official, high or petty, can prescribe what shall be orthodox in politics, nationalism, religion or other matters of opinion or force citizens to confess by word or act their faith therein."

I mention this example because it is an important instance of the Court resisting majoritarian pressures and enforcing the Constitution. I am not contending that the Supreme Court always fails or that all of its decisions are flawed. That, of course, would be an absurd contention. My point is that in crucial areas, the Court historically has failed to uphold the Constitution or resist majoritarian pressures, such as with regard to race, rights during times of crisis, and allowing government economic regulations. But even in these areas, not every Court decision has been misguided. *West Virginia State Board of Education v. Barnette,* decided in the midst of a war, is almost universally regarded as a terrific decision.

The Warren Court

As I have shared the thesis of this book, the most common response I have received is "What about the Warren Court?" In fact, over the years, as I have responded to those who argue that the Court has largely been a failure, I point to the successes of the Warren Court. The Warren Court began in 1953, when President Dwight Eisenhower made a recess appointment of Earl Warren to be chief justice of the United States, replacing Fred

Vinson, who had died of a heart attack. Warren, who had been a prosecutor and attorney general in California, was elected governor of California three times. He even once ran for governor with the nominations of both the Democratic and Republican Parties, something hard to imagine today.

When Warren joined the bench, it already had two liberal justices, Hugo Black and William O. Douglas, who had been appointed by President Franklin Roosevelt. Two years after Warren's appointment, Republican president Dwight Eisenhower chose a Democrat—New Jersey Supreme Court justice William Brennan. Often, these four justices could persuade one of the moderate justices to join them. In 1962, President John F. Kennedy appointed Arthur Goldberg to the Court and created a liberal majority.

The Warren Court ended in 1969 when Warren Burger was nominated by President Richard Nixon to replace Earl Warren, who had submitted his resignation. Between 1969 and 1971, Nixon was able to replace four members of the Warren Court (Warren, Black, Harlan, and Fortas) with individuals who were much more conservative (Burger, Blackmun, Powell, and Rehnquist). In the four decades since, a majority of the justices have been Republican appointees, and the Supreme Court has not again had a liberal majority.

The Warren Court is widely thought of as having been liberal, based on its decisions on topics such as desegregation, school prayer, protections for criminal defendants, and reapportionment of state legislatures. Richard Nixon ran for president in 1968 and repeatedly attacked the Warren Court's decisions, calling for the appointment of "strict constructionists" for the Court. Bumper stickers and billboards in the South called for Warren's impeachment. Although many of the Warren Court's decisions were regarded as liberal at the time they came down, many of its most important rulings are regarded in hindsight as clearly correct by liberals and conservatives alike. Examples of such widely applauded decisions by the Warren Court are those regarding race, voting, and criminal procedure. Few today, even among the staunchest conservatives, question these rulings or call for them to be overruled.

The Warren Court and Race

As I explained in chapter 1, the Warren Court was the first since the adoption of the Fourteenth Amendment to use the Equal Protection Clause in a significant way. Perhaps most important, in 1954, in *Brown v. Board of Education*, the Court held that separate schools are inherently unequal.

From *Plessy v. Ferguson*, in 1896, until *Brown*, in 1954, not once had the Supreme Court called into question its holding that "separate but equal" was consistent with the Constitution. On a few occasions, the Court held that a state's treatment of whites and blacks was so unequal as to violate the Equal Protection Clause of the Fourteenth Amendment. For example, in 1938, in *Missouri ex rel. Gaines v. Canada*, the Supreme Court held that it was unconstitutional for Missouri to refuse to admit blacks to its law school but instead to pay for blacks to attend out-of-state law schools. In response, Missouri did not admit blacks to its law school but instead created a new law school for blacks.

In *Sweatt v. Painter*, in 1950, the Supreme Court for the first time ordered that a white university admit a black student, but it did so without questioning the "separate but equal" doctrine. The University of Texas School of Law had denied Heman Sweatt admission on the ground that he could attend the recently created Prairie View Law School. Although the Court was urged to reconsider *Plessy v. Ferguson*, it refused and instead found that the schools obviously were not equal. The state university's law school had sixteen full-time faculty members and substantial facilities; Prairie View had opened in 1947 with no full-time faculty and no library, though by the time the Court decided the case, there were five full-time professors and a small library. The Court concluded, "[W]e cannot find substantial equality in the educational opportunities offered white and Negro law students by the State. . . . It is difficult to believe that one who had a free choice between these law schools would consider the question close."

Brown v. Board of Education came before the Supreme Court during

October Term 1952. It was in fact a review of five separate cases that challenged the doctrine of separate but equal in the context of elementary and high school education. At the time, seventeen states and the District of Columbia required segregation of public schools. The school systems challenged in the five cases before the Supreme Court involved schools that were unequal by tangible measures.

The five cases were argued together during October Term 1952. Tradition holds that the Court decides by the end of June all of the cases argued during a term. Occasionally, though, the justices can't or don't decide by the end of the term and ask for new arguments the following year. The justices could not agree on a decision in *Brown,* and the cases were set for reargument the following year. After they were argued on October 13, 1953, an intense effort by Chief Justice Warren persuaded all of the justices to join a unanimous decision holding that separate but equal was impermissible in the realm of public education.

On May 17, 1954, the Supreme Court released its decision in *Brown v. Board of Education.* The named plaintiff, Oliver Brown, was one of thirteen parents who were challenging the segregation of the Topeka, Kansas, public schools. The Court said, "In approaching this problem, we cannot turn the clock back to 1868 when the Amendment was adopted, or even to 1896 when Plessy v. Ferguson was written. We must consider public education in the light of its full development and its present place in American life throughout the Nation."

The Court did not focus on the obvious inequalities between the black and white schools in the cases before it. Rather, it said that "there are findings below that the Negro and white schools involved have been equalized, or are being equalized, with respect to buildings, curricula, qualifications and salaries of teachers, and other 'tangible factors.' Our decision, therefore, cannot turn on merely a comparison of those tangible factors in the Negro and white schools involved in each of the cases. We must look instead to the effect of segregation itself on public education."

The Court probably characterized the issue this way because there had been factual findings by some of the district courts that equalization was occurring between the black and white schools. Also, the Court wanted to address the basic question: Is separate but equal constitutional in public education? By assuming the schools to be equal, even when they weren't, the Court could state the issue as "Does segregation of children in public schools solely on the basis of race, even though the physical facilities and other 'tangible' factors may be equal, deprive the children of the minority group of equal educational opportunities?"

The Court answered this question by declaring that state-mandated segregation inherently stamps black children as inferior and impairs their educational opportunities. Chief Justice Warren wrote, "To separate them from others of similar age and qualifications solely because of their race generates a feeling of inferiority as to their status in the community that may affect their hearts and minds in a way unlikely ever to be undone." The Court supported this conclusion with a citation from psychology literature that purported to show that segregation causes black children to feel inferior and interferes with their learning.

The Court ended its relatively short opinion by declaring, "We conclude that in the field of public education the doctrine of 'separate but equal' has no place. Separate educational facilities are inherently unequal." The Court did not prescribe a remedy but rather asked for reargument in the next term on that issue. A year later, in *Brown II,* the Supreme Court remanded the cases to the lower courts, to use traditional principles to fashion remedies "to admit to public schools on a racially nondiscriminatory basis with all deliberate speed the parties to these cases."

Brown's significance cannot be overstated. Richard Kluger eloquently wrote:

> Every colored American knew that Brown did not mean that he would be invited to lunch with the Rotary the following week. It meant something more basic and more important. It meant that black rights had suddenly been redefined; black bodies had suddenly been reborn under a new law. Blacks' value as human beings had been changed overnight by the

declaration of the nation's highest court. At a stroke, the Justices had severed the remaining cords of de facto slavery. The Negro could no longer be fastened with the status of official pariah. No longer could the white man look right through him as if he were, in the title words of Ralph Ellison's stunning 1952 novel, Invisible Man. No more would he be a grinning supplicant for the benefactions and discards of the master class; no more would he be a party to his own degradation. He was both thrilled that the signal for the demise of his caste status had come from on high and angry that it had taken so long and first exacted so steep a price in suffering.

Brown began the process of the Supreme Court's invalidating the Jim Crow laws that segregated every aspect of southern life. After Brown, in a series of short, unsigned opinions, the Supreme Court affirmed lower-court decisions declaring unconstitutional state laws requiring segregation in all of the remaining areas of southern life. For example, in Mayor and City Council of Baltimore City v. Dawson, in 1955, the Supreme Court, without an opinion, affirmed a lower-court decision declaring unconstitutional a law requiring segregation in the use of public beaches and bathhouses. The Court did the exact same thing in Holmes v. City of Atlanta, also in 1955, declaring unconstitutional the segregation of municipal golf courses; in Browder v. Gayle, in 1956, declaring unconstitutional the segregation of a municipal bus system; in Turner v. City of Memphis, in 1962, declaring unconstitutional the segregation of public restaurants; and in Johnson v. Virginia, in 1963, declaring unconstitutional segregation of courtroom seating. Interestingly, in all of these cases, laws requiring racial segregation were declared unconstitutional, but without judicial opinions.

The result, however, was that the Court never wrote an opinion explaining why government-mandated segregation inherently denies equal protection. Brown focused solely on why segregation of schools violates the Constitution, but none of the other cases had opinions. The Court thus squandered the chance to explain why it is inimical to the very notion of equal protection for the white majority to mandate segregation: such laws are based on the assumption of the superiority of one race and the inferiority of another.

That said, no one today is likely to criticize the holding in *Brown* or the results in the other decisions declaring segregation unconstitutional. These cases dramatically changed society and are a powerful example of what the Court exists to accomplish.

The Warren Court and Equality in Voting

A second area where the Warren Court made a huge positive difference was in the area of voting. Prior to the 1960s, many state legislatures were badly malapportioned—one legislative district often was far more populous than another district for the same body. Likewise, states' U.S. congressional districts often were significantly malapportioned. Such malapportionment usually was a result of population shifts from rural to urban areas. Districts often were not redrawn after urban migration, causing cities to be underrepresented compared with more rural areas. Legislators who benefited from the malapportionment were highly unlikely to change the districting.

Initially, when the first challenges reached the Supreme Court in the 1940s, it ruled that challenges to malapportionment posed an issue that could not be decided by the courts. However, in *Baker v. Carr*, in 1962, the Warren Court concluded that equal protection objections to malapportionment *could* be decided by federal courts. Justice William Brennan wrote the opinion for the Court and opened the door to challenges to the tremendous disparities that existed in districts for city councils, state legislatures, and the House of Representatives.

Soon after, the Court articulated the rule of one person, one vote; that is, for any legislative body, all districts must be about the same size in population terms. The first case to announce this principle was *Gray v. Sanders*, in 1963. *Gray* involved a challenge to the Georgia system of selecting representatives for the House of the Georgia General Assembly on a county basis. An inequality resulted because counties varied widely in population size. Justice Douglas, writing for the Court, explained why this is unconstitutional:

> How then can one person be given twice or ten times the voting power of another person in a statewide election merely because he lives in a rural area or because he lives in the smallest rural county? Once the geographical unit for which a representative is to be chosen is designated, all who participate in the election are to have an equal vote—whatever their race, whatever their sex, wherever their occupation, whatever their income, and whatever their home may be in that geographic unit. This is required by the Equal Protection Clause of the Fourteenth Amendment.

Thus, the Court said that equal protection requires that all districts be about the same in population size; anything else impermissibly dilutes the voting power of those in the more populous districts. In its conclusion, the Court declared, "The conception of political equality from the Declaration of Independence, to Lincoln's Gettysburg Address, to the Fifteenth, Seventeenth, and Nineteenth Amendments can mean only one thing—one person, one vote."

In *Reynolds v. Sims,* in 1964, the Warren Court applied these principles to declare the malapportionment of a state legislature unconstitutional and to order its reapportionment. Under then-existing law, the Alabama legislature had a thirty-five-member state senate elected from thirty-five districts that varied in population from 15,417 to 634,864. There also was a one-hundred-member state house of representatives with districts varying from 31,175 to 634,864.

Chief Justice Warren, writing for the Court, explained that geographical area made no sense in drawing districts; only population was a permissible basis. He said, "Legislators represent people, not trees or acres.

Legislators are elected by voters, not farms or cities or economic interests. As long as ours is a representative form of government, and our legislatures are those instruments of government elected directly by and directly representative of the people, the right to elect representatives in a free and unimpaired fashion is a bedrock of our political system."

Malapportionment inevitably means vote dilution; voters in the more populous districts have proportionately less influence in the political process than those in the small districts. Malapportionment systematically favored rural areas and disfavored urban ones in the legislative process.

Earl Warren said that of all the decisions during his time as chief justice, the reapportionment cases were the most important. There is no doubt that the reapportionment decisions have had an enormous effect on American government by changing the composition of city councils, state legislatures, and congressional delegations. Although they were extremely controversial in the 1960s, since the 1980s they have been seen as a paradigm instance of the judiciary acting to perfect the political process and reinforce democracy. Reapportionment was very unlikely to occur without judicial action, because officeholders were not going to give up their seats voluntarily. The decisions dramatically changed the composition of legislatures and thus undoubtedly affected the laws adopted.

And the Warren Court did much more to expand protection of the right to vote. The Twenty-fourth Amendment prohibits poll taxes—the requirement that a person pay a fee in order to vote—in elections for federal offices. The Supreme Court in *Harper v. Virginia State Board of Elections* held that poll taxes are unconstitutional as a denial of equal protection for all other elections. The Court concluded that limiting voting to those who paid a poll tax was impermissible discrimination. Justice Douglas, writing for the Court, explained that "a State violates the Equal Protection Clause . . . whenever it makes the affluence of the voter or payment of any fee an electoral standard. Voter qualifications have no relation to wealth nor to paying or not paying this or any other tax." The Court rejected the state's argument that the poll tax of $1.50 was minimal and thus not a significant burden on voters.

In a democracy, the right to vote is obviously critically important. The Warren Court's decisions significantly expanded equality in voting, and today few would question their desirability. The Court was performing its essential function: acting to protect a basic right when the political process would not do so. It is so different from today, when, as discussed in chapter 7, we have a Supreme Court that declared unconstitutional a key provision of the Voting Rights Act of 1965—a case of the political process protecting equality with regard to a basic right, and a Court that invalidated it.

The Warren Court and the Rights of Criminal Defendants

Another area where the Warren Court was a success, but one that is more controversial than its race or voting decisions, was the expansion of the rights of criminal defendants. The Warren Court did this in a number of ways. One of the most important was its holding that the provisions of the Bill of Rights protecting criminal suspects and defendants applied to state and local governments.

The Bill of Rights, of course, in many ways safeguards those accused of crimes. The Fourth Amendment prohibits unreasonable searches and arrests. The Fifth Amendment requires that a person be indicted by a grand jury before being tried for a crime, prohibits double jeopardy (being tried twice for the same crime), protects the privilege against self-incrimination, and ensures due process of law.

The Sixth Amendment guarantees a defendant the right to a speedy and public jury trial. It also requires that the defendant be given an opportunity to confront the witnesses against him or her and to call witnesses in his or her defense. The most important right that the defendant enjoys under the Sixth Amendment is the right to assistance of counsel. Through counsel's diligent efforts, a defendant can preserve his or her other rights. Finally, the Eighth Amendment prohibits excessive bail and fines and forbids cruel and unusual punishment.

These are essential protections to ensure that any person accused of a crime is treated fairly. The provisions help protect against the conviction of innocent people and ensure that all are treated with dignity by the criminal justice system. The government, through the criminal justice system, possesses enormous power to take away a person's liberty or even life. These provisions regulate how that can be done.

But it was not until well into the twentieth century that these provisions were applied to state and local police and prosecutors. And this occurred almost entirely through the decisions of the Warren Court.

Early in the nineteenth century, the Court held that the Bill of Rights was meant to apply only to the federal government, not to state or local governments. In *Barron v. Mayor & City Council of Baltimore*, in 1833, the Court said, "The constitution was ordained and established by the people of the United States for themselves, for their own government, and not for the government of the individual states." In that case, the Court said that a local government that took someone's private property did not have to pay just compensation, even though the Fifth Amendment to the Constitution explicitly says that when the government takes private property for public use, it must pay compensation. The Supreme Court held that this constitutional right, like all of those in the Bill of Rights, applies only to the federal government.

The Court came to this conclusion even though some provisions of the Bill of Rights do not, by their terms, limit themselves to the federal government. The Fifth Amendment begins, "No person shall," and concludes, "nor shall private property be taken for public use, without just compensation." It does not say that the federal government cannot commit such a taking. The provisions protecting the rights of criminal defendants—the Fourth, Fifth, and Sixth Amendments—are not by their language limited to the federal government. The First Amendment, by contrast, begins, "Congress shall make no law." That would imply that when the framers wanted a Bill of Rights position to be limited in its application to the federal government, or a part of it, they said so.

If the Bill of Rights applies only to the federal government, the obvious concern is that state and local governments are therefore free to infringe on even the most precious liberties. Chief Justice John Marshall responded to this concern by saying that state constitutions provided an adequate check on state and local governments, so it wasn't necessary for the Bill of Rights to be applied to them. But it so often did not work this way. Even when state constitutions had provisions like those in the United States Constitution, often they were not enforced against state and local governments. States often did not provide counsel for those accused of crimes, even capital crimes. States punished individuals for invoking the privilege against self-incrimination. Some states had official state churches.

A crucial failing of the Supreme Court was its not applying the Bill of Rights—the protection of the nation's most precious liberties—to state and local governments for the first century and a half of American history. How many innocent people were convicted and incarcerated and even executed because they did not have basic protections, such as the right to counsel, in state court proceedings? It is unthinkable to us today that the most fundamental rights contained in the Bill of Rights simply could not be applied to protect people from state and local governments through most of American history.

In the early twentieth century, the Supreme Court suggested that at least some of the rights protected in the Bill of the Rights are among the liberties protected from state interference by the Due Process Clause of the Fourteenth Amendment. Section 1 of the Fourteenth Amendment prevents state governments from depriving people of life, liberty, or property without due process of law. As discussed in the prior chapter, in the early twentieth century, the Court aggressively used the Due Process Clause to protect economic liberties. At this same time, the Court also suggested that among the rights protected under due process could be provisions of the Bill of Rights that were deemed "fundamental" liberties.

In 1908, in *Twining v. New Jersey,* the Court expressly recognized the possibility that the Due Process Clause of the Fourteenth Amendment incorporates provisions of the Bill of Rights and thereby applies them to state and local governments. The Court rejected a criminal defendant's claim that a state court had violated his constitutional rights by instructing the jury that it could draw a negative inference from his failure to testify at trial. However, the Court said that it "is possible that some of the personal rights safeguarded by the first eight Amendments against National action may also be safeguarded against state action, because a denial of them would be a denial of due process of law."

This opened the door for the Court, giving it a way to apply the Bill of Rights to state and local governments. The Court began to find that the Due Process Clause of the Fourteenth Amendment, which applies to state and local governments, includes protection for fundamental rights found in the Bill of Rights. In 1925, in *Gitlow v. New York*, the Court for the first time said that the First Amendment's protection of freedom of speech applies to the states through its incorporation into the Due Process Clause of the Fourteenth Amendment. The First Amendment, like all of the Bill of Rights, was adopted in 1791. So for the first 134 years of American history, state and local governments that infringed on freedom of speech, even egregiously so, could not be challenged as acting unconstitutionally.

Even more astounding, it was not until 1932, in *Powell v. Alabama*, that the Court found that it was a violation of due process and the Constitution to sentence a person to death when the individual was not represented by a lawyer. The infamous Scottsboro trial involved two African American men who were convicted of rape without the assistance of an attorney at trial and by a jury from which all blacks had been excluded. The Supreme Court reiterated that the Due Process Clause of the Fourteenth Amendment protects fundamental rights from state interference and that this can include Bill of Rights provisions. The Court held that in a capital case, "it [is] clear that the right to the aid of counsel is of this fundamental character." It is deeply disturbing that until 1933, a person could be convicted in a state court, sentenced to death, and executed without an attorney being provided.

Powell v. Alabama involved the right to counsel only in a case where a defendant faced a possible death sentence. It was not for another thirty years, until the Warren Court in 1963, in *Gideon v. Wainwright,* that the Court held that all criminal defendants facing possible imprisonment are entitled to an attorney. Clarence Earl Gideon, a fifty-one-year-old native of Florida, had been convicted of breaking and entering. He was indigent and could not afford a lawyer, and none was provided to him. He was sentenced to five years in prison. After losing his appeals in the Florida courts, he filed a handwritten petition for Supreme Court review. The Court decided to hear his case and appointed renowned Washington attorney (and later Supreme Court justice) Abe Fortas to represent Gideon.

The Court held that the government is obligated to provide an attorney to any criminal defendant who, if convicted, could be imprisoned. *Gideon*'s assurance of counsel to all facing a prison sentence undoubtedly has meant that many who otherwise would have been convicted and imprisoned, some wrongly, were able to be free. In fact, there have likely been countless instances of prosecutors not even going forward simply because of the presence of defense counsel. In a criminal justice system in which almost all cases are disposed of by guilty pleas—97 percent in federal court and 94 percent in state court—the presence of defense attorneys surely frequently makes an enormous difference in the nature of the plea deal and the length of the sentence.

None of these effects can be measured. It is not possible to know the number of people who were acquitted who otherwise would have been convicted or the number of cases not brought or the sentences not imposed. But nor can these benefits be denied by anyone with even a passing familiarity with the criminal justice system.

The importance of *Gideon* as a symbol also cannot be overstated. An adversary system of justice requires some semblance of equality between the two sides. *Gideon* is a crucial attempt to make that a reality. It holds that all facing the power of the state to take away their liberty, however poor, are entitled to representation. Under a Constitution that often is described as being a charter of negative liberties and restrictions on government power, rather than affirmative rights, *Gideon* holds that there is something the government must pay for and provide: an attorney to those who cannot afford one and who face the loss of their liberty by imprisonment. As the Court powerfully declared in *Gideon*:

> [R]eason and reflection require us to recognize that in our adversary system of criminal justice, any person haled into court, who is too poor to hire a lawyer, cannot be assured a fair trial unless counsel is provided for him. This seems to us to be an obvious truth.... The right of one charged with crime to counsel may not be deemed fundamental and essential to fair trials in some countries, but it is in ours. From the very beginning, our state and national constitutions and laws have laid great emphasis on procedural and substantive safeguards designed to assure fair trials before impartial tribunals in which every defendant stands equal before the law. This noble ideal cannot be realized if the poor man charged with crime has to face his accusers without a lawyer to assist him.

The Warren Court also took the important step of applying to the states other key provisions of the Bill of Rights that protect criminal defendants. Quite important, though not without controversy, was *Mapp v. Ohio*, in 1961, in which the Court held that the exclusionary rule—the principle that evidence gained via an illegal search must be excluded from use against a criminal defendant—applies to the states. A half-century earlier, the Supreme Court had ruled that the federal government cannot take advantage of illegally obtained evidence in a criminal prosecution. In part, this was to deter police from violating the Fourth Amendment, and in part it was about protecting the integrity of the judicial system and keeping it from being tainted through the use of illegally obtained evidence. Without the exclusionary rule, there is little to discourage police from engaging in illegal searches and arrests. Applying the exclusionary rule to the states was crucial to increasing compliance with the Fourth Amendment by state and local police.

The Warren Court also applied to the states the Fifth Amendment's prohibition of double jeopardy and its protection against self-incrimination. Key provisions of the Sixth Amendment—such as the requirement for a trial by an impartial jury, the right to confront adverse witnesses, and the right to subpoena witnesses to testify—also were applied in state courts during the Warren era. The Warren Court additionally held that states cannot impose cruel and unusual punishment in violation of the Eighth Amendment.

Today, these decisions applying the Bill of Rights to state and local governments seem unassailable and are hardly criticized. I have rarely heard anyone call for these cases to be reconsidered or overruled. The Bill of Rights is regarded as our charter of fundamental rights that all individuals possess. It is unthinkable that state and local governments could violate them and not be held accountable. Yet it was not until 1963 that states had to provide an attorney in cases involving possible prison sentences, and it was not until 1964 that the states were required to obey the privilege against self-incrimination.

The Warren Court also expanded the rights of criminal defendants through its interpretation of Bill of Rights provisions. Most famously, in *Miranda v. Arizona,* in 1966, the Court found that police questioning of a suspect in custody is inherently coercive. The Court said that the remedy is that police in-custodial interrogation must be preceded by the administration of now famous warnings to the suspect: "You have the right to remain silent. Anything you say can and will be used against you in a court of law. You have the right to an attorney. If you cannot afford an attorney, one will be provided for you." The Court's stated goal was to limit the pressure during questioning in the coercive environment of the police station house by reminding suspects of their constitutional rights.

Initially, *Miranda* was very controversial, with critics seeing it as unduly limiting police questioning and fearing that it would let criminals off on a technicality. Yet over time, it has become widely accepted. In 2000, the Court had the chance to overrule *Miranda* and declined to do so. Even police organizations filed a brief urging the Court to keep *Miranda.* They explained to the Court that the *Miranda* warning provides clear guidance to the police about what to do in questioning a suspect. So long as officers read the few simple precautions, there is a presumption that any incriminating statements were voluntarily obtained and are admissible. Also, police had discovered that *Miranda* did not keep them from gaining confessions, perhaps because the Court had allowed so many ways around it. In *Dickerson v. United States,* in 2000, with conservative chief justice William Rehnquist writing for the majority, the Court, by a 7–2 margin, reaffirmed that *Miranda* is constitutionally required in order to protect the Fifth Amendment's privilege against self-incrimination.

Why These Decisions Matter

These three areas—ending segregation, increasing equality in voting, and expanding the rights of criminal defendants—are unquestionably successes for the Supreme Court that made American society better. The political process would not have enforced the Constitution in any of these areas. Southern states would not have ended segregated schools or any of the other areas of apartheid in the 1950s, or likely in the 1960s. State legislators who benefited from malapportionment were not about to voluntarily redraw election districts to take themselves out of office. Legislatures virtually never expand the rights of criminal defendants; there is no political constituency to do so. Thus, in each of these areas, the Supreme Court was performing its core mission: enforcing the Constitution to protect minorities in areas where otherwise the Constitution would have been unenforced.

But at the same time, I do not want to overstate the successes of the Warren Court. Even in the areas that I have identified, the Warren Court could have done much more. In fact, its failure to do so has serious adverse consequences to this day. The case against the Supreme Court, while tempered by all of the positive things done by the Warren Court, must include recognition that it did not do all that it could have or all that was necessary, even in the key areas that I have identified. Consider two crucial examples: school desegregation and the right to counsel. No Warren Court decisions are more celebrated than *Brown v. Board of Education* and *Gideon v. Wainwright*. Yet, with regard to each, the Warren Court did too little.

The Failure to Achieve Equal Educational Opportunity

Ironically, the area of society that remains most segregated, where the Supreme Court has most failed, is the one that was the focus of *Brown:* public school education. American public schools are racially separate, and this segregation is increasing at an accelerating rate. The overall statistics for major-city public schools could not be more discouraging for those who believe in desegregation. In 2012–13, in the Boston public schools, only 12 percent of the students were white. In Chicago, just 8.8 percent of children in the schools were white. In Los Angeles, the number was 9.2 percent, while in Dallas it was only 4.8 percent. In Washington, D.C., 85 percent of children were black or Hispanic, and 11 percent were white.

The simple and tragic reality is that American schools are separate and unequal. To a very large degree, education in the United States is racially segregated. By any measure, predominantly minority schools are not equal in their resources or their quality. Wealthy suburban school districts are almost exclusively white; poor inner-city schools are often exclusively composed of African American and Hispanic students. Studies have shown that across the United States, significantly more is spent on the average white child's education than on the average black child's schooling. Moreover, disproportionately more white children than minority children attend private schools, which have more resources and far better student-to-faculty ratios. According to recent national statistics, private elementary schools are 86 percent white, and private high schools are 87 percent white.

The causes of racial segregation in education are complex, but the Supreme Court, including the Warren Court, deserves a good deal of the blame. The problem began with *Brown v. Board of Education* itself. In *Brown*, in 1954, the Court found that separate but equal is unconstitutional in the realm of public education, but it did not order a remedy. The Court asked for new briefs and arguments in the following years on the question of the appropriate remedy. A year later, in *Brown II,* the Court considered the issue of remedy but did virtually nothing: it sent the case back to the lower courts to achieve desegregation "with all deliberate speed." I have always thought that this phrase was an oxymoron, and it certainly gave no real instructions to the lower courts that would be responsible for implementing *Brown* about what they were supposed to do. The Court gave no deadlines or timetables; it prescribed no techniques or approaches to desegregating schools to comply with the Constitution. The NAACP had asked the Court to order an immediate end to segregated schools. The Court did not do so, and tellingly, the day after *Brown II,* southern state officials were quoted in the press declaring victory.

For a decade after *Brown,* the Supreme Court largely stayed out of the desegregation effort. In 1958, in *Cooper v. Aaron,* the Court ruled that the governor of Arkansas could not disregard the Constitution and obstruct the desegregation of the Little Rock public schools. It was a powerful opinion, signed individually by each justice. But it was the only Supreme Court decision about school segregation in the decade following *Brown.* It wasn't until 1964, a decade after *Brown,* that the Court lamented, "There has been entirely too much deliberation and not enough speed" in achieving desegregation.

The result was that a decade after *Brown,* virtually no desegregation had occurred. In the South in 1964, just 1.2 percent of black schoolchildren were attending school with whites. In South Carolina, Alabama, and Mississippi, not one black child attended a public school with a white child in the 1962–63 school year. In North Carolina, only one-quarter of 1 percent of the black students attended desegregated schools in 1961, and the figure did not rise above 1 percent until 1965. Similarly, in Virginia in 1964, only 1.63 percent of blacks were attending desegregated schools.

It was not until seventeen years after *Brown,* in 1971, in *Swann v.*

Charlotte-Mecklenburg Board of Education, that the Supreme Court finally attempted to provide guidance to lower courts in structuring remedies to desegregate schools. The Court prescribed such techniques as redrawing attendance zones and busing students to achieve desegregation.

I always ask my students whether it would have made a difference had the Supreme Court, in *Brown II* or another case soon thereafter, mandated timetables for desegregation and detailed the remedies to be imposed.

There obviously is no way of knowing whether such Supreme Court efforts would have hastened desegregation. But it is too easy to assume that they would have made little difference in the face of massive resistance. Had the Court dictated timetables, outlined remedies, and been more actively involved between 1954 and 1964, results might well have been different, at least in some places. None other than Justice John Paul Stevens has argued, in a recent book, that the Warren Court made a huge mistake by choosing to ensure unanimity among the justices and not doing more to desegregate schools. Southern states would have defied judicial orders, but they did that anyway, and the Court could have done much more to give lower federal court judges guidance on what they needed to do to desegregate schools.

Subsequent Supreme Court decisions have contributed greatly to the separate and unequal schools that exist today. Just after the end of the Warren Court, in two decisions in 1973 and 1974, the Court dealt critical blows to the effort to create equal education for all children.

In *San Antonio Independent School District v. Rodriguez,* the Court held that inequalities in school funding do not deny equal protection, and the Court concluded that education is not a fundamental right under the Constitution. *Rodriguez* involved a challenge to the Texas system of funding public schools largely through local property taxes. The litigation involved the San Antonio metropolitan area, where there were great disparities in the funding of schools depending on the wealth of the school district.

There were seven public school districts in the San Antonio area. The Edgewood Independent School District, with approximately 22,000 students enrolled in its twenty-five elementary and secondary schools, was one of the poorer in the area. It was in the core of San Antonio, in a residential neighborhood that had little commercial or industrial property. The residents were predominantly of Mexican American descent: approximately 90 percent of the student population was Mexican American, and more than 6 percent was African American. It had the lowest average property value ($5,960) and the lowest median annual family income ($4,686) in the metropolitan area. It also taxed its property at the highest rate in the area: an equalized tax rate of $1.05 per $100 of assessed property. The result, when combined with state and federal funds, was an expenditure of $356 per pupil annually.

By contrast, Alamo Heights was the most affluent school district in the San Antonio metropolitan area. Its six schools, educating approximately five thousand students, were situated in a very different residential area than Edgewood. The school population was overwhelmingly white, having only 18 percent Mexican Americans and fewer than 1 percent African Americans. Its local property tax rate was $.85 per $100, significantly lower than that in Edgewood. But it was able to yield more revenue and spend significantly more on each child's education: Alamo Heights spent $594 per pupil.

Such disparities in school funding were common all across the country, with white suburban school districts spending far more on education than did predominantly minority city schools. In 1972, education expert Christopher Jencks estimated that on average, 15 to 20 percent more was being spent on each white student's education than on each black child's. This was true throughout the country. For example, in the early 1970s, the Chicago public schools, where the majority of students were African American, spent $5,265 for each student's education, but in the Niles school system (91.6 percent white), just north of the city, the figure was $9,371. In Camden, New Jersey, $3,538 was spent on each pupil, while in predominantly white Princeton, New Jersey, $7,725 was spent.

There is an easy explanation for the disparities in school funding. In most states, education is substantially funded by local property taxes.

Wealthier suburbs have significantly larger tax bases than poorer inner cities. The result is that suburbs can tax at a lower rate and still have a great deal to spend on education. Cities must tax at a higher rate and nonetheless often have much less to spend on schools.

The Court had the opportunity to remedy this inequality in education in *San Antonio Independent School District v. Rodriguez*. But the Court profoundly failed and expressly concluded that inequalities in school funding do not deny equal protection. The Court rejected the claim that education is a fundamental right. The Court said, "Education, of course, is not among the rights afforded explicit protection under our Federal Constitution. Nor do we find any basis for saying it is implicitly so protected."

This makes little sense. Education obviously is inextricably linked to the exercise of constitutional rights such as freedom of speech and voting. If America ever becomes a more equal society, it will be through education. Chief Justice Warren eloquently expressed this view in *Brown v. Board of Education*:

> Today, education is perhaps the most important function of state and local governments. . . . It is required in the performance of our most basic public responsibilities, even service in the armed forces. It is the very foundation of good citizenship. Today it is a principal instrument in awakening the child to cultural values, in preparing him for later professional training, and in helping him to adjust normally to his environment. In these days, it is doubtful that any child may reasonably be expected to succeed in life if he is denied the opportunity of an education.

The Court in *Rodriguez* nonetheless decided that education is not a fundamental right. From the Court's perspective, education is like nutrition or medical care: it is very important, but it is not a right provided by the Constitution. Thus, the Court concluded that the significant disparities in school funding did not offend the U.S. Constitution.

While *Rodriguez* meant that there would be unequal schools, another decision, a year later, *Milliken v. Bradley,* ensured that they would be racially separate. The case involved the segregation of the Detroit public schools. Following the common pattern, Detroit had a student population that was almost entirely minority, but it was surrounded by suburbs that were almost entirely white. For example, of the fourteen schools that opened in Detroit in 1970–71, eleven opened with more than 90 percent African American students, and one opened with less than 10 percent African American students. Many of the surrounding suburbs had school systems comprising almost entirely white students. The federal district court found that without including the suburbs in the desegregation plan, many schools in Detroit would inevitably remain between 75 and 100 percent black.

A federal district court devised a remedy for the racial separation in the schools that included both the city and the suburbs. The plan included Detroit and fifty-three of eighty-seven suburbs in that metropolitan area. No one in the litigation disputed that the area-wide remedy would have been very successful in achieving desegregation.

Nonetheless, the Supreme Court ruled this impermissible and held that courts generally cannot create interdistrict desegregation plans. In almost every metropolitan area, without the ability to assign students from city schools to suburban ones, and from suburban schools to city ones, there is no practical way to achieve desegregation. If 90 percent of a city's school system is made up of minority students, no amount of busing or shifting students can achieve desegregation. *Milliken* thus has had a devastating effect on the ability to achieve desegregation in many areas. Duke professor Charles Clotfelter, in a careful study of American schools, concluded that 60 percent of segregation is a result of *Milliken v. Bradley.* Put another way, American schools would be 60 percent less segregated if interdistrict remedies were possible.

The segregated pattern in major metropolitan areas—blacks in the city and whites in the suburbs—did not occur by accident, but rather was the product of both private choices and myriad government policies.

Moreover, *Milliken* had the effect of encouraging white flight. Whites who wish to avoid sending their children to racially integrated schools can do so by moving to the suburbs. If *Milliken* had been decided differently, one of the incentives for such moves would have been eliminated.

The combined effect of *Milliken* and *Rodriguez* has been enormous. *Milliken* helped to ensure racially separate schools, and *Rodriguez* meant that they would be unequal. American public education is characterized by wealthy white suburban schools spending a great deal on education, surrounding much poorer black and Latino city schools that spend much less on education. The promise in *Brown* of equal educational opportunity has been unfulfilled because of the Supreme Court's failures.

And subsequent decisions have made it worse. In *Board of Education of Oklahoma City Public Schools v. Dowell,* in 1991, the Court said that desegregation orders should be lifted even when their end will mean a resegregation of the public schools. Oklahoma schools had been segregated under a state law mandating separation of the races in education. It was not until 1971—seventeen years after *Brown*—that desegregation was ordered by a federal court judge. The federal court order was very successful in desegregating the Oklahoma City public schools. Evidence proved that ending the desegregation order would result in dramatic resegregation of these schools. The ending of the federal court's remedy would mean that more than half of Oklahoma City's elementary schools would have student bodies that were either 90 percent African American or 90 percent non–African American.

Nonetheless, the Supreme Court held that the school desegregation order should be lifted. As a result of this decision, many successful federal court desegregation orders were ended, resulting in the resegregation of school systems. Cases like *Milliken* and *Oklahoma City* limited the ability of federal courts to desegregate school systems.

Even after these cases, there was still the possibility of school districts implementing desegregation plans on their own. The Supreme Court's decision in *Parents Involved in Community Schools v. Seattle School District No. 1,* in 2007, ended many of these efforts. It was a 5–4 decision, with the five most conservative justices—Roberts, Scalia, Kennedy, Thomas, and Alito—making up the majority.

The case involved two school systems, in Seattle and Louisville, that had adopted desegregation plans. The Seattle plan applied at the high school level. The district operates ten regular public high schools. Under a plan adopted in 1998, students get to pick the school they wish to attend. If too many students list the same school as their first choice, the district uses a series of "tiebreakers" to determine who will gain admission to the oversubscribed school. The first factor to be considered gives preference to students who have a sibling currently enrolled in the school. The second factor looks to race if the school is not racially balanced. In other words, race is one factor considered in assigning students if the schools are oversubscribed.

Unlike Seattle, where the schools had never been segregated by law, the Jefferson County schools in Louisville had been racially segregated until this was declared unconstitutional, in 1973. A desegregation order was imposed by the federal court in 1975. In 2000, undoubtedly as a result of the Supreme Court's decisions from the 1990s, the federal court lifted its desegregation order. The school board then adopted its own desegregation plan. Approximately 34 percent of the district's 97,000 students were black; most of the remaining 66 percent were white. The desegregation plan adopted by the school board required all non-magnet schools to maintain a minimum black enrollment of 15 percent and a maximum black enrollment of 50 percent. In both the elementary schools and the high schools, race was one factor used to assign students to schools to achieve desegregation.

The Supreme Court struck down both programs and created a significant obstacle to school boards implementing their own desegregation programs in the future. The Court said that the government can use race in assigning students to schools only if there is no other way to achieve diversity, and Chief Justice Roberts's opinion, joined by three other justices, rejected the importance of diversity in the classroom. As discussed in chapter 1, these justices see no difference in the meaning of the Equal Protection Clause between the government using race to discriminate against African Americans and the government using race to desegregate its public schools.

The decision will create a significant obstacle to school systems adopting desegregation plans. For obvious reasons, desegregating schools often requires taking into account the race of the students. Assigning students randomly, without regard to their race, cannot achieve the goal. Justice Breyer, in his dissenting opinion, attached an appendix listing dozens of voluntary desegregation plans that will be in jeopardy after the Court's holding. Many have been ended since the decision. The earlier Supreme Court decisions greatly limited what courts could do to desegregate schools and equalize educational opportunity. *Parents Involved v. Seattle* is important because it significantly restricts the ability of school districts to create effective voluntary desegregation plans on their own.

There are many reasons why American public schools are separate and unequal—why there are what public education advocate Jonathan Kozol has termed "savage inequalities." But a share of the blame must go to the Supreme Court. It has persistently failed to do all it could, and it has, in so many ways, made the problem worse.

The Failure to Provide Adequate Counsel in Criminal Cases

Another area where the promise of the Warren Court has gone unfulfilled is the right to counsel for criminal defendants, so importantly assured by *Gideon v. Wainwright.*

As someone who handles criminal appeals, I have represented clients whom I believe to be innocent who were convicted because of ineffective assistance of counsel, and I have represented clients who I am convinced received death sentences because of this. In instances like these, I wonder whether these individuals really were better off because of *Gideon.* Perhaps if they had been left to represent themselves, they would have done better, or maybe the courts would have looked more closely at their cases. *Gideon* creates a strong presumption that the presence of counsel has ensured adequate representation, when the reality is so very different. As Senator Patrick Leahy remarked, "Too often individuals facing the ultimate punishment are represented by lawyers who are drunk, sleeping, soon-to-be disbarred or just plain ineffective. Even the best lawyers in these systems are hampered by inadequate compensation and insufficient resources to investigate and develop a meaningful defense."

The reality is that the quality of representation often matters in criminal cases, and money often is crucial in determining the quality of representation. Of course there are instances in which the outcome will be the same no matter how good or bad the defense lawyer. Of course there are instances in which the best-paid lawyer does a poor job or the inadequately compensated attorney is terrific. But that said, any one of us facing criminal charges would want the best lawyer we could get, and being able to pay for it matters.

The most powerful evidence of this comes from studies that have compared the outcomes of cases on the basis of how the lawyer is compensated. The Bureau of Justice Statistics found that those with publicly funded counsel are more likely to be convicted than those with privately paid attorneys. It concluded, "Of defendants found guilty in federal district courts, 88% with publicly financed counsel and 77% with private counsel received jail or prison sentences; in large state courts, 71% with public counsel and 54% with private attorneys were sentenced to incarceration."

Moreover, among those with publicly paid attorneys, the outcome varies depending on whether there is a public defender or appointed counsel—such as whether, in federal court, there is a federal defender or an attorney appointed under the Criminal Justice Act to represent a criminal defendant. Professor Radha Iyengar concluded that "[d]efendants with CJA panel attorneys are on average more likely to be found guilty and on average to receive longer sentences. Overall, the expected sentence for defendants with CJA panel attorneys is nearly 8 months longer."

The same difference has been found in state courts. Professors James M. Anderson and Paul Heaton compared the outcomes in murder cases in Philadelphia courts on the basis of whether there is a public defender or an appointed counsel. They found that, compared with appointed counsel, public defenders reduce their clients' murder conviction rate by 19 percent and lower the probability that their client will receive a life sentence by 62 percent. Public defenders, as compared with appointed counsel, reduce overall expected time served in prison by 24 percent. To state the obvious, these are dramatic differences.

Many studies have been done in capital cases, and they are remarkably consistent in documenting that a conviction and death sentence in a capital case is least likely with a privately paid lawyer, and that those with government-paid attorneys are much better off with public defenders than with appointed counsel.

The best advice to give a person facing prosecution, especially for a serious crime, is clear: If you can, hire your own attorney. Failing that, do all you can to get representation by a public defender rather than by a court-appointed attorney. Why? Anderson and Heaton offer a compelling explanation:

> We find that, in general, appointed counsel have comparatively few resources, face more difficult incentives, and are more isolated than public defenders. The extremely low compensation for appointed counsel reduces the pool of attorneys willing to take the appointments and makes extensive preparation economically undesirable. Moreover, the judges selecting counsel may be doing so for reasons partly unrelated to counsel's efficacy. In contrast, the public defenders' steady salaries, financial and institutional independence from judges, and team approach to indigent defense avoid many of these problems. These longer-term institutional differences lead to the more immediate cause of the difference in outcomes: less preparation by appointed counsel.

Simply put, the identity of the lawyer matters, and the method of compensating the lawyer is often crucial in determining who will provide representation. It is in this context that the many studies done on the inadequacy of representation in criminal cases can be understood. The American Bar Association's Standing Committee on Legal Aid and Indigent Defendants concluded:

> Quality legal representation cannot be rendered unless indigent defense systems are adequately funded. Attorneys who do not receive sufficient compensation have a disincentive to devote the necessary time and effort to provide meaningful representation or even participate in the system at all. With fewer attorneys available to accept cases, the lawyers who provide services are often saddled with excessive caseloads, further hampering their ability to represent their clients effectively.

The ABA committee concluded that "inadequate compensation for indigent defense attorneys is a national problem, which makes the recruitment and retention of experienced lawyers extraordinarily difficult."

The report of the National Right to Counsel Committee similarly concluded that "inadequate financial support continues to be the single greatest obstacle to delivering 'competent' and 'diligent' defense representation." It noted that "the most visible sign of inadequate funding is attorneys attempting to provide services while carrying astonishingly large caseloads. Frequently, public defenders are asked to represent far too many clients." Appointed counsel are often paid so little that only those who cannot find other work are available, and their compensation is so inadequate as to provide insufficient incentives for the needed work.

This basic notion, that one gets what one can pay for in representation, is reflected in studies done on the quality of representation in capital cases. Professor Douglas Vick explained:

> Several observers have noted that poor compensation will not attract the best attorneys to represent indigents in death penalty cases. . . . For example, as of January 1990, the Alabama attorneys

who represented defendants sentenced to death had been subject to disciplinary action, including disbarment, at a rate twenty times that of the Alabama bar as a whole. For those attorneys whose clients were executed, the rate of disciplinary sanctions was almost forty times that of the bar as a whole. One-quarter of the inmates on Kentucky's death row were represented at trial by attorneys who subsequently were disbarred or resigned rather than face disbarment. As of January 1990, nearly 13% of the defendants executed in Louisiana had been represented by lawyers who had been disciplined, while the disciplinary rate for the Louisiana bar as a whole was 0.19%. In Texas, the attorneys who represented defendants sentenced to death have been disciplined at a rate nine times that of the Texas bar as a whole; similar disparities exist in Georgia, Mississippi, and Florida.

All of this has been exacerbated by the fiscal crisis facing state governments—and thus state courts—all across the country. The report of the National Right to Counsel Committee concluded that "the country's current fiscal crisis, which afflicts state and local governments everywhere, is having severe adverse consequences for the funding of indigent defense services, which already receives substantially less financial support compared to prosecution and law enforcement." A study by the National Center for State Courts found that from 2008 to 2011, forty-two states cut funding for their state court systems. Funding for defense lawyers and the support they need has been cut from its previously inadequate levels.

By every measure, then, there are gross inadequacies in the provision of counsel to indigent defendants. The constitutional assurance of the right to counsel is rendered illusory, and innocent people are convicted as a result.

Why has the promise of *Gideon* been so poorly realized? I believe two interrelated phenomena explain this. First, the Supreme Court imposed an unfunded mandate on state and local governments, with the only realistic enforcement mechanism being the finding of ineffective assistance of counsel in individual cases. Second, the Court created a test for ineffective assistance of counsel that makes it very difficult for a convicted individual to get relief, even when counsel's performance is quite deficient.

Gideon creates an affirmative constitutional duty for the government to provide something to individuals: counsel in criminal cases where there is a possible prison sentence, if necessary at the government's expense. The Court, however, imposed this duty without providing a funding source or even suggesting one. It was left to each state—and in many instances each country—to provide funds for attorneys for indigent criminal defendants.

In the decades following Gideon, this burden grew tremendously as a result of an enormous increase in criminalization, prosecution, and incarceration. Nationally, five times more prisoners are incarcerated today than just a few decades ago. The nation's incarceration rate is among the world's highest—five to ten times higher than the rates in other industrialized nations. Whatever burden on state treasuries was envisioned by the Gideon Court, the dramatic growth in criminal laws and criminal prosecutions made it vastly greater than expected.

Among the many interests competing for scarce government resources, indigent criminal defendants are hardly a powerful political constituency. Professor Vick notes that in the context of inadequate representation for those facing death sentences, "[t]he individuals adversely affected by this crisis—those accused of aggravated murder—are the most hated and the least politically powerful in the country, and political actors, including judges, are not highly motivated to make unpopular decisions that would benefit them." It is not surprising, then, that the result is the inadequacy in funding of defense counsel described above. The Supreme Court left it to the states to provide defense lawyers, and states often will choose the most inexpensive way to meet this obligation.

Actually, the problem is more subtle and more difficult. Gideon must mean more than just a right to a lawyer: to have any meaning, it must be that there is a right to competent counsel. The Supreme Court has recognized that the Sixth Amendment of the U.S. Constitution guarantees a criminal defendant effective assistance of counsel. This means that no criminal defendant is to be left to the "mercies of incompetent counsel." It is relatively easy to provide some attorney for a criminal defendant; if nothing else, courts can appoint lawyers to provide representation, and attorneys are ethically required to accept such appointments. Ensuring competency is far more difficult. State courts have not been receptive to claims that their systems of compensating lawyers are inadequate overall for ensuring competent counsel, and, "to date, a federal forum has not been available to indigent defendants seeking to vindicate their Sixth Amendment right to counsel on a systemic basis."

The primary mechanism, then, for enforcing *Gideon*'s promise has been the ability of an individual criminal defendant to argue that he or she received ineffective assistance of counsel. But the Supreme Court, in *Strickland v. Washington,* made it difficult for courts to find ineffective assistance of counsel, even when representation is very deficient. Justice Sandra Day O'Connor, writing for the conservative majority, set a standard that means that only rarely will a conviction be overturned for inadequacy of representation. The Court said that a finding of ineffective assistance of counsel requires demonstrating two things. First, it must be shown that the attorney's performance was so deficient that "counsel was not functioning as the 'counsel' guaranteed by the Sixth Amendment." But even gross deficiency by a defense counsel is not sufficient for overturning a conviction or a sentence for ineffective assistance of counsel. Second, the defendant must show prejudice; that is, the defendant has to demonstrate that the "counsel's deficient performance more likely than not altered the outcome in the case." In other words, relief for ineffective assistance of counsel requires that a convicted defendant show that the result of the trial likely would have been different if only the attorney had acted competently.

This is usually an insurmountable burden. It is far too easy for later judges to say that they think that the judge or jury would have come to the same conclusion anyway. Justice Thurgood Marshall explained

exactly this problem in his dissent in *Strickland*. "[I]t is often very difficult to tell whether a defendant convicted after a trial in which he was
ineffectively represented would have fared better if his lawyer had been
competent. Seemingly impregnable cases can sometimes be dismantled
by good defense counsel." In a death penalty appeal I handled, the court
of appeals conceded that counsel's performance was seriously deficient
but rejected the claim of ineffective assistance of counsel by summarily
concluding that the jury would have come to the same conclusion anyway.

My former colleague and Yale law professor Dennis Curtis said that
under *Strickland*, an attorney will be found to be adequate so long as a
mirror put in front of him or her at trial would have shown a breath.
Professor Curtis overstates, but not by much. I can identify only two
cases in the twenty-five years since *Strickland* in which the Supreme
Court has found ineffective assistance of counsel. The latter of these, in
2005, was a 5–4 decision, with Justice O'Connor in the majority, revers-
ing an opinion written by then federal appeals court judge Samuel Alito.

The Court's more recent decision in *Cullen v. Pinholster*, in 2011, calls
into question even these rulings in favor of criminal defendants and
shows how difficult it is to demonstrate ineffective assistance of counsel.
Scott Lynn Pinholster was convicted of murder. In capital cases, after a
defendant is found guilty of murder, there is a penalty phase in which the
jury is asked to decide whether it believes that the aggravating factors
outweigh the mitigating circumstances and whether it recommends a
death sentence. Pinholster's defense lawyers had not been notified that
the prosecutor planned to present aggravating circumstances in a penalty
phase and therefore did not prepare to present mitigating evidence.
Nonetheless, the judge overruled their objection and said that there
would be a penalty phase. The judge offered the defense additional time
to prepare for the next phase, when the jury would decide whether to
impose a death sentence. The defense lawyers declined this offer and presented only one witness, Pinholster's mother. By all accounts, she was not
an effective witness.

After Pinholster was sentenced to death and exhausted his appeals in

California state court, his new lawyers filed a writ of habeas corpus in federal court. The lawyers provided declarations showing substantial new evidence that supported the claim of ineffective assistance of counsel. The federal court granted a hearing, and the new evidence documented that the defense counsel at trial had undertaken no investigation of mitigating circumstances, and had they done so they would have learned that Pinholster suffered from a brain injury, a seizure disorder, and personality disorders. The evidence also included testimony from family members and school officials about Pinholster's abuse as a child. All of this is strong mitigating evidence that might have caused the jury to refrain from imposing the death penalty.

The federal district court granted the writ of habeas corpus, and ultimately the Ninth Circuit affirmed. The Supreme Court, though, in an opinion by Justice Clarence Thomas, reversed. The Court concluded that the inadequacy of the defense lawyers was not sufficient to show ineffective assistance of counsel. The Court stressed the need for great deference to the state courts and concluded that Pinholster could not prove that he was prejudiced by the failings of counsel. But if this total failure of defense counsel to investigate can be rationalized as a strategic choice of counsel and not prejudicial, there will be very few instances in which ineffective assistance of counsel can be demonstrated.

Taking all these things into account, it is possible to explain the failure to implement *Gideon:* the Supreme Court created a mandate without ensuring adequate funding, state and local governments lacked political or legal incentives to provide sufficient resources, and systemic litigation was unsuccessful, leaving as the only remedy the determination of ineffective assistance of counsel in individual cases. But the Court adopted a standard for this in *Strickland v. Washington* that makes it exceedingly difficult for a defendant to establish ineffective assistance of counsel. The result is that, as death penalty lawyer Stephen Bright declared, "[n]o constitutional right is celebrated so much in the abstract and observed so little in reality as the right to counsel."

Conclusion

The Warren Court is a symbol for both liberals and conservatives. For liberals, it is seen as the one time in history when there was a progressive Court and an era in which the Supreme Court fulfilled its constitutional role of protecting minorities and enforcing the Constitution. For conservatives, it is regarded as a time of liberal judicial activism and is remembered with great disdain.

Both of these reactions have some basis, but both are also fundamentally mistaken. It was, of course, a liberal era for the Court, though it was shorter than we might remember. The Warren Court—the time during which Earl Warren was chief justice—lasted only fifteen years, from 1954 to 1969, and for only seven of those years was there a liberal majority, beginning in 1962, when Arthur Goldberg joined the Court.

The conservative reaction to the Warren Court is much more about the idea of a liberal Court than it is criticism of specific decisions. Conservatives, in law-review articles, op-eds, and speeches, no longer criticize *Brown v. Board of Education* or the voting decisions requiring reapportionment and striking down poll taxes or the rulings applying the Bill of Rights to the states. I find that even my most conservative students agree with these decisions.

The liberal reaction to the Warren Court overlooks that it did so much less than it needed to and should have done, even in the areas of its greatest accomplishments, such as school desegregation and ensuring counsel for criminal defendants. The Court was surely right in holding that state laws requiring segregation were unconstitutional, but American schools today are increasingly separate and unequal. The Warren Court and its successors deserve some of the blame. The Court was undoubtedly correct in interpreting the Constitution to require that every criminal defendant facing a possible jail or prison sentence be provided an attorney. But for so many defendants, including those facing a possible death sentence, the lawyers are incompetent, and the resources in many states are grossly inadequate for providing adequate representation. Once more, the Warren Court and its successors deserve a great deal of the blame.

The question we must ask, then, is why did the Warren Court not do more? It is possible that this reflects the inherent limits of what the judiciary can do. Massive resistance to desegregation, as well as white flight, were enormous obstacles to school desegregation. Lack of money, and the difficulty in the Court requiring expenditures, has undermined providing adequate counsel. Perhaps the country would not have accepted the Supreme Court going any further.

But I think this is again making excuses for the Supreme Court. The Warren Court could have done much more to bring about desegregation. It did not need to wait a decade after *Brown*, in 1954, before declaring that there had been all too much deliberation and not enough speed, and finally taking action to enforce *Brown*. It could have written opinions explaining why segregation was inconsistent with the Constitution, rather than invalidating laws requiring segregation without judicial opinions or explanation. It could have outlined the steps to be taken in desegregating schools, something that did not happen until 1971, two years after the end of the Warren Court.

The Court could have focused more on the need for competent counsel and developed a meaningful standard for determining ineffective assistance of counsel. It could have provided systemic remedies for state systems that are grossly inadequate in providing representation for criminal defendants.

It is uncomfortable to criticize the Warren Court because it was a success in many ways. But it could have and should have done so much more.

PART II

THE PRESENT:

THE ROBERTS COURT

CHAPTER 5

Employers, Employees, and Consumers

On Wednesday, December 4, 2013, I stood before the justices to argue a free speech case, *United States v. Apel*. My client, Dennis Apel, had been barred from California's Vandenberg Air Force Base because of prior misconduct during antiwar protests. A federal statute, 18 U.S.C. Section 1381, makes it a federal crime to reenter a base after having received a bar order. The issue was whether this applied to Apel's participating in protests on a fully open public road, in an officially designated protest zone, outside of the closed base, because it is land owned by the federal government.

The justices emerged from behind curtains at exactly 10:00 a.m. They have seats that are assigned by seniority. The chief justice always sits in the center and presides over the argument. John Roberts was appointed chief justice in 2005 by President George W. Bush after William Rehnquist died. A person can be nominated for the seat of chief justice, as Roberts was, without ever having served as an associate justice. Roberts, a graduate of Harvard College and Harvard Law School, had impeccable professional credentials. After law school, he clerked for a federal appeals court judge and then for Rehnquist. Roberts then worked in the Reagan administration before joining a major Washington, D.C., firm; he specialized in representing businesses before the Supreme Court. During the administration of President George H. W. Bush, Roberts was a deputy solicitor general of the United States, the second in command to Solicitor

General Ken Starr in the office responsible for representing the United States before the Supreme Court. He was regarded as one of the best Supreme Court advocates of his generation.

The elder President Bush had nominated Roberts for the United States Court of Appeals for the District of Columbia Circuit, but his nomination languished and he was not confirmed by the end of the Bush presidency. President George W. Bush successfully nominated Roberts to that court in 2003, and two years later to the Supreme Court.

By all measures, throughout his career Roberts has been politically conservative, and such has been the case during his time as a Supreme Court justice, though he famously disappointed conservatives by casting the fifth vote to uphold the Affordable Care Act. It was, though, a rare instance in which Roberts did not join with the conservative bloc on the Court.

Immediately to Roberts's right on the bench sits the most senior associate justice: Antonin Scalia. Scalia, a graduate of Georgetown University and Harvard Law School, was an attorney in a Cleveland law firm before working in the Nixon and Ford administrations. He then became a law professor at the University of Chicago, a position he held until he was appointed by President Reagan to the United States Court of Appeals for the District of Columbia Circuit and then, in 1986, to the Supreme Court. He almost always votes in a way that conservatives favor and is frequently caustic and sarcastic in his written opinions and comments from the bench.

To Roberts's immediate left sits Anthony Kennedy. Kennedy grew up in Sacramento and attended Stanford University and Harvard Law School. He then returned to Sacramento, where he practiced law and taught constitutional law at McGeorge School of Law. In 1975, President Gerald Ford appointed him to the United States Court of Appeals for the Ninth Circuit. In 1987, after the Senate rejected President Reagan's nomination of Robert Bork for the Supreme Court and after Douglas Ginsburg's nomination was withdrawn when it was revealed that he had smoked marijuana, Kennedy was picked.

Kennedy is regarded as the "swing justice" on the current Court and often has disappointed conservatives, such as in casting the fifth vote in

1992 to reaffirm *Roe v. Wade*. But when the Court is ideologically divided
5–4, Kennedy is much more likely to be with the conservatives than the
liberals. For example, in October Term 2012 (the term that began on
Monday, October 1, 2012, and ended on Thursday, June 27, 2013), there
were sixteen 5–4 decisions that were ideologically divided, with Roberts,
Scalia, Thomas, and Alito on one side and Ginsburg, Breyer, Sotomayor,
and Kagan on the other. Kennedy was with the conservatives in ten of
the cases and with the liberals in six. Overall, since John Roberts became
chief justice, in 2005, Kennedy has been with the conservatives about 70
percent of the time in ideologically divided 5–4 rulings.

To Justice Scalia's immediate right sits the justice who is next in seniority: Clarence Thomas. During oral arguments, it is easy to forget that
Thomas is even present, because he virtually never asks a question. Thomas
goes years between questions, and no one is quite sure why. A graduate of
Holy Cross and Yale Law School, he worked for Missouri senator John
Danforth before going into the Reagan administration as an assistant secretary of education and then as chair of the Equal Employment Opportunity Commission (EEOC). In 1990, President George H. W. Bush
nominated him for the D.C. Circuit and a year later to the Supreme
Court, to fill the vacancy created by Thurgood Marshall's retirement.

Liberal groups strongly opposed Thomas's confirmation because of his
conservative writings and speeches. The hearings were tense and conten-
tious. *After* the hearings concluded, allegations surfaced that Thomas had
sexually harassed Anita Hill while at the EEOC. The hearings were re-
convened, and the nation was mesmerized as Hill recounted what she
had experienced while working for Thomas and then as Thomas denied
all of the accusations and labeled the hearings a "high-tech lynching for
uppity blacks." Thomas was confirmed by a vote of 52–48, the closest vote
to approve a justice in American history.

Since coming onto the Court, Thomas virtually always has voted in a
conservative direction and more than any other justice has urged the
Court to overrule earlier decisions. For example, Thomas has taken the
position that the Establishment Clause of the First Amendment does not

apply to state and local governments, so there should be no constitutional limit on their ability to advance religion. He has said in dissent that children should have no First Amendment rights. He has gone much further than any contemporary justice in saying that Congress should be very limited in its ability to regulate commerce, which would mean the invalidation of countless federal laws. Each would be a radical change in the law, and no justice ever has joined Thomas's views on these topics.

On the opposite side of the bench, both literally and ideologically, next to Justice Kennedy, sits Justice Ruth Bader Ginsburg. A graduate of Cornell University, she attended Harvard Law School until she transferred to attend Columbia Law School when her husband took a job with a New York law firm. Ginsburg was a professor at Rutgers School of Law and Columbia Law School and was a preeminent advocate for women's rights. She cofounded the ACLU's women's rights project and in 1973 became a general counsel of the ACLU. She argued a number of landmark cases before the Supreme Court concerning gender equality.

She was appointed to the D.C. Circuit by President Jimmy Carter and then to the Supreme Court in 1993 by President Bill Clinton. She almost always has voted in a liberal direction and has been a powerful voice especially on issues affecting women, such as cases involving sex discrimination, employment, and abortion rights. She is the oldest member of the Court and was eighty when I argued the *Apel* case in December 2013.

Justice Stephen Breyer sits on the opposite side from Justice Ginsburg, just to the right of Clarence Thomas. Breyer grew up in San Francisco and attended Stanford University and then Harvard Law School. He clerked for Supreme Court Justice Arthur Goldberg before becoming a Harvard law professor, specializing in administrative and regulatory law. He worked for Senator Edward Kennedy as counsel for the Senate Judiciary Committee before being nominated by President Jimmy Carter to the United States Court of Appeals for the First Circuit. In 1994, President Bill Clinton nominated him for the Supreme Court. Overall, he has been a liberal justice, though in some notable cases he has joined with the conservatives, such as in upholding the ability of the United States to detain an American citizen as an enemy combatant, in allowing random drug testing for students participating in extracurricular activities, and (in a case I argued) allowing a six-foot-high, three-foot-wide Ten Commandments monument at the corner between the Texas State Capitol and the Texas Supreme Court.

From 1994 until 2005, there were no vacancies on the Court. In 2005, when William Rehnquist died and Sandra Day O'Connor left the Court, President Bush selected John Roberts as chief and Samuel Alito to replace O'Connor. Alito graduated from Princeton University and Yale Law School. He had a distinguished career as an attorney, an assistant U.S. attorney, a deputy solicitor general, and a U.S. attorney. President George H. W. Bush nominated him for the United States Court of Appeals for the Third Circuit in 1990. In fifteen years as a judge on that court, Alito had a reputation for being very conservative, and it is hard to think of an instance in which he has not taken a position favored by conservatives since joining the Supreme Court in January 2006.

At each end of the bench sit the two newest justices, both appointees of President Barack Obama. Justice Sonia Sotomayor sits in the seat farthest to the right of the chief justice. Sotomayor grew up in New York and attended Princeton University and Yale Law School. She served as an assistant district attorney in New York before joining a law firm there. She was nominated for the federal district court by President George H. W. Bush at the urging of Democratic senator Daniel Patrick Moynihan and then to the United States Court of Appeals for the Second Circuit by President Bill Clinton. In 2009, President Obama appointed her to the Supreme Court to fill the vacancy created by Justice David Souter's resignation. She is the first Latina to serve on the Supreme Court and wrote a bestselling autobiography, *My Beloved World,* in 2013. She has been a consistent liberal since joining the Supreme Court.

Finally, at the opposite end of the bench is Justice Elena Kagan. Born in 1960 and nominated for the Court in 2010 at age fifty, she is the youngest justice on the current Court. Kagan attended Princeton University and Harvard Law School. She then clerked for a federal appeals court judge and Justice Thurgood Marshall. She was a law professor at the

University of Chicago Law School before working in the Clinton administration. After that, she taught at Harvard Law School before becoming its first female dean. In 2009, President Obama named her solicitor general of the United States, and in 2010 she was nominated to the Supreme Court when Justice John Paul Stevens announced his resignation after thirty-five years on the high court. Kagan has been a consistent liberal vote in her short time on the Supreme Court.

These were the justices I stood before to argue the *Apel* case, and they are the current version of the Roberts Court. Since John Roberts was only fifty years old when he became chief justice, in 2005, he likely will be in that position for decades to come, and the Roberts Court will have many versions, with its future ideology depending on when vacancies occur and the president who fills them.

The current Court, though, is six men and three women. All attended Harvard or Yale Law School, and a majority grew up in New York. In fact, every borough of New York except Staten Island had a current justice grow up there. Only two were raised west of the Mississippi. The current Court has six Catholic justices and three Jewish justices; for the first time in history, there are no Protestants on the Court. It has four conservative justices, four liberal justices, and a swing justice who votes with the conservatives much more often than not.

In this part of the book, I want to assess the Roberts Court. I will focus on three major areas: its decisions concerning regulation of business, its rulings regarding the ability to sue government entities and government officers when they violate the Constitution, and its cases affecting the political process. In each area, I believe that the Court has done great harm and has failed to fulfill its most important constitutional roles.

The Risk in Taking Generic Drugs

If you are injured by a generic prescription drug—even horribly injured—you cannot sue the maker of the drug. You can't sue for having not been adequately warned of the side effects of the drug. You can't sue for defects in the design of the drug. You can't sue in federal court, and you can't sue in state court. You can't sue the maker of the generic drug, even if you could have sued had you taken the brand-name version instead.

How can this possibly be the law? It is the result of two recent Supreme Court cases, from 2011 and 2013, that have foreclosed suits against makers of generic drugs, no matter how terrible the harms they cause. Paradoxically, the decisions, both 5–4 with the conservative justices in the majority, are a result of the Supreme Court's interpreting a statute that was meant to protect consumers.

The first case was *Pliva, Inc. v. Mensing* and involved patients who took metoclopramide, a drug designed to speed the movement of food through the digestive system. The drug is often prescribed for those with diabetes. The Food and Drug Administration (FDA) first approved metoclopramide tablets, under the brand name Reglan, in 1980. Five years later, generic manufacturers also began producing metoclopramide. Studies have shown that long-term metoclopramide use can cause tardive dyskinesia, a severe, often irreversible neurological disorder. Tardive dyskinesia involves repetitive, involuntary, purposeless movements, such as grimacing, tongue protrusion, lip smacking, puckering and pursing of the lips, and rapid eye blinking. Rapid, involuntary movements of the limbs, torso, and fingers also may occur. Studies have demonstrated that up to 29 percent of patients who take metoclopramide for several years will develop this condition.

The case involved two women who used the drug for a long time and developed tardive dyskinesia. Both women took the generic version of metoclopramide. They sued the drug manufacturer under their states' laws for failing to provide adequate warnings. In 1985, the label was modified to warn that "tardive dyskinesia ... may develop in patients treated with metoclopramide," and the drug's package insert added that "[t]herapy longer than 12 weeks has not been evaluated and cannot be recommended." But it was not until 2009, after the plaintiffs, Gladys Mensing and Julie Demahy, took the drug, that the FDA ordered a black-box warning—its strongest—which states: "Treatment with metoclopramide can cause tardive dyskinesia, a serious movement disorder that is often irreversible. . . . Treatment with metoclopramide for longer than 12 weeks should be avoided in all but rare cases."

The drug company argued that it could not be sued for failing to adequately warn patients because the drug had the warning label that had been approved by the FDA. The drug company said that such a state law claim for failing to warn was "preempted" by federal law. The Constitution, in Article V, says that the Constitution and laws and treaties made pursuant to it are the supreme law of the land. Thus, if there is a conflict between federal law and state law, federal law wins out; this is termed "preemption." The drug company said that its compliance with federal law—its having the warning label approved by the FDA—meant that it could not be held liable.

But the problem for the drug company was that just two years earlier, in *Wyeth v. Levine*, the Court had ruled that drug companies could be sued on a failure-to-warn theory, even if their warning label had been approved by the FDA. That case had been brought by Diana Levine, a musician in Vermont who went to a hospital emergency room with a severe migraine. She was given Demerol to counteract her pain and Phenergan to lessen the nausea she was suffering from. Phenergan is known to be highly corrosive and is supposed to be given diluted in a saline solution through an IV. Levine, though, was administered the Phenergan via a shot into her vein. Because of Phenergan's corrosive effect, Levine developed gangrene in her arm, and it had to be amputated. She sued the drug company for failing to provide adequate warnings to patients. Wyeth, the drug company, said that its warning label had been approved by the FDA and that therefore a state could not allow recovery; it said that the approval of the warning label by the FDA preempted any liability under state tort law.

The Supreme Court ruled in favor of Levine, finding that allowing tort liability would further the federal regulatory goal: informing doctors and patients of the dangers of prescription drugs. The Court concluded that nothing in federal law precludes drug companies from providing more information and that allowing drug companies to be sued would further the federal objective of ensuring drug safety. Drug companies always can engage in more speech—via advertisements, "Dear Doctor" letters, and requests to the FDA to change the warning label. Justice Stevens concluded the majority opinion by declaring, "In short, Wyeth has not persuaded us that failure-to-warn claims like Levine's obstruct the federal regulation of drug labeling. Congress has repeatedly declined to pre-empt state law."

Wyeth v. Levine was clearly right. In interpreting federal laws, the Supreme Court should seek to implement Congress's purpose. Allowing drug companies to be sued for failing to adequately warn consumers furthers Congress's goals of safer drugs and better informed patients.

This should have made *Pliva v. Mensing* an easy case; it was a claim against a drug company for failure to warn, and the Court had just ruled that such suits can go forward. But instead the Supreme Court, in a 5–4 decision, held that such claims against the manufacturers of *generic* drugs are preempted by federal law. *Wyeth,* the Court said, involved a *brand*-name drug, and that was completely different from a suit against a generic-drug maker. Justice Clarence Thomas wrote the opinion for the Court and was joined by Chief Justice Roberts and Justices Scalia, Kennedy, and Alito.

Justice Thomas based his opinion denying relief to the injured women on a federal law, the Hatch-Waxman Amendments, which ironically were meant to protect consumers by making it easier for companies to sell generic drugs, which are generally less expensive. The Hatch-Waxman Amendments say that generic drugs can gain FDA approval by showing equivalence to a drug that has already been approved by the FDA. Under this law, warning labels for generic drugs are to be the same as those for the non-generic drug approved by the FDA. The Court quoted the federal regulation, which states that the generic drug's "labeling must be the same as the listed drug product's labeling because the listed drug product is the basis for [generic drug] approval."

The Court said that the makers of *generic* drugs could not change these warnings because the content of the warnings for generic drugs must be the same as the warning that has been approved for non-generic drugs.

Nor could manufacturers send "Dear Doctor" letters to inform physicians of the harms. The Court explained, "A Dear Doctor letter that contained substantial new warning information would not be consistent with the drug's approved labeling." The Court thus decided that suits against makers of generic drugs for failing to adequately warn patients of side effects are preempted by federal law. If someone is injured after taking a brand-name version of a drug, the victim can sue the drug company; but if someone is injured after taking the generic version of the drug, the Supreme Court said that the person cannot sue the company that made that drug. Nor can the victim sue the company that made the brand-name version of the drug, because the person did not use that company's product.

The Court's reasoning is questionable on many levels. First, whether a suit can be brought against a drug company now depends entirely on whether the drug is a generic or a non-generic, brand-name version. This makes no sense. Even the majority conceded this and declared, "We recognize that from the perspective of Mensing and Demahy, finding preemption here but not in *Wyeth* makes little sense. Had Mensing and Demahy taken Reglan, the brand-name drug prescribed by their doctors, *Wyeth* would control and their lawsuits would not be pre-empted. But because pharmacists, acting in full accord with state law, substituted generic metoclopramide instead, federal law pre-empts these lawsuits." The Court then said that, despite this irrationality, the plaintiffs were out of luck: "We acknowledge the unfortunate hand that federal drug regulation has dealt Mensing, Demahy, and others similarly situated. But 'it is not this Court's task to decide whether the statutory scheme established by Congress is unusual or even bizarre.'"

But nothing in federal law or the law of preemption requires this distinction. The Court blames Congress, but no federal law—not the Hatch-Waxman Amendments or any other—precludes suits against the makers of generic drugs. Under federal law, makers of generic drugs could ask the Food and Drug Administration to change the warning labels to provide the needed information to patients and doctors. Makers of generic drugs, like manufacturers of brand-name drugs, could take out ads to warn consumers of the risk. As Justice Sotomayor objected in her dissent, "[The Court] invent[ed] new principles of pre-emption law out of thin air."

Second, the premise of the Court's decision is that the Hatch-Waxman Amendments require that warning labels on generic drugs be the same as the warning labels the FDA has approved for non-generic drugs. If so, then it would make sense that generic-drug companies would face the same liability for failure to warn and be required to have the same content on their warning labels as is required for non-generic-drug companies. The point of the Hatch-Waxman Amendments was to *help* consumers by facilitating the marketing of generic drugs by allowing them to copy the warning labels approved by the FDA. A statute that was meant to protect patients and to treat generic drugs the same as non-generic drugs was interpreted by the Court to prevent suits by patients and to have generic drugs treated dramatically differently from their non-generic equivalents.

Third, preemption analysis is always a question of legislative intent: did Congress intend to preempt state law under the circumstances? The Supreme Court has said that "[t]he purpose of Congress is the ultimate touchstone in every preemption case." But there is no indication whatsoever that Congress ever meant to preempt tort liability for generic drugs in the exact same situations in which failure to warn suits could be brought against their non-generic equivalents. As Justice Sotomayor stated: "If Congress had intended to deprive injured parties of [this] long available form of compensation, it surely would have expressed that intent more clearly. Given the longstanding existence of product liability actions, including for failure to warn, [i]t is difficult to believe that Congress would, without comment, remove all means of judicial recourse for those injured by illegal conduct."

But the Court went even further in protecting generic-drug companies in its 2013 decision in *Mutual Pharmaceutical Co. v. Bartlett*, where the Court held that makers of generic drugs cannot be sued for design defects in their products. Karen Bartlett took a generic form of the prescription pain reliever sulindac. She then experienced a horrific side effect called toxic epidermal necrolysis. Sixty to sixty-five percent of the surface of her skin deteriorated, was burned off, or turned into an open wound. She spent months in a medically induced coma, underwent twelve eye surgeries, and was tube-fed for a year. She is now severely disfigured, has a number of physical disabilities, and is nearly blind. She sued Mutual Pharmaceutical on a design-defect claim, arguing that the design of the drug made it unduly risky. The jury ruled in her favor and awarded her $21 million.

Her lawyers were careful to present this not as a claim about failure to warn of side effects, which no longer was available after *Pliva v. Mensing*, but as one about defects in the design of the drug. It didn't matter. The Supreme Court, in a 5–4 decision, held that this claim, too, was preempted by federal law. Justice Alito wrote for the Court and was joined by the same justices as in *Pliva v. Mensing*.

The Court explained that New Hampshire law requires that manufacturers not sell drugs or other products that are "unreasonably dangerous." The Court said that in the context of prescription drugs, it would be necessary to redesign a drug to increase its usefulness or reduce its risk of danger. But the maker of a generic drug cannot redesign it; federal law—the Hatch-Waxman Amendments—requires that for a generic drug to be sold, it must be identical to the brand-name version. Therefore, Justice Alito reasoned that the only way for a generic-drug company to reduce the risk would be to strengthen the warning for consumers. *Pliva v. Mensing*, though, held that generic-drug companies cannot change the warning label but instead must have exactly the same warning label approved for the brand-name drug. The Court thus concluded that a generic-drug maker could avoid liability only by either changing the chemical compound or by strengthening the warning label, and that both of these options were precluded by federal law.

The practical effect is to give broad immunity to suit for makers of generic drugs, and it means that patients who are hurt, even severely, are out of luck. Justice Breyer wrote a dissenting opinion joined by Justice Kagan and disputed the majority's contention that it is impossible to comply with both federal and state law. He said that there *was* a way for the drug company to do this: cease selling the product in the state or decide to pay the penalty for doing so.

Justice Sotomayor wrote a dissent joined by Justice Ginsburg and strongly objected to the Court extending *Pliva* to design-defect claims. She said that it was not impossible for a drug company to comply with both federal and state law. She explained that "[a] manufacturer of a drug that is unreasonably dangerous under New Hampshire law has multiple options: It can change the drug's design or label in an effort to alter its risk-benefit profile, remove the drug from the market, or pay compensation as a cost of doing business." She recognized that this may be an "unwelcome choice" for a manufacturer, but she said that "it is a choice that a sovereign State may impose to protect its citizens from dangerous drugs or at least ensure that seriously injured consumers receive compensation."

The Court's decisions in *Pliva v. Mensing* and *Mutual Pharmaceutical Co. v. Bartlett* are very disturbing. Makers of generic drugs cannot be sued for failure to warn of a design defect, no matter how badly the drugs injure people. From the perspective of preemption law, this makes no sense, because it was Congress's goal to protect consumers from the harms of prescription drugs. The Court has taken a statute that was meant to protect consumers and used it to deny any relief to those who are severely injured. It was precisely for this reason that *Wyeth v. Levine* held that tort liability of drug companies furthered the underlying regulatory goals of the Pure Food and Drug Act.

The Court's decision cannot be based on the statute used to find preemption. Nothing in it says a word about preemption. The Court's decision cannot be justified as fulfilling Congress's purpose in enacting the Hatch-Waxman Amendments, since that was done to protect consumers. The Court's decision can be understood only as protecting big business at the expense of all of us.

According to the FDA, nearly 80 percent of all prescriptions are filled with generic drugs. When there is a generic equivalent to a brand name, more than 90 percent of the time a generic is prescribed. All who take generic drugs are at risk; if they are injured from the drug, they will not be able to recover.

The Supreme Court and Statutes Regulating Business

The Court's recent decisions protecting generic-drug companies from liability did not involve issues of constitutional law, but rather were about the Court interpreting a federal statute. About half of all Supreme Court decisions each year concern federal statutes and do not pose constitutional questions. There are, of course, thousands of federal laws regulating every aspect of the economy and society. Many statutes are criminal prohibitions.

Federal laws regulate business practices in countless ways—ranging from how things are manufactured (such as occupational safety and health standards) to how employees are treated (such as minimum-wage and maximum-hours laws and prohibitions on employment discrimination) to how things are marketed (such as the prohibitions of false and deceptive advertising) to how businesses operate (such as securities regulations and antitrust laws).

What is striking about the recent decisions of the Roberts Court, such as in the area of generic drugs, is how they have interpreted statutes to protect business in a way that undermines Congress's purpose. Simply put, the Roberts Court is the most pro-business Court since the mid-1930s, and this has been especially evident in its decisions concerning federal laws. Putting aside conservative and liberal labels, to understand the Roberts Court, it is important to see it in this light.

This Court's strong pro-business orientation has been at the expense of consumers, employees, and patients. In addition to the generic-drug cases, this is also evident in the Roberts Court's recent decisions regarding arbitration and class action suits and in its employment discrimination rulings.

Protecting Corporations from Litigation

Vincent and Liza Concepcion purchased cellular telephones from AT&T Mobility LCC. Like most of us, they had to sign an agreement for their cell phone service. The form contract they signed provided for arbitration of all disputes between the parties. In other words, if they had a legal dispute with AT&T, they could not sue in court, but instead their claim would go before a private arbiter. Such clauses are increasingly common in consumer contracts, employment contracts, and even medical contracts.

Businesses would much prefer that suits against them by injured consumers or aggrieved employees never get before a jury. Juries are perceived as pro-plaintiff and too likely to be swayed by emotions. (Whether this is an accurate perception is much debated in the scholarly literature.) Professional arbiters are strongly favored by corporate defendants as more likely to rule in their favor and likely to award less in damages when ruling for plaintiffs.

Also, scholars such as Yale law professor Judith Resnik have explained another reason that businesses prefer arbitration: an institutionalized bias among arbiters in favor of repeat players in the system. Resnik explains that professional arbiters depend for their work on selection—or at least not being rejected—by the parties. Arbiters know that if they develop the reputation of being pro-plaintiff, businesses will be sure not to use them in the future. The corollary is that those arbiters who develop a reputation for being pro-business are much more likely to be high on the defendants' list of possible arbiters. The repeat players in the system—businesses—thus gain a real advantage.

AT&T had advertised that the phones were free but charged the Concepcions $30.22 in sales tax. The Concepcions' suit was consolidated with other similar claims in a class action suit in federal court alleging that AT&T had engaged in false advertising and fraud by charging sales tax on phones that it had advertised as free.

AT&T moved to compel arbitration under the terms of its contract with the Concepcions. The federal district court and the United States Court of Appeals for the Ninth Circuit, however, rejected this, explaining that California law was clear that such a contractual provision was not enforceable because there was no meaningful waiver of the right to sue and because arbitration of a dispute between two parties is no substitute for a class action remedy. The California Supreme Court said that these clauses were "contracts of adhesion," and that is exactly what they were: AT&T imposed this condition on consumers, and a person who wanted a cell phone has no choice but to sign an agreement mandating arbitration of any dispute. There is a long-standing principle of contract law that such "contracts of adhesion" are not enforceable.

The Federal Arbitration Act is a law, adopted in 1925, that requires enforcement of arbitration clauses in contracts, but it specifically provides that such clauses are not enforceable where state law provides for the revocation of the contractual provision. Both the federal district court and the federal court of appeals said that the Concepcions did not have to go to arbitration and could sue AT&T because of this exception to the Federal Arbitration Act. California law was clear, and there was a California Supreme Court case on point decreeing that such arbitration clauses in consumer contracts are not enforceable.

Nonetheless, Justice Scalia, writing for the Supreme Court in a 5–4 decision, ruled that the California law allowing consumer class actions in such circumstances was preempted by federal law and that arbitration was required under the Federal Arbitration Act. The Court stressed the efficiency benefits of arbitration over court litigation and said that it was important to protect defendants, such as corporations, from the "in terrorem" effects of class action, which pressure them into settlements. The Court's desire to protect business and its hostility to class action suits could not have been more clearly stated.

The Court said that the Federal Arbitration Act requires that claims be arbitrated on an individual basis and that class arbitration is not allowed. Nowhere does the Federal Arbitration Act say or imply this. It is debatable whether arbitration should be required at all, since the act specifically says that arbitration clauses are not to be enforced when state law would not do so. But even if the matter must go to arbitration, nothing in the text or history of the Federal Arbitration Act implies that this must be individual as opposed to class arbitration. The pro-business majority simply read this significant protection of business into the federal law.

The effect is to keep those injured from an allegedly illegal practice from getting any recovery. Justice Breyer described the practical reality: "What rational lawyer would have signed on to represent the Concepcions in litigation for the possibility of fees stemming from a $30.22 claim? The *realistic* alternative to a class action is not 17 million individual suits, but zero individual suits, as only a lunatic or a fanatic sues for $30." As a federal court of appeals said in another case invalidating class action waivers, absent unusual circumstances, "only a fanatic or a lunatic" would litigate a case worth only a few hundred dollars. Since the overwhelming majority of lawyers are neither fanatics nor lunatics, and since AT&T presumably knew this when it included the class action waiver in its agreement, the agreement effectively insulates the company from judicial review and civil liability for its practices.

Class actions exist precisely for this situation, where a large number of people each lose a small amount of money and none is likely to bring an individual claim. The effect of the Supreme Court's decision is to make it far less likely that corporations engaged in even brazen, extensive fraud will be held accountable in situations where many people lose a small amount.

Indeed, in a subsequent case, in 2013, the Court again said that an arbitration clause is to be enforced even when the effect surely will be to immunize a defendant's wrongful conduct from any remedy. In *American Express v. Italian Colors Restaurant,* the Court said that an arbitration clause in a contract must be enforced even if it means that an antitrust suit realistically has no chance of going forward.

Italian Colors Restaurant, a small business, accepted American Express cards. The restaurant wanted to bring a class action against American

Express for antitrust violations. Italian Colors alleged that American Express used its monopoly power in the market to force merchants to accept their credit cards at rates approximately 30 percent higher than the fees for competing credit cards. It claimed that this violated federal antitrust law.

American Express sought to prevent this litigation by invoking a clause in its agreement that requires all disputes between parties to be resolved by arbitration. The agreement also provides that "[t]here shall be no right or authority for any Claims to be arbitrated on a class action basis." In other words, the agreement between American Express and Italian Colors Restaurant requires that any dispute between them go to arbitration, and that it had to be individual, not class, arbitration. The terms of the agreement, of course, were dictated by American Express.

Italian Colors said that the antitrust suit realistically could not go forward except as a class action. Successfully suing for an antitrust violation costs hundreds of thousands, if not millions, of dollars. Recovery for a claim under the antitrust law, though, is limited to $39,000, including treble damages. No one is going to spend hundreds of thousands or millions of dollars to bring a lawsuit to collect $39,000. On the other hand, a class action on behalf of all similarly situated is economically viable. Like *AT&T Mobility v. Concepcion*, this was a situation in which a class action was needed because a large number of parties had each suffered a relatively small injury.

The Court, in a 5–4 decision with an opinion written by Justice Scalia, said that the Federal Arbitration Act required that the arbitration clause be strictly enforced, even if it meant that the antitrust claims otherwise would not be brought. As in *AT&T Mobility*, two years before, the Court's conservative majority required enforcement of an arbitration clause even though it would likely completely immunize the defendant from liability for illegal conduct. In fact, Justice Scalia declared, "Truth to tell, our decision in *AT&T Mobility* all but resolves this case."

There is a long-standing principle under the Federal Arbitration Act that arbitration clauses are not to be enforced if they prevent "effective vindication" of a claim. This seems obviously relevant to Italian Colors' claim. But the Court refused to allow the exception to apply in situations

like this, in which the costs of litigation meant that no claim ever would
be brought.

Justice Kagan wrote a powerful dissent and declared:

> Here is the nutshell version of this case, unfortunately ob-
> scured in the Court's decision. The owner of a small restaur-
> ant (Italian Colors) thinks that American Express (Amex)
> has used its monopoly power to force merchants to accept a
> form contract violating the antitrust laws. . . . So if the arbitra-
> tion clause is enforceable, Amex has insulated itself from anti
> trust liability—even if it has in fact violated the law. The
> monopolist gets to use its monopoly power to insist on a con-
> tract effectively depriving its victims of all legal recourse. And
> here is the nutshell version of today's opinion, admirably
> flaunted rather than camouflaged: Too darn bad.

Kagan lamented that this conclusion was "a betrayal of our precedents, and of federal statutes like the antitrust laws." It creates the power
of big businesses to enter into agreements violating antitrust law and then
keeping themselves from being held liable by having clauses requiring
arbitration and precluding class action suits. That certainly was not Congress's intent in adopting the Federal Arbitration Act or in enacting the
federal antitrust laws.

These, though, are not the first instances in which the Court, split
along ideological lines, has broadly construed the Federal Arbitration Act
to protect big business in a way that thwarts congressional intent. Consider a decision from a decade ago. Saint Clair Adams worked for a Circuit City store in Southern California. When he applied for work, the
application said that any grievances, including discrimination claims,
with Circuit City would go to arbitration. Two years after being hired,
Adams sued Circuit City for discrimination. Adams's lawyer decided it
was best to keep the case in California state courts and sued entirely under California law, eschewing any claims under federal civil rights laws.

Circuit City then filed a separate action in federal district court to compel arbitration under the Federal Arbitration Act. There is an exception to the Federal Arbitration Act that says that arbitration is not required for claims by "contracts of employment of seamen, railroad employees, or any other class of workers engaged in foreign or interstate commerce." Under the literal language of the statute, Adams was an employee in interstate commerce. Many federal laws regulating the workplace that have been adopted by Congress under its commerce power—such as the Fair Labor Standards Act, which requires a minimum wage, and Title VII of the Civil Rights Act of 1964, which prohibits employment discrimination—explicitly treat those, like Adams, who work for major companies as employees in interstate commerce. The Supreme Court would not even question in these contexts that someone like Adams is an employee in interstate commerce.

The Federal Arbitration Act plainly says that arbitration is not required in an employment dispute for somebody who is in interstate commerce. The United States Court of Appeals for the Ninth Circuit said that the Federal Arbitration Act does not apply to Adams's claim. Also, there are important public policy reasons for wanting civil rights claims to be litigated in court rather than handled before private arbiters.

The Supreme Court, 5–4, reversed the Court of Appeals and held that the employment discrimination claim had to go to arbitration. Justice Kennedy wrote the opinion, which was joined by the four most conservative justices then on the Court: Rehnquist, O'Connor, Scalia, and Thomas. The Court interpreted the statute to say that "employees in interstate commerce" refers only to transportation workers. Under the Court's interpretation, contractual clauses requiring arbitration are not enforceable for those working in the transportation industry. But all other employees are compelled to have their employment disputes, including discrimination claims, resolved through arbitration. That is not what the statute says; it creates an exception for all "employees in interstate commerce."

Moreover, it is hard to see there really having been a contractual agreement between Adams and Circuit City. A clause on an employment application, where the employee had no choice but to sign, is not a contract in any meaningful sense of the word. As the California Supreme Court said with regard to arbitration clauses in consumer contracts, they are contracts of adhesion.

This decision, of course, does not just apply to Saint Clair Adams. It means that countless other employees with claims of race or gender or age discrimination will be deprived of their chance to go to court. As Justice Stevens lamented in his dissenting opinion, the Supreme Court has "pushed the pendulum far beyond a neutral attitude and endorsed a policy that strongly favors private arbitration."

Each of us is affected by these decisions, because these arbitration clauses are increasingly common. When we are injured—whether as consumers or employees or patients—we will not be able to go to court, and often, practically speaking, we will not be able to get any recovery at all.

In *AT&T Mobility v. Concepcion, American Express v. Italian Colors Restaurant,* and *Circuit City v. Adams,* the Court strictly enforced the Federal Arbitration Act, including clauses to prevent class action suits and to protect business. In *Concepcion,* Justice Scalia expressed concern over the terrorizing effect of class actions, which supposedly could force businesses to settle non-meritorious suits. He made this assertion without support. Justice Scalia and the majority expressed no concern for the adverse effects on those who never will have their day in court.

The Court's hostility toward class actions also was evident in its ruling in *Wal-Mart Stores, Inc. v. Dukes,* in 2011. The case was a class action of 1.5 million women who alleged sex discrimination by Wal-Mart in pay and promotions. The Court said that their class action suit could not go forward because the plaintiffs could not show sufficient commonality to their claims. It was one of the largest class action suits in history, but it also was brought against the largest corporation in American history. For a class action suit to go forward, a judge must find that certain requirements are met, including "commonality." Commonality means that there are significant common issues of law or of fact such that it makes sense to try the case as a class action suit rather than require that each claim be adjudicated separately.

The Court concluded that the women who alleged sex discrimination by Wal-Mart lacked sufficient commonality for the matter to be litigated as a class action suit. Justice Scalia, again writing for the majority in a 5–4 decision, explained that Wal-Mart had an official nondiscrimination policy and that therefore any employment decisions had been made by different individuals in stores around the country. The Court's majority held that a class action alleging intentional employment discrimination could not be brought when the allegedly discriminatory decisions had been made by individual supervisors at different Wal-Mart stores.

The Court came to this conclusion despite the fact that the plaintiffs presented a great deal of evidence to show that Wal-Mart had company-wide practices and policies that caused the sex discrimination throughout its large enterprise. The plaintiffs had statistical studies that showed that female Wal-Mart employees nationwide were paid less and were less likely to be promoted. The plaintiffs had expert witnesses who talked about Wal-Mart's practices and how they led to discrimination against women. The plaintiffs presented a large number of affidavits from female employees across the country, detailing their experience and the discrimination they'd suffered in working at Wal-Mart. It is impossible to imagine that the significant differences between the pay for men and pay for women was just a mass coincidence.

But the Court rejected all of this evidence as insufficient to allow the class action even to go forward. The issue before the Court was not whether the plaintiffs proved enough to win their case; the only question was whether this was enough to show common issues and permit a class action suit. First, the Court found the plaintiffs' statistical evidence of nationwide gender disparities "insufficient." It speculated—and it was entirely speculation by Justice Scalia—that the pay disparities between men and women "may be attributable to only a small set of Wal-Mart stores." Second, the majority found the plaintiffs' expert witness not worthy of belief and thus "disregard[ed]" his testimony about the ways in which Wal-Mart's personnel policies and corporate culture allowed gender bias to infect thousands of pay and promotion decisions. Scalia's majority opinion rejected the expert's entire testimony just because he could not determine how often Wal-Mart's individual employment decisions were "determined by stereotyped thinking." Third, the majority dismissed the 120 affidavits recounting evidence of discriminatory statements and decisions as insufficient, given Wal-Mart's size and the size of the plaintiff class. Having thus brushed aside the evidence of bias, and twice pointing out that Wal-Mart had a written policy prohibiting sex discrimination, the Court found that the gender disparities were the result of individual supervisors' decisions and must be litigated individually.

The result is that it will be very difficult for employment discrimination claims to be litigated as class actions. If workers have a complaint in a small workplace, one that has a single decision maker, then there is unlikely to be a sufficient number of plaintiffs to warrant a class action suit. Another requirement for a class action is "numerosity"—that there are enough suffering the same injury that it makes sense to try the matter as a class action rather than as individual suits. But if it is a larger workplace, where multiple people are making pay and promotion decisions, then, based on the Court's decision in *Wal-Mart v. Dukes*, there is unlikely to be sufficient commonality for it to be litigated in a class action. Consider a university. Hiring, pay, and promotion decisions are made in separate departments and schools all across campus. Under the reasoning of *Wal-Mart v. Dukes*, no class action suit would be permitted, even if the school were blatantly discriminating based on race or gender, in violation of federal law.

The effect again will often be to prevent any recovery by those who have been treated illegally and suffered great harms. Often, the amount lost by an individual employee does not justify his or her bringing a separate lawsuit. At times, an employee may be reluctant to bring an individual suit against the employer, for fear of retaliation and adverse consequences. Sometimes, even if employees want to sue, they cannot get lawyers to handle the matter.

The effect of *Wal-Mart*, like *AT&T Mobility v. Concepcion* and

American Express v. Italian Colors Restaurant, is to dramatically reduce the ability to bring a class action against businesses. Why does that matter? With the rise of the large corporation in the early twentieth century, courts and legislatures developed class actions as a procedural device to protect individuals from the harms of exploitation by large entities. Courts and legislatures realized that large entities have incentives to engage in widespread but small violations of law, because corporations know that most people cannot afford to sue over a small violation of a law. When individual litigation is not economically rational, the threat of litigation is not an effective deterrent to illegal behavior. Absent a robust government bureaucracy dedicated to enforcing consumer- or employee-protection laws, class actions are an essential aspect of law enforcement. And even the most aggressive enforcement agency cannot deal with even a significant fraction of law violations. Litigation is essential for deterring wrongdoing, and class action suits are necessary when a large number of people each suffer a relatively small injury.

Large entities, including employers and sellers of consumer goods and services, face both costs and benefits of the market power that comes from being large. Among the benefits are access to legal expertise and the market power to use that expertise to craft company-favorable standardized terms on which to contract with employees and consumers. Another benefit of bigness is economy of scale: a company has every reason to think and act in the aggregate; squeezing a few extra cents or dollars of profit out of the tens of thousands or millions of consumers or employees (including by legally questionable methods) benefits the company hugely, even if it hurts each individual slightly. Thus, if the company wants to sell mobile phone service contracts by giving away phones but does not want to pay the sales tax on the phones, it will say a mobile phone is free when in fact it is shifting to the consumer the $30 in sales tax, knowing that it will save the company millions of dollars across tens of thousands of consumers. Similarly, if a company adopts a set of personnel policies that results in employees being paid a few cents less per hour than the law requires, the company will, in the aggregate, save millions in labor costs.

Even if it's illegal to fail to disclose the full cost of the sales gimmick or to misclassify an employee as ineligible for overtime or not qualified to receive the minimum wage, most consumers and employees won't sue. Most don't know it is illegal. Even those who suspect it is illegal will not go to the trouble of finding and consulting a lawyer, because it's stressful and time-consuming. Occasionally, but not often, there is a consumer advocate who will sue; usually there is no one. Most employees will not sue their current employer, for fear of retaliation. And, assuming the person passes those obstacles, no lawyer will take a case worth $30 or $300 or even $3,000. So it's economically rational for a company to cheat a con sumer or employee. In short, large corporations have the market power and the legal expertise to shade the law in their benefit, and they have the incentive to do it in a million small transactions that add up to big profits.

But with size and uniformity of contract relations comes the risk that when employees or consumers discover that they all have been the victims of a similar practice, and a lawyer is willing to file a suit on behalf of a class alleging that the practice is illegal, the potential damages can be substantial. The larger the company, the greater the damages.

Just as the bigness of the standardized and aggregated profits from illegalities in millions of small transactions tempt some companies, so, too, does the bigness of class actions tempt some plaintiffs' lawyers. Some will file a suit for the settlement value rather than with the goal of obtaining meaningful relief for every class member. Even those lawyers determined to recover relief to benefit every member of the plaintiff class know that class actions are sufficiently large and expensive to litigate that it may be in the company's interest to settle rather than to try to win it all. The reality is that a consumer class action, like *AT&T Mobility v. Concepcion*, will yield relatively little for each consumer; after all, each lost only $30. 22 to begin with, and a successful class action will recoup only a fraction of this. But the lawyers' fees are substantial. The image of lawyers being greatly enriched while individual consumers get relatively little makes such class actions an easy target. If, however, such class actions are thought of as being about law enforcement and deterrence, then the lawyers are being rewarded for enforcing the law and protecting consumers by preventing future violations.

Conservative courts and commentators tend to worry about the risks to companies of the large class action. Progressive courts and commentators tend to worry more about the risks to consumers and employees of large companies. The weight of scholarly opinion has struck a middle ground, focusing on preserving the deterrent effects of class actions to curb the incentives of large companies to act improperly while reforming the treatment of settlement class actions to reduce the incentives for plaintiffs' lawyers to act improperly. But the Supreme Court majority in *Wal-Mart* and *AT&T* abandoned any pretense of equilibration and handed huge victories to large companies. The significance, of course, is not simply that Wal-Mart's employees who suffered sex discrimination are unlikely to ever recover damages or that AT&T Mobility has been unjustly enriched by millions of dollars. The larger importance is that big companies know that it will be much harder to sue them in class actions, and in the future they will more often make the choice to do something harmful or even illegal that will enrich them at the expense of consumers and employees.

It is ironic that the Court in cases like *Wal-Mart* has been openly troubled by the size of the class action but unconcerned about the size of the companies being protected. Wal-Mart, AT&T, and American Express are enormous companies—among the largest in American history. An effective remedy against a large company also must be large. The Supreme Court's recent decisions have greatly protected business at the expense of all of us, as consumers, employees, and patients.

Employment Discrimination

Until 1964, no federal law prohibited employment discrimination based on race, gender, or religion. The Civil Rights Act of 1964 was the first major federal civil rights law to be adopted since the end of Reconstruction. The act was initially proposed by President John F. Kennedy. His successor, Lyndon Johnson, appealed to Congress to enact the law as a tribute to the slain president. Johnson, a southerner from Texas, had particular credibility in urging the law's enactment. Also, Johnson had been majority leader of the Senate and was a master at its procedures.

All of this came together in the Civil Rights Act of 1964, which I regard as one of the most important statutes adopted in my lifetime. Title II of the act prohibits hotels and restaurants from discriminating based on race. Title VI says that recipients of federal funds cannot discriminate on the basis of race. Because virtually every school district in the country takes federal money, this provision was crucial in ending government-mandated segregation of public schools; the then Department of Health, Education, and Welfare said that any school system segregated by law could not receive federal dollars.

Title VII of the act prohibits employers from discriminating based on race, gender, or religion. There is no doubt that Congress intended that this statute be construed broadly to protect employees from discrimination. Yet it is striking that the Supreme Court consistently ignores this legislative objective and repeatedly construes the statute to favor business at the expense of employees. In 1989, there was a series of Supreme Court decisions interpreting Title VII in a very narrow way, and Congress in 1991 adopted a law to overturn these restrictive rulings.

In recent years, the Roberts Court, too, has interpreted the statute narrowly, so as to protect corporations over individuals. An important victory for businesses over employees came in *Ledbetter v. Goodyear Tire and Rubber Co., Inc.*, in which the Court made it much more difficult for employees to sue for pay discrimination under Title VII of the Civil Rights Act of 1964.

Lilly Ledbetter worked as a supervisor for Goodyear Tire and Rubber Company at its Gadsden, Alabama, plant from 1979 until 1998. In March 1998, Ledbetter submitted a questionnaire to the Equal Employment Opportunity Commission alleging sex discrimination, and in July of that year she filed a formal EEOC charge.

For most of her years with Goodyear, Ledbetter worked as an area manager, a position largely occupied by men. The evidence at trial indicated that Ledbetter's salary initially was similar to those of male employees, but over time a significant discrepancy developed. By "the end of 1997, Ledbetter was the only woman working as an area manager and the pay discrepancy between Ledbetter and her 15 male counterparts was stark: Ledbetter was paid $3,727 per month; the lowest paid male area manager received $4,286 per month, the highest paid, $5,236." A jury found for Ledbetter, and a judgment was entered in her favor for $3.3 million.

The Supreme Court, however, found that her claims under Title VII were time-barred. Writing for the Court, Justice Alito—who was joined by Chief Justice Roberts and Justices Scalia, Kennedy, and Thomas—held that the statute of limitations for pay discrimination claims under Title VII of the Civil Rights Act of 1964 begins running at the time when the pay is set.

Generally, discrimination claims must be filed with the EEOC within 180 days of the discriminatory act. Often, however, individuals do not know the salary of other employees in their workplace. Justice Ginsburg, in her dissenting opinion, pointed out that "one-third of private sector employers have adopted specific rules prohibiting employees from discussing their wages with co-workers; only one in ten employers has adopted a pay openness policy."

The Court expressly rejected Ledbetter's claim that each additional paycheck is a new discriminatory act that separately triggers the statute of limitations. The Court's holding in *Ledbetter* was a very significant obstacle for many pay discrimination claims under Title VII. The decision was not based on the text of the law, and it certainly did not further Congress's broad purpose of protecting workers.

In 2009, just nine days after taking office, President Obama signed the Lilly Ledbetter Fair Pay Act, to overturn the Supreme Court's decision. The act reinstates prior law and makes clear that pay discrimination claims on the basis of sex, race, national origin, age, religion, and disability "accrue" whenever an employee receives a discriminatory paycheck, as well as when a discriminatory pay decision or practice is adopted, when a person becomes subject to the decision or practice, or when a person is otherwise affected by the decision or practice. This is important, because women today are paid, on average, only seventy-seven cents for every dollar paid to men. On average, "African-American women earn only 62% and Hispanic women earn only 53% of the income of Caucasian, non-Hispanic males," according to professor Marianne DelPo Kulow.

There is no way to understand the Court's decision in *Ledbetter* other than as the Court interpreting a statute meant to protect employees in a manner that protected businesses. The decision simultaneously reflects the majority's bias in favor of business and its skepticism, if not hostility, toward employment discrimination plaintiffs. That has been evident in other Roberts Court employment discrimination decisions as well. In 2013, the Court once more adopted very restrictive interpretations of federal employment discrimination statutes in a way that very much favored employers over employees.

Harassment in the workplace based on race and sex is widespread. Surveys indicate that almost half of all working women have experienced some form of harassment on the job. Sexual harassment might take the form of unwelcome sexual advances, where an employee is given a quid pro quo ("sleep with me or you are fired"), or an environment made hostile by sexual tension (such as a workplace that is so offensive as to make the reasonable woman feel unwelcome). Very few harassed women formally report problems of harassment to members of management or to fair-employment agencies. There are many reasons why victims of sexual harassment don't file complaints: fear of retribution in losing their jobs or otherwise hurting their careers, worry that they will be blamed even though they were the victim, and the concern that nothing can or will be done about the harassment.

In 1986, the Supreme Court held that sexual harassment is a form of employment discrimination that violates Title VII of the Civil Rights Act of 1964. Federal law is similarly clear that harassing an employee on the basis of race is a form of employment discrimination. Holding employers liable for harassment in the workplace is critical for ensuring that there is an incentive for them to do everything possible to prevent harassing behavior or a hostile work environment.

In two cases in 1998, the Court articulated the standard for when an employer could be held liable if an employee is harassed. The Court drew a distinction between harassment by a fellow employee and harassment by a supervisor. If an employee is harassed by another employee based on race or sex, the employer can be held liable only if it is proven that the employer was negligent in controlling the workplace. That is, the employer is liable for harassment of one of its employees by another employee only if the employer did not act as a reasonable employer would, under the circumstances, to prevent and remedy sexual harassment. But if the harassment is by a supervisor, and the employee is subject to some tangible action such as firing, demotion, or a decrease in pay, then the company is automatically liable; in legal terms, the employer is said to be "strictly liable" under such circumstances. It always is much easier for a plaintiff to recover under strict liability, as opposed to having to prove that the defendant was so careless as to be negligent.

In practical reality, then, the determination of who is a fellow employee and who is a supervisor makes all the difference in many cases. It is far easier to hold an employer liable for harassment by a supervisor than for harassment by other employees. In 2013, the Supreme Court adopted a restrictive test to determine who is a supervisor that significantly protects businesses.

Maetta Vance, an African American woman, began working for Ball State University in 1989 as a substitute server in the University Banquet and Catering division of Dining Services. In 1991, Ball State promoted Vance to a part-time catering assistant position, and in 2007 she applied and was selected for a position as a full-time catering assistant.

Over the course of her employment with Ball State University, Vance lodged numerous complaints of racial discrimination and retaliation. In this case, Vance alleged that Saundra Davis, a white woman who was employed as a catering specialist in the Banquet and Catering division, repeatedly harassed her because of her race. Vance complained that Davis "gave her a hard time at work by glaring at her, slamming pots and pans around her, and intimidating her."

The Court concluded that Davis could not be considered a supervisor. Justice Alito, writing for the majority in a 5–4 decision, said, "We hold that an employer may be vicariously liable for an employee's unlawful harassment only when the employer has empowered that employee to take tangible employment actions against the victim, *i.e.*, to effect a significant change in employment status, such as hiring, firing, failing to promote, reassignment with significantly different responsibilities, or a decision causing a significant change in benefits." Because Davis could not fire or demote or cut the pay of Vance, Davis was not a supervisor under the law, even though in every practical way Davis was Vance's supervisor.

Under this definition, it will be much more difficult to identify someone as a supervisor and to impose liability on businesses. Imagine, for example, that a senior associate in a law firm, or even a partner, sexually harasses a more junior associate whom he is supervising. Under the court's decision, the senior associate or even the partner is likely not to be deemed a supervisor, because he probably does not have the authority to fire or cut the pay of the junior associate. In law firms, such tangible actions are virtually never left to a supervisor; such decisions are made by the partners as a group or by a firm committee. Practically speaking, the senior associate or partner is a supervisor; he is the one giving the work to the junior associate, overseeing her work, and evaluating her work. But to the Supreme Court he is not a supervisor. The result is that it will be much more difficult to hold the law firm liable, because it will be necessary to prove that the firm was negligent in its actions in controlling the workplace. As Justice Ginsburg noted in her dissent, the majority's opinion "ignores the conditions under which members of the work force labor, and disserves the objective of Title VII to prevent discrimination from infecting the Nation's workplaces."

Once more, what the majority has done is interpret a statute clearly intended by Congress to broadly protect against workplace discrimination, including harassment, so as to protect businesses. As Ginsburg pointed out, "Trumpeting the virtues of simplicity and administrability, the Court restricts supervisor status to those with power to take tangible employment actions. In so restricting the definition of supervisor, the Court once again shuts from sight the 'robust protection against workplace discrimination Congress intended Title VII to secure.'"

Conclusion

We all take generic drugs, enter into cell phone agreements, go to work. Any of us might be injured by side effects from a prescription drug or lose some money from fraud by a major corporation or experience discrimination in the workplace. Congress acted to provide protections against harmful business practices in each of these areas. The goal of these laws was clear: safeguarding consumers and employees.

But in each area, as well as many others, the Court has nullified Congress's purpose by narrowly interpreting the federal statutes. The Court's decisions cannot be understood based on the words of the laws or their intent. In each instance, it has been about a pro-business Court construing federal statutes to protect business.

An important study was published in 2013 by three prominent scholars: Lee Epstein, who teaches law and political science at the University of Southern California; William M. Landes, an economist at the University of Chicago; and Judge Richard A. Posner, of the federal appeals court in Chicago, who also teaches law at the University of Chicago. The study examined the thirty-six justices who have served on the Court over the past sixty-five years by the proportion of their pro-business votes; all five of the current Court's more conservative members were in the top ten. The study found that the two justices most likely to vote in favor of business interests since 1946 are the most recent conservative additions to the court, Chief Justice Roberts and Justice Samuel A. Alito Jr., both appointed by President George W. Bush. *New York Times* reporter Adam Liptak wrote:

But the business docket reflects something truly distinctive about the court led by Chief Justice John G. Roberts Jr. While the current court's decisions, over all, are only slightly more conservative than those from the courts led by Chief Justices Warren E. Burger and William H. Rehnquist, according to political scientists who study the court, its business rulings are another matter. They have been, a new study finds, far friendlier to business than those of any court since at least World War II.

Federal statutes, like all laws, inevitably have ambiguities. Statutes should be construed to accomplish the legislature's underlying purpose. But the pattern for the Roberts Court has been to interpret statutes to favor businesses over employees and consumers, even when it means that the protections provided by the laws are rendered meaningless.

Supreme Court decisions interpreting statutes are different from those dealing with the Constitution, because Congress can amend the law to override what the Court says. That is what happened in the *Ledbetter* case. Congress could amend the Food and Drug Act to make clear that generic drug makers can be held liable for failing to provide adequate warnings or for design defects in their products. Congress could amend the Federal Arbitration Act to make clear that it does not apply to language in form agreements requiring arbitration or where the requirement for arbitration will effectively nullify the ability to gain relief. Congress could amend the employment discrimination statutes to broaden the definition of "supervisor."

It is at best uncertain whether such laws have a chance to get adopted. In the meantime, people are hurt and left without a remedy, and congressional intent to provide protections is thwarted. It is part of a much larger pattern that has occurred throughout American history—of the Supreme Court siding with business at the expense of individuals.

CHAPTER 6

Abuses of Government Power

Thomas Lee Goldstein spent twenty-four years in prison for murders that he did not commit. When Goldstein was tried, there were no eyewitnesses to the murders, and there was no confession. There was no physical evidence, like DNA, linking him to the murder site. The primary evidence against him was the false testimony of a longtime jailhouse informant, Edward Floyd Fink. As the federal court of appeals explained, "Thomas Goldstein spent 24 years in prison after being convicted for murder based largely upon the perjured testimony of an unreliable jailhouse informant, the aptronymic Edward Fink."

Fink was a heroin addict with a long criminal record. He testified that he had been in a cell with Goldstein in the Long Beach City Jail and that he had heard Goldstein admit to the murders. At the time, in 1979, Goldstein was an engineering student and a Marine Corps veteran with no criminal history. As the California Supreme Court explained:

He became a murder suspect after an eyewitness to an unrelated shooting saw the gunman enter Goldstein's apartment building. No witness or forensic evidence connected Goldstein with the murder victim, but Long Beach police detectives showed Goldstein's photograph, among others, to Loran Campbell, an eyewitness to the homicide. Campbell did not recognize anyone in the photo lineup, and Goldstein did not match Campbell's description of the suspect. However, a detective asked if Goldstein could have been the person Campbell saw running from the scene. Campbell said it was possible, though he was not certain.

Once arrested on this basis, Goldstein had the misfortune of being placed in a cell with Edward Fink. Fink had a long history of getting deals from prosecutors, such as reduced sentences, in exchange for giving testimony against his fellow inmates. Fink testified at Goldstein's trial that Goldstein had admitted to the murders while they were together in the jail cell. It was on the basis of this testimony that Goldstein was convicted and ultimately spent twenty-four years in prison.

In fact, Goldstein was not the first person wrongly convicted based on Fink's testimony. Thomas Thompson was executed on the basis of Fink's perjured testimony. As federal appeals court judge Stephen Reinhardt noted, "It is unlikely that Thompson was death-eligible for his part in the crime, if he was guilty at all of any offense." As Judge Reinhardt wrote, "Despite a request to reverse Thompson's conviction by seven California prosecutors with extensive death penalty experience, including the author of California's death penalty statute, the Supreme Court refused to consider Fink's perjured testimony or any of the constitutional violations."

In 1963, in *Brady v. Maryland,* the Supreme Court held that prosecutors have the constitutional duty to turn over to criminal defendants any evidence that might help show the defendant's innocence. Police and prosecutors, in their investigations, often uncover information that is exculpatory, and they should not be able to hide this evidence. The Supreme Court held, and often has reaffirmed, that it violates due process of law for a prosecutor to fail to disclose to the defense evidence that could materially assist them at trial or at sentencing. Additionally, in every state, the code of professional responsibility that regulates lawyer behavior requires that prosecutors turn over to the defense any potentially exculpatory information, including any that might help reduce the defendant's sentence. In light of this, many years prior to Goldstein's arrest, the Supreme

Court held that prosecutors' offices have a constitutional obligation to establish "procedures and regulations . . . to insure communication of all relevant information on each case"—including promises made to informants in exchange for testimony in that case—"to every lawyer who deals with it."

There is no dispute that the prosecutors in Goldstein's case had the constitutional duty to inform his defense counsel of Fink's long history of making deals in exchange for a reduction of charges and sentences. This would have provided a crucial basis for impeaching the key witness against Goldstein. Obviously, there were lawyers in the Los Angeles County district attorney's office who knew of these deals—they had negotiated them—and Goldstein's attorneys could have been informed about Fink. The disclosure, though, never happened.

After more than two decades in prison, a federal district court granted Goldstein's habeas corpus petition. The court concluded that there was no reliable evidence linking Goldstein to the murders and that Fink's testimony was so lacking in credibility that it could not be the basis for a conviction. The federal court of appeals agreed, and finally Tommy Lee Goldstein was a free man.

Goldstein then sued the district attorney of Los Angeles County, John Van de Kamp, and other top officials, claiming that they had violated his constitutional rights "by purposefully or with deliberate indifference" failing to create a system that would ensure that key evidence would be turned over to defendants as required by the Constitution. Goldstein also argued that the district attorney had violated Goldstein's constitutional rights by failing to adequately train and supervise deputy district attorneys to ensure that they shared information regarding jailhouse informants with their colleagues.

The federal court of appeals ruled that Goldstein's suit could go forward against Van de Kamp and others in his office. The U.S. Supreme Court, though, unanimously reversed and ordered Goldstein's case dismissed. Justice Breyer wrote the opinion for the Court and said that prosecutors have absolute immunity to suits for money damages—they cannot be sued at all—and this extends even to the administrative practices that Goldstein says led to his wrongful conviction. Tommy Lee Goldstein spent twenty-four years in prison for murders he did not commit, and the Supreme Court's response to him was "Tough luck."

It is tempting to dismiss Goldstein's case as an aberration, but consider another recent Supreme Court case with remarkably similar facts. John Thompson was convicted and spent eighteen years in prison, and fourteen years on death row, because of egregious prosecutorial misconduct. One month before he was to be executed, Thompson's defense lawyers found blood evidence that prosecutors possessed at the time of his trial, but did not disclose, that exonerated him for an armed robbery for which he had been convicted and that greatly affected his murder trial.

Two days before Thompson's murder trial in New Orleans, the assistant district attorney had received the crime lab's report, which stated that the perpetrator had blood type B and that Thompson's blood was type O. The defense was not told of this—not at the trial and not until the report was discovered, shortly before Thompson's scheduled execution.

The assistant district attorney who had the blood report simply hid it. Many years later, when that assistant district attorney was dying of cancer, he told another assistant district attorney about it. That person, too, told no one. That attorney was subsequently disciplined by the Louisiana State Bar Association for not informing Thompson and his lawyers immediately about the blood evidence.

All the while Thompson remained on death row with his execution date coming ever closer. Through a series of coincidences, Thompson's lawyer discovered the blood evidence soon before the scheduled execution and learned that it was still available to be examined. New testing was done, and the blood of the perpetrator didn't match Thompson's DNA or even his blood type. Thompson's conviction was overturned, and he was retried for the murders. He was acquitted of all charges.

The district attorney's office conceded that it had violated its constitutional obligations under *Brady v. Maryland* in not turning over the blood evidence. There was no way to argue otherwise. Thompson's lawyers knew that they could not sue the district attorney or the prosecutors themselves, because the Supreme Court had ruled, including in *Van de Kamp v. Goldstein*, that they had absolute immunity. So Thompson sued the local government, New Orleans, which employed them. The Orleans Parish district attorney's office has a notorious history of not disclosing exculpatory information to defendants, as required by the Constitution. The jury ruled in favor of Thompson and awarded him $14 million.

But the Supreme Court reversed, in a 5–4 decision, and held that the local government could not be held liable for the prosecutorial misconduct. Justice Thomas, writing for the Court, said that a single instance of prosecutorial misconduct was not enough to show sufficient deliberate indifference to allow the city to be sued. Thompson, like Goldstein, suffered one of the worst harms a government can inflict on a person, and the Court once more refused to allow any remedy.

As Justice Ginsburg pointed out in her dissenting opinion, what Thompson suffered was not a single instance of prosecutorial misconduct. She wrote that throughout the trial, the prosecutors "hid from the defense and the court exculpatory information Thompson requested and had a constitutional right to receive." For more than two decades, despite many opportunities, they did not set the record straight. What happened here, the Court's opinion obscures, was no momentary oversight, no single incident of a lone officer's misconduct. Instead, the evidence demonstrated that misperception and disregard of *Brady*'s disclosure requirements were pervasive in Orleans Parish.

In fact, this was not the only serious *Brady* violation in this case. Soon after the murder, the police interviewed an eyewitness who described the assailant as having short hair. At that time, Thompson had a large Afro. That, too, never was disclosed to the defense.

Tommy Lee Goldstein and John Thompson were convicted thousands of miles apart, in Los Angeles and New Orleans. Each spent years in prison for crimes they did not commit. Each was the victim of clearly unconstitutional abuse of power by the government, in that the district attorneys' offices did not make disclosures that the Supreme Court has held are constitutionally required. In neither case did the Supreme Court deny—nor could it—that the Constitution had been violated. The legal issues in their cases were somewhat different—Goldstein sued the individuals in the district attorney's office, while Thompson sued the local government. But the Supreme Court ruled against both. The result is that a person who is wrongly convicted and spends years in prison generally cannot sue the officers responsible or the government. The Supreme Court has failed at one of its most important functions: protecting people from abuse of government power.

Holding the Government Accountable

Long ago, in *Marbury v. Madison,* in 1803, Chief Justice John Marshall wrote, "The very essence of civil liberty certainly consists in the right of every individual to claim the protection of the laws, whenever he receives an injury." The Court said that "[t]he government of the United States has been emphatically termed a government of laws, and not of men." The Court thus declared that no one, not even the government or its top officials, is above the law, and that it is elemental that the law must provide a remedy to those who have been injured.

One of the most important functions of the courts is to protect people from abuses of government power. The government has enormous power and can inflict great injury on people. Those who face injury must be able to sue for injunctions to stop the government from acting illegally and unconstitutionally. Those who are injured must be able to sue to recover money damages from government entities and government officials who violate their rights. Damages provide compensation to victims of government wrongdoing and also are a way to deter such conduct. The realistic possibility of being held liable for money damages hopefully provides a deterrence against violations of the law.

What is striking about the Supreme Court, and especially the Roberts Court, is that it has systematically made it more difficult for people to sue the government when it acts wrongly. Tommy Lee Goldstein and John

Thompson were victims of unconstitutional abuses of power by prosecutors. No one, including the government officials, denies that. But the Roberts Court said in both instances that they were entitled to no remedy. Not only are they denied monetary compensation—not that any amount of money ever could restore the years they lost from their lives—but also prosecutors are sent a message that they cannot be sued for money damages for their misconduct. A vital check on wrongdoing is lost.

If a person is injured by government wrongdoing, as Goldstein and Thompson were, there are only a couple of possibilities: sue the individual officer who violated the Constitution and/or sue the government entity, the state or local government, that is responsible for the wrong. What is striking is that the Roberts Court (and, to be fair, its decisions follow from those of the Rehnquist and Burger Courts before it) has closed the courthouse doors on the ability to sue either individual wrongdoers or government entities for money damages. At the same time, the Supreme Court has made it much harder for those facing injury from government unconstitutional actions to get an injunction to stop such conduct.

The result is a failure on the part of the Supreme Court to provide essential remedies for those who suffer—even terribly suffer, as Goldstein and Thompson did—from government misconduct. The Court has rendered hollow its assurance in *Marbury v. Madison* that "[t]he very essence of civil liberty certainly consists in the right of every individual to claim the protection of the laws, whenever he receives an injury."

To see this, consider the various ways in which a person might seek recovery and how the Court has thwarted them: damages against individual government officers, damages against government entities, and injunctions to prevent wrongdoing.

Damages Against Individual Government Officers

The Constitution, of course, provides rights to individuals, but it does not speak to the remedies that can be provided to those whose rights have been violated. In 1871, Congress passed a federal law—18 U.S.C. Section 1983—which allows suits for money damages or injunctions by those whose rights have been violated "under color of state law." A Section 1983 suit can be brought against a state or local official or a local government that violates a person's rights. As explained below, state governments cannot be sued under Section 1983—or under almost any other federal law—because they are deemed to possess "sovereign immunity."

Both Tommy Lee Goldstein and John Thompson brought Section 1983 suits to recover damages for the violation of their constitutional rights. If a police officer uses excessive force and injures a person, a Section 1983 suit is brought, because the Supreme Court has said that excessive police force violates the Fourth Amendment. If a local government violates the free speech rights of demonstrators, a Section 1983 suit is the vehicle for redress. If a local government takes someone's property without just compensation, again it is a Section 1983 suit. Section 1983 is said to create the "cause of action" for money damages or injunctions against state and local officers and local governments for violating the Constitution. Virtually all civil suits for constitutional violations by these defendants are brought as Section 1983 actions.

Section 1983 was adopted in 1871. Following the Civil War and the adoption of the Thirteenth, Fourteenth, and Fifteenth Amendments, violence against blacks was endemic throughout the South. The U.S. Senate conducted extensive investigations of this lawlessness, focusing especially on the role of the Ku Klux Klan. A six-hundred-page Senate report detailed the unwillingness or inability of southern states to control the activities of the Klan. In response to this report, Congress adopted the Civil Rights Act of 1871, Section 1 of which is now embodied in Section 1983. The law, titled "An Act to enforce the Provisions of the Fourteenth Amendment to the Constitution, and for other Purposes," was a direct result of "the campaign of violence and deception in the South, fomented by the Ku Klux Klan, which was denying decent citizens their civil and political rights."

There were lengthy discussions in Congress concerning the uncontrolled violence in the South and the failure of state police and state courts to adequately control the problem. Section 1983 thus was meant to substantially alter the relationship of the federal government to the states. The statute empowered the federal government, and especially the federal courts, with the authority necessary to prevent and redress violations of federal rights. As the Supreme Court declared, "[t]he very purpose of §1983 was to interpose the federal courts between the States and the people, as guardians of the people's federal rights—to protect the people from unconstitutional action under color of state law, whether that action be executive, legislative, or judicial."

Section 1983, though, cannot be used to sue the federal government or federal officers. There actually is no federal law that authorizes suits against the federal government or its employees when they violate the Constitution. The federal government itself generally cannot be sued, because of its sovereign immunity, though there are a few federal statutes that waive this sovereign immunity and permit suits in limited instances. As for federal officers, in 1971, in *Bivens v. Six Unknown Named Federal Agents,* the Supreme Court held that federal officers who violate constitutional rights may be sued for money damages directly under the Constitution.

Wesley Bivens had been subjected to an illegal and humiliating search, in violation of the Fourth Amendment, by agents of the Federal Bureau of Narcotics. He could not sue the United States because of its sovereign immunity, so instead he sought to sue the agents themselves. The Supreme Court ruled in his favor and said that a right to sue federal officials for money damages could be inferred directly from the U.S. Constitution. Justice John Marshall Harlan, in an eloquent concurring opinion, explained that for someone in Bivens's shoes, it is such a damages remedy or nothing. Even though there is not a federal law, like Section 1983, permitting suits against federal government officials for constitutional violations, the Court said that the ability to sue is inferred directly from the Constitution. After all, how else could those injured get compensation, and how else could wrongdoing by government officials be deterred?

Section 1983 is written in seemingly absolute language. It says, "Every person who, under color of any statute, ordinance, regulation, custom, or usage of any State or Territory or the District of Columbia, subjects, or causes to be subjected, any citizen of the United States or other person within the jurisdiction thereof to the deprivation of any rights, privileges, or immunities secured by the Constitution and laws, shall be liable to the party injured in an action at law, suit in equity, or other proper proceeding for redress." No exceptions are stated in the law.

But the Supreme Court has said otherwise. The Court has ruled over many decades that all government officials who are sued for money damages possess an immunity from liability. Some government officials have absolute immunity; that is, they cannot be held liable at all, no matter how egregious their conduct or how horrible the injury they inflict. All other government officials are said to have "qualified immunity" and can be held liable only if they violate clearly established law that the reasonable officer should know. The Roberts Court did not invent these doctrines; they were created by the Supreme Court in earlier eras. But the Roberts Court has greatly expanded them and made it much more difficult for those injured to sue government officers who violate the Constitution.

Immunity doctrines are extremely important. The availability of relief against individual officers is often crucial, because the governmental entity frequently is completely protected from liability. As explained below, state governments generally cannot be sued in federal court because of the Eleventh Amendment, and municipal governments are not liable unless their official policy caused the unconstitutional conduct. Hence, if injured individuals are to receive compensation, and if there is to be deterrence of wrongdoing, it frequently must take the form of suits against the individual officers.

It is widely believed that some degree of immunity for individual officers is necessary. At minimum, it seems unfair to hold an officer personally liable if he or she had no way of knowing that the actions taken were illegal. As the Supreme Court remarked, official immunity reflects "the injustice, particularly in the absence of bad faith, of subjecting to liability an officer who is required by the legal obligations of his position, to exercise discretion." Additionally, there is concern that the absence of immunity might make it more difficult to attract people into government service, or at least would chill the exercise of discretion. Thus, I am not arguing against the existence of some immunity for government officers who are sued for money damages; instead I am objecting to the great expansion of immunity, and how, accompanied by the increased protection of state and local governments from suit, this often has left those injured with no recourse at all.

Absolute Immunity. The Supreme Court has said that some tasks by government officials are protected by absolute immunity and thus cannot be the basis for a lawsuit for money damages. Specifically, the Court has said that judges performing judicial tasks, prosecutors performing prosecutorial tasks, legislators performing legislative tasks, law enforcement personnel testifying as witnesses, and the president performing executive tasks can never be held liable for money damages. Period. It does not matter how awful or clearly wrong or illegal the conduct. It does not matter how horrific the injury suffered. These individuals have absolute immunity and cannot be sued.

Absolute immunity is not mentioned in Section 1983. The Supreme Court created it. The goal of absolute immunity is to protect the exercise of discretion by government officials. But it is highly questionable whether absolute immunity is necessary for achieving these goals. The choice is not limited to selecting between absolute immunity and no immunity. For example, certain functions could be protected by according immunity except for malicious acts, or immunity except for intentional violations of rights. Admittedly, such a standard would open the door to litigation, but it would be preferable to protect officials from meritless suits by other procedural devices rather than by according them absolute immunity for even egregious misconduct.

The cases in which the Court has found absolute immunity illustrate the great problem in creating a complete bar to any recovery. For example, the Court has said that a judge cannot be sued for money damages for any judicial act. It is this doctrine that explains why, in *Stump v.*

Sparkman, as discussed in the introduction, Linda Sparkman could not sue the judge who ordered her surgical sterilization, even though he unquestionably violated her constitutional rights and permanently took away her ability to have children.

In *Mireles v. Waco,* a judge was upset that a lawyer did not show up in court despite a subpoena. The judge told the bailiff to go find the lawyer, Howard Waco, and forcibly bring the lawyer to court. The judge instructed the bailiff to rough Waco up so that he would learn a lesson. Waco's complaint against the judge alleged that the officers "by means of unreasonable force and violence seize[d] plaintiff and remove[d] him backwards" from another courtroom where he was waiting to appear, cursed him, and called him "vulgar and offensive names," then "without necessity slammed" him through the doors and swinging gates into Judge Raymond Mireles's courtroom.

The Supreme Court said that Waco's suit had to be dismissed because the judge possessed absolute immunity and could not be sued at all. The Court accepted as true Waco's allegations but said that it didn't matter, because "judicial immunity is not overcome by allegations of bad faith or malice." I understand why judges need some protections from being sued, but not for this type of conduct, and not for ordering a girl's sterilization without any legal authority. When a judge acts maliciously or without authority, the judge should be held liable—those injured by the wrongdoing deserve compensation, and judges should be deterred from engaging in such behavior.

Prosecutors, too, have absolute immunity from suits for damages resulting from their prosecutorial misconduct. It was on this basis that the Supreme Court ruled against Tommy Lee Goldstein, despite his allegations that the Los Angeles County district attorney had violated the Constitution by failing to adopt a policy to ensure that exculpatory evidence be disclosed to criminal defendants.

Van de Kamp v. Goldstein was not the first Supreme Court case to recognize absolute immunity for prosecutors. In *Imbler v. Pachtman,* the Supreme Court accorded absolute immunity to a prosecutor who was sued for damages for knowingly using perjured testimony that resulted in an innocent person's conviction and incarceration for nine years. The Court concluded that anything other than absolute immunity risked "harassment by unfounded litigation [that] would cause a deflection of the prosecutor's energies from his public duties, and the possibility that he would shade his decisions instead of exercising the independence of judgment required by his public trust." However, it again must be asked whether something less than absolute immunity might achieve this goal. For example, would prosecutorial liability for intentional use of known perjured testimony really chill discretion in an undesirable way?

A third category of government officials possessing absolute immunity is legislators performing legislative tasks. The Court has broadly construed which individuals are protected by this. In *Bogan v. Scott-Harris,* an individual who worked as a police psychologist had his job eliminated by the mayor and city council as part of the city's budget process. He sued and alleged that his firing was racially motivated and was in retaliation for speech activities. The Supreme Court found that the lawsuit, against the mayor and the members of the city council, had to be dismissed based on absolute legislative immunity. The Court unanimously concluded that the process of proposing, voting for, and signing a budget are "integral steps in the legislative process" and thus safeguarded by absolute immunity.

The case is most remarkable in extending absolute legislative immunity to the acts of the mayor in the budget process. The mayor obviously is an executive official, and it is notable that the Court found that all aspects of the budget process, even those traditionally done in the executive branch, should be deemed legislative in nature. The result was that even if the firing was blatantly unconstitutional, there was no remedy available to the person who was fired.

Fourth, the Supreme Court has held that police officers have absolute immunity for the testimony they give as witnesses, even if an officer commits perjury. In general, police officers have only qualified, good-faith immunity to suits against them pursuant to Section 1983. However, in *Briscoe v. LaHue,* the Court concluded that police officers who commit perjury have absolute immunity in suits against them for money damages. The Court reasoned that officers should be able to testify as witnesses without fear of possible civil litigation and argued that if absolute immunity did not exist, officers would be sued frequently. Thus, the Court concluded that allowing officers to be sued for their testimony as witnesses "might undermine not only their contribution to the judicial process but also the effective performance of their other public duties." The Court emphasized that police officers, like all other witnesses, could be criminally prosecuted for perjury and believed that this provided an adequate deterrent to perjury

I find it quite disturbing that a police officer could intentionally lie under oath, cause an innocent person to be convicted and imprisoned, and then be totally immune to any civil liability for money damages. In 2000, I was asked to do an extensive report on the Los Angeles Police Department in the wake of the Rampart scandal. This scandal involved police officers planting evidence on innocent people whom they thought to be gang members and then lying in court to gain convictions. One high-profile case involved Javier Francisco Ovando. Ovando, nineteen years old at the time, had the misfortune of coming into contact with two of the officers who were at the center of the Rampart scandal, Rafael Perez and Nino Durden. After a verbal altercation, Ovando was shot in the head by the officers and permanently paralyzed. The officers planted a sawed-off .22-caliber rifle on Ovando and claimed that he had attacked them. The two men lied in court to get Ovando's conviction. The teenager was sentenced to twenty-three years in prison for assaulting the police officers. At sentencing, the judge stressed that Ovando had not shown any remorse for his crime.

It was learned as part of the Rampart investigation that Ovando was not alone in being convicted as a result of police perjury. More than a hundred convictions were overturned as a result of the investigation into Rampart. But those imprisoned because the police lied could not sue the officers for their misconduct.

Unfortunately, the Roberts Court recently extended this immunity

beyond police officers to all witnesses for law enforcement, and beyond trials to all stages of criminal proceedings. Charles Rehberg, a certified public
accountant, sent anonymous faxes to several recipients, including the management of a hospital in Albany, Georgia, criticizing the hospital's management. In response, apparently as a favor to the hospital's leadership, the
local district attorney's office began a criminal investigation of Rehberg.
The investigation was undertaken solely in retaliation for Rehberg's speaking out about the hospital's management; there was no indication that Rehberg had committed any crime. The investigation was conducted by James
Paulk, the chief investigator in the district attorney's office.

Paulk went before a grand jury and lied about Rehberg. He told the
grand jury that Rehberg had assaulted a hospital physician, Dr. James
Hotz, after unlawfully entering the doctor's home. Rehberg was then indicted for aggravated assault, burglary, and six counts of making harassing telephone calls. Rehberg challenged the indictment, and a judge
dismissed it for lack of any evidence to support it.

A few months later, Paulk returned to the grand jury, and Rehberg
was indicted again for assaulting Dr. Hotz and for making harassing
phone calls. Rehberg challenged the sufficiency of this second indictment, and told the court that he was "nowhere near Dr. Hotz" on the date
in question and that "[t]here was no evidence whatsoever that [he] committed an assault on anybody." Again the indictment was dismissed.

Undaunted, Paulk appeared before a grand jury for a third time, and
yet another indictment was returned. Rehberg was again charged with
assault and making harassing phone calls. This final indictment was ultimately dismissed as well.

Rehberg then sued Paulk for malicious prosecution in violation of the
Fourth Amendment. This should have been an easy case. Paulk had abused
his power by three times lying before a grand jury to get a person indicted.
Rehberg had financial costs, for the lawyer he had to retain, and emotional
costs, from being thrice falsely indicted. But the Supreme Court, in 2012,
unanimously ruled that Paulk was protected by absolute immunity.

In an opinion by Justice Alito, the Court held that *Briscoe v. LaHue* was controlling and that it did not matter that the testimony was before a grand jury rather than at trial or by an investigator rather than a police officer. Justice Alito declared, "[W]e conclude that grand jury witnesses should enjoy the same immunity as witnesses at trial. This means that a grand jury witness has absolute immunity from any §1983 claim based on the witness' testimony." Moreover, the Court said that there could not be a claim that a grand jury witness had conspired to present false testimony or any other claim that used the witness's testimony to recover for the initiation or maintenance of a prosecution. The Court said, "In the vast majority of cases involving a claim against a grand jury witness, the witness and the prosecutor conducting the investigation engage in preparatory activity, such as a preliminary discussion in which the witness relates the substance of his intended testimony. We decline to endorse a rule of absolute immunity that is so easily frustrated."

So police and prosecutors' investigators can go to court and lie about any of us, for whatever reason, and cause us to be indicted and have to spend large sums on attorney fees and go through the anguish of being dragged through the criminal justice system. The victim of this, though, cannot sue and get compensation, even if the wrongdoer would admit to misconduct.

The final area in which the Supreme Court has found absolute immunity is suits against the president for money damages for acts done while in office. A. Ernest Fitzgerald was an analyst in the Defense Department and testified before Congress about cost overruns in building a transport plane. President Nixon was furious at him for embarrassing the Defense Department and ordered that Fitzgerald be fired. Fitzgerald subsequently sued Nixon for violating his First Amendment rights to freedom of speech and to petition Congress for a redress of grievances.

The Supreme Court, though, in 1982 ruled that the president has absolute immunity and cannot be sued for money damages for actions done in carrying out the presidency. In a 5–4 decision, the Court held that the president's "unique status under the Constitution" and the "singular importance" of the duties of the office justified absolute immunity. As in other cases according absolute immunity, the Court emphasized the likelihood of frequent suits as a justification for providing more than good-faith immunity.

However, it should be noted that in a subsequent case, involving President Bill Clinton, the Court held that this immunity does not extend to actions taken prior to taking office. Paula Jones sued Bill Clinton for sexual harassment that had allegedly occurred when he was governor of Arkansas. Clinton sought to have the suit dismissed or at least stayed until after the completion of his presidency. The U.S. Supreme Court disagreed and ruled that presidential immunity extends only to acts while in office. The Court explained that immunities exist to protect the exercise of discretion in office; therefore, they do not extend to conduct before taking office. The Court said that trial courts should manage litigation against a president to minimize interference with presidential tasks. (Of course, it was the Court's ruling in *Clinton v. Jones* that led to President Clinton's being deposed in the Paula Jones case and to Clinton's denial of a sexual relationship with Monica Lewinsky.)

Judges, prosecutors, legislators, police officers, and the president have enormous power and the ability to inflict tremendous harms. I understand the need to provide them with protection from frivolous suits. But what I don't agree with is that this protection requires a complete bar on litigation—absolute immunity. If they act maliciously, they, like all the rest of us, should be held liable so as to compensate victims and deter such wrongdoing. Otherwise, what is left of the assurance in *Marbury v. Madison* that no one is above the law and that "[t]he government of the United States has been emphatically termed a government of laws, and not of men"?

Qualified Immunity. As one reads the absolute immunity cases, there is a sense that the Court is worried that without such protection, it would be far too easy to hold these government officials liable. The reality is just the opposite. All government officials—local, state, and federal—who are sued for money damages for constitutional violations are protected by qualified immunity if they do not have absolute immunity. The Roberts Court has recently redefined qualified immunity to make it very difficult for plaintiffs to recover under this standard.

The test for qualified immunity was articulated in *Harlow v. Fitzgerald*, in 1982. This was a companion case to *Nixon v. Fitzgerald*. Ernie Fitzgerald, an analyst in the Air Force who claimed that his job had been eliminated in retaliation for his exposing cost overruns in the Defense Department, sued not only the president but also a top aide, Bryce Harlow. The Court said that the president's absolute immunity did not extend to others in the government, but it said that these other officers were protected by qualified immunity. The Court stated the legal test that still controls: "government officials performing discretionary functions generally are shielded from liability for civil damages insofar as their conduct does not violate clearly established statutory or constitutional rights of which a reasonable person would have known."

For three decades, the Supreme Court and lower courts have struggled with what it means to say that government officers are liable only if they violate clearly established law that the reasonable person would have known. There are thousands of cases in the lower courts interpreting and applying this test. It has great importance in determining whether those harmed by government misconduct can recover at all. Because the government itself usually cannot be sued, the only recovery is from the individual officer. Except for those government officials with absolute immunity, liability of all others, for all constitutional violations, requires showing that there was a violation of clearly established law that the reasonable person would know.

For a time, it appeared that the Court would define this in a way that would allow those injured to recover even if there was not a prior court decision exactly on point holding that the specific actions violated the Constitution. Otherwise, some of the worst behavior by a government official would be protected from liability simply because no one had ever done it before.

In 1995, Larry Hope was a prisoner at the Limestone Correctional

Facility, in Alabama. At the time, Alabama was the only state in the country that handcuffed prisoners to "hitching posts" if they disrupted work squads or refused to work. On two occasions, Hope was tied to a hitching post by prison guards. On May 11, 1995, he was tied to a post for two hours because of an altercation with another inmate. During this time, he was offered drinking water and a bathroom break every fifteen minutes. A month later, on June 7, Hope was again tied to a post, this time for getting into a scuffle with a prison guard. He was left tied to the hitching post for seven hours, during which he was given no access to a bathroom and was given water only once or twice. Officers taunted him by giving water to some dogs and pouring water on the ground. Guards took away Hope's shirt and left him to burn in the hot sun.

Hope sued the three guards responsible for tying him to the post. The federal district court and the federal court of appeals both agreed with Hope that his constitutional rights had been violated by the infliction of cruel and unusual punishment, but they said that the officers were protected by qualified immunity because there was not a case on point holding that the use of the hitching post violated the Constitution.

In *Hope v. Pelzer*, in a 6–3 decision, the Supreme Court ruled that the officers who had tied Hope to a hitching post were *not* entitled to qualified immunity and could be held liable. The Supreme Court, like the federal court of appeals, found that the use of the hitching post was unconstitutional. The Court long has held that "the unnecessary and wanton infliction of pain . . . constitutes cruel and unusual punishment forbidden by the Eighth Amendment." The Court said that, based on the facts alleged by Hope, "the Eighth Amendment violation is obvious. . . . Despite the clear lack of an emergency situation, the respondents knowingly subjected him to a substantial risk of physical harm, to unnecessary pain caused by the handcuffs and the restricted position of confinement for a 7-hour period, to unnecessary exposure to the heat of the sun, and to a deprivation of bathroom breaks that created a risk of particular discomfort and humiliation." The Court said, "This punitive treatment amounts to gratuitous infliction of 'wanton and unnecessary' pain that our precedent clearly prohibits."

The Court then turned its attention to whether the officers were protected by qualified immunity. Justice Stevens said that the lower courts' insistence that there be a prior decision on point was unsupported by Supreme Court precedents. The Court stressed that qualified immunity operates "to ensure that before they are subjected to suit, officers are on notice that their conduct is unlawful." Thus, the key inquiry is whether the officers had "fair notice" that the conduct was a violation of rights. Justice Stevens explained that the central question in determining whether the prison officials could be held liable to Hope was "whether the state of the law in 1995 gave [them] fair warning that their alleged treatment of Hope was unconstitutional." The Court then reviewed the law as it existed in 1995 and said that the officers had fair warning that their conduct was unconstitutional.

This is exactly right. If an officer has "fair notice" that his or her conduct is unlawful and proceeds to violate a person's constitutional rights, the officer should be held responsible and a victim should be able to recover. There is no need for a specific case on point. But in the more than a decade since *Hope v. Pelzer*, the Roberts Court repeatedly has found qualified immunity based on the absence of a case on point. The Court has not distinguished *Hope v. Pelzer*. The Court has not overruled *Hope v. Pelzer*. The Court has just ignored it and denied recovery to injured individuals.

Savana Redding was a seventh-grade student at a public school in Arizona. She was suspected by a teacher of having given prescription-strength ibuprofen to another student. Two female school officials took Savana into another room and subjected her to a strip search. Savana was required to remove all of her outer clothes and to pull out her bra and underpants so that school officials could look in them for the drugs. Nothing was found.

Savana and her parents sued the school officials who had subjected her to this degrading and humiliating search. They contended that it was a search that violated the Fourth Amendment of the Constitution. It wasn't a close question—subjecting a seventh-grade girl to a strip search to look for ibuprofen violates the Constitution. In an 8–1 decision, the Court said that the intrusiveness of the search violated the Fourth Amendment, especially given the relatively minor nature of the suspected offense and the lack of any reason to believe that the girl had hidden drugs in her underwear.

But the Court then proceeded to rule, 7–2, that the school officials could not be held liable because of qualified immunity. The Court said that the law concerning strip searches was not clearly established at the time of their search, because the lower-court cases were conflicting on when strip searches in schools are permissible. But wouldn't any reasonable teacher or school official have "fair notice" that it is wrong to strip-search a seventh-grade girl, including looking in her underwear and at her breasts and genitals in order to find ibuprofen, especially without any reason to believe she was hiding it there?

In *Ashcroft v. al-Kidd*, in 2011, the Court again found qualified immunity based on the absence of a case on point, and it changed the law to make it much harder to hold government officers accountable. Abdullah al-Kidd, a U.S. citizen and a married man with two children, had been arrested in 2003 at a Dulles International Airport ticket counter. Over the next sixteen days, he was confined in high-security cells—lit twenty-four hours a day—in Virginia, Oklahoma, and then Idaho, during which he was strip-searched on multiple occasions. Each time he was transferred to a different facility, al-Kidd was handcuffed and shackled about his wrists, legs, and waist. He was released on "house arrest" and subjected to numerous restrictions on his freedom. By the time al-Kidd's confinement and supervision ended, fifteen months after his arrest, he had been fired from his job as an employee of a government contractor and had separated from his wife.

Al-Kidd was arrested and detained not because he had committed a crime or even because there was probable cause to believe he had done so. Rather, he was held under the federal material witness statute, which allows the government to hold a material witness who has essential testimony and who otherwise is likely to be unavailable to testify. But the government was not holding al-Kidd because it wanted to secure his testimony, as that statute requires. His detention had absolutely nothing to do with obtaining testimony from him. He was detained in order that the government could investigate him, and the material witness statute was used because the government did not have enough evidence to arrest him.

Al-Kidd was never charged with any crime, or ever used as a material witness. He sued Attorney General John Aschroft, who had authorized the detention. Ashcroft claimed that he was protected by qualified immunity and moved to dismiss the lawsuit. The federal court of appeals rejected this, saying that any government official, and especially the attorney general of the United States, should know that it violates the Fourth Amendment to arrest and detain a person as a material witness if there is no desire to use the person as a witness and no probable cause that the person has committed any crime.

The Supreme Court, however, reversed and held that al-Kidd had no claim upon which he could recover. Justice Scalia wrote for the Court. First, Scalia said that al-Kidd's Fourth Amendment rights had not been violated, because a valid warrant had been issued by a magistrate judge, and it is inappropriate for courts to consider the subjective reasons why the attorney general chose to detain al-Kidd.

There are many flaws in Justice Scalia's reasoning. As Justice Ginsburg observed, there was no valid warrant for al-Kidd's arrest. She explained:

> Is a warrant "validly obtained" when the affidavit on which it is based fails to inform the issuing Magistrate Judge that "the Government has no intention of using [al-Kidd as a witness] at [another's] trial," and does not disclose that al-Kidd had cooperated with FBI agents each of the several times they had asked to interview him? Casting further doubt on the assumption that the warrant was validly obtained, the Magistrate Judge was not told that al-Kidd's parents, wife, and children were all citizens and residents of the United States.

Al-Kidd was arrested as a material witness, not for committing any crime, and there was never any reason to believe that he would be a witness at all. Thus there was no probable cause for the arrest, and his seizure violated the Fourth Amendment.

Second, Justice Scalia said that former attorney general John Ashcroft was protected by qualified immunity because there were no cases on point indicating that his conduct was unconstitutional. But *Hope v. Pelzer* had expressly held that there need not be a case on point to overcome qualified immunity. Surely it does not take a case on point for the attorney general of the United States to know that it is unconstitutional to detain a person as a material witness if there is no desire to use the person as a material witness. It is clearly established law that it violates the Fourth Amendment to detain a person without probable cause, and this is exactly what was done to al-Kidd.

Al-Kidd should have been a simple case for the Supreme Court. But the Court found in favor of Ashcroft and went even further in protecting government officials from liability. Justice Scalia's majority opinion significantly changed the law of qualified immunity. Writing for the Court, Justice Scalia stated: "A Government official's conduct violates clearly established law when, at the time of the challenged conduct, '[t]he contours of [a] right [are] sufficiently clear' that every 'reasonable official would have understood that what he is doing violates that right.' We do not require a case directly on point, but existing precedent must have placed the statutory or constitutional question beyond debate." Never before had the Supreme Court said that the test is whether "every reasonable official" would have known that the conduct was impermissible. Never before had the Court said that a plaintiff could recover for a constitutional violation only if existing law placed the question "beyond debate."

This is a standard that is quite different from *Hope v. Pelzer*'s conclusion that government officials could be held liable to long as they had "fair notice" that their conduct was unconstitutional. It is a legal test that is going to make it extremely difficult to successfully sue government officials when they violate constitutional rights, even if they inflict great injuries. An illustration of this is found in a subsequent, recent decision of the United States Court of Appeals for the Ninth Circuit.

As explained in chapter 2, José Padilla, an American citizen, was apprehended at Chicago's O'Hare Airport in May 2002 and held as an enemy combatant until January 2006. During this time, he was charged with no crime, indicted by no grand jury, and convicted by no jury. The government claimed the authority to hold an American citizen indefinitely as an enemy combatant.

While being held as an enemy combatant, Padilla was subjected to what was euphemistically called "extreme interrogation." As the Ninth Circuit explained, Padilla alleged that he was subjected to "extreme isolation; interrogation under threat of torture, deportation and even death; prolonged sleep adjustment and sensory deprivation; exposure to extreme temperatures and noxious odors; denial of access to necessary medical and psychiatric care; substantial interference with his ability to practice his religion; and incommunicado detention for almost two years, without access to family, counsel or the courts."

Padilla sued John Yoo, who was the deputy assistant attorney general in the Office of Legal Counsel in the U.S. Department of Justice. The complaint alleged that Yoo's conduct, including memos he wrote, had been responsible for the abuses that Padilla suffered. In fact, Yoo, now a law professor at the University of California, Berkeley, wrote a book defending exactly these actions. Yoo moved to dismiss Padilla's suit based on, among other grounds, qualified immunity. The district court denied Yoo qualified immunity, and he appealed.

This should have been an easy case: What was done to Padilla was unconstitutional, and anyone should know that, especially a deputy assistant attorney general of the United States. But the Ninth Circuit, in an opinion by Judge Raymond Fisher, came to the opposite conclusion. The court gave two reasons for ordering Padilla's suit be dismissed.

First, the Ninth Circuit said that "the Supreme Court had not, at the time of Yoo's tenure at OLC, declared that American citizens detained as enemy combatants had to be treated at least as well, or afforded at least the same constitutional and statutory protections, as convicted prisoners." This, though, misses the point: even if American citizens detained as enemy combatants do not have the same rights as convicted prisoners, surely they have the right not to be tortured. In fact, Judge Fisher's opinion recognizes this when he states, "We agree with the plaintiffs that the unconstitutionality of torturing a United States citizen was 'beyond debate' by 2001."

Thus, it is the second reason given by the appeals court that was the key to its decision. The court stated: "Yoo is entitled to qualified immunity, however, because it was not clearly established in 2001–03 that the treatment to which Padilla says he was subjected amounted to torture." The court said that there was a debate over what constitutes torture and that there were not cases on point specifically holding that what the government did to Padilla constituted torture. Judge Fisher stated:

> We assume without deciding that Padilla's alleged treatment rose to the level of torture. That it was torture was not, however, "beyond debate" in 2001–03. There was at that time considerable debate, both in and out of government, over the definition of torture as applied to specific interrogation techniques. In light of that debate, as well as the judicial decisions discussed above, we cannot say that any reasonable official in 2001–03 would have known that the specific interrogation techniques allegedly employed against Padilla, however appalling, necessarily amounted to torture.

The court thus used the new restrictive language from *Ashcroft v. al-Kidd* to deny Padilla recovery.

But reading the allegations in Padilla's complaint leaves no doubt that by any definition, what was done to him was torture. The complaint alleged that Padilla suffered "severe physical pain" and "profound disruption of his senses and personality."

It is incomprehensible that the Ninth Circuit could say that this would not clearly have been regarded as torture from 2001 to 2003 or that any reasonable government official would not recognize it as such. Although there might not have been specific cases on point stating that this was torture, *Hope v. Pelzer* was clear that there need not be a case on point in order to say that there is clearly established law for purposes of qualified immunity. What was done to Padilla was far worse than what occurred in *Hope v. Pelzer,* and there the Court denied qualified immunity.

There are times when what we need from our judges most of all is humanity and common sense. Both were seriously lacking in the Ninth Circuit's holding that John Yoo could not be sued for the role he played in causing José Padilla's torture. What was done to Padilla was cruel, inhumane, and torture by any definition. Those responsible should be held liable. Yet the Supreme Court's restrictive approach to qualified immunity—now seemingly requiring a case on point, that "every reasonable official" would have known of the right, and that the right be "beyond debate"—is going to make it difficult for anyone who is injured by government officials to recover.

A person whose rights have been violated and who seeks compensation for the injuries, even enormous injuries, often has no recourse except to sue the government officer for money damages. But the Supreme Court has made such suits impossible in the instances in which it has created absolute immunity, and very difficult in all other instances because of its expansive definition of the protections of qualified immunity.

Damages Against Government Entities

The response to this might be that it is good to protect government officers from suits for money damages, but not to worry, because the government entity itself can be sued. A rational system might be devised wherein the choice is made to put liability on the government rather than its employees. I worry about whether such a system would do enough to deter wrongdoing, especially for malicious and egregious violations of rights, but making the government liable would ensure compensation for the victim and would give the government a powerful incentive to do all it could to prevent abuses.

Unfortunately, the Supreme Court has made suits against government entities difficult and in many instances impossible. The Court has said that both the federal government and state governments have sovereign immunity and generally cannot be sued for money damages. Even those who are horribly hurt usually are barred from suing for money damages. Consider, for example, the story of James Stanley.

In February 1958, James B. Stanley, a master sergeant in the Army stationed at Fort Knox, Kentucky, volunteered to participate in a program in which, he was told, the effectiveness of protective clothing and equipment as defenses against chemical warfare would be tested. He was released from his duties and went to the Army's chemical warfare laboratories, at Aberdeen Proving Ground, in Maryland. Four times that month, Stanley was secretly administered doses of lysergic acid diethylamide (LSD), pursuant to an Army plan to study the effects of the drug on human subjects.

Stanley was not told that he was being subjected to human experimentation or given LSD. He said that as a result of the LSD, he "suffered from hallucinations and periods of incoherence and memory loss, was impaired in his military performance, and would on occasion 'awake from sleep at night and, without reason, violently beat his wife and children, later being unable to recall the entire incident.'" He said that his marriage ended because of the personality changes as a result of his being given LSD.

It was not until 1975 that Stanley was told that he had been given LSD. The Army sent Stanley a letter soliciting his cooperation in a study of the long-term effects of LSD on those who had participated in the 1958 tests. As the Supreme Court noted, "This was the Government's first notification to Stanley that he had been given LSD during his time in Maryland."

What was done to Stanley violates the Constitution and the most basic principles of international human rights law. As Justice O'Connor forcefully argued in her dissent, this was exactly the type of human experimentation that is condemned by international law and has been universally decried since the Nazis engaged in such reprehensible behavior.

But the Supreme Court, in an opinion by Justice Scalia, held that Stanley could not recover for his injuries. He could not sue the U.S. government, because of its sovereign immunity. There is a federal statute, the Federal Tort Claims Act, that allows the United States to be sued for money damages for torts committed by its employees. But there are about two dozen exceptions to this, including one the Court created for injuries arising from military service. And the Court said that the individual military officials who subjected Stanley to the experimentation could not be sued, either. James Stanley was left without any remedy for the injuries he suffered.

Suing States. There also has been a dramatic expansion of sovereign immunity, keeping state governments from being sued even when they violate federal law and injure people. The Eleventh Amendment says that a state cannot be sued in federal court by citizens of other states or by citizens of foreign countries. By its terms, this is a limited provision that was meant to keep states from being sued based solely on the fact that the claimant was from elsewhere in the country or the world. It was meant to repeal a provision in Article III of the Constitution that says that a state can be sued by a citizen of a different state. The Eleventh Amendment, by its terms and history, does not keep a state from being sued for violating the Constitution or federal laws. But the Supreme Court has said that the Eleventh Amendment is part of a larger constitutional principle: states have sovereign immunity and generally cannot be sued without their consent, even on constitutional claims or for violating federal laws.

This means that a state can violate the law, inflict great harms, and not be held accountable. Consider a few recent examples. In *Florida Prepaid v. College Savings Bank,* the Supreme Court held that state governments cannot be sued for patent infringement. College Savings Bank, a New

Jersey company, devised a system, which it patented, that allowed students to save money to later pay for their college education. Florida Prepaid, an agency of the Florida government, copied this system so that Florida residents could save money to attend Florida schools. College Savings Bank sued Florida Prepaid for, among other things, patent infringement.

In 1992, Congress expressly amended the patent laws to authorize suits against state governments for patent infringement. But in *Florida Prepaid,* in 1999, the Court held, 5–4, that Congress lacked the authority to authorize such suits against state governments. The result is that a state can violate a patent, or for that matter a copyright, with impunity and avoid any liability. To better understand this principle, I give my students the example of a hypothetical law professor who has written several textbooks that are used in many law schools. I ask them to imagine that a law school at a state university has decided to copy the books and give them to its students for free. I ask them to further imagine that this hypothetical law professor is using the royalties to pay for his four children's college educations. He is simply out of luck. Although law professors don't usually get large amounts in royalties, this also would mean that a state medical school could infringe on patents worth millions of dollars and not be held accountable.

A year after *Florida Prepaid,* in *Kimel v. Florida Board of Regents,* the Court held that state governments could not be sued for age discrimination in violation of the federal Age Discrimination in Employment Act. *Kimel* involved a suit by current and former faculty and librarians at Florida State University, including J. Daniel Kimel Jr. They alleged that the university's failure to provide promised pay adjustments discriminated against older workers and thus violated the federal law prohibiting age discrimination in the workplace.

The Supreme Court held that the Eleventh Amendment barred these claims against state agencies in federal court. The Court ruled that Congress lacked the power to authorize suits against states that violate the federal law prohibiting age discrimination in employment. Where does this leave state employees who are victims of age discrimination? Justice O'Connor concluded the majority opinion by saying that their recourse is under state law in state courts. But that, of course, assumes that the state courts will hear such suits. More important, why should enforcement of an important federal statutory right—the protection against age discrimination in employment—depend on state courts?

A year later, in *Board of Trustees of University of Alabama v. Garrett*, the Court ruled that state governments may not be sued for violating Title I of the Americans with Disabilities Act, which prohibits employment discrimination against the disabled and requires reasonable accommodation for disabilities by employers. Patricia Garrett was the director of nursing for women's services and neonatology at the hospital of the University of Alabama at Birmingham. She was diagnosed with breast cancer and took time off work to have surgery, chemotherapy, and radiation. When she returned to work, she was informed that her position as director of nursing was no longer available. She sued under Title I of the Americans with Disabilities Act. But once more the Court ruled, 5–4, that state governments were immune from suit in federal court and that Patricia Garrett could not sue and recover, even though her treatment violated a federal statute.

The Court in these cases said that precluding such litigation in federal courts was not that big a deal, because states could be sued in state court. After all, the Eleventh Amendment speaks only of suits against states in federal court. Well, not so fast. When confronted with the question of whether state governments could be sued in state courts to enforce a federal law, the Court said this could be done only if the state chose to consent to being sued.

In *Alden v. Maine*, in 1999, the Court held that state governments cannot be sued in state court without their consent. Probation officers in Maine sued, claiming that they were owed overtime pay under the federal Fair Labor Standards Act. The suit was initially filed in federal court, but it was dismissed based on the Eleventh Amendment. The probation officers then sued in Maine state court. The Supreme Court, in a 5–4 decision, ruled that the state had sovereign immunity and could not be sued in state court, even on a federal claim, without its consent. Justice

Kennedy wrote for the Court and acknowledged that the Constitution and its framers were silent about the ability to sue state governments in state courts. Kennedy said, though, that it was unthinkable that the states would have ratified the Constitution had they thought that it made them subject to suit without their consent. The Court declared, "We hold that the powers delegated to Congress under Article I of the United States Constitution do not include the power to subject nonconsenting States to private suits for damages in state courts."

Sovereign immunity wrongly favors government power over individual freedom and protects government immunity over government accountability. State governments can violate the Constitution and federal laws and inflict great harm—as they did to College Savings Bank, J. Daniel Kimel, and Patricia Garrett—yet nowhere be held accountable. It is inconsistent with the very notion of a government under law. People can be deprived of life, liberty, or property but be left with no remedy and thus no due process. In *Alden v. Maine,* Justice Kennedy expressly addressed concerns about accountability when he declared:

> The constitutional privilege of a State to assert its sovereign immunity in its own courts does not confer upon the State a concomitant right to disregard the Constitution or valid federal law. The States and their officers are bound by obligations imposed by the Constitution and by federal statutes that comport with the constitutional design. We are unwilling to assume the States will refuse to honor the Constitution or obey the binding laws of the United States. The good faith of the States thus provides an important assurance that "[t]his Constitution, and the Laws of the United States which shall be made in Pursuance thereof . . . shall be the supreme Law of the Land."

This is a truly amazing statement. The Court says that there is no need to be able to sue state governments to ensure compliance with the

Constitution and federal laws. Trust in the "good faith" of state governments is sufficient to uphold federal law. It is hard to imagine that the Court would have said in the 1950s or '60s that there was no need to have federal courts enforce desegregation orders—that trust in the good faith of state governments was enough. James Madison remarked that if people "were angels, no government would be necessary." State governments will violate the Constitution and federal laws, and sovereign immunity means that they can get away with it, even when they severely injure people and violate basic rights.

The irony is that the conservative Justices on the Court, who profess to want to strictly follow the text and the original intent of the Constitution, ignore that imperative in creating a principle of sovereign immunity nowhere mentioned in that document. And they then use it to bar suits against states that seek to enforce the Constitution.

Suing Local Governments. Although the federal and state governments have sovereign immunity and rarely can be sued, the Court has held that local governments—cities and counties—do not have sovereign immunity. However, the Court has also made it very difficult to sue these governments. It has ruled that a local government can be held liable only if its own policies violate the Constitution; a city or county cannot be held liable when its employees act unconstitutionally. This is different from all other areas of law. A nongovernment employer is always liable if its employees, within the scope of their duties, injure someone. If a UPS driver gets in an accident while on the job, UPS is liable. This ensures that the victim gets compensation and that the employer has an incentive to do all it can to prevent harms. The principle is termed "respondeat superior" liability, and it means simply that employers are liable for the harms inflicted by their employees. But the Supreme Court has been emphatic that local governments cannot be held responsible on this basis; they are liable only if their own policies violate the Constitution.

The problem is that the Court has made it very difficult to prove the existence of a municipal policy. No city is going to have an official policy that its police officers should use excessive force, even if the unstated policy and culture in a police department condones and encourages it. The story of James Thompson, at the beginning of this chapter, illustrates the difficulty of proving municipal policy. Thompson spent eighteen years in prison, fourteen of them on death row, for a murder he did not commit, because the local prosecutors hid key blood evidence from him. And yet he could not recover from the local government, because the Court said that he had failed to prove that it had a policy that prosecutors should hide evidence from criminal defendants.

Another illustration of how difficult it is to prove municipal policy is the Court's decision in *Bryan County, Oklahoma v. Brown*. The Bryan County sheriff, B. J. Moore, had hired his nephew's son, Stacy Burns, as a deputy, despite Burns's having a long criminal record that included driving infractions and guilty pleas for misdemeanors such as assault and battery, resisting arrest, and public drunkenness. Moore obviously had great concerns about Burns and authorized him to make arrests but not to carry a weapon or to operate a patrol car.

On one occasion, after a high-speed chase, Burns violently pulled Jill Brown from the automobile in which she was a passenger and caused serious and permanent damage to her knees. As the Supreme Court noted, Burns "used an 'arm bar' technique, grabbing [Brown's] arm at the wrist and elbow, pulling her from the vehicle, and spinning her to the ground. Respondent's knees were severely injured, and she later underwent corrective surgery. Ultimately, she may need knee replacements."

This should be an easy case for holding the local government liable. The jury found that the sheriff, Moore, was "deliberately indifferent" in his hiring and supervision of Burns. But the Court, in a 5–4 decision, said that there was not sufficient proof that the local government had caused the injuries to Jill Brown. The Court said that "a finding of culpability simply cannot depend on the mere probability that any officer inadequately screened will inflict constitutional injury. Rather, it must depend on a finding that this officer was highly likely to inflict the particular injury suffered by the plaintiff. The connection between the background of the particular applicant and the specific constitutional violation must be strong." In other words, a plaintiff has to meet a remarkably high burden in order to hold the local government liable: the plaintiff must demonstrate that it was "highly likely" that the officer would inflict that "particular injury." Usually, this burden will be insurmountable.

The Court's decision is troubling, because the jury had found that the sheriff's deliberate indifference in hiring caused the injuries to Brown. The jury's decision was supported by the record: failing to review a prospective deputy's criminal records risks hiring violent individuals who can cause great harm. It is unclear how much worse the criminal record would have needed to be for the Supreme Court to allow the verdict of liability to stand. It should have been obvious that Burns, based on his long criminal record, would likely cause harms as a deputy, but it is an impossible obstacle to liability to say that it had to be foreseeable that he would cause that "particular injury."

Suits for Injunctions

The Supreme Court has thus made it very difficult, and often impossible, for those whose rights have been violated to sue for money damages. It is often not possible to sue the individual officer or the government itself, even for serious violations of rights that cause great harms. Tommy Lee Goldstein and John Thompson are without any recourse for all of the years they spent wrongly imprisoned.

A response might be that at least the government can be sued for an injunction to stop future wrongdoing. Unfortunately, the Supreme Court has made that, too, very difficult and often impossible.

On October 6, 1976, at approximately 2:00 a.m., Adolph Lyons, a twenty-four-year-old African American man, was stopped by four Los Angeles police officers for driving with a burned-out taillight. The officers ordered Lyons out of his car and confronted him with drawn revolvers as he emerged from it. Lyons was told to face his car and spread his legs. He did this and was then ordered to clasp his hands and put them on top of his head. He again complied. After one of the officers completed a pat-down search, Lyons dropped his hands, but he was ordered to place them back above his head. One of the officers grabbed Lyons's hands and slammed them onto his head. Lyons complained about the pain caused by the key ring he was holding in his hand. Within five to ten seconds, the officer began to choke Lyons by applying a forearm against his throat. As Lyons struggled for air, the officer handcuffed him, but he continued to apply the chokehold until Lyons blacked out. When Lyons regained consciousness, he was lying facedown on the ground, choking, gasping for air, and spitting up blood and dirt. He had urinated and defecated. He was issued a traffic citation and released. He suffered an injured larynx as a result of being choked by the officer.

The chokehold was commonly used at this time by Los Angeles police officers, as well as by police departments across the country, to subdue suspects. A survey in 1980 revealed that 53 percent of departments authorized the bar-arm hold, the hold that had been used on Lyons, and 90 percent authorized the carotid hold, which is considered less dangerous. Los Angeles Police Department (LAPD) policy manuals expressly authorized officers to use the chokehold as a way to subdue suspects. Officers were trained in its use at the police academy.

Lyons did some research and learned that, up to that point, sixteen people had died from the use of the chokehold by LAPD officers; almost all, like him, were African American men. This led to one of the more infamous moments during Daryl Gates's tenure as chief of the LAPD. When asked why almost all of those who died had been African American, Gates responded that it was because of physiological differences between black people and "normal people," specifically that "veins or arteries of blacks do not open up as fast as they do in normal people."

Lyons sued the City of Los Angeles for an injunction to keep police officers from using the chokehold except where necessary to protect the officers' lives or their safety. In a 5–4 decision, the Supreme Court ruled that Lyons's suit had to be dismissed. The Court explained that Lyons could not show that he, personally, was likely to be choked again in the future. Justice White, writing for the five most conservative justices, declared that "[a]bsent a sufficient likelihood that he will again be wronged in a similar way, Lyons is no more entitled to an injunction than any other citizen of Los Angeles; and a federal court may not entertain a claim by any or all citizens who no more than assert that certain practices of law enforcement officers are unconstitutional." The Court articulated a rule that plaintiffs seeking an injunction must show a likelihood of being harmed again in the future.

I have been part of countless discussions with civil rights lawyers, the conclusion of which has been that no one can sue for an injunction, because no one can show that he or she personally will be injured in the future. There are hundreds and hundreds of reported decisions of cases being thrown out of court because of *Lyons*. For example, two federal district courts ruled that women who had been strip-searched when stopped by police for routine traffic violations did not have standing to sue for an injunction. These women could not sue for an injunction because neither could show a likelihood of their personally being subjected to this illegal and terribly degrading practice in the future. There have been countless instances of the government allegedly engaging in an unconstitutional practice and individuals being injured, but no one can show that it is likely to happen to him or her again. Injunctions are not available in all of these instances.

Conclusion

What, then, is left of Chief Justice John Marshall's famous words that "[t]he very essence of civil liberty certainly consists in the right of every individual to claim the protection of the laws, whenever he receives an injury"? One of the most important functions of the Constitution is to limit government power, and thus one of the most crucial responsibilities for the Supreme Court is to ensure remedies for abuses of this authority.

The government at all levels has tremendous power to harm people.

Individuals can suffer the horrors inflicted on Tommy Lee Goldstein and John Thompson and be falsely incarcerated, or even wrongly executed. The government can take away our most precious liberties, as it did when Carrie Buck and Linda Sparkman were surgically sterilized without their consent.

It is the Supreme Court's role to assure that those who are hurt can gain injunctions to prevent wrongdoing and sue for damages when they are injured. But in a series of cases involving individual officer immunity, sovereign immunity, and standing, the Court has undermined the ability to hold governments accountable when they and their officers violate basic constitutional rights and even inflict great harm. Cases on these topics do not make headlines. Few, other than lawyers, realize that because of sovereign immunity, neither state governments nor the federal government generally can be sued for money damages, even when they cause serious injuries.

Our rights are meaningless if they cannot be vindicated. And that is exactly what the Supreme Court has done: it has, far too often, kept those who have been injured by unconstitutional government conduct from having any remedy. In this way, the Court has failed at one of its most important functions under the Constitution and in our government system.

CHAPTER 7

Is the Roberts Court Really So Bad?

E dith Windsor and Thea Spyer met in 1963, and four years later they moved in together. For forty-two years, until Spyer passed away in 2009, they lived together in Manhattan and also owned a house on Long Island. Windsor was a computer programmer at IBM and reached the highest technical rank in the company. Spyer, who had a doctorate in clinical psychology, maintained an active private practice.

In 1977, Spyer was diagnosed with multiple sclerosis, and her disability progressively worsened. She required a cane, then crutches, then a manual wheelchair, and then a motorized wheelchair that she could operate with her one usable finger. Their life together was the focus of an award-winning 2009 documentary film, *Edie and Thea: A Very Long Engagement.*

After Canada changed its law to allow same-sex marriage, Spyer, then seventy-five, and Windsor, seventy-seven, flew to Toronto, where they were wed on May 22, 2007. They lived together for two more years, until Spyer passed away on February 5, 2009.

In 2011, New York adopted a law permitting and recognizing same-sex marriages. New York law recognizes the marriage between Spyer and Windsor, even though it occurred before the New York statute was enacted. But federal law would not recognize the marriage because of Section 3 of the federal Defense of Marriage Act.

The Defense of Marriage Act (DOMA) was adopted in 1996. In 1993,

the Hawaii Supreme Court held that it might violate the Hawaii constitution to deny marriage licenses to same-sex couples. The Hawaii Supreme Court said that prohibiting same-sex marriage was sex
discrimination; the only reason a woman could not marry a woman was
because of her sex. The Hawaii Supreme Court remanded the case to the
lower court to decide whether the sex discrimination was justified. Congress reacted by enacting DOMA. Section 2 of the act says that a state is
not required to recognize a same-sex marriage from another state. Even
though no state had yet allowed same-sex marriage—that did not occur
until Massachusetts did so in 2003—there was concern in Congress that
a state might take this step, and then other states would have to recognize
those marriages.

Section 3 of DOMA provides: "In determining the meaning of any
Act of Congress, or of any ruling, regulation, or interpretation of the
various administrative bureaus and agencies of the United States, the
word 'marriage' means only a legal union between one man and one
woman as husband and wife, and the word 'spouse' refers only to a person
of the opposite sex who is a husband or a wife." There are more than a
thousand federal laws that give benefits to married couples that are not
available to others. For example, section 3 of DOMA prevents same-sex
married couples from filing joint federal tax returns, prevents the surviving spouse of a same-sex marriage from collecting Social Security sur-
vivor benefits, and leaves federal employees unable to share their health
insurance and other medical benefits with same-sex spouses.

Section 3 of DOMA became crucial after Spyer passed away and left
her entire estate to Windsor. The federal estate tax imposes a tax on es-
tates that are worth more than a specific dollar amount. There is, however, an unlimited deduction for property that passes from the decedent
to the surviving spouse. If the federal government recognized their marriage, Spyer's estate would not owe any taxes.

Although New York recognized the marriage between Windsor and
Spyer, the federal government would not do so because of Section 3 of
DOMA. As a result, Spyer's estate owed $363,053 in federal estate taxes,

which Windsor paid. If Spyer had been married to a man, her estate's tax bill would have been zero.

Windsor brought a lawsuit arguing that Section 3 of DOMA unconstitutionally discriminates against gays and lesbians. On June 26, 2013, in a 5–4 decision, the Supreme Court agreed and declared this provision unconstitutional. Justice Kennedy wrote the opinion for the Court, joined by Justices Ginsburg, Breyer, Sotomayor, and Kagan. The Court began by noting that marriage has traditionally been defined by the states. It said that "DOMA seeks to injure the very class New York seeks to protect. By doing so it violates basic due process and equal protection principles applicable to the Federal Government." The Court explained that DOMA is unconstitutional, because it was based on an impermissible desire to disadvantage gays and lesbians. Justice Kennedy quoted the House report on DOMA, which said that the act was based on "both moral disapproval of homosexuality, and a moral conviction that heterosexuality better comports with traditional (especially Judeo-Christian) morality."

The Supreme Court had earlier held that the government cannot base a law on disapproval of homosexuality. Such animus is not a legitimate government purpose sufficient to justify a discriminatory statute. The Court concluded that Section 3 of DOMA denied equal protection to gays and lesbians. The Court's decision in *United States v. Windsor* means that same-sex couples who are lawfully married in the states that allow this can take advantage of the more than one thousand federal laws that benefit married couples.

In *Windsor*, the Supreme Court performed its proper constitutional role: it acted to protect a minority from discrimination. The Court's decision in *Windsor* was about giving equal dignity and respect to gays and lesbians by allowing them to express love and commitment and get the tangible benefits of marriage, just as heterosexual couples always have been able to do. I have debated the issue many times, and I'm still perplexed about what government interest is served by denying gays and lesbians the ability to marry. Likely someday, maybe even fairly soon,

Congress will repeal the Defense of Marriage Act. But fundamental rights—and the Supreme Court has said on many occasions that marriage is a fundamental constitutional right—should not depend on protection from the political process. Minorities—and gays and lesbians are obviously a minority—should not have to rely on the political majority to safeguard them from arbitrary discrimination. That is a preeminent role of the federal judiciary.

I imagine that many readers of this book have thought of *Windsor* as they have read these pages and wondered how I could make a case against the Supreme Court at a time when the Court has done something that I very much applaud. It makes sense to ask, "Is the Roberts Court really so bad?"

Over the time that John Roberts has been chief justice—since the fall of 2005—both liberals and conservatives have won some key victories. Liberals, for example, are pleased with the Court's decision upholding most of the Affordable Care and Patient Protection Act, the Court's ruling striking down key provisions of Arizona's restrictive immigration law (SB 1070), and, of course, its declaring Section 3 of DOMA unconstitutional. By contrast, conservatives applaud the Court's striking down the Medicaid provisions of the Affordable Care Act, its declaring unconstitutional key provisions of the Voting Rights Act of 1965, its upholding the federal Partial Birth Abortion Ban Act, and its finding a Second Amendment right for individuals to possess guns in their homes.

It seems that there have been decisions for those on both sides of the political aisle to cheer about and to decry from the Roberts Court. My thesis, of course, is not that the Supreme Court always fails. My central point is that it has often failed—and at some of the most important times in American history, at some of the most important tasks that it exists to perform.

I readily concede that a large number of Supreme Court decisions each term are unobjectionable. Each year, a significant percentage of the decisions are unanimous. In October Term 2012, thirty-three of seventy-three cases were decided unanimously. Simply counting how often one agrees or disagrees with the Supreme Court is not a basis for evaluation, because not all cases are of equal significance in the law or in society. Also, in assessing the impact of the Court, its decisions striking down laws are particularly important, because these are the actions through which the Court usually makes the greatest difference. Laws that are upheld would be on the books whether or not there were a Supreme Court.

As I assess the Roberts Court and its predecessor, the Rehnquist Court, one area weighs especially heavily in my case against the Supreme Court: its decisions concerning the political process. These cases deserve significant attention in evaluating the Supreme Court, because they affect who governs the country. The Court has had a significant and long-lasting negative effect on the American political system in its rulings in *Bush v. Gore,* in striking down campaign finance laws, and in declaring unconstitutional a key provision of the Voting Rights Act of 1965. In *Bush v. Gore,* the Supreme Court made George W. Bush the president of the United States, deciding a presidential election for the first time in American history and ignoring basic constitutional principles. In finding that corporations can spend unlimited amounts of money in election campaigns, the Court, in *Citizens United v. Federal Election Commission,* changed the nature of the political process in a way that will alter who will run for office and who will be elected. In declaring unconstitutional a provision of the Voting Rights Act, the Court eliminated a key weapon against race discrimination in voting.

All three of these areas strongly favor Republicans over Democrats. Bush, of course, was the Republican candidate for president. Republicans benefit from corporate expenditures far more than Democrats. And Democrats gain from voting by racial minorities much more than Republicans.

These cases are important because they will affect how American democracy works and will affect the outcome of elections, at all levels of government, often in a decisive way.

Bush v. Gore

If it is possible to get past the partisan context and look at the legal issues, it should be clear that the Court had no business deciding *Bush v. Gore* and that its decision to take the matter out of the hands of the Florida courts was inconsistent with principles of federalism that conservatives have consistently advocated. *Bush v. Gore* is a powerful example in the case against the Supreme Court.

Although the 2000 election was not so long ago, in appraising the Supreme Court's performance, it is important to remember what happened. The presidential election of Tuesday, November 7, 2000, was one of the closest in American history. By early Wednesday morning it was clear that the Democratic candidate, Vice President Al Gore, had won the national popular vote but that the outcome of the electoral vote was uncertain. The presidency hinged on Florida and its twenty-five electoral votes. Early on election night, the television networks had called Gore the winner in Florida, only to retract their projection later in the evening. Not long after midnight on Wednesday, November 8, the networks declared Bush the winner of Florida and the presidency, only to recant *that* a short time later and to conclude that the outcome in Florida, and thus of the national election, was too close to call.

On November 8, the Florida Division of Elections reported that Bush had received 2,909,135 votes and Gore had received 2,907,351 votes. Florida law provides for a recount of votes if the election is decided by less than one-half of a percent of the votes cast. Because the margin was far closer than that—only .061 of 1 percent—Gore immediately asked for a machine recount of the tally of votes in four counties: Volusia, Palm Beach, Broward, and Miami-Dade. On November 9, Florida's secretary of state, Katherine Harris, declined to extend the statutory deadline for county vote totals beyond November 14. By this point the machine recount had narrowed Bush's lead to a mere 327 votes.

Upon learning of the close margin between himself and Bush, Gore petitioned and received permission to have a hand recount in the four counties in question. On Saturday, November 11, Bush sued in federal district court to block the manual recount, but his request was denied.

However, Secretary of State Harris—who also was the campaign manager for Bush in Florida—declared that she would enforce the November 14 deadline and that she would not accept late recounts from counties in Florida. She said that the Florida election statute required counties to report their votes within one week of the election unless one of the statutory exceptions was met. The four counties submitted their response and requested acceptance of late completion of totals; each was denied by Harris. Gore's supporters brought a suit against Harris in a Florida trial court to compel her to extend the time for the reporting of the results. On Friday, November 17, the Florida trial court ruled in favor of Harris. On Monday, November 20, the Florida Supreme Court held a nationally televised hearing in the case. On Tuesday night, November 21, that court unanimously reversed the trial court and ordered that the secretary of state accept hand recounts from the four counties if they were completed by Sunday, November 26, at 5:00 p.m., or by Monday morning if the secretary of state was not open for business on Sunday afternoon. The Florida Supreme Court ruled that Florida's secretary of state had abused her discretion in refusing to extend the deadline for certifying elections so as to provide the needed time for the recounts.

On Friday, November 24, the day after Thanksgiving, the United States Supreme Court granted review in the case and scheduled oral argument for the following Friday, December 1. In a highly unusual order, the Court permitted the broadcast of the oral argument immediately after it was finished. A few days later, in *Bush v. Palm Beach County Canvassing Bd.*, the U.S. Supreme Court remanded the case back to the Florida Supreme Court for clarification of its earlier decision. The U.S. Supreme Court said that it was unclear whether the Florida court's decision had been based on its interpretation of the Florida constitution or of Florida statutes. The former apparently would be an impermissible basis for decision, while the latter would be acceptable, based on the U.S. Supreme Court's interpretation of federal election laws. On Monday, December 11—the same day the U.S. Supreme Court held oral argument in *Bush v. Gore*—the Florida Supreme Court issued a statement saying that its decision was based on interpretation of Florida's statutes, not its constitution.

Meanwhile, on Sunday, November 26, some counties had asked for additional time to complete their counting. Harris refused all requests for extensions. That night, Florida's Elections Canvassing Commission certified the election results: Bush was determined to be the victor in Florida by 537 votes and thus the winner of Florida's twenty-five electoral votes.

On Monday, November 27, Gore filed suit in Florida under the Florida law providing for "contests" of election results. This provision, Section 102.168(3)(c) of the Florida statutes, provides that "[r]eceipt of a number of illegal votes or rejection of a number of legal votes sufficient to change or place in doubt the result of the election" shall be grounds for a contest. The statute authorizes a court, if it finds that there are successful grounds for a contest, to "provide any relief appropriate under such circumstances."

On Saturday and Sunday, December 2 and 3, a Florida state trial court held a hearing on whether Gore had met the statutory requirements for a successful contest. On Monday, December 4, the court ruled against Gore on the grounds that he had failed to prove a "reasonable probability" that the election would have turned out differently if not for problems in counting ballots.

The Florida Supreme Court granted review and scheduled oral arguments for Thursday, December 7. On Friday afternoon, December 8, the Florida Supreme Court, by a 4–3 decision, reversed the trial court, ruling that the trial court had used the wrong standard under Florida law in insisting that Gore demonstrate a "reasonable probability" that the election would have been decided differently. The Florida Supreme Court said that the statute requires only a showing of "[r]eceipt of a number of illegal votes or rejection of a number of legal votes sufficient to change or place in doubt the result of the election."

The Florida Supreme Court ordered "the Supervisor of Elections and the Canvassing Boards, as well as the necessary public officials, in all counties that have not conducted a manual recount or tabulation of the undervotes . . . to do so forthwith, said tabulation to take place in the individual counties where the ballots are located." The Florida Supreme Court also determined that Palm Beach County and Miami-Dade County, in their earlier manual recounts, had identified a net gain of 215 and 168 legal votes, respectively, for Vice President Gore, and that these should be included in the vote total, even though they were reported after the deadline of Sunday, November 26.

Just hours after the Florida Supreme Court's decision, on Friday night, December 8, a Florida trial court judge ordered that the counting of the uncounted votes commence the next morning and that it be completed by Sunday afternoon, December 9, at 2:00 p.m. The judge said that he would resolve any disputes.

On Saturday morning, counting commenced as ordered. C-SPAN provided live coverage of the officials counting ballots. At the same time, Bush asked the U.S. Supreme Court to stay the counting and to hear the case. In the early afternoon on Saturday, the U.S. Supreme Court, in a 5–4 ruling, stayed the counting of the votes in Florida. Justice Stevens dissented on the grounds that the requirements for a stay had not been met. The law is that a higher court can issue a stay—a halt of a lower court's order—only if there is an "irreparable injury," a harm that cannot later be undone. Justice Stevens said that there would be no such harm in allowing the counting to continue, as ordered by the Florida Supreme Court, while the U.S. Supreme Court considered the matter.

Justice Scalia wrote a short opinion, not joined by any other justice, in which he said that the requirements for a stay *had* been met. He said that Bush had shown a likelihood of prevailing on the merits and also of irreparable injury. Scalia said that there were two such harms: First, there would be a cloud over the legitimacy of a Bush presidency if the counting showed Gore ahead but the counting was disallowed by the Supreme Court; and second, handling of the ballots would lead to their degradation and prevent a more accurate counting later if that were ordered by the Court. Both of these are highly questionable rationales for the stay. As for the former, it is not the Court's role to protect the legitimacy of a particular candidate's presidency; besides, if anything could cast a cloud over the legitimacy of the presidency, it was the Court's ending the counting itself—the uncounted ballots never were tallied in Florida, and no one will ever know who won that state. As for the latter claim, there was absolutely nothing in the record of the case to suggest that counting the ballots would do any harm to them. This was invented by Justice Scalia without any basis.

On Monday, December 11, the U.S. Supreme Court held oral arguments. Again, they were broadcast immediately after their completion. On Tuesday, December 12, at approximately 10:00 p.m. Eastern time, the Court released its opinion in *Bush v. Gore*.

In a per curiam opinion—an opinion of the Court in which the author is not identified by name—the Supreme Court, in a 5–4 decision, held that the counting of the ballots violated equal protection and ordered an end to the counting based on its understanding of Florida law. The per curiam opinion was joined by Chief Justice Rehnquist and Justices O'Connor, Scalia, Kennedy, and Thomas.

The Court's opinion began its analysis by reiterating that the right to vote is a fundamental right and that "[w]hen the state legislature vests the right to vote for President in its people, the right to vote as the legislature has prescribed is fundamental; and one source of its fundamental nature lies in the equal weight accorded to each vote and the equal dignity owed to each voter."

The Court said that the central problem was that the Florida Supreme Court had ordered the counting of the uncounted ballots but failed to prescribe standards for doing so. It said that this would result in similar ballots being treated differently. The Court also objected to the procedures being followed in the recount:

> In addition to these difficulties the actual process by which
> the votes were to be counted under the Florida Supreme

Court's decision raises further concerns. That order did not specify who would recount the ballots. The county canvassing boards were forced to pull together ad hoc teams comprised of judges from various Circuits who had no previous training in handling and interpreting ballots. Furthermore, while others were permitted to observe, they were prohibited from objecting during the recount.

The Court thus concluded that counting the uncounted ballots pursuant to the order of the Florida Supreme Court would deny equal protection, because similar ballots could be treated differently. The Court was explicit that it was deciding just the matter before it and was not setting a general precedent and declared: "Our consideration is limited to the present circumstances, for the problem of equal protection in election processes generally presents many complexities." It was extraordinary for the Court to declare that its decision was not a precedent for the future; I cannot think of another instance of the Supreme Court doing this. Indeed, no Supreme Court decision ever has cited to *Bush v. Gore*.

The Court then confronted the key question: Should the case be remanded to the Florida Supreme Court for it to set standards for the counting, or should the Court order an end to the counting process? The Court said that Florida indicated that it wished to observe the December 12 date set by federal law, which created a conclusive presumption that a state's electors chosen by that date would be recognized by Congress. The Court thus stopped the counting, stating:

> The Supreme Court of Florida has said that the legislature intended the State's electors to "participat[e] fully in the federal electoral process," as provided in 3 U.S.C. §5. That statute, in turn, requires that any controversy or contest that is designed to lead to a conclusive selection of electors be completed by December 12. That date is upon us, and there is no recount procedure in place under the State Supreme

Court's order that comports with minimal constitutional standards. Because it is evident that any recount seeking to meet the December 12 date will be unconstitutional for the reasons we have discussed, we reverse the judgment of the Supreme Court of Florida ordering a recount to proceed.

What is often forgotten about *Bush v. Gore* is that the Court ordered an end to the counting of votes in Florida based on its interpretation of the Florida election law.

Chief Justice Rehnquist wrote a separate opinion, which was joined by Justices Scalia and Thomas. The Rehnquist opinion focused on 3 U.S.C. Section 5, which provides that the state's selection of electors "shall be conclusive, and shall govern in the counting of the electoral votes" if the electors are chosen under laws enacted prior to Election Day, and if the selection process is completed six days prior to the meeting of the Electoral College. Rehnquist said that this prevents a state from changing its electoral process after the election and that Florida's Supreme Court had done this by usurping the authority Florida law had vested in the Florida secretary of state and the Florida circuit courts. The chief justice concluded that the Florida Supreme Court had "significantly departed from the statutory framework in place on November 7, and authorized open-ended further proceedings which could not be completed by December 12, thereby preventing a final determination by that date."

Each of the other four justices wrote a dissenting opinion. Justice Stevens, joined by Justices Ginsburg and Breyer, challenged the Court's premise that there was a denial of equal protection. He argued that the procedure created by the Florida Supreme Court, with a trial judge resolving disputes, could prevent unequal treatment of like ballots.

Justice Stevens said that if the lack of standards for counting was the problem, the solution was to send the case back to Florida for the creation of standards and subsequent counting. He concluded his dissent in powerful language:

The endorsement of that position by the majority of this court can only lend the credence to the most cynical appraisal of the work of judges throughout the land. It is confidence in the men and women who administer the judicial system that is the true backbone of the rule of law. Time will one day heal the wound to that confidence that will be inflicted by today's decision. One thing, however, is certain. Although we may never know with complete certainty the identity of the winner of this year's Presidential election, the identity of the loser is perfectly clear. It is the Nation's confidence in the judge as an impartial guardian of the rule of law.

Justice Souter's dissenting opinion, joined by the other three dissenting justices, objected to the Court's hearing the case at all. Souter argued that there were no significant federal issues raised and that the case should have been left to the Florida courts to resolve under Florida law. Justice Ginsburg's dissent argued that there were was no denial of equal protection and that, in any event, the appropriate solution was to have the case sent back to Florida for the counting to continue.

Finally, Justice Breyer said that he saw equal protection problems with counting votes without standards, but he argued that the Court was wrong in ending the counting rather than remanding the case for counting with standards to be developed by the Florida courts. He stressed that there was nothing magical about the December 12 deadline—states could still choose their electors after that date and could be confident that Congress would recognize them. He ended his opinion forcefully:

I fear that in order to bring this agonizingly long election process to a definitive conclusion we have not adequately attended to that necessary "check upon our own exercise of power," "our own sense of self-restraint." Justice Brandeis once said of the Court, "The most important thing we do is not doing." What it does today, the Court should have left undone. I would repair the damage done as best we now can, by permitting the Florida recount to continue under uniform standards.

What, then, was so bad about *Bush v. Gore* that I put it among the worst decisions in history? I want to be clear about what I am not saying. I do not believe that *Bush v. Gore* was a corrupt decision or that the five justices who voted to stop the counting wanted Bush to be president—or that the four who voted against it favored Gore. Some have suggested exactly that: that *Bush v. Gore* was a baldly partisan choice by Republican justices to make the Republican candidate the next president. Vincent Bugliosi and Alan Dershowitz have advanced this view. Indeed, Bugliosi argued that the justices in the majority should be subjected to impeachment proceedings.

But I believe that the role of politics was both more subtle and more profound. On Friday, December 8, after the Florida Supreme Court ordered the counting of uncounted votes, everyone I knew who had voted for Gore praised the decision and said that every ballot should be counted, and everyone I knew who had voted for Bush decried the ruling and said that there had to be an end to the proceedings. I immediately realized that there was no reason to think that the justices on the Supreme Court would be any different in the way they perceived the matter.

In other words, it was not that the five justices in the majority set out to make sure that Bush became president and the four dissenters acted to make sure that Gore would be president. I accept that each of the nine justices believed that he or she was making a ruling on the law, not on partisan grounds. But how each justice saw the case was entirely a product of his or her views. In fact, it would have been much easier for the dissenting justices on the Court to embrace the equal protection argument, given their other opinions on equality and the Constitution. Part of the irony of *Bush v. Gore* is that it is virtually the only case in which Justice Scalia or Justice Thomas has found an equal protection violation, except in striking down affirmative action programs.

This is important for how we think about constitutional law and the

Supreme Court. We are all results-oriented, consciously or unconsciously, much of the time. We come to conclusions and then look for arguments to support them. We constantly hear criticisms of judges or academics for being result-oriented. Yet there is no way to avoid this. The premises we begin with influence, if not determine, the conclusions we come to. *Bush v. Gore* unquestionably seemed a results-oriented decision in the sense that each of the nine justices came to a result that was consistent with his or her political views, so far as we know them. That does not mean that it was corrupt or even unique among judicial decisions. In the vast majority of important cases, the justices' conclusions are a reflection of the views with which they begin.

Bush v. Gore was a bad decision, first, because the Court clearly had no business hearing and deciding the case. For several reasons, the issues before the Supreme Court in *Bush v. Gore* were not appropriate for review at the time the case was heard and decided. The Court long has held that Article III of the Constitution prevents a federal court, including the Supreme Court, from deciding a case that is not "ripe"—that is, not ready for judicial review. The central legal issue addressed by the Supreme Court was whether the counting of votes in Florida would deny equal protection. But there would be a constitutional violation only if similar ballots were treated differently in the counting process. It could not be known if this had happened until after the counting occurred and the trial judge in Florida, Judge Terry Lewis, ruled on all of the challenges. Until then, the question of whether there would be a problem with similar ballots being treated differently was purely speculative.

The Supreme Court focused on inequalities that already had occurred in Florida. The Court's opinion pointed to differences in the counting that had occurred in Miami-Dade County and Palm Beach County. But the counting that already had been done was not the issue before the Supreme Court. The only question was whether the counting should continue. The prior experience was not predictive of what was to occur because of a key change: a single judge had been appointed to oversee all of the counting under the Florida Supreme Court's decision. This judge was to hear all of the disputes and potentially could eliminate any inequalities by applying a uniform standard.

Justice Stevens emphasized exactly this point in his dissent. He wrote, "Admittedly, the use of differing substandards for determining voter intent in different counties employing similar voting systems may raise serious concerns. Those concerns are alleviated—if not eliminated—by the fact that a single impartial magistrate will ultimately adjudicate all objections arising from the recount process." Only after the counting was completed could the parties claim that there was inequality, and thus a constitutional violation. Only then would the case be ripe for review under traditional principles of federal court jurisdiction.

The case was not ready to be decided by the Supreme Court for an even more basic reason: George W. Bush might well have ended up ahead after the counting. In that event, there obviously would have been no need for the Supreme Court to decide his appeal. The Supreme Court repeatedly has held that a case cannot be decided when it is unknown whether an injury will be suffered.

Bush v. Gore was not ripe for review on December 9, when the stay was issued, or on December 11, when the case was heard, or on December 12, when the case was decided. The case would have been ripe only after all the counting was done, and only if (a) Gore had come out ahead in Florida *and* (b) Bush could present evidence of inequalities in how the ballots had actually been counted. Until and unless these eventualities occurred, the case was not appropriate for federal judicial review and should have been dismissed. It is the conservatives on the Court who long have emphasized limits on federal power, such as ripeness and standing. But here they abandoned them.

Also, the Supreme Court should have found that *Bush v. Gore* posed a political question that it should not decide. Since early in American history, the Court has said that matters posing "political questions" should be dismissed and not decided by the federal courts. The political-question doctrine says that some allegations of constitutional violations should be left to the other branches of government to resolve. For instance, challenges to the president's use of troops in a foreign country consistently have been dismissed as political questions. More than two dozen lawsuits were brought arguing that the Vietnam War was unconstitutional, because the president was waging war without a congressional declaration of war, and they all were dismissed based on the political-question doctrine.

The most famous articulation of the political-question doctrine was provided by the late Yale law professor Alexander Bickel. Bickel wrote:

> Such is the foundation, in both intellect and instinct, of the political-question doctrine: the Court's sense of lack of capacity, compounded in unequal parts of (a) the strangeness of the issue and its intractability to principled resolution; (b) the sheer momentousness of it, which tends to unbalance judicial judgment; (c) the anxiety, not so much that the judicial judgment will be ignored, as that perhaps it should but will not be; (d) finally ("in a mature democracy"), the inner vulnerability, the self-doubt of an institution which is electorally irresponsible and has no earth to draw strength from.

Although Bickel wrote these words more than five decades ago, they seem almost prescient when applied to *Bush v. Gore*. Certainly in terms of (a), there is "strangeness of the issue" and intractability to a principled resolution. Never before in history had the Supreme Court decided a presidential election. The Court said that counting the ballots without uniform standards would be unequal, but no prior decision had ever found variations among counties in election practices to be unconstitutional. Nor did the Court explain why this inequality was impermissible while many other differences in elections in Florida, such as differences in voting machines, in ballots, and in access to polling places, were constitutional.

The Court seemed aware of the problems with applying equal protection to such variances among counties and with opening the door to challenges to virtually every election because of reliance on local election officials. That is likely why the Court took the extraordinary step of declaring that its opinion was not a precedent for future decisions. This certainly confirms Professor Bickel's concerns about the strangeness of the issue and the lack of principles for resolution of it.

Bickel's second factor is even more relevant: "the sheer momentousness of [the issue], which tends to unbalance judicial judgment." If any case fits this description, it surely is *Bush v. Gore.*

Bickel's last two criteria point to a concern over which issues should be decided by unelected judges. Bickel's worry was about how involvement in some political issues could compromise the legitimacy of the Court. Although I am critical of Bickel's view and of many of the uses of the political-question doctrine, *Bush v. Gore* obviously cost the Supreme Court in terms of its credibility. More than forty-nine million people voted for Al Gore, and likely almost all of them regard the Court's decision as a partisan ruling by a Republican majority in favor of the Republican candidate. Few cases, if any, in American history have been more widely perceived as partisan than *Bush v. Gore.*

Second, the Court abandoned long-standing principles of federalism in ending the counting of the uncounted ballots in Florida based on Florida law, rather than allowing the Florida courts to interpret Florida law. The supreme irony of the case is that the majority was comprised of five justices who, as explained in chapter 3, were at the time repeatedly striking down federal laws based on their commitment to federalism and states' rights. But in *Bush v. Gore,* these justices showed no deference to the Florida state court.

The Supreme Court's opinion made two arguments. First, counting the uncounted votes without standards violates equal protection. Second, Florida law prevented the counting from continuing past December 12. This second point is indispensable to the Court's decision to end the counting. Assuming that there were inequalities in the counting that violated the Constitution, there were two ways to remedy this situation: count none of the uncounted ballots, or count all of the ballots with uniform standards. The latter would involve remanding the case to the Florida Supreme Court for development of standards and for such relief as that court deemed appropriate. It would not have been difficult for the Florida Supreme Court to quickly develop such standards; the question was how many corners of the "chad"—the little piece of cardboard that is punched out of the ballot—had to be detached in order for the ballot to count.

It must be emphasized that the Supreme Court did not hold that federal law prevented the counting from continuing. The only reason for not remanding the case—which Justices Souter and Breyer argued for—was the Court's judgment that Florida law prevented this. The Supreme Court was quite explicit that it was ordering a stop to the counting based entirely on Florida law: "Because the Florida Supreme Court has said that the Florida Legislature intended to obtain the safe-harbor benefits of 3 U.S.C. §5, Justice Breyer's proposed remedy—remanding to the Florida Supreme Court for its ordering of a constitutionally proper contest until December 18—contemplates action in violation of the Florida Election Code, and hence could not be part of an 'appropriate' order authorized by Fla. Stat. Ann. §102.168."

Although the Court's only reason for ending the counting was based on its interpretation of Florida law, no Florida statute stated or implied that the counting had to be done by December 12. The sole authority for the Supreme Court's conclusion was one brief statement by the Florida Supreme Court.

That statement, however, was made in a very different context, when the Florida Supreme Court was not faced with the issue posed by the Supreme Court's ruling. After the Supreme Court decided on December 12 that the counting without standards violated equal protection, the issue was what remedy was appropriate under Florida law: to continue the counting past December 12, or end the counting to meet the December 12 deadline? Federal law set December 12 as the deadline for states to designate their electors if they wanted a certainty that they would be part of the Electoral College. But in prior elections, other states had picked their electors later than this deadline and had been allowed to participate in the Electoral College, which votes in early January.

The Supreme Court could not possibly know how the Florida Supreme Court would resolve this issue, because it had never before arisen. Prior Florida decisions emphasized the importance of making sure that every vote is accurately counted. The Florida Supreme Court might have relied on these decisions to continue the counting past December 12. Alternatively, the Florida Supreme Court might have ended the counting, treating December 12 as a firm deadline in Florida.

After *Bush v. Gore* was decided, the Florida Supreme Court issued a decision dismissing the case. Justice Leander Shaw, in a concurring opinion, declared, "[I]n my opinion, December 12 was not a 'drop-dead' date under Florida law. In fact, I question whether any date prior to January 6 is a drop-dead date under the Florida election scheme. December 12 was simply a permissive 'safe-harbor' date to which the states could aspire. It certainly was not a mandatory contest deadline under the plain language of the Florida Election Code."

Perhaps a majority of the Florida Supreme Court would have followed this view; perhaps not. The point is that this was a question of Florida law, to be decided by the Florida Supreme Court. It is clearly established that state supreme courts get the final word on the interpretation of state law. In *Murdock v. City of Memphis,* in 1875, the Supreme Court held that it could review only questions of federal law, and that the decisions of the state's highest court are final on questions of state law.

It is inexplicable why the five justices in the majority—usually the advocates of states' rights on the Court—did not remand the case to the Florida Supreme Court to decide under Florida law whether the counting should continue. The Supreme Court impermissibly usurped the Florida Supreme Court's authority to decide Florida law in this extraordinary case.

In *Bush v. Gore,* the Supreme Court for the first and only time in American history decided a presidential election. It was unnecessary. The Court could have allowed the counting to continue. It is quite possible that Bush would have come out ahead in Florida and the matter would have been over. But even if there had been a dispute, the law provided procedures for resolving who the electors from Florida were. This situation had happened before, such as in 1960, when Hawaii designated two sets of electors—one for John F. Kennedy and one for Richard M. Nixon. In *Bush v. Gore,* the Court decided a case that it did not need to hear and in the process ignored basic, long-standing principles of constitutional law. The consequences were enormous: the Court made George W. Bush the president of the United States.

Citizens United v. Federal Election Commission

Citizens United v. Federal Election Commission, in 2010, significantly changed the American political system. Corporations and unions now can spend unlimited amounts of their funds to elect or defeat candidates for federal, state, and local office. At the very least, this often will have the effect of increasing the cost of running for elected office, which will influence who chooses to run. The additional dollars will sometimes determine the outcome of elections. Although there has been only one major election year since *Citizens United,* the decision's effects were manifest in the development of super PACs (political action commitees) and in the unprecedented amount of money spent in election campaigns. Although it was a 5–4 decision, with the Court split along ideological lines, I have been surprised at how much both liberals and conservatives I speak to disagree with the decision.

In *Citizens United,* the Supreme Court declared unconstitutional a provision of the Bipartisan Campaign Finance Reform Act of 2002. The law sought to diminish the corrupting and corrosive effects of money in federal elections. It was a truly bipartisan bill, passed by Congress after lengthy study and debate and co-sponsored by Republican senator John McCain and Democratic senator Russ Feingold.

This, of course, was not Congress's first attempt to regulate campaign spending. In 1907, Congress adopted a law prohibiting corporations from contributing money to candidates for federal elective office. After being elected in 1904, in response to criticisms that he had taken corporate money in his campaign, President Theodore Roosevelt called for the prohibition of such contributions. He declared, "All contributions by corporations to any political committee or for any political purpose should be forbidden by law; directors should not be permitted to use shareholders' money for such purposes; and, moreover, a prohibition of this kind would be, as far as it went, an effective method of stopping the evils aimed at in corrupt practices acts." In 1946, this ban was extended to unions.

The concern, in part, was that corporations and unions were using the money of their shareholders and members for political purposes with which they might disagree; Roosevelt was explicit in saying that "directors should not be permitted to use shareholders' money for such purposes." But there was also great concern about the tremendous wealth of these entities and the distorting effect that it could have on elections. There was a concern that contributions from corporations and unions directly to candidates would inevitably lead to the appearance, if not the reality, of undue influence over those elected. The laws also reflected a desire to limit the ability of corporations and unions to influence the outcomes of elections through their spending.

Corporations and unions learned to circumvent the ban on contributions by taking out their own ads supporting and opposing candidates. In the wake of the Watergate scandal and the abuses of campaign financing that it revealed, Congress amended federal election law in 1974 to ban this as well.

Once more, corporations and unions were clever and figured out a way around the law. They began running issue ads around the time of elections in which they would attack or support a candidate's position on a particular high-profile issue. Never did the ads call for the election or defeat of a specific candidate, but that message usually was clear. In 2002, in the Bipartisan Campaign Finance Reform Act, Congress prohibited issue ads on broadcast media by corporations or unions that support or oppose an identifiable candidate if they appear thirty days before a primary election or sixty days before a general election. It was this provision that was before the Court in *Citizens United.*

The Supreme Court had expressly considered the constitutionality of this provision and had upheld it in *McConnell v. Federal Election Commission,* in 2003, just seven years before the decision in *Citizens United.* Before that, the Court had upheld state laws limiting corporate spending in state and local election campaigns in *Austin v. Michigan Chamber of Commerce.* In both cases, the Court expressed the concerns that had animated restrictions on corporate and union political spending from the outset: the desire to protect corporate shareholders and union members from having their money spent against their wishes and the worry that corporations and unions would have undue influence in the political process, including being able to drown out other voices. In *Citizens United,* the Supreme Court expressly overruled both of these earlier decisions.

Citizens United arose out of a conservative political action committee making a video-on-demand movie very critical of then Democratic presidential candidate Hillary Clinton. The issue came to the Supreme Court in 2009, to decide whether the provision of the Bipartisan Campaign Finance Reform Act limiting broadcast advertisements by corporations applied to this format, video on demand. Rather than deciding this issue, on June 29, 2009, the Court, on its own, asked for new briefing as to whether the provision should be declared unconstitutional and whether *McConnell* and *Austin* should be overruled. None of the parties to the case had asked the Court to consider this constitutional issue.

In a 5–4 decision, the Court did exactly that and declared this key provision of the Bipartisan Campaign Finance Reform Act unconstitutional. The Court broadly held that corporations have the same First Amendment rights as individuals and that restrictions on corporate spending in election campaigns are unconstitutional. The Court focused only on "independent expenditures" by corporations—the ability of corporations to spend money on their own in election campaigns. The constitutionality of restrictions on corporate contributions directly to candidates, which were created by the Tillman Act in 1907, was not before the Court.

The Court was split along ideological lines, with Justice Kennedy writing for the Court, joined by Chief Justice Roberts and Justices Scalia, Thomas, and Alito. Justice Stevens wrote a lengthy dissent, vehemently disagreeing with every aspect of the majority opinion. The key difference from seven years earlier, when the Court decided *McConnell,* was that Justice O'Connor, who had been in the five-justice majority in that case, had retired. She was replaced by Justice Alito, who joined the *McConnell* dissenters to create the majority to overrule that decision.

Justice Kennedy, writing for the Court, said that it had been established by prior cases that corporations possess free speech rights and that expenditures in election campaigns are core political speech. The Court explained that "[p]olitical speech is indispensable to decisionmaking in a democracy, and this is no less true because the speech comes from a corporation rather than an individual." The Court rejected *Austin*'s concern with preventing corporate wealth from distorting elections.

The Court concluded that the restrictions on independent expenditures by corporations and unions violated the First Amendment. The Court stated:

> The censorship we now confront is vast in its reach. The Government has "muffle[d] the voices that best represent the most significant segments of the economy." And "the electorate [has been] deprived of information, knowledge and opinion vital to its function." By suppressing the speech of manifold corporations, both for-profit and nonprofit, the Government prevents their voices and viewpoints from reaching the public and advising voters on which persons or entities are hostile to their interests.

The Court, though, in an 8–1 ruling, upheld the disclosure requirements in the Bipartisan Campaign Finance Reform Act, and Justice Kennedy's opinion stressed that these were a key way of preventing corruption or the appearance of corruption from large independent expenditures.

He wrote, "The Court has explained that disclosure is a less restrictive alternative to more comprehensive regulations of speech."

There is much that is deeply disturbing about this case. First, the premise that spending money is pure speech is dubious, though it is one that the Court has followed since 1976. Spending money is conduct, not expression in itself. There is First Amendment protection for conduct that communicates, but the Supreme Court has long said that it is much more subject to government regulation than "pure speech," which is how the Court has treated spending money in election campaigns. Money in elections facilitates speech, such as in the form of political advertisements, but many things that facilitate speech—such as education—are not regarded by the Court as constitutional rights. The Court has taken far too literally the figurative expression "Money talks" in finding that restrictions on campaign expenditures violate the First Amendment. As Justice Stevens explained, "Money is property; it is not speech. . . . These property rights are not entitled to the same protection as the right to say what one pleases."

Second, the Court's premise that corporations should have the same speech rights as individuals is just wrong. It is ironic that the conservative justices, such as Scalia and Thomas, who believe that the meaning of a constitutional right is limited to its "original understanding," could find a First Amendment right for corporations to spend unlimited amounts of money on political ads. There is no evidence that the framers of the First Amendment meant to protect corporations or campaign spending, let alone bestow a right for corporations to spend unlimited sums in election campaigns.

The Supreme Court has explained that the First Amendment protects speech especially because of its importance to the autonomy and dignity of each person, something that has no meaning when it comes to corporations. Justice Stevens powerfully stated:

> In the context of election to public office, the distinction between corporate and human speakers is significant. Although

they make enormous contributions to our society, corporations are not actually members of it. They cannot vote or run
for office.... The financial resources, legal structure, and in-
strumental orientation of corporations raise legitimate concerns about their role in the electoral process. Our lawmakers
have a compelling constitutional basis, if not also a democratic duty, to take measures designed to guard against the
potentially deleterious effects of corporate spending in local
and national races.

Third, there are important reasons for allowing restrictions of corporate expenditures in election campaigns. The Court previously had allowed restrictions on corporate expenditures; among others, seven years
earlier it had upheld the very provision that was struck down in *Citizens
United*. In doing so, the Court had expressed concern that corporate
wealth could distort the outcome of elections, since corporations often
can outspend all others. In some elections, this can make all of the difference in terms of the results. Also, some candidates might choose not to
run because of the knowledge of the corporate wealth that will be against
them. Although presidential campaigns are the most visible, corporate
spending can also be decisive in local elections, where there is less visibility and therefore expenditures are all the more important. At the very
least, when a corporation spends a large amount of money to get a candidate elected, there will be the perception—if not the reality—that the
government official is beholden to the donor.

The Court had also earlier allowed restrictions on corporate expenditures as a way of protecting corporate shareholders. It is their money that
is being spent in corporate political expenditures, and they may well disagree with how their money is being used. In 2012, the Supreme Court
emphasized that unions should not be able to spend their members'
money without their consent; this should apply with equal force to corporations.

It is important to remember that the restrictions on corporate expenditures, such as in the Bipartisan Campaign Finance Reform Act, did not mean that corporations were prohibited from spending money in federal election campaigns. Corporations could create political action committees and raise money, and the PACs could spend it as they wished. The limit was on spending from the vast coffers of corporate treasuries.

Justice Stevens concluded his dissent in *Citizens United* by declaring:

> At bottom, the Court's opinion is thus a rejection of the common sense of the American people, who have recognized a need to prevent corporations from undermining self-government since the founding, and who have fought against the distinctive corrupting potential of corporate electioneering since the days of Theodore Roosevelt. It is a strange time to repudiate that common sense. While American democracy is imperfect, few outside the majority of this Court would have thought its flaws included a dearth of corporate money in politics.

Other campaign finance laws seem very vulnerable after *Citizens United*. The Supreme Court's decision rested on two key premises: that spending money in election campaigns is political speech under the First Amendment and that corporations have the same free speech rights as citizens. But these assumptions and the Court's holding in *Citizens United* can be used to challenge other campaign finance laws. Although the Court dealt only with corporate spending, the decision surely applies to union expenditures as well.

More dramatically for the future, federal law long has prohibited corporations from contributing money directly to candidates for federal elective office. Many state and local governments have similar restrictions for their elections. *Citizens United v. Federal Election Commission* concerned only independent expenditures by corporations and not their right to make contributions directly.

But it is hard to see a basis for a distinction once it is held that corporations are entitled to the same free speech rights as citizens, and that this includes spending money to influence elections. The Court also did not consider the constitutionality of restrictions on campaign spending by foreign corporations. A distinction seems difficult, because foreign corporations, like American ones, have the capacity to inform the public and increase discussion and debate.

In fact, the Court in *Citizens United* implicitly rejects any notion that free speech is limited to citizens. Corporations obviously are not citizens, and yet they are accorded First Amendment protection in *Citizens United*. This is in marked tension with earlier cases that held that the First Amendment protects only speech by citizens. In fact, just four years earlier, in *Garcetti v. Ceballos,* the Supreme Court held that there is no First Amendment protection for the speech of government employees on the job in the scope of their duties. As was the case in *Citizens United,* the opinion was written by Justice Anthony Kennedy and joined by Chief Justice Roberts and Justices Scalia, Thomas, and Alito.

Justice Kennedy stressed that such speech by government employees is not protected because it is not speech by "citizens." He wrote, "We hold that when public employees make statements pursuant to their official duties, the employees are not speaking as citizens for First Amendment purposes, and the Constitution does not insulate their communications from employer discipline."

But if corporations have full First Amendment rights, then it makes no sense to limit free speech protection to expression by citizens. Indeed, the claim for free speech protection by government employees is even stronger than that for corporations—government employees do not relinquish their citizenship when they enter their workplace.

Citizens United v. Federal Election Commission should put to rest the constant conservative attack on "judicial activism." Since Richard Nixon ran for president in 1968, conservatives have railed against supposed judicial activism. By any measure, *Citizens United* was stunning in its judicial activism. The deference to the democratic process so often preached by conservatives in attacking liberal rulings protecting rights was nowhere in evidence as the conservative majority struck down restrictions on corporate spending that had existed for decades.

Conservatives have lambasted prior decisions protecting rights not stated in the Constitution or intended by its framers. But there is no evidence that the First Amendment's drafters contemplated spending money in election campaigns as a form of protected speech. Nor did they intend the First Amendment, or any of the Bill of Rights, to protect corporations. It was not until 1978, in *First National Bank of Boston v. Bellotti,* that the Court first found any First Amendment protection for speech by corporations.

Few Supreme Court decisions are as important on as many different levels as *Citizens United.* It has changed elections all across the country. It portends even greater changes in campaign finance in the years ahead, as other laws are now far more vulnerable to challenge.

Since *Citizens United,* in 2010, the Court has continued to invalidate campaign finance laws and to keep the government from limiting the corrosive effects of money in the political system. One alternative to the traditional way of funding election campaigns is public funding. Many suggested after *Citizens United* that public funding of elections was a way to avoid the undesirable consequences of corporate spending. But a year after *Citizens United,* the Court invalidated a public funding system and made it much more difficult for such an approach to exist in a manner that has a chance to succeed.

The Supreme Court's decision in *Arizona Free Enterprise Club's Freedom Club PAC v. Bennett,* in 2011, reflects the conservative majority's hostility toward campaign finance regulation and its desire to protect the influence of the wealthy in the electoral process. The case involved an Arizona-voter-passed initiative law, adopted after a major political scandal, that provided for public funding of elections for state offices.

Under the Arizona Citizens Clean Elections Act, no candidate was required to accept public funding for his or her election. A candidate wishing to receive such money could qualify for public funds by obtaining a specified amount of donations. Candidates choosing to take public funds had to agree, among other things, to limit their expenditure of personal funds to $500, to participate in at least one public debate, to adhere to an overall expenditure cap, and to return all unspent public monies to the state.

The concern, though, was that if the amount of public funds was fixed, it could be exceeded by an opponent who did not take public funds. The Arizona law said that if an opponent not taking public funds spent more than a designated sum, a publicly financed candidate would receive roughly one additional dollar for every dollar spent by the opposing, privately financed candidate. The publicly financed candidate would also receive roughly one dollar for every dollar spent by independent expenditure groups to support the privately financed candidate or to oppose the publicly financed candidate. But there was a cap on these additional funds; matching funds topped out at two times the initial authorized grant of public funding to the publicly financed candidate.

The Supreme Court, in a 5–4 decision, declared this law unconstitutional. Chief Justice Roberts wrote for the Court and was joined by Justices Scalia, Kennedy, Thomas, and Alito. These, of course, were the five justices in the majority in *Citizens United*. The Court said that the Arizona law was unconstitutional because it penalized candidates who spent their own money in elections. The "penalty" was that their increased spending would be met with greater public funds for an opponent accepting public money. The Court said that the Arizona law violated the First Amendment, because it would chill candidates and their supporters from spending money in elections. The Court rejected the argument that the laws served a compelling interest in preventing corruption or the appearance of corruption or in equalizing influence in the electoral process.

The Court's reasoning and holding are questionable and troubling on many levels. First, the Arizona law in no way restricted or regulated any speech. The sole effect of the Arizona Citizens Clean Election Act was to increase money for candidates taking public funds. As Justice Kagan noted in her dissent, Chief Justice Roberts's majority opinion repeatedly characterizes the act as limiting speech, but "Arizona's matching funds provision does not restrict, but instead subsidizes, speech."

No candidate's speech was limited. No one's spending was curtailed.

Arizona's law just provided for additional funds to those taking public money. This was not a restriction on expression in any way.

Second, if one accepts that spending money in elections is a form of speech protected by the First Amendment, then the Arizona law actually increases speech. In repeatedly striking down campaign finance laws, such as in *Citizens United v. Federal Election Commission*, the Court has based its decisions on the premise that spending money in elections is speech protected by the First Amendment. If so, then Arizona's law should be applauded by the conservatives on the Court who made up the majority in *Citizens United*, because it increases the amount of money spent in elections and thus the amount of expression through all of the things that money can buy, such as advertising, mailers, and rallies.

But that is not how the Court's conservative majority saw the Arizona law; they saw it as likely to decrease speech by chilling candidates from spending their own money. There is little evidence that this occurs. In fact, the law could well have the opposite effect by causing candidates not taking public funding (and their supporters) to spend even more in response to the greater public dollars. Thus, the public funding scheme could quite possibly have a multiplier effect in increasing spending and speech.

Ultimately, though, this is a factual question: Had Arizona's law resulted in a net decrease in campaign expenditures because the wealthy and their supporters were chilled from spending, or had it caused more net spending because of the additional funds to candidates receiving public funding and expenditures made in response to them? The law was unconstitutional only if there was proof of the former, and no such evidence exists.

In the absence of such evidence, the Court simply made a value choice that it was more important to protect rich people and their supporters from being chilled from spending money than it was to further the speech of candidates receiving public funds. This is a disturbing choice and little more than a naked preference for some over others in the election system.

Finally, the Court left open the possibility that other public funding systems might be allowed. It would seem that in order to be constitutional, these would need to provide a lump sum to all candidates receiving public funding; there could be no increase based on the amount spent by an opponent. The problem with this is that it makes it far harder to design a public funding system that will attract the participation of candidates. The amount needed for a successful campaign varies tremendously depending on the election, the opponents, the overall spending, and the like. It is much less likely that candidates will choose to participate in public funding if that funding won't be increased when candidates not taking such money can spend far more.

Arizona voters adopted the initiative after revelations of significant corruption in its state legislature. Almost one-third of the states have some form of public funding of elections. Many of these are now unconstitutional even though they do not restrict or punish any speech but rather just provide for more speech. It really does turn the First Amendment upside down.

Shelby County, Alabama v. Holder

The Voting Rights Act of 1965 is one of the most important federal laws adopted in my lifetime. Section 2 prohibits state and local governments from having election practices or systems that discriminate against minority voters. Lawsuits can be brought to enforce it. But Congress believed that this would not be sufficient to stop discrimination in voting. Congress knew that litigation is expensive and time-consuming. Congress also knew that southern states, in particular, had the practice of continually changing their voting systems to disenfranchise minority voters.

Section 5 of the Voting Rights Act provides that jurisdictions with a history of race discrimination in voting may change their election systems only if they get "preclearance" from the attorney general or a three-judge federal district court. Congress believed that this was a key prophylactic mechanism for preventing race discrimination in voting systems. Section 4(b) of the act defines those jurisdictions that must get preclearance. Under the most recent version of this formula, nine states and many local governments scattered across the country must get preclearance. Almost all of these states are in the South, though the local governments are all over the country.

Each time the law was about to expire, Congress extended it. Lawsuits were brought challenging the constitutionality of each extension, but in every instance the Supreme Court upheld the law. For example, these provisions were scheduled to expire in 1982, and Congress extended them for another twenty-five years.

Most recently, the law was set to expire in 2007, and Congress held twenty-one hearings and produced a record of almost sixteen thousand pages in considering whether to extend it again. Congress documented continued discrimination against minority voters in jurisdictions covered by the preclearance requirement. For instance, it found that there were 650 instances between 1982 and 2006 in which preclearance was denied to the covered jurisdictions. There likely were thousands of other situations in which covered jurisdictions did not even seek to put plans into place because they knew that they would be denied preclearance. Also, far more suits for race discrimination in voting had been successfully brought against jurisdictions covered by Section 5 of the Voting Rights Act.

The Senate voted 98–0 to extend the law for another twenty-five years, and there were only thirty-three "no" votes in the House of Representatives. President George W. Bush signed the extension into law.

In *Shelby County, Alabama v. Holder*, the Court, in a 5–4 decision, held that Section 4(b)—the provision that determines which jurisdictions need to get preclearance—was unconstitutional. This had the practical effect of nullifying Section 5 of the Voting Rights Act; without Section 4(b), there are no state or local governments that need to get preclearance. No longer will state or local governments need to get preapproval from the attorney general before changing their election systems, no matter how long or how pernicious their pattern of race discrimination in voting.

It is the first time since the nineteenth century that the Court has declared unconstitutional a federal civil rights statute concerning race. Chief Justice Roberts wrote for the Court and stressed that the formula in Section 4(b) rested on data from the 1960s and '70s. Congress did not change Section 4(b) when it extended the law in 2006, but rather kept the formula it had adopted in 1982. Roberts said that times had changed—race discrimination in voting does not exist as it used to, and some covered jurisdictions had higher registration rates for minority voters than places where preclearance is not required.

The Court said that it was an intrusion on state and local sovereignty to require that they "beseech" the attorney general to approve their election systems. Roberts said that it violated a principle of equal state sovereignty to treat the states differently with regard to the requirement for preclearance.

Chief Justice Roberts's opinion was puzzling; it was not clear about the constitutional basis for the decision. What part of the Constitution did Section 4(b) violate? When it declares a law unconstitutional, the Court is expected to explain the constitutional provision or principle that has been infringed. But here the Court didn't say. Was it that the extension exceeded the scope of Congress's power? If so, there is a test for that previously created by the Court, but the chief justice's majority opinion never mentions it.

The Court said that there is a principle of equal sovereignty—that all states must be treated the same by the federal government. But what is the constitutional basis for this? Nowhere does the Constitution say this. How could justices like Scalia and Thomas, who consider themselves originalists who want to follow the Constitution's original meaning, come to such a conclusion? The Congress that ratified the Fourteenth Amendment also imposed Reconstruction and military rule on southern states, the antithesis of treating all states the same. And if such a constitutional rule exists, countless federal laws, especially spending programs, are constitutionally vulnerable, because they treat some states differently from others.

In theory, Congress can overcome the Court's decision in *Shelby County* by enacting a new version of Section 4(b) with a new formula based on contemporary data for determining which states need to get preclearance. In reality, it is hard to imagine members of Congress ever being able to agree on a new formula to require that some of their jurisdictions get preclearance. Moreover, it would seem that any formula that treats some states differently from others would violate the Court's principle of equal state sovereignty.

The Court's decision in *Shelby County, Alabama v. Holder* is likely to change the political process in many state and local governments. Effectively ending the preclearance requirement likely will mean that many election systems will go into place that otherwise would have been rejected because of their impact on minority voters. As soon as the Court handed down its decision, Texas immediately sought to put in place an election system that previously had been denied preclearance. There can still, of course, be lawsuits challenging discriminatory election systems, but a key protection against race discrimination in voting—the requirement that jurisdictions with a history of such bias get preclearance—no longer exists.

Conclusion

I believe that throughout American history, the Court's most important decisions have included those that have changed the nature of the political process. The Court's triumphs over the course of American history have included its rulings to make the democratic process work and become more inclusive, especially of minority voters. For example, as discussed in chapter 4, the Warren Court's decisions ordering reapportionment of legislatures and expanding who can vote, such as by declaring poll taxes unconstitutional, are among the best decisions in American history. Legislatures were not going to adopt these reforms on their own, and the Court acted to make democracy work.

But Court decisions also can do great damage to the political process. It is for this reason that I regard *Bush v. Gore, Citizens United,* and *Shelby County* as among the worst decisions in recent times. The consequences of the latter two rulings will be felt for many years to come as unlimited corporate expenditures change the nature of election campaigns at all levels of government and as the invalidation of the preclearance requirement in the Voting Rights Act will lead to many more discriminatory election systems.

In assessing the Rehnquist and Roberts Courts, these decisions deserve great weight. They are key aspects of the case against the Supreme Court.

PART III

THE FUTURE:
WHAT TO DO ABOUT
THE SUPREME COURT?

CHAPTER 8

The Question of Judicial Review

I t is tempting to conclude from all of the Court's failures that it would be better to simply get rid of the Supreme Court. But then I think of instances in which the Court has played a crucial role in upholding the Constitution. I think here of *United States v. Nixon* and what it would have been like without the Court having the power to rule against the president. I was in college during the years when the Watergate scandal played out, and my perception of judicial review is undoubtedly shaped by the Supreme Court's essential role in upholding the Constitution.

On June 17, 1972, a burglary occurred at the Democratic National Headquarters, in the Watergate complex in Washington, D.C. It was quickly discovered that the burglars were connected to the Committee to Re-elect the President, and over the next year it was learned that high-level White House officials were involved in a cover-up. In the summer of 1973, Senator Sam Ervin, of North Carolina, chaired closely watched, nationally televised hearings of the Senate Select Committee on Watergate. One of the dramatic moments occurred when a presidential aide, Alexander Butterfield, revealed that there was a secret taping system in the Oval Office and that presidential conversations were routinely recorded.

Because top Justice Department officials, including the former attorney general, John Mitchell, were suspected of involvement in the cover-up, there was political pressure for an independent investigation. Attorney

General Elliot Richardson appointed Harvard law professor Archibald Cox to serve as a special prosecutor.

Cox subpoenaed tapes of White House conversations, and the president challenged the subpoena in courts. On October 12, 1973, the United States Court of Appeals for the District of Columbia sided with the special prosecutor and gave the president one week to file an appeal. On October 19, President Nixon announced that he would turn over edited transcripts of the tapes and that he would ask Senator John C. Stennis (who was reported to be quite hard of hearing) to listen to the tapes and verify their accuracy. Nixon also announced that he would comply with no additional subpoenas and turn over no additional tapes.

On Saturday, October 20, special prosecutor Archibald Cox declared Nixon's position unacceptable; there was a court order to turn over tapes, not transcripts. More important, Cox said that he would seek whatever tapes he needed. President Nixon ordered Attorney General Richardson to fire Cox; Richardson refused and resigned. Nixon then asked the Justice Department's number-two official to fire Cox; William Ruckelshaus also refused and resigned. The request was then made to the number-three person in the Justice Department, Solicitor General Robert Bork. Bork fired Cox. This ugly episode came to be known as the Saturday Night Massacre.

The first resolutions calling for Richard Nixon's impeachment were introduced into the House of Representatives, and intense political pressure caused the appointment of a new special prosecutor, former American Bar Association president Leon Jaworski. On March 1, 1974, a grand jury for the United States District Court for the District of Columbia indicted seven top officials of the Nixon administration and the Committee to Re-elect the President for obstruction of justice and conspiracy to defraud. President Nixon was named an "unindicted co-conspirator." The grand jury explained that it would have indicted Nixon, but it did not know whether a sitting president could be indicted.

On April 18, 1974, a subpoena was issued, at the request of the special prosecutor, for the president to turn over tapes and other materials to use as possible evidence in the upcoming criminal trial. On April 30,

President Nixon announced that he was disclosing edited transcripts of forty-three conversations, including twenty that were the subject of the subpoena. On May 1, the president moved to quash the subpoena. On May 20, the district court denied the motion to quash and directed the president to provide all of the items, including the tapes, that had been subpoenaed; edited transcripts were not deemed sufficient. In a relatively unusual but not unprecedented action, the Supreme Court agreed to hear the case prior to its being considered by the Court of Appeals.

Meanwhile, the House Judiciary Committee was considering articles of impeachment against President Nixon. Impeachment hearings were held in July 1974, while the Nixon case was pending before the Supreme Court. The Court announced its decision in *Nixon* on July 25, 1974, unanimously ruling that the president had to comply with the subpoena. By coincidence, the House Judiciary Committee voted its first article of impeachment on July 25, for obstruction of justice in connection with the Watergate break-in and cover-up. On July 29 and 30, the committee voted two additional articles of impeachment, for abuse of power and failure to comply with a Judiciary Committee subpoena.

The Supreme Court, by an 8–0 vote, ruled against President Nixon and ordered him to comply with the subpoena and produce the tapes. The opinion was written by Chief Justice Warren Burger, a Nixon appointee. Also in the majority were Nixon appointees Harry Blackmun and Lewis Powell. William Rehnquist, the final Nixon appointee to the Supreme Court, was recused because he had been part of the Nixon Justice Department.

The Court made three major points. First, it held that it is the role of the Court to decide whether the president has executive privilege and, if so, its scope. Nixon claimed that the Constitution gave the president executive privilege and that the president alone determined its reach. The Court flatly rejected this contention: "The President's counsel, as we have noted, reads the Constitution as providing an absolute privilege of confidentiality for all Presidential communications. Many decisions of this Court, however, have unequivocally reaffirmed the holding of *Marbury v. Madison,* that '[i]t is emphatically the province and duty of the judicial department to say what the law is.'"

Second, the Court recognized the existence of executive privilege, even though this is nowhere mentioned in the Constitution. The Court acknowledged that the need for candor in communications with advisers justified executive privilege, averring that the need for confidentiality was "too plain to require further discussion." Although Article II of the Constitution does not expressly grant this power to the president, the Court said that "the privilege can be said to derive from the supremacy of each branch within its own assigned area of constitutional duties. Certain powers and privileges flow from the nature of enumerated powers; the protection of the confidentiality of Presidential communications has similar constitutional underpinnings."

Third, the Court held that executive privilege is not absolute, but rather must yield when there are important countervailing interests. It explained that "neither the doctrine of separation of powers, nor the need for confidentiality of high-level communications, without more, can sustain an absolute, unqualified presidential privilege of immunity from judicial process under all circumstances."

More specifically, the Court said that an absolute privilege would interfere with the ability of the judiciary to perform its constitutional function. The opinion explained: "The impediment that an absolute, unqualified privilege would place in the way of the primary constitutional duty of the Judicial Branch to do justice in criminal prosecutions would plainly conflict with the function of the courts under Article III." The Court thus concluded that the need for evidence at a criminal trial outweighed executive privilege and said that allowing "the privilege to withhold evidence that is demonstrably relevant in a criminal trial would cut deeply into the guarantee of due process of law and gravely impair the basic function of the courts."

On August 6, 1974, President Nixon complied with the subpoena, turned over the tapes to the Court, and made the transcripts of the tapes available to the public. The tapes and transcripts showed that Nixon had obstructed justice by ordering the Federal Bureau of Investigation not to investigate the

Watergate matter. Three days later, on Thursday, August 9, 1974, Richard Nixon became the only president in United States history to resign.

Nixon is a powerful reaffirmation of the essential principle that no person, not even the president, is above the law. *United States v. Nixon* also is an example in which the Court did not fail and performed its crucial function in enforcing the Constitution. Without the Supreme Court's decision, Nixon likely would have been impeached. But that would have been far more divisive for the country; it would have seemed partisan and political. Once Nixon produced the tapes, his criminal activity became clear, and even Republicans and political allies realized he had to resign. The Supreme Court's unanimous decision applied basic constitutional principles about checks and balances and, most of all, about the president's obligation to follow the law.

Asking the Right Question

Although *United States v. Nixon* is an important example of the Court succeeding in performing its constitutional role, in light of all of the Supreme Court's failures throughout American history, it is reasonable to ask whether we should eliminate the Supreme Court, or at least dramatically lessen its role. There is an inherent discomfort in vesting so much power in nine individuals who have their positions for life and are directly accountable to no one. The Court's performance over the past two hundred years provides a basis for questioning whether it is desirable to keep the institution, given that the Court has failed, at some of the most important times, at some of the most important tasks assigned to it under the Constitution. There is a strong temptation to add my voice to those of some prominent academics who have called for ending the power of the Court to declare laws and executive actions unconstitutional.

Actually, to focus on whether to eliminate the Supreme Court's power of judicial review is to ask the wrong question. The right question must be whether to eliminate the power of all federal courts to engage in judicial review of the constitutionality of the acts of the other branches of government. If there were not a Supreme Court, or at least not one with the power to declare laws unconstitutional, that would just leave matters to the lower federal courts and the state courts. If those courts continued to possess the power of judicial review, the power to declare laws and executive actions unconstitutional, the absence of the Supreme Court would be highly problematic. The Constitution would mean different things in each part of the country as courts came to varying interpretations of its meaning and of what is unconstitutional. The same federal law might be constitutional in one part of the United States and unconstitutional in another. The idea of a Constitution and of federal laws with a uniform meaning across the country would be lost. Commercial transactions and interstate conduct would be very difficult under those circumstances. Eliminating judicial review by the Supreme Court would make no sense if other federal courts continued to exercise that power.

More important, all of the criticisms of the Supreme Court's exercise of judicial review could be directed at the lower courts. There is no reason to believe that they are better at the task of interpreting the Constitution than Supreme Court justices are. With much less visibility for their decisions and with far more cases to handle, perhaps they do worse.

The vast majority of constitutional litigation never reaches the Supreme Court. In October Term 2012, the Supreme Court decided only seventy-three cases after briefing and oral argument; the year before, it was sixty-five cases. Focusing exclusively on the Supreme Court ignores the huge quantity of lower-court decisions enforcing the Constitution that never make it to the Supreme Court. They, too, must be evaluated in assessing the desirability of judicial review. It must be remembered that these include all of the easy cases wherein lower courts strike down clearly unconstitutional government actions based on well-established law.

Thus, the real question raised by the Supreme Court's failures must be whether the power of judicial review should be eliminated. This would leave the Supreme Court and the lower courts in place, and they would interpret and apply statutes but lack the power to declare laws and executive actions unconstitutional. Professor James MacGregor Burns, who, as discussed below, has urged the elimination of judicial review, explains that there still would be a role for the Supreme Court and the lower federal judiciary. They would "still be called upon to interpret ambiguous statutes, adjust conflicting laws, clarify jurisdiction, police the boundaries of federal-state power—virtually all of it present responsibilities except that of declaring federal laws unconstitutional. It would simply be brought closer to the role the Framers originally envisioned for it."

The Calls to Eliminate Judicial Review

The Constitution does not expressly give to the courts the power to review the constitutionality of laws and executive actions. No court had this power in England, and it might be expected that if the framers meant to change government in such an important way, the Constitution would have said so. The power of judicial review was created by the Supreme Court's decision in *Marbury v. Madison,* in 1803, which held that the courts may declare unconstitutional both federal laws and executive actions. Chief Justice John Marshall explained that the Constitution exists in order to impose limits on government and that those limits are rendered meaningless if not enforced. He famously declared that "it is the province and duty of the judicial department to say what the law is."

Judicial review has existed for almost all of American history, but it is not an inevitable aspect of having a constitution. The Netherlands, for example, has a written constitution, but that document explicitly states that it does not empower the courts to strike down government actions. The Netherlands has functioned as a democracy and without tyranny even though its courts do not have the power of judicial review.

In recent years, some prominent scholars have argued for eliminating judicial review in the United States. Harvard law professor Mark Tushnet in 1999 wrote a book titled *Taking the Constitution Away from the Courts.* His premises are quite similar to the arguments I have made in this book about the serious failures of the Supreme Court over the course of American history. In a chapter titled "Against Judicial Review," he asks what would happen if the Court overruled *Marbury v. Madison* and said, "We will no longer invalidate statutes, state or federal, on the ground that they violate the Constitution." He argues that over time, "[t]he effects of doing away with judicial review, considered from a standard liberal or conservative perspective, would probably be rather small, taking all issues into account."

Professor Tushnet says that the experiences in other democracies that have no judicial review show that a nation without judicial review need not look like Stalinist Russia. He points out, "The examples of Great Britain and the Netherlands show that it is possible to develop systems in which the government has limited powers and individual rights are guaranteed, without having U.S.-style judicial review." Tushnet argues that a "popular constitutionalism" would develop, in which the people and their elected officials would feel more need to comply with the Constitution, knowing that the courts were not engaged in judicial review. He believes that the results of "popular constitutionalism" would be more progressive than the constitutional law that results from Supreme Court decisions.

Tushnet is not alone among prominent constitutional scholars in making this argument. Former Stanford Law School dean Larry Kramer wrote a well-received book espousing what he also terms popular constitutionalism. Although Kramer does not define popular constitutionalism with any precision, and he does not go so far as to call for the elimination of judicial review, he does call for an end to "judicial supremacy" and a return of constitutional interpretation to the people. He argues, for example, that the people can be trusted, and he defends the deliberative processes of Congress as at least equal to those of the judiciary. He rightly points out that if Congress makes a mistake, the error can be corrected by that Congress or a future one. The change can be based on public pressure or election returns. But if the Court makes a mistake, the only way to overturn it is by way of a constitutional amendment or by waiting until the Supreme Court changes its mind.

Influential political scientists, too, have advocated the elimination of judicial review, Pulitzer Prize winner James MacGregor Burns, a professor of government at Williams College, urges the elimination of judicial review,

> based on the fact that the Constitution never granted the judiciary a supremacy over the government, nor had the Framers ever conceived it. It would remind Americans that the court's vetoes of acts of Congress are founded in a ploy by John Marshall that was exploited and expanded by later conservatives until the court today stands supreme and unaccountable, effectively immune to the checks and balances that otherwise fragment and disperse power throughout the constitutional system.

Burns, like Tushnet and Kramer, argues that without judicial review, elected government officials would be more vigilant about their duties to uphold the Constitution. Echoing an argument made in the nineteenth century by Harvard professor James Bradley Thayer, they contend that the existence of judicial review causes the other branches of government to take less seriously their duty to interpret and uphold the Constitution. Politicians can push for what is popular, even if it is unconstitutional, because they know that courts will take care of it and enforce the Constitution.

Voices such as Mark Tushnet, Larry Kramer, and James MacGregor Burns must be taken seriously. And they are not alone among contemporary academics who have called for an elimination, or at least substantial curtailment, of judicial review. In light of all that I have written in the earlier chapters about the failures of the Supreme Court, I am tempted to join them.

But on careful reflection, I think that the case for eliminating judicial review is not persuasive. There are compelling reasons why the existence of judicial review is important in achieving the missions of the Constitution. The focus should be on what can be done to reform the Court and its processes for the future.

Why Keep Judicial Review?

The classic—and, I believe the most powerful—argument for judicial review is the one first made for it: the need to enforce the limits of the Constitution. This is the primary argument advanced in *Marbury v. Madison,* early in American history, to justify constitutional judicial review. Chief Justice John Marshall explained that allowing the government to violate the Constitution without a judicial check "would subvert the very foundation of all written constitutions. . . . It would be giving to the legislature a practical and real omnipotence." The Constitution limits government power, but these limits are meaningless if the legislature and executive can ignore them.

Those who advocate eliminating judicial review argue that the benefits of judicial review in enforcing the limits of the Constitution are minimal, because there are incentives for the political branches to comply with the Constitution, and existing political checks on the judiciary make it unlikely to depart far from the popular will. But this ignores the instances in which the political process lacks the incentives to comply with the Constitution. These situations, which often involve the most vulnerable in society, are where the federal judiciary is especially needed.

Most dramatically, those without political power have nowhere to turn except the judiciary for the protection of their constitutional rights. In a telling passage, Tushnet admits, "My wife is Director of the National Prison Project of the American Civil Liberties Union. She disagrees with almost everything I have written in this chapter." The reality is that the political process has no incentive to be responsive to the constitutional rights of prisoners. Prisoners lack political power—they do not give money to political candidates, they generally are prohibited from voting, and they are unpopular and often unsympathetic. Admittedly, the Rehnquist and Roberts Courts have less-than-stellar records of protecting prisoners' rights, but there is no doubt that judicial review has dramatically improved prison conditions for countless inmates who would be abandoned by the political process. When was the last time a legislature adopted a law to expand the rights of prisoners or criminal defendants? In competition for scarce dollars, legislatures have every political incentive to spend as little as possible on prisoners. Moreover, how much worse might it be if politicians and prison officials knew that the constitutionality of their actions could not be reviewed by the courts?

A recent example in California and the Supreme Court illustrates the importance of judicial review for prisoners and the unwillingness of the political process to protect them. The litigation over California prison overcrowding has a long history. A lawsuit was initiated in 1990 alleging that the state was deliberately indifferent to the mental-health-care need of inmates, and in 1995 a federal district court ruled that there was "overwhelming evidence of the systematic failure to deliver necessary care to mentally ill inmates" in California prisons. The court found that mentally ill inmates "languished for months, or even years, without access to necessary care."

In 2007, a special master reported that the state of mental health care in California's prisons was deteriorating as a result of increased overcrowding. The rise in the prison population had led to a greater demand for care, and existing programming space and staffing levels were inadequate to keep pace.

A separate lawsuit was filed in 2001, concerning the inadequate medical care provided to inmates. The district court found that "the California prison medical care system is broken beyond repair," resulting in an "unconscionable degree of suffering and death." The court found that "it is an uncontested fact that, on average, an inmate in one of California's prisons needlessly dies every six to seven days due to constitutional deficiencies in the [California prisons'] medical delivery system."

At the request of the federal district courts, a three-judge court was appointed by the chief judge of the Ninth Circuit, as required by the Prison Litigation Reform Act, to consider the release of inmates as a remedy. The three-judge court heard fourteen days of testimony and issued a 184-page opinion, making extensive findings of fact. The court ordered California to reduce its prison population to 137.5 percent of the prisons' design capacity within two years. Unless additional prisons were built, the order required a population reduction of 38,000 to 46,000 persons, from the 156,000 who were then incarcerated in California prisons.

California aggressively contested this and took the matter to the Supreme Court. In 2011, the Supreme Court, in *Brown v. Plata,* affirmed the decision of the three-judge federal district court ordering the release of inmates as a necessary remedy for the prison overcrowding and the unconstitutional deliberate indifference to the prisoners' medical needs. Justice Kennedy wrote for the Court, in a 5–4 decision, and spoke forcefully of the rights of prisoners: "Prisoners retain the essence of human dignity inherent in all persons. Respect for that dignity animates the Eighth Amendment prohibition against cruel and unusual punishment. The basic concept underlying the Eighth Amendment is nothing less than the dignity of man."

Did the State of California comply with the Supreme Court decision? Unfortunately, no; even after the Court's decision, the state's lawyers repeatedly refused to agree to a plan or a timetable to ensure compliance with the order to release inmates. On January 8, 2013, Governor Jerry Brown announced that the problem was over and that "prison crowding no longer poses safety risks to prison staff or inmates, nor does it inhibit the delivery of timely and effective health care services to inmates." He said that as of July 2013, he no longer would use his powers to help comply with the court's order. He announced that he believed that California had done all it needed to to comply with the judges' mandate and the state was not going to take further steps to reduce the prison population.

In April 2013, the three-judge court issued a seventy-three-page opinion rejecting the state's arguments and mandating compliance with its order, which had been affirmed by the Supreme Court, to release inmates to bring the prison to within 137.5 percent of its planned capacity. The court made clear that disobedience with its order would be punishable, including by contempt.

Rather than comply, Governor Brown again asked the judges to delay the need for the state to comply. They once more refused. He went to the Supreme Court and once more asked them to hear the case, but the request for review was denied. The governor has continued to try to avoid compliance. His defiance of the federal court is reminiscent of the southern governors of the 1950s in their reactions to federal court orders to desegregate the schools. Even a relatively progressive Democratic governor, Jerry Brown, when confronted with all of the competing demands California faces, does not want to spend more money on prisoners or accept the political consequences of releasing some of them.

The case illustrates why the political process cannot be relied upon to protect a powerless, unpopular group like prisoners. Prisoners will often lose in the federal courts and the Supreme Court as well. But that is not always the case, as *Brown v. Plata* shows, and they have nowhere else to turn to vindicate their constitutional rights.

Prisoners are an example of how disfavored groups without political clout must rely on the judiciary if their rights are to be protected. Similarly, criminal defendants generally are unpopular and rarely can succeed in the legislative process. Even protecting the most basic right at criminal trials—the right to an attorney—did not occur until the Supreme Court mandated it. Even then, as I described in chapter 4, legislatures have provided grossly inadequate resources for providing criminal defendants with competent counsel.

More generally, there is little incentive for the political process to protect unpopular minorities, such as racial or political minorities. How long would it have been before southern state legislatures declared segregation of public facilities unconstitutional if not for *Brown v. Board of Education*? How long would it have taken Congress, dominated by southerners in key committee chairs, to have acted in this regard? The political process had an obviously dismal record in protecting racial minorities and advancing racial equality through most of American history. From the end of Reconstruction, almost a century went by without a major federal civil rights law.

Another, less dramatic example where political incentives fail is in situations where state and local governments choose to discriminate against out-of-staters. The political process has little incentive to protect noncitizens from discrimination, but it has great incentive to impose burdens on those who cannot vote and thereby to benefit those citizens who do.

Sometimes these cases arise in the context of the right to travel. California adopted a law that said that those moving into the state would, for their first year of residency, receive welfare benefits at the level of those in the state from which they moved. A lawsuit was brought by a woman referred to as "Roe," who moved from Mississippi to California. Under the terms of this law, she would receive Mississippi-level welfare benefits for a year, even though California had a far higher cost of living. This demonstrated how the effect of the California law was to discourage interstate migration; in fact, its likely purpose was to discourage people from moving to the state. The Supreme Court declared the California law unconstitutional as infringing on the fundamental right to interstate travel. In a case forty years earlier, the Court had similarly struck down a Pennsylvania law that said a person could not receive welfare benefits from the state until the individual had lived in the state for a year. There, too, the Court found that the state had violated the right to travel.

Such discrimination against out-of-staters occurs frequently when state and local governments adopt laws that favor in-state businesses at the expense of those from other states. The Court has found that such laws are unconstitutional if they unduly burden interstate commerce. There are a great many cases about this. A fairly recent example involved a Michigan law that allowed in-state wineries to sell wine directly to consumers through the mail, while out-of-state wineries could not. Michigan was acting entirely to help its own businesses at the expense of those from other states. The political process can't be trusted when a state is imposing burdens on those who are out of state and have no representation in the state's political process.

Sometimes the political process will even fail the majority. Reapportionment is the classic example here. As discussed in chapter 4, by the 1960s, many state legislatures were badly malapportioned, with legislative districts of vastly different sizes. The migration of population from rural to urban areas was not accompanied by a redrawing of election districts. The result was that urban districts were much more populous than the rural districts but had less representation. Malapportioned state legislatures were not about to reapportion themselves so as to decrease the political power of those in office. Every incentive led those legislators who benefited from malapportionment to retain the existing system. Realistically, only judicial review could institute one person, one vote.

These, of course, are just some of the examples where the political process cannot be relied on to comply voluntarily with the Constitution. In all of these areas, it is likely the courts or nothing when it comes to enforcing and upholding the Constitution and the key social values that are embodied in it.

Judicial review also is essential for ensuring that state and local governments comply with the Constitution. The nature of the federalist structure of American government is that there are fifty states and tens of thousands of local governments that can violate the Constitution. These include not only the city council or board of supervisors of every town, city, and county, but also every school board, zoning commission, water district, and so on. Scholars who advocate the elimination of judicial review focus especially on Congress and the president in discussing the incentives for voluntary compliance with the Constitution. Dean Kramer, for example, compares favorably the deliberative process in Congress to that of the Supreme Court.

This focus ignores, however, the likelihood of constitutional infringements by all of the other levels of government and the need for judicial review of their actions. A few examples illustrate this point. Without judicial review, the Bill of Rights would not be applied to the states. As discussed in chapter 4, it was not until well into the twentieth century that the Supreme Court held that the Bill of Rights applies to state and local governments. Although most states might voluntarily comply with most of the Bill of Rights, some states certainly would not follow all of its provisions, especially where it was expensive or politically unpopular to do so. For instance, many states did not provide free attorneys in felony cases until *Gideon v. Wainwright,* in 1963. How many local governments would advance religion in all sorts of ways if not for courts enforcing the First Amendment's prohibition of laws "respecting the establishment of religion"?

Nor is it an answer to say that state court judges can enforce the

Constitution against state and local governments. If judicial review is to be eliminated, there is no reason why state courts, any more than their federal counterparts, should have the power to declare government actions unconstitutional. Also, it must be remembered that in the vast majority of states, judges face some form of electoral review; in some states, judges run for office in partisan elections, and in many others judges face retention elections. How long would it have been before the elected judges in southern states ended the laws requiring segregation of the races?

There also is a larger point that is often overlooked in the debate over judicial review: its effects must be measured not only in terms of what is actually decided by the courts, but also by what governments and government officials don't do because they know that courts would strike down those actions if taken. Eliminating judicial review assumes that there would be much more voluntary compliance with the Constitution because government officials wouldn't have the assurance that courts would strike down unconstitutional acts. But the opposite effect seems more plausible: knowing that there was no judicial review would embolden government and government officials to ignore the Constitution. Its limits, so eloquently described by *Marbury v. Madison,* would be lost. In chapter 2, I described the actions taken by the government in times of crisis and the failure of the courts to invalidate them. But how much worse might those actions have been without government officials knowing that there was judicial review?

Popular constitutionalists and others who would eliminate judicial review justify doing so for review of the actions of, at most, elected officials. The claim is that the popular political process would be enough to ensure compliance with the Constitution. Although I am skeptical of that claim, it is important to remember that eliminating judicial review would also mean that the actions of unelected government officials would not be subject to constitutional scrutiny. Much actual governance in the United States is done by unelected officials: police officers, prison guards, zoning-board members, and regulatory agencies at all levels of government. Critics of judicial review stress the desirability of majority rule, but decisions by these officials are not majoritarian in any sense. Even if one could accept the popular constitutionalists' trust in the majoritarian process, it seems far-fetched to say that police officers or prison guards or zoning-board members will have compliance with the Constitution at the forefront of their concerns.

In fact, on reflection, it is not at all clear what it would mean to eliminate judicial review. Certainly, it would take away from courts the ability to declare unconstitutional a statute or an executive action in a lawsuit brought before them. But it is much more complicated than that. Would there be a bright line rule that all constitutional challenges are to be dismissed by courts? This would mean that the government would always prevail against a constitutional claim.

What would this mean in criminal cases? Would courts simply ignore the Constitution in evaluating whether to issue a warrant or to provide a jury trial or in determining what evidence to admit? Much of the Bill of Rights is concerned with criminal procedure. These cases cannot be taken out of the courts without a radical change in American government (and not one that anyone would advocate). Surely it cannot mean that the courts should do whatever the government (i.e., the prosecutors) wants in criminal cases. The undesirability of this is obvious and enormous. Would eliminating judicial review mean that in criminal prosecutions, courts would apply criminal statutes even when they are patently unconstitutional?

The point of these examples is that it is not realistic, or desirable, to eliminate constitutional decision making by the courts, including the U.S. Supreme Court. So long as there is a Constitution that is controlling over all other government actions, the courts will need to interpret and enforce it, notwithstanding all of the bad decisions by the Supreme Court throughout American history.

Those who argue for popular constitutionalism and the elimination of judicial review contend that society would be better off without courts being able to declare laws and executive actions unconstitutional. Mark Tushnet, for example, says that a populist constitutional law will advance the "principle of universal human rights justifiable by reason in the service of self-government." He says, "Populist constitutional law rests on the idea that we all ought to participate in creating constitutional law through our actions in politics." But what does this idea actually mean in practice? Who will be participating, and what will they be doing?

Also, scholars who argue for "popular constitutionalism" never explain why judicial review prevents a populist constitutional law from developing. Tushnet implies that the complex body of judicially created law precludes populist constitutional law. But people, of course, often speak in terms of their "basic" rights, even with judicial review and complicated court decisions.

In fact, it is quite possible that without judicial review, there would be less of a populist constitutional law. Without judicial review to enforce the Constitution—and to reinforce it in the public's consciousness—it is conceivable that the Constitution would become ever less important in society.

A populist constitutional law, almost by definition, would reflect popular attitudes. But why believe that this would be better than the courts in enforcing the Constitution? The judiciary can be a moral leader and protect our core values from hostile public pressure, although, as I have argued in this book, it often has failed to do so.

As a simple example, popular attitudes in many parts of the country strongly support school prayer and government support for religious institutions. The courts have been far more willing to resist this pressure and enforce the Establishment Clause, as compared with any conceivable populist constitutional law. The Texas town that wanted student prayers at high school football games certainly never would have embraced a popular constitutional law prohibiting them. In fact, it is not only conceivable, but likely, that some places would require prayers in schools and other public events.

My conclusion, then, is that despite the Supreme Court's many serious failures, society is better off with an institution—the federal judiciary—that is largely immune from direct accountability, with the responsibility of interpreting and enforcing the Constitution. The focus must be on how to change things to make it more likely in the future that the Court will succeed in fulfilling its core constitutional responsibilities.

Does Judicial Review Make a Difference?

Those who call for the elimination of judicial review make another argument that must be taken seriously: that judicial review fails to make much of a difference, so there is really no problem with eliminating it. Those who make this argument, including Tushnet and others, rely heavily on a famous book, published in 1991, by Professor Gerald Rosenberg, *The Hollow Hope: Can Courts Bring About Social Change?* Rosenberg's thesis is that the Supreme Court, and more generally the judiciary, can't really make much of a difference. Rosenberg points to failures that I discussed earlier, such as in bringing about desegregation, and says that successes, such as protecting abortion rights, would have happened anyway.

History and the examples in this book show that the Supreme Court's decisions sometimes make a huge difference in society, both positively and negatively. *Dred Scott,* in invalidating the Missouri Compromise, helped precipitate the Civil War. *Brown v. Board of Education* played a key role in fueling the civil rights movement. The Court's decision in *Korematsu* meant that the government could evacuate and intern tens of thousands of Japanese Americans during World War II. The Court's striking down of the federal child labor law meant that countless children had to work long hours in inhumane conditions. The Court's decision in 2012 upholding the key provisions of the Affordable Care Act may affect how we all will receive medical care. The Court's striking down Section 3 of the Defense of Marriage Act in 2013 means that gay and lesbian couples who are married in the states that allow it will now get benefits pursuant to more than a thousand federal laws previously available only to heterosexual married couples.

In fairness, Rosenberg's thesis is more subtle. He argues that courts cannot really bring about positive social change, and that the good they do likely would have happened anyway.

Of course, this assumes that litigation and decisions are to be evaluated solely in terms of the social change that results. Even if court decisions brought about no social change, they still might serve important ends. Perhaps most important, court decisions can provide redress to injured individuals, which, as I described in chapter 7, is a crucial function of the courts, even if the Supreme Court often has failed in this regard. Even if laws forbidding employment discrimination are shown to have had little net impact in eradicating workplace inequalities, the statutes still serve a crucial purpose if they provide compensation to the victims of discrimination. Similarly, even if tort law does not succeed in deterring dangerous products and practices, it can be successful in compensating those injured. Moreover, the redress might be noneconomic. Court decisions can provide vindication to those who have suffered from unconstitutional or illegal practices. *Brown v. Board of Education* was a vitally important statement of equality, even if public schools remain largely racially segregated.

Those, like Gerald Rosenberg, who say that judicial review has little positive effect underestimate all of the instances where court decisions clearly make a difference. The most obvious examples are when a court's decision is essentially self-executing, meaning that no further action of any government official or even of the courts is necessary. In the Pentagon Papers case, for instance, the Court refused to enjoin the publication of a study of the United States' involvement in the Vietnam War. No further action of any government official was necessary, and yet government policy changed and the Pentagon Papers were published. The First Amendment was vindicated, and the American people learned a great deal about how the country got enmeshed in the Vietnam War.

Also, there are those instances in which the judiciary can fully enforce a court's decision through its power to dismiss future cases. For example, if the Supreme Court declares unconstitutional a criminal statute, the judiciary can enforce that decision simply by dismissing any future prosecutions brought under the law. The Court, by definition, has changed governance by altering the law and by ending a set of criminal prosecutions. A simple illustration of this is the Supreme Court's decision in *United States v. Lopez*, discussed in chapter 3, which invalidated a federal law making it a crime to have a firearm within one thousand feet of a school. The federal government can no longer use that statute. If the government tried to enforce it, any court would dismiss the case. The judiciary can enforce the Supreme Court's decisions invalidating laws prohibiting the use of contraceptives and forbidding abortion just as effectively by dismissing any prosecutions brought against those violating the statutes.

Supreme Court decisions can encourage government action by upholding the constitutionality of laws or government practices. By stepping aside, the Court encourages other governments to act in the same manner. The Court's decision in *Plessy v. Ferguson* upholding "separate but equal" encouraged laws segregating the races throughout the country. The results were tragic, but it is indisputable that the Court's decision had a great effect.

There are Court decisions that require compliance by others but that the judiciary can enforce through its contempt power. This is typified by the classic injunction: the court issues an injunction and punishes violations by contempt. Usually, the threat of contempt is sufficient to gain the government's compliance. If an employer is sued for using a racially discriminatory test in hiring, then the court, upon finding a violation of the law, can enjoin future use of the test. If the employer is recalcitrant and continues to use the test, then the court can hold the employer in contempt of court.

Additionally, there are Court decisions that are enforced through the award of money damages that are likely to change government conduct. An obvious example is the law of the Takings Clause, the provision of the Fifth Amendment that says the government may take private property for public use, but it must pay just compensation. The award of money when there is a taking of private property is an essential protection for property owners, and the knowledge of such liability limits what governments choose to do. More generally, damages can deter wrongful government conduct. Part of the purpose of Section 1983 litigation, discussed in chapter 6, is to deter government from violating constitutional rights. For instance, the possibility of money damages for sexual harassment provides strong encouragement for government employers to refrain from such behavior.

Finally, there are Court decisions that require substantial actions by other branches of government in compliance and implementation and therefore continuing judicial monitoring and enforcement. The litigation discussed above concerning prison conditions and prison overcrowding is an illustration of this. Another example is the school desegregation litigation. Changing the government laws that segregated parks or water fountains simply required taking down the WHITES ONLY sign. If the government failed to do this, then the court could impose contempt. Although there was a period of massive resistance in the mid-1950s, compliance with these court orders was obtained in a relatively short time. Desegregating schools, however, was a far more daunting challenge, because it required affirmative steps ranging from changing pupil assignments to redrawing attendance zones to busing. Ongoing court involvement has not succeeded in desegregating schools, but one still has to wonder how much worse it would have been without the courts.

These examples are not exhaustive, but they are illustrative of the many ways in which courts can change government and make a difference. It is too glib, and just wrong, to say that judicial review can be eliminated because it never really makes much difference.

Critics of judicial review argue that the social changes that have followed Supreme Court decisions would have occurred even without judicial review. For example, in *The Hollow Hope,* Rosenberg argues that there was a trend toward increased numbers of legal abortions even before *Roe v. Wade.*

The difficulty with such arguments is that they are projections of a world that never existed (and I think likely never would have existed). In 1973, when *Roe* was decided, abortion was legal in only four states; about half of the remaining states allowed it in limited circumstances, and half prohibited it in all instances. There was no trend toward a large number of states allowing abortion. It is conceivable that over time, state legislatures would have loosened restrictions on access to abortion if *Roe* had not invalidated such laws. But it is also conceivable that as pro-choice forces gained political strength, anti-abortion groups would have mobilized, just as they did after *Roe.* Yale Law School professors Linda

Greenhouse and Reva Siegel have written a detailed analysis refuting both that there was a trend toward greater protection of abortion rights before *Roe v. Wade* and the claim that the decision was responsible for a backlash against abortion rights after it was decided.

Also, a key problem with such projections is that they often fail to account for time or geography. *Roe v. Wade* made abortion legal in 1973 for the entire country. How long would it have been before abortion was legal everywhere in the nation without this decision? Almost surely this would never have happened. As soon as the Supreme Court gave signals that it might reconsider *Roe*, Utah, Idaho, and Guam adopted laws prohibiting almost all abortions. I realize, of course, that *Roe* is enormously controversial. I am just questioning those, like Rosenberg, who say that it made little difference. Tens of millions of women have had safe, legal abortions that would not have occurred without *Roe v. Wade*. Both supporters and critics of the decision believe it made a huge difference; that is why it has been at the center of American politics for decades.

The Argument from Democracy

There is a final argument that is often made for eliminating, or substantially reducing, judicial review: an argument from democracy. The claim is that the United States is a democracy, meaning majority rule, and judicial review—allowing unelected judges to strike down the elections of popularly elected officials—is incompatible with democracy. Alexander Bickel, in one of the most famous books about constitutional law, *The Least Dangerous Branch*, published in 1962, called this the "countermajoritarian difficulty" and referred to judicial review as a "deviant institution" in American democracy. It is an argument that has been used by all sides of the political spectrum to criticize the Supreme Court and judicial review. In the 1920s and '30s, liberals made this argument to criticize the *Lochner*-era decisions described in chapter 3. In the 1960s and '70s, conservatives used it to criticize the Warren Court decisions.

Countless books and articles have been written criticizing judicial review as being anti-democratic, and many theories have been advanced for ways to reconcile judicial review and democracy. Some of the most prominent constitutional scholars define "democracy" as majority rule and see judicial review as inherently problematic. Professor Jesse Choper noted that the procedure of judicial review conflicts with the fundamental principle of democracy—majority rule under conditions of political freedom. Similarly, the late professor John Hart Ely based his analysis on the premise that majority rule "is the core of the American governmental system" and defined his task as describing a judicial rule consistent with this definition of democracy. Professor Michael Perry also began his book by observing that democracy means that decisions among competing values "ought to be subject to control by persons accountable to the electorate."

But it is impossible to reconcile this definition of democracy—as majority rule—with the U.S. Constitution. The framers openly and explicitly distrusted majority rule; virtually every government institution they created had strong anti-majoritarian features. As historian Charles A. Beard remarked, "majority rule was undoubtedly more odious to most of the delegates to the Convention than was slavery." The design of government institutions reflects the framers' distrust of majority rule. Under the original Constitution, the president was chosen by the Electoral College, the Senate was composed of two senators elected by each state legislature, and the federal judiciary was selected by the president, was approved by the Senate, and was assured life tenure. Although the right of the people to issue binding instructions to representatives was common until the 1780s and was originally included in the proposed amendments that constituted the Bill of Rights, James Madison and Alexander Hamilton led the fight against such mandates. They argued that representatives should exercise independent judgment and not be bound to follow the preferences of the voters. Elected officials were to deliberate and follow their consciences, not slavishly obey public sentiment.

Even more important, the Constitution exists primarily to shield some matters from easy change by political majorities. The body of the Constitution reflects a commitment to separation of powers and individual liberties (for example, no ex post facto laws or bills of attainder, no state impairment of the obligation of contracts, no congressional suspension of the writ of habeas corpus except in times of insurrection). Furthermore, as Justice Robert Jackson eloquently stated: "The very purpose of a Bill of Rights was to withdraw certain subjects from the vicissitudes of political controversy, to place them beyond the reach of majorities and officials and to establish them as legal principles to be applied by the courts. One's right to life, liberty, and property, to free speech, a free press, freedom of worship and assembly, and other fundamental rights may not be submitted to vote: they depend on the outcome of no elections."

If judicial review is always slightly suspect because it is not expressly mentioned in the Constitution's text, majority rule should be even more so because the Constitution is heavily oriented against it. Taking the Constitution as the baseline in understanding American government and in determining the place of majority rule avoids such an anomaly. Judicial review implementing a counter-majoritarian document is inherently counter-majoritarian; but such court review is not deviant if the Constitution's values are the major premise in analysis.

Put another way, the United States is not a democracy if that term is defined as majority rule. Rather, it is a constitutional democracy, where majority rule exists so long as it is consistent with the Constitution. In this way, judicial review enforcing the Constitution is consistent with democracy once that term is properly understood.

The task necessarily becomes deciding the appropriate content of American democracy—which matters should be decided by majoritarian processes and which values are so important that they should be deemed protected by the Constitution and safeguarded by the judiciary. The concept of majority rule obviously can provide no answer to this question. But nor does a belief in the importance of majority rule justify the elimination of judicial review.

Conclusion

I have spent the past thirty-five years arguing appeals, in the federal courts of appeals and in the Supreme Court, on behalf of those who have been convicted of crimes and those whose civil liberties have been violated. The first Supreme Court case I argued was on behalf of a man who was sentenced to life in prison, with no possibility of parole for fifty years, for stealing $153 worth of videotapes from Kmart Stores. (I lost 5–4, with the Court rejecting my argument that the sentence was cruel and unusual punishment.) The second Supreme Court case I argued was on behalf of a homeless man challenging a six-foot-high, three-foot-wide Ten Commandments monument that sits at the corner between the Texas State Capitol and the Texas Supreme Court. (I lost 5–4, with the Court rejecting my argument that this violated the Establishment Clause of the First Amendment.)

Having so often lost in the Supreme Court and the lower federal courts, and believing that the Court has frequently failed, it is tempting to conclude this book by arguing that judicial review should be eliminated. But then I imagine a world without judicial review and realize it would be much worse.

As someone who often argues cases on behalf of prisoners or those whose rights have been violated, I have the sense that popular constitutionalism is the product of an academic detachment that fails to recognize that, for clients like mine, it is often the courts or nothing. Prisoners and civil rights litigants very well might lose in the courts, but generally they have no recourse except in the courts. As I think about calls to eliminate judicial review, I remember *United States v. Nixon,* in which the Court stood up to the president, enforced the Constitution, and reminded us that no one is above the law.

But if the Court has failed so often throughout American history and the solution is not to eliminate the Court or judicial review, what can be done?

CHAPTER 9

Changing the Court

Why did the Court, in an 8–1 decision, uphold the involuntary sterilization of Carrie Buck, with Justice Oliver Wendell Holmes offensively declaring that "three generations of imbeciles are enough"? Why did the Supreme Court uphold "separate but equal" and then take fifty-eight years to overrule it? Why, in World War II, did the justices not see that evacuating and interning Japanese Americans solely on the basis of their race violated the most elemental notions of equal protection and human decency? Why has the current Court so favored business at the expense of consumers and employees and all of us? Simply put, why has the Supreme Court failed so often at times when it has been most needed?

There is no single or easy answer to these questions. Of course, a part of the answer is that the justices live in society and thus are likely to reflect its attitudes and values at any point in time. A majority of the justices who struck down the Missouri Compromise in *Dred Scott* were or had been slave owners. The justices who approved "separate but equal" in *Plessy* lived in a society that was racially segregated. The justices who approved evacuation of Japanese Americans in *Korematsu* had lived through the early days of World War II, when the outcome was uncertain and patriotism meant supporting the government's war efforts. Also, more subtly, they all had been appointed by President Roosevelt, and all in reaction to a prior group of justices who were reviled for having repeatedly struck down New Deal programs.

The Constitution exists to protect our long-term values from the passions of the moment. The Supreme Court is there to enforce the limits of the Constitution, and the justices are given life tenure to help insulate them from majoritarian pressures. But history gives reason to doubt that they will be able to do so, especially at particularly critical moments. Harvard law professor Mark Tushnet said, "Looking at judicial review over the course of U.S. history, we see the courts being more or less in line with what the dominant national political coalition wants. Sometimes the courts deviate a bit, occasionally leading to better political outcomes and occasionally to worse."

It must be remembered that the justices are elites and reflect the values of elites in society. Look at the current Court. As I mentioned earlier, all were educated in elite schools. John Roberts, Antonin Scalia, Anthony Kennedy, Ruth Bader Ginsburg, Stephen Breyer, and Elena Kagan all went to Harvard Law School, while Clarence Thomas, Samuel Alito, and Sonia Sotomayor went to Yale. As undergraduates, Roberts, Ginsburg, Kagan, Alito, and Sotomayor went to Ivy League colleges, while Kennedy and Breyer went to Stanford.

I, of course, am not against presidents appointing graduates of prestigious law schools. (I went to Harvard Law School.) But it is striking how similar the educational backgrounds of the justices are and how many of them come from relatively privileged families. On the current Court, Clarence Thomas and Sonia Sotomayor are exceptions to that. The point is not that there is anything wrong with picking justices with these credentials, but that the justices have remarkably similar educational backgrounds, and their experiences generally reflect that of a small part of society.

The Court has, throughout history, largely ruled in favor of the elites, and especially in favor of the interests of business. Given the backgrounds of the justices—not just these, but those throughout American history—is this any surprise?

The justices on the current Court obviously have impeccable academic and professional qualifications. The competence and ability of these justices cannot be questioned; nor can it be argued that they were picked because of cronyism or their friendships with the presidents who nominated them. But that has not always been so over the course of American history. There have been many justices who never should have been on the nation's highest court.

More than twenty years ago, University of Chicago law professor David Currie and Judge Frank Easterbrook (also a law professor) published a fascinating exchange about who the most insignificant justice in history was. There were many rivals for this dubious distinction. Currie identified Gabriel Duvall. He served on the Court for twenty-five years, from 1811 until 1835. As Currie noted, "In constitutional cases he was recorded as having delivered one opinion in twenty-five years, and it can be quoted in full: 'DUVALL, Justice, dissented.'" Thus, "Duvall sat for twenty-five years and wrote three words."

Currie notes that Justice John McKinley, from Kentucky, served on the Court from 1837 to 1852 and authored "not one opinion for the Court in a constitutional case; as Professor [Carl] Swisher has succinctly observed, McKinley 'seldom wrote opinions of any kind.'"

But such justices are not limited to the nineteenth century. Charles Evans Whittaker was on the Supreme Court from 1957 until 1962, when he had a nervous breakdown. I cannot think of any opinion he wrote as a justice. Sherman Minton, who served on the Supreme Court from 1949 to 1957, was appointed primarily because he was a close friend of President Harry Truman from the time they served in the Senate together. He, too, was undistinguished as a justice, and a survey of academics put him and Whittaker on a list of the "failures" among justices in the first two hundred years of American history.

The point is that there are many examples of individuals who served on the Court without distinction. Conversely, in every generation, some who would be terrific justices, who are truly the best and the brightest legal minds of their time, don't get picked, because the politics and timing are wrong. I think of Judge Learned Hand, one of the most respected jurists in American history, and California Supreme Court justice Roger Traynor as easy examples. I think of the most brilliant law professors and lawyers of their time who never made it onto the bench but likely would have been great justices. Being nominated to the Supreme Court is so much about the accidents of history. Sandra Day O'Connor was a state appeals court judge in Arizona, not even on the Arizona Supreme Court, when President Ronald Reagan nominated her to be the first female justice. I am not criticizing her ability or her performance as a justice, but only pointing out that her choice reflects the fortuities of timing. Clarence Thomas had only briefly been a federal appeals court judge when Thurgood Marshall retired from the Court. Wanting to pick an African American and a solid conservative, President George H. W. Bush nominated Thomas.

Law students assume that the Supreme Court justices are there because they are the smartest and the best lawyers and judges. Some unquestionably are, but many are there because fate smiled on them. They are no better qualified than so many others who could have been picked, and likely less qualified than many who were passed over.

It is easy to forget how easily the history of the Court could have been different. If Hubert Humphrey rather than Richard Nixon had won in 1968, Humphrey would have had four picks for the Court in his first years, and a liberal court—a continuation of the Warren Court—would have been secured for another generation. If Al Gore or John Kerry had been president in 2005, rather than George W. Bush, a Democrat would have picked the replacements for William Rehnquist and Sandra Day O'Connor. The new justices certainly would have been more liberal than those they replaced and those who were selected, John Roberts and Samuel Alito. The Supreme Court would be vastly different today. On the other hand, if John McCain had won in 2008 and replaced David Souter and John Paul Stevens, the Court would be far more conservative; for example, there almost certainly would now be a majority on the Court to overrule *Roe v. Wade*.

Some of the Court's failures are the result of justices being far out of step with the times. There is a benefit to having justices picked by different presidents at varying times; it creates a Court that does not necessarily reflect the majority's passions at any moment. But if justices remain for decades, as so many do, there is a real danger that they will come to reflect dangerously outmoded values and views. This was certainly evident with regard to the *Lochner* era, discussed in chapter 3. Justices who came on the Court in the late nineteenth and early twentieth centuries reflected the economic and moral conservatism of that time and were deeply committed to a laissez-faire, unregulated economy, which was in vogue when they were appointed. Some of these justices remained on the Court well into the 1930s, when the Great Depression made their views outmoded and dangerous. Whenever the Court deals with emerging technology, as it often does, I worry about a bench filled with justices who have little grasp of it. In one recent case about the privacy of text messages, it was clear at oral arguments that some of the justices did not grasp the distinction between text messages and e-mail.

Reforms That Might Make a Difference

I know of no single reform that could have prevented all of the failures identified in the earlier chapters. The Court is a human institution, and like any other human institution, it will have successes and failures. But I can identify a number of changes, some large and some small, that could make a difference in the future. Together, they would change the Court significantly for the better.

Clarify the Role of the Supreme Court. I believe that many of the Court's failures stem from the lack of a clear articulation and recognition of the role of the Court. The Constitution simply says that there will be a Supreme Court and such inferior courts as Congress "shall ordain and establish." Since the Constitution does not mention the authority of courts to review the constitutionality of executive and legislative acts, it obviously also says nothing about how it should go about this task.

The justices, individually and collectively, should articulate and

embrace the idea that the most important role of the Supreme Court is
to enforce the Constitution against the will of the majority. The Court
should recognize that the two preeminent purposes of the Court are to
protect the rights of minorities who cannot rely on the political process
and to uphold the Constitution in the face of repressive desires of political majorities. I do not expect disagreement from liberals or conservatives
that these are core aspects of the Supreme Court's role, even though there
will be disagreement as to what these obligations mean in practice.

Social psychologists long have documented that how a role is defined
has a strong effect on behavior. If the Court had seen itself as having a
duty to protect minorities, many of its race cases might have come out
differently. If the Court had accepted that its role was especially to enforce the Constitution in times of crisis, its rulings upholding repressive
government actions in war times might have been different. If the Court
saw its role as being to ensure redress for constitutional violations, it likely
would craft a very different set of doctrines to allow people to recover
from the government and government officials.

One of the most important ways of preventing the failures of the past
is for all—justices, lawyers, academics, society—to more clearly and explicitly define the purposes of the Constitution and of the Supreme Court.

Merit Selection of Justices. Every year since 1990, I have spoken at the
annual conference of the Alaska judges and lawyers. Each year, I do a
review of the Supreme Court's decisions and also a review of the decisions
of the Alaska Supreme Court and its Court of Appeals on constitutional-
law and criminal-law issues. As I read the decisions of these courts every
year, I am struck by their high quality. Alaska has had some very
conservative governors in recent years, most notably Sarah Palin, but the
justices and judges on the Alaska courts are not particularly conservative.
For example, Palin appointed Morgan Christen to the Alaska Supreme
Court. Christen was opposed by anti-abortion groups because of her
work on the board of Planned Parenthood. President Barack Obama
then picked Christen for the United States Court of Appeals for the

Ninth Circuit, where she now sits. More recently, Marjorie Allard, a public defender, was picked for the Alaska Court of Appeals by conservative governor Sean Parnell.

I have been fascinated at how this has happened, and I learned that the answer is merit selection. The Alaska Constitution creates a Judicial Council whose task is to nominate candidates for judgeships at all four levels of the state court system. The council is made up of seven individuals: three attorney members appointed by the Alaska Bar Association Board of Governors, three non-attorney members appointed by the governor and confirmed by a majority of the members of the legislature in joint session, and the chief justice of the Alaska Supreme Court, who serves as the ex-officio chair.

The Alaska Judicial Council must provide the governor with a list of at least two qualified applicants for each vacancy. Any candidate who gets four votes on the Judicial Council is on the list given to the governor; if there are fewer than two candidates who get four votes, no names are given to the governor, and a new search is begun. As I have spoken to individuals in Alaska, I have gotten the strong sense that the Judicial Council sees its task as identifying those who will be outstanding judges, without regard to their political party or ideology.

The governor must use this list in choosing whom to appoint. The Alaska Constitution is explicit in this regard: "The governor shall fill any vacancy in an office of supreme court justice or superior court judge by appointing one of two or more persons nominated by the judicial council."

After selection, a judge in Alaska serves a three-year term and then must run for reelection. The judge runs unopposed, and voters cast a "yes" or "no" vote on the judge's retention. Following retention, Alaska Supreme Court justices serve a term of ten years, appeals court judges serve for eight years, superior court judges serve for six years, and district court judges serve for four years. At the end of each term, the judge then faces another retention election, with the voters once more asked to vote "yes" or "no" on retention.

My sense is that over time, this has truly been a merit-selection process and has produced courts with excellent judges. Alaska is not the only state with such a merit-selection commission, though the methods of selecting state judges vary widely across the country. In Texas, for example, judges run in partisan elections for fixed terms. In California, a vacancy on the California Supreme Court is filled by a nomination from the governor, confirmation by a three-person panel (comprising the chief justice of the California Supreme Court, the attorney general, and the most senior judge on the court of appeals), and then a retention election. But without question, I think the best selection process is one that truly emphasizes merit, and Alaska's has succeeded in this regard.

There is nothing in the U.S. Constitution that prevents the president from creating a merit-selection panel for judicial vacancies on the Supreme Court and the federal courts and then promising to pick an individual from the names forwarded to him. President Jimmy Carter (who never got to select a justice for the Supreme Court) did exactly this for federal court of appeals vacancies, and the results were stunning. When Carter ran for president, he promised to appoint judges based on merit and to increase the diversity of the federal bench. Within a month of taking office, by executive order, he created a United States Circuit Judge Nominating Commission, charged with nominating judges for the federal courts of appeals.

The U.S. Department of Justice developed detailed guidelines for the operation of these nominating commissions. Each commission had to be composed of lawyers and non-lawyers and, it was assumed, had to have an equal balance of Democrats, Republicans, and independents. When a vacancy occurred on a circuit court of appeals, the commission, following the prescribed procedures and criteria, was to recommend three to five well-qualified persons to the president. There was a commission in each circuit, plus an additional one in the Ninth Circuit because of its size. (It covers the western quarter of the United States, encompassing Alaska, Arizona, California, Hawaii, Idaho, Montana, Oregon, and Washington.)

President Carter encouraged senators to create merit-selection plans for federal district court vacancies. Traditionally, senators have been responsible for recommending individuals to the president to fill vacancies on the district court, particularly when the senator is from the same political party as the president. Often senators have made recommendations based on merit, but sometimes it has been a matter of patronage, and those with dubious qualifications have been picked. Carter urged merit selection for the federal district courts and, while many senators rebelled, some created merit-selection panels.

At the very least, President Carter's approach substantially increased the diversity of the federal bench. To that point, in all of American history, only two women had sat on federal courts of appeals in the United States. Carter appointed nine, including Ruth Bader Ginsburg for the United States Court of Appeals for the District of Columbia Circuit. More generally, when Carter took office, in 1977, there were only eight women (1.4 percent of all federal court judges at that time), twenty African Americans (3.5 percent), and five Hispanics (0.9 percent) on the entire federal bench—including the district courts, the courts of appeals, and the Supreme Court. Carter's merit-selection system made significant progress toward achieving a diverse bench, appointing forty-one women (15.7 percent of the Carter appointees and 3.7 percent of all judges by the end of his term), thirty-seven African Americans (14.2 percent and 5.6 percent), and sixteen Hispanics (6.1 percent and 2.3 percent).

Assessing quality of nominees obviously is more subjective, but my sense is that Carter's picks to the federal courts of appeals were the best in terms of consistent merit of any president, at least in the several decades that I have been observing. I think of the nine women he appointed to the federal courts of appeals: Ruth Bader Ginsburg, Betty Fletcher, Amalya Kearse, Carolyn Dineen King, Phyllis Kravitch, Dorothy Nelson, Stephanie Seymour, Mary Schroeder, and Patricia Wald. By any measure, they had superb qualifications and have been outstanding judges.

Thus, I recommend that the president of the United States adopt a merit-selection approach to filling vacancies on the Supreme Court and the lower federal courts. The president should promulgate an executive order, like that of President Carter, creating a merit-selection panel for

Supreme Court vacancies and similar panels for vacancies on the federal courts of appeals and the district courts. Each merit-selection panel should be ideologically diverse, including Democrats and Republicans and independents, lawyers and non-lawyers. The role of the panel should be to present the president with the most qualified individuals to consider for each vacancy. The merit-selection panel should be charged with giving the president at least two names for each vacancy and the president should promise that he or she will pick a nominee from this list.

This would need to be done voluntarily by the president. For Congress to try to require this by statute would likely be unconstitutional as an infringement of the president's powers. A constitutional amendment to mandate this is obviously unlikely. But a president could create such a merit-selection process and then hope that his or her successors will follow suit. That, of course, is a risk; President Ronald Reagan eliminated President Jimmy Carter's merit-selection panels, and no subsequent president has revived them. A president may fear that going to such a system is like unilateral disarmament: there is no assurance that a subsequent president from a different political party will continue with merit selection. But my hope is that once a courageous president creates the system, especially for high-profile Supreme Court nominations, political pressure will be great for others to follow the practice of merit selection.

Of course, many of those who have sat on the Supreme Court likely would have been picked through a merit-selection process. John Roberts and Ruth Bader Ginsburg, for instance, would have been on any list based on merit. But others, throughout history, of lesser qualifications likely would not have made it through the process.

Such merit selection also would likely change the confirmation process (which I discuss below). Candidates chosen through such a merit-selection process would come to the Senate with a stronger presumption of competence and perhaps be more likely to receive bipartisan support.

Changing the Confirmation Process. In January 2006, I testified before the Senate Judiciary Committee against the confirmation of

Samuel Alito to the Supreme Court. At a recess in the hearing, then chair
(and now vice president) Joe Biden said to me that it was all an exercise in
"Kabuki theater." He was right. Everyone in the room, Republicans and
Democrats alike, knew that Alito was very conservative and would be a
very conservative Supreme Court justice. Alito had been a federal appeals
court judge for fifteen years, and studying his opinions left no doubt
about where he was on the ideological spectrum. But Alito presented
himself at the hearings as an open-minded moderate without a judicial
ideology. The Democrats spent the hearings trying to pin him down with
their questions and get him to express his conservative ideology. Alito, of
course, was far too smart for that. The Republicans used their questions
to give Alito the chance to present himself as he wished to be seen.
Democrats and Republicans each had their witnesses to describe Alito
based on his past opinions.

Alito was confirmed by the Senate, though with forty-two "no" votes.
He got on the Supreme Court and has turned out to be every bit as conservative as everyone expected him to be. Conservatives are thrilled to
have him there and—since he was fifty-five years old at the time of his
confirmation—to likely have him on the bench for a few decades. Liberals realize they got exactly what they feared.

Of course, the same thing happens when a Democrat is picked. Sonia
Sotomayor and Elena Kagan spent their confirmation hearings denying
that they were liberals and presenting themselves as open-minded moder-
ates. Republicans tried to use questions to pin them down as having liberal positions, but both, like Alito, were too smart for that. Democrats
used their questions to emphasize the qualifications of the nominees and
to help them seem fair and open-minded.

These recent confirmation hearings have lasted several days and served
little purpose beyond allowing the senators of both parties to use the
televised hearings to appeal to their constituents. The lengthy hearings
and intense questioning also let the public get some sense of the person
who will be serving on the high court for years to come. But not much
beyond this is accomplished.

It should be acknowledged that the confirmation process seldom will be very meaningful when the president and the majority of the Senate are from the same political party. Rarely will the Senate reject a nominee from a president of the same political party. The only hope for the Democrats to block Samuel Alito was by a filibuster, and even with forty-two votes against him, this was not something they were willing to do. There were forty-eight votes against Clarence Thomas, but Democrats were unwilling to use a filibuster to stop his confirmation.

It is time to create a more meaningful confirmation process. It is now custom that, at their confirmation hearings, nominees refuse to answer questions about their views on any issues that might come before them. Their reticence makes sense, though, only if their views don't matter. Senators have come to respect this position.

I believe this is wrong. It is appropriate for the president and the Senate to ask nominees for their views on key constitutional issues—though not how they would vote in a specific case, which obviously would depend on the record of the case, the briefs, the arguments, and the deliberations. For example, a nominee can be asked whether he or she believes that the Constitution protects the right of a woman to have an abortion or, more generally, whether the Constitution includes a right to privacy. This is not inconsistent with the merit selection I argued for above. From among those of the highest merit, the president can select the individual whose views he or she most wants on the Supreme Court. The Senate can and should do the same thing in deciding whether to confirm the nominee.

The confirmation process is the most important check on the unelected judiciary. Given that a nominee's views will matter significantly in how he or she decides cases, those views should be explored by the senators responsible for confirming the nominee. The Senate should insist, as a condition for confirmation, that the nominee answer detailed questions about his or her views on important constitutional questions.

There are several possible reasons why nominees' ideologies are not explored more thoroughly, but none are persuasive. One possibility is that nominees simply don't have views on topics like abortion, affirmative action, separation of church and state, and so on. At their confirmation hearings in 1990 and 1991, respectively, David Souter and Clarence Thomas both said that they had not thought about the abortion issue and had no views on it. This led Patricia Ireland, then president of the National Organization for Women, to quip that there were two adults in the country who did not have views about abortion and they were both on the Supreme Court. Thomas made this claim despite having written several articles arguing that *Roe v. Wade* had been wrongly decided. Of course, there is also the question of whether we really want someone on the Supreme Court who has no views on one of the most important constitutional questions of our time.

Another possibility is that the harm of asking and knowing is greater than the benefits—that publicly airing future justices' views destroys the appearance of judicial impartiality. But judges do not become more impartial by pretending that they don't have views. There can be little doubt regarding how Justice Scalia or Justice Ginsburg will rule the next time a party asks the Court to overrule *Roe v. Wade*. But no one would suggest that this disqualifies them. Nor would knowing a nominee's views create any greater problems. As a lawyer, I would much rather know the judge's views than pretend that the judge is a blank slate.

Yale law professors Robert Post and Reva Siegel propose an elegant solution: insist that the nominee answer how he or she would have voted in cases already decided. It is possible that the same issues might again come before the Court, but the views would have been known if the person already had been on the bench at the time of the prior case, whether as an associate justice or as a lower-court judge.

I have heard some say that this is inappropriate, because it is not really possible to predict what someone will do as a justice. There are examples of justices changing over time: Felix Frankfurter, a liberal law professor, became a conservative justice; Harry Blackmun, a conservative in his first several years as a justice, had become the Court's most liberal member by the time he retired. But such conversions are exceedingly rare. Few individuals have major ideological conversions in their fifties and sixties.

Antonin Scalia and Clarence Thomas have not changed in their time on the Court; neither have Ruth Bader Ginsburg or Stephen Breyer.

This open focus on ideology in the selection and confirmation process is not a radical idea. Presidents, of course, have always considered ideology in making their picks for the federal judiciary. Every president has appointed primarily, if not almost exclusively, individuals from his own political party. Ever since George Washington, presidents have looked to ideology in making judicial picks. Some presidents are more ideological than others; not surprisingly, these presidents focus more on ideology in their judicial nominations. Franklin Roosevelt, for example, wanted judges who would uphold his New Deal programs, and Ronald Reagan emphasized selecting conservative jurists.

Senates always have done the same, using ideology as a basis for evaluating presidential nominees for the federal bench. Early in American history, President George Washington appointed John Rutledge to be the second chief justice of the United States. Rutledge was impeccably qualified; he already had been confirmed by the Senate as an associate justice (although he never actually sat in that capacity). The Senate rejected Rutledge for the position of chief justice because of its disagreement with Rutledge's views on the United States' treaty with Great Britain.

During the nineteenth century, the Senate rejected twenty-one presidential nominations for the U.S. Supreme Court. The vast majority of these individuals were defeated because of Senate disagreement with their ideologies. Professor Grover Rees explains that "during the nineteenth century only four Supreme Court Justices were rejected on the ground that they lacked the requisite credentials, whereas seventeen were rejected for political or philosophical reasons."

During the twentieth century, nominees for the Supreme Court also were rejected solely because of ideology. In 1930, a federal appeals court judge, John Parker, was denied a seat on the high court because of his anti-labor, anti-civil-rights views. In 1970, the Senate rejected federal appeals court judge Clement Haynsworth largely because of his anti-union views. The Senate then rejected President Nixon's next pick for the Supreme Court, federal appeals court judge G. Harrold Carswell.

In 1987, the Senate rejected Robert Bork, even though he had impeccable professional qualifications and unquestioned ability. Bork was denied, 42–58, because of his unduly restrictive views of constitutional law, including rejecting constitutional protection of a right to privacy, limiting freedom of speech to political expression, and denying protection for women under equal protection. The defeat of Robert Bork was in line with a tradition as old as the republic itself.

Those who contend that ideology should play no role in judicial selection are arguing for a radical change from how the process has worked from the earliest days of the nation. Never has the selection or confirmation process focused solely on whether the candidate has sufficient professional credentials.

There is a widespread sense that the focus on ideology has increased in recent years. Confirmation fights occur when there are deep ideological divisions over issues likely to be decided by the courts. Now, for example, conservatives and liberals disagree over countless issues: the appropriate method of constitutional interpretation; the desirable scope of Congress's power and the judicial role in limiting it; the content of individual rights, such as privacy. It is widely recognized that the outcomes of cases concerning these questions will be determined by who is on the bench. Therefore, senators know, and voters recognize, that the confirmation process is enormously important in deciding the content of the law. Interest groups on both sides of the ideological divide have strong reasons for making judicial confirmation a high priority; they know what is at stake in who occupies the federal bench.

Opponents to the use of ideology in the judicial selection process must sustain one of two arguments: either that an individual's ideology is unlikely to affect his or her decisions on the bench or that, even if ideology will influence decisions, it should not be examined, because disadvantages to such consideration will outweigh any advantage.

The former argument, that a person's ideology is unlikely to affect performance in office, is impossible to sustain. Supreme Court justices possess great discretion, and the exercise of this discretion is strongly influenced by a justice's preexisting ideological beliefs. In cases involving questions of constitutional or statutory interpretation, the language of the document and the intent of the drafters often will be unclear. Judges have to decide the meaning, and this often will be a product of their views. Many cases, especially in constitutional law, require a balancing of interests. The relative weight assigned to the respective claims often turns on the judge's values. Given the reality of judicial decision making, it is impossible to claim that a judge's ideology will not affect his or her decisions.

Opposition to considering ideology must be based on the latter argument: that even though ideology matters, it is undesirable to consider it. One argument is that having the Senate consider ideology will undermine judicial independence. Professor Stephen Carter makes this argument: "[I]f a nominee's ideas fall within the very broad range of judicial views that are not radical in any nontrivial sense—and Robert Bork has as much right to that middle ground as any other nominee in recent decades—the Senate enacts a terrible threat to the independence of the judiciary if a substantive review of the nominee's legal theories brings about a rejection."

But Professor Carter never explains why judicial independence requires blindness to ideology during the confirmation or selection of a federal judge. Judicial independence means that a judge should feel free to decide cases according to his or her view of the law and not in response to popular pressure. As such, Article III's assurance of life tenure and its protection against a reduction in salaries provide independence. Each judge is free to decide a case according to his or her conscience and best judgment; they need not worry that their rulings will cause them to be ousted from office. Carter never explains why this is insufficient for protecting judicial independence. He subtly shifts the definition of "independence" from autonomy while in office to autonomy from scrutiny before taking office. But he does not justify why the latter, freedom from evaluation before ascending to the bench, is a prerequisite for judicial independence in the former, far more meaningful sense.

Another argument against considering ideology is that it will deadlock the selection process—liberals will block conservatives, and vice versa. The reality is that this is a risk only when the Senate majority and the president are from different political parties. But this happens, and there have been times when a number of nominations have been rejected, such as the Senate's defeating every pick for the Supreme Court by President Tyler and rejecting two nominations in a row by President Nixon. But in more than two hundred years of history, deadlocks have been rare.

Most important, even when the Senate and the president are controlled by different parties, the solution to deadlocks is in the president's hands: nominate individuals who will be acceptable to the Senate. Presidents in this circumstance have to select more moderate individuals than if the Senate were controlled by their party. President Clinton undoubtedly was forced to select less liberal, more moderate judges because the Senate was Republican-controlled for the last six years of his presidency. A merit-selection approach, such as I described above, might make such deadlocks even less likely, if the Senate perceived that the candidate had impeccable credentials and was chosen based on merit.

Finally, some suggest that using ideology is undesirable because it will encourage judges to base their rulings on ideology. The argument is that ideology has to be hidden from the process to limit the likelihood that, once on the bench, judges will base their decisions on it. This argument is based on numerous unsupportable assumptions. It assumes that it is possible for judges to decide cases apart from their views and ideology; it assumes that judges do not already decide cases because of their views and ideology; and it assumes that considering the views of the nominee in the selection process will increase this in deciding cases. All of these are simply false. Ideology often matters enormously in how the Court decides cases, so let's have a confirmation process that recognizes this.

How much of a difference will this actually make in who is chosen for and confirmed to the Supreme Court? When the president and the Senate majority are from the same political party, it won't matter much, because nominees are virtually always approved. But when the president and the Senate majority are from opposing parties, changing the confirmation process could matter greatly. Also, a confirmation process that is based on a recognition of the importance of ideology in Supreme Court decision making would help eliminate the myth that justices are just umpires calling balls and strikes or applying the law in a mechanical way.

Term Limits for Justices and Regularized Vacancies. Increasingly, I've been finding that I am asked, by lawyers and non-lawyers, whether there should be term limits for Supreme Court justices. During the 2012 Republican primaries, Texas governor Rick Perry advocated eighteen-year term limits for Supreme Court justices. I rarely find myself in agreement with Governor Perry, but here I think he, and others who have proposed this, are on to something.

The idea is that each justice would be appointed for an eighteen-year, nonrenewable term. A vacancy thus would occur every two years. Vacancies that occur through resignation or death would be filled by interim appointments to serve the unfinished part of the term.

There are many virtues to this approach. Life expectancy is dramatically longer today than when the Constitution was written, in 1787. The result is that Supreme Court justices are serving ever longer. From 1789 until 1970, justices served an average of fifteen years. From 1970 until early 2005, the average tenure was almost twenty-six years. The four justices leaving since then had served an average of twenty-eight years.

William Rehnquist, who died in 2005, was appointed by Richard Nixon in 1971. John Paul Stevens, who retired in 2010, was appointed by Gerald Ford in 1975.

Clarence Thomas was forty-three when he was appointed to the Court, and John Roberts and Elena Kagan were each fifty at the time of their appointment. If these justices serve until they are ninety—the age at which Justice Stevens retired—Thomas will have been a justice for forty-seven years and Roberts and Kagan for forty years. A person should not exercise that much power for such a long time. Term limits also make it less likely that we will have a Court dominated by views that are far out of step with society's needs, as occurred during the 1920s and '30s.

The only democratic check on the Supreme Court is the appointment and confirmation process. This is as it should be, because the Court was meant to be a constraint on the majoritarian process and to be largely insulated from direct political accountability. But the democratic control of the Court cannot work when justices are serving for three decades or more.

The absence of term limits also means that a president's ability to select justices is based on the fortuity of when vacancies occur. Jimmy Carter, for example, had no vacancies to fill, whereas Richard Nixon got to select four justices in his first two years in office and reshaped the Supreme Court in a way that lasted for decades. President William Howard Taft got to fill five vacancies in four years in office. Having a vacancy every two years would give all presidents the chance to equally influence the Court.

Eighteen years is long enough to allow a justice to master the job, but not so long as to risk a Court that reflects political choices from decades earlier. Eighteen-year terms, with regular vacancies, should allow the Court to have both the wisdom of experienced justices and the turnover to allow fresh perspectives. Making the appointment nonrenewable helps ensure that a justice won't decide cases in a way to help ensure reappointment.

Although this would be a change from how things have been done, it is not a radical proposal. No other major countries give life tenure to their high-court justices. Neither do any of the fifty states.

This does not mean that the justices would have to leave judicial service after their terms ended. Throughout American history, retired justices have served as lower federal court judges. Sandra Day O'Connor and David Souter still regularly hear cases on federal courts of appeals. Also, a procedure could be created such that if a Supreme Court justice could not participate in a case, a retired justice would be chosen at random from among those available to fill in. Today, if a justice cannot participate in a case because of disqualification or illness, the Court decides with eight justices, which sometimes results in a tie.

Liberals might bemoan that term limits would push a Ruth Bader Ginsburg (who has served since 1993) off the Court, while conservatives could lament the loss of an Antonin Scalia (who has served since 1986). But this proposal would treat all justices the same, and knowing which vacancies will occur during a coming presidential term likely would make Supreme Court appointments much more important in presidential elections.

Would term limits for justices require a constitutional amendment? Article III of the Constitution says, "The Judges, both of the supreme and inferior Courts, shall hold their Offices during good Behaviour." Professors Paul Carrington and Roger Cramton have argued that term limits could be imposed by a federal statute defining the phrase "hold their offices." They contend that it would be constitutional because the law would not take away the justice's life tenure—the individual would continue to be a federal judge, just not sitting on a regular basis on the Supreme Court.

I am skeptical of this interpretation, and I think that a constitutional amendment would be needed to create term limits. The Constitution says that they "hold their offices" until death, resignation, or impeachment and removal. A justice is not holding his office if he has been confirmed as a Supreme Court justice but is not participating on the Supreme Court. For more than two centuries it has been accepted by everyone that a federal judge has his or her office for life. Changing that understanding necessitates a constitutional amendment, not a statute.

Of course, requiring a constitutional amendment makes it far less likely that there will be term limits for Supreme Court justices. But as I speak to audiences, liberals and conservatives alike are asking more and more about term limits, and perhaps enough support will develop for such a constitutional amendment. After all, if Rick Perry and I agree, likely many others will, too.

Changing Communications. On Tuesday, December 12, 2000, at about 10:00 p.m. Eastern time, the Supreme Court released its decision in *Bush v. Gore.* We all vividly remember the image of reporters standing outside the Supreme Court, fumbling with copies of the opinion and trying to figure it out while speaking. Some got it drastically wrong. In hindsight, it was a monumental failure to communicate by the Court. The public learned that night that the Court had ruled in favor of Bush, but there was not a clear explanation of why. This helped to fuel—though certainly was not entirely responsible for—the sense that the Court had decided the outcome of the presidential election on a partisan basis.

Bush v. Gore, of course, is an extreme and obvious example of the Court's failing to communicate effectively with the American people. Yet in a sense, history repeated itself in June 2012, when CNN and Fox News initially reported that the Supreme Court had declared unconstitutional the individual mandate in the Patient Protection and Affordable Care Act. This was arguably the most anticipated and perhaps the most important Supreme Court decision since *Bush v. Gore,* and two major media outlets got it wrong and misinformed the American public.

Although these errors in reporting are not typical, and the press certainly deserves a great deal of the blame for hasty and inaccurate reporting, they reflect a larger problem. The U.S. Supreme Court is guilty of a serious failure to communicate with the American public.

A starting point in discussing communication by the Supreme Court is to ask: Why does it write opinions at all? Neither legislatures nor executives are required to give reasons for their decisions, though reasons are often provided. But the expectation is that when the Supreme Court decides a case, there will be a written opinion explaining the rationale. A written opinion serves many functions.

A judicial opinion provides an explanation to the parties and their attorneys for why a court came to its conclusion. Judicial opinions at all levels of the court system are a way for judges to make it seem that their rulings are not arbitrary and to tell the parties why they won or lost. A large percentage of opinions issued by lower courts are not published and therefore exist solely to explain the rationales for the decisions to the litigants. Judicial opinions are also thought to improve decision making. The need to write out a rationale requires more careful thought than simply announcing a result; there may even be instances in which judges change their minds when they try to write out an explanation for their decisions. Also, written opinions increase the legitimacy of a court's decisions for both the litigants and society—the result seems less arbitrary when reasons are given for it. For the Supreme Court, and for appellate courts more generally, written opinions provide guidance for lower courts and for government officials who must adhere to the decisions. In a system like ours, where precedent is given weight, written opinions facilitate this; it is hard to imagine following precedents without written opinions.

It is possible, then, to identify many audiences for Supreme Court decisions. The effectiveness of the Court's communication can be assessed relative to each of these audiences.

One audience, of course, is the parties. In a criminal case, an opinion for the government explains to a person why he or she will be imprisoned or even executed. In a civil case, an opinion explains why a person wins or loses money or has his or her constitutional rights vindicated or not. Yet, in reading opinions, there is little explicit recognition that the parties are an audience for the opinions. Supreme Court opinions, like those of every court, are densely written, often using jargon and technical language. This may be necessary for meeting the needs of other audiences, but it also means that the opinions will be difficult for most of the parties to understand.

A second audience for Supreme Court opinions is the press—and, through the press, the public. My sense is that relatively few in the public actually read the Supreme Court's opinions. The public thus learns of the Court's actions through the press. I would guess that a very small percentage of the American public, or even lawyers, read the Supreme Court's 193-page opinion concerning the constitutionality of the Affordable Care Act. People learned of what the Court did and why from the media.

A third audience is the scholarly community. The justices know that their opinions will be carefully read by academics who will write about them. Justices may be publicly disdainful of law-review articles, but they also know that there will be scholarly attention to their judicial opinions. It is hard for me to believe that justices are totally indifferent to how their opinions are analyzed, praised, and criticized. After all, four of the current justices—Scalia, Ginsburg, Breyer, and Kagan—were primarily academics before going onto the bench.

A fourth audience for Supreme Court opinions, and one of the most important, is the lower courts that must follow them and apply them to future cases. This imposes a crucial duty on the Court to write its opinions so as to provide guidance to lower courts.

A fifth audience is the government officials who must apply and follow the Court's rulings. Because the Constitution applies only to the government, constitutional decisions virtually always involve the government as one of the parties. Government officials at all levels must understand the Supreme Court's decisions and follow them in future actions. This imposes an important duty on the Court to write opinions in a way that guides these officials on what is permissible and what is not allowed. Sometimes, such as in criminal procedure cases, the audience is the police, who need guidance about what is permissible investigative behavior. Sometimes the audience is the legislatures that need to be guided with regard to what future laws in the area will be permissible and not struck down.

Finally, it is important to see the Court itself, in subsequent cases and in future configurations, as a crucial audience for Supreme Court opinions. As explained above, in a system based on precedent, judicial opinions are crucial. The justices are aware that the language of their opinions shapes the law and future decisions. Concurring and dissenting opinions often seem to be written with the hope of influencing future cases.

At all four stages of the process—taking and denying cases, hearing cases, releasing decisions, and writing opinions—the Supreme Court fails to effectively communicate.

First, the Court poorly communicates about its choices to grant or deny review. In October Term 2011, the Supreme Court decided sixty-five cases after briefing and oral argument. In October Term 2012, seventy-three cases were decided after briefing and oral argument. The Court had more than eight thousand petitions for review each year. Therefore, the Supreme Court's decision in the overwhelming majority of cases is a loss for the party seeking review. The Supreme Court always has said that the denial of certiorari—that is, the denial of review of a decision of a lower court—is not a decision on the merits. It is just a refusal by the Court to hear the case and cannot be interpreted as the Court agreeing with the lower court. But for the lawyer and the party, it is usually the end, the final loss.

While working on this book, I filed a petition for a writ of certiorari on behalf of Morton Berger, an Arizona man who had received a sentence of two hundred years in prison for possessing twenty pictures of child pornography; he was sentenced to ten years in person for each picture, to run consecutively, with no possibility of parole or clemency. He received this sentence even though he never had been accused of molesting a child or of making child pornography. In virtually no other state besides Arizona could he have received such a sentence. The Supreme Court, without explanation, denied review. Berger has nowhere else to turn and now will spend the rest of his life in prison.

The Supreme Court never gives reasons why it is denying certiorari. Usually only an order is issued refusing to hear the case, though occasionally there will be a dissent from the denial of review. The lawyers and the parties are left to guess about why they lost. Sometimes it is possible to speculate that the Court did not take a matter because there was not a split among the lower courts or because the Court wanted to wait for the issue to further "percolate" or because there was not a significant federal question. But there are so many instances from virtually every conference in which the Court denies certiorari despite the presence of a split among the circuits and in cases presenting important, unresolved issues of federal law.

As a lawyer who has been in this situation time after time, including in capital cases, the denial of certiorari is intensely frustrating. It feels arbitrary, because no reason is given or even hinted at. All of the benefits of written opinions described above are missing. A decision has been made—the Court has decided not to take the case, and thus the lower-court ruling stands—but it seems random, and there is nothing to say to a client, even one facing life in prison or death, except that the Court takes few cases and didn't take his or hers.

Second, it is inexplicable and inexcusable that Supreme Court proceedings are not broadcast live. Supreme Court proceedings, of course, are government events, and there should be a strong presumption that people are entitled to watch government proceedings. Arguments in the Supreme Court always have been open to the public, but relatively few can attend in person. There are only 250 seats, and people literally camp out all night or even longer in order to attend arguments in high-profile cases.

Broadcasting Supreme Court arguments would allow the entire nation to watch a crucial branch of government at work. Allowing broadcasts of Supreme Court arguments would help society understand the issues before the Court. For example, many thought that the central question before the Court with regard to the Affordable Care Act was whether people had a right to not purchase health insurance. That, of course, was not the issue at all; the Court's focus was entirely on the scope of congressional power and the ability to force states to comply with federal requirements. Hearing the oral arguments would have made this much clearer for people.

Broadcasting Supreme Court arguments would also help society understand the judicial process. Cases are in the Supreme Court because there is no clear right or wrong answer; every case presents a choice, and rarely, if ever, does the Court hear a case in which there are not reasonable arguments on each side. Allowing people to listen to and watch oral arguments would make this clear and apparent.

And broadcasting arguments would allow people to better understand the Court. They would see that cases are heard and decided by nine human beings, with nine different personalities. I believe that people of all political persuasions would be impressed and would see that the Court is composed of nine very intelligent individuals who work very hard to decide cases based on their best understanding of the law.

Unfortunately, though, the Supreme Court's rules prohibit live broadcasting of oral arguments. I have always felt that many of the arguments against allowing cameras in the courtroom are really arguments against allowing the public and reporters to be there at all, something that is thankfully unthinkable as well as unconstitutional.

At least since *Bush v. Gore,* the Supreme Court has on occasion, in high-profile cases, allowed broadcasting of the audiotapes of oral arguments immediately after they conclude. This occurred after the oral arguments concerning the constitutionality of the Patient Protection and Affordable Care Act and the cases involving the right to marriage equality for gays and lesbians. C-SPAN has taken advantage of this opportunity, broadcasting the audiotapes as soon as they become available and showing still photographs of the justices and advocates as their voices are heard. But if people can hear the tapes just minutes after the arguments conclude, it is impossible to see the harm in allowing them to watch the proceedings live an hour or two earlier. What is the difference between watching the arguments live from 10:00 a.m. until noon and watching them, with still photographs of the participants, from noon until 2:00 p.m.?

What rationale is there for excluding cameras from Supreme Court proceedings? One concern is that broadcasting arguments might change the behavior of lawyers and justices. Perhaps that concern has some basis in trial courts, where there is worry about the effect of cameras on witnesses. Even there, however, the experiences of many jurisdictions with cameras in the courtrooms and many studies refute any basis for concern.

But especially in the Supreme Court, there seems little reason to worry. The lawyers, who are focused on answering intense questioning from the justices, are unlikely to alter their arguments to play to the cameras. Besides, anyone who has witnessed a Supreme Court argument knows that the justices are firmly in control of the proceedings. Justices and lawyers know that the arguments, especially in high-profile cases, are

going to be extensively covered in the media. In this context, there is no
reason to think that live broadcasting will change behavior. And again,
justices and lawyers know that audiotapes of the arguments will be available, sometimes immediately after they conclude. It is hard to believe that
live as opposed to tape-delayed broadcasts will affect the behavior of justices and lawyers.

I have heard justices express concern that if television cameras were
allowed, the media might broadcast excerpts that offered a misleading
impression of arguments and the Court. But that is true of any government proceeding and any event that reporters cover. A newspaper or television reporter already can quote a justice's question or a lawyer's answer
out of context. The Supreme Court should not be able to protect itself
from misreporting any more than any other government institution can.

Or the justices might be afraid that an excerpt from an oral argument
might appear on Jon Stewart's or David Letterman's show and be used for
entertainment purposes; perhaps they will even be mocked. But that is a
cost of being part of a democratic society and of holding a prominent
position in government. In no other context would Supreme Court justices say that government officials can protect themselves from possible
criticism by cutting off public access.

More than anything, though, the Court's decision to prohibit live broadcasts seems to be about protecting its own credibility. More than a decade
ago, there was a panel discussion at the Ninth Circuit Judicial Conference
about cameras in the courtroom. Fred Graham, from Court TV, challenged
Justice Stephen Breyer about why Supreme Court proceedings could not be
broadcast. Breyer responded by saying, "Compare the public approval rat-
ings of the Court with that of the other branches of government."

But this mistakenly blames the messenger. There is no reason to believe that the Supreme Court's legitimacy is helped by prohibiting live
broadcasts. Quite to the contrary, I believe that the Court's credibility
would only be enhanced if more people saw the justices at work. Anyone
who watches a Supreme Court argument will see nine highly intelligent,
superbly prepared individuals grappling with some of the nation's hardest

questions. The public would see, too, that there are no easy answers to most constitutional questions and that there are usually compelling arguments on both sides. That would likely increase the public's understanding of the law and its appreciation for the Court.

Third, from a communications perspective, there are many problems with how the Supreme Court releases its decisions. The Court gives no notice of which cases will be announced on which day. Unless it is the last day of the term, in which case all of the remaining decisions are expected, there is no way to know which cases will come down on a given day. I never have understood why the Court can't reveal—say, the day before—which cases will be handed down. The California Supreme Court does this, and I've never heard about any problem with it. Giving prior notice would allow reporters and commentators to be better prepared; they could review the cases that are about to be handed down and be in a better position to discuss them. Especially in a world where instant reporting and instant commenting occur, better advance preparation can only help in more accurately informing the public.

Also, when the Court announces a decision, there is no clear, intelligent summary of the decision. I have always thought that a decision should be accompanied by a one-paragraph description of what the Court did. This would not be authoritative or part of the decision, and it would be much less technical and much clearer than the "syllabus" that now accompanies every decision. Providing such a summary could avoid mistaken reports like those that occurred when the Affordable Care Act decision was released. It would have been easy to release a paragraph that read, "The individual mandate was upheld, by a 5–4 margin, as a valid exercise of Congress's taxing power. Five justices said that the individual mandate was not within the scope of Congress's commerce power or necessary and proper clause authority. The Court ruled 7–2 that forcing states to comply with the new Medicaid requirements by tying all Medicaid funds to compliance was unduly coercive." The description could have been more elaborate than this, but even a short summary like this would have helped tremendously.

There is no broadcast—even a tape-delayed one—of the announcing of decisions. Justices announce their decisions from the bench, often briefly, sometimes in detail. Occasionally dissents are read from the bench, often quite dramatically. Sometimes justices say things in these oral pronouncements that are not in the written opinions. I do not understand why the announcing of decisions is not broadcast. As explained above, the primary argument against cameras in the Supreme Court is that it will adversely affect the behavior of lawyers and judges. This concern has no basis if all the justices are doing is announcing their decisions.

Additionally, too many decisions are announced per day at the end of the term. Often during the last week of the term, multiple decisions are announced over a few days; between June 24 and 26, 2013, for example, exactly a dozen decisions were handed down. In some years, several major, enormously important cases come down on the last day of the term. Having multiple major cases on the same day makes it harder for reporters to cover—and harder for people to understand—what the Court has done. Why not have the decisions spread out more that week, releasing one or two decisions each day of the week, rather than multiple decisions in just a couple of days? This would allow for more in-depth reporting and greater understanding on the part of the public. The annual end-of-term flurry is unnecessary; the release of opinions could be spread out over another several days.

Fourth, Supreme Court opinions can do a better job of giving guidance to those who must follow them. Obviously, it's easy to wish that more justices wrote like Robert Jackson or Louis Brandeis. But beyond that, there are ways in which Court opinions fail to adequately communicate.

Supreme Court opinions have become much too long and thus far more difficult for lower courts and government officials to read and rely upon. Adam Liptak wrote in the *New York Times* of how October Term 2009 set the all-time record with regard to length of opinions. Liptak wrote:

Brown v. Board of Education, the towering 1954 decision that held segregated public schools unconstitutional, managed to do its work in fewer than 4,000 words. When the Roberts court returned to just an aspect of the issue in 2007 in *Parents Involved v. Seattle* [a case about school desegregation, which I discussed in chapter 1], it published some 47,000 words, enough to rival a short novel. In more routine cases, too, the court has been setting records. The median length of majority opinions reached an all-time high in the last term.

The opinions have not gotten shorter since then. The decision in the Affordable Care Act case was 193 pages long. Opinions over a hundred pages long occur in far less prominent cases, too. I've long believed that the Court would benefit from word and page limits, like those imposed on litigants.

Too often, the Court fails to give guidance for the lower courts that will need to follow its decisions. As I explained above, this is one of the most important audiences for the Court. Yet I often have the sense that the Court does not focus nearly enough on the need for clarity to guide lower court judges. Examples are plentiful. In *Crawford v. Washington,* the Court significantly changed the rules of evidence in criminal trials, holding that prosecutors cannot use "testimonial" statements of unavailable witnesses, even if they are reliable. This was a really big deal: the Court ruled that the Confrontation Clause in the Sixth Amendment— the right that a person be able to confront his or her accuser—is violated if the prosecutor uses testimonial statements from a witness who is not in court. The issue of what is "testimonial" is something that arises constantly, on a daily basis, in state and federal trial courts all across the country. But the Court made no effort to give guidance to the lower courts and define it.

Another example comes from the area of civil litigation: *Philip Morris USA v. Williams.* For the third time in eleven years, the Court imposed significant constitutional limits on punitive-damage awards. *Philip Morris USA,* though, seemed to go further than the earlier rulings in restricting punitive damages. The Supreme Court, in a 5–4 decision, held that juries can base punitive damages against a defendant only on the harms suffered by that plaintiff; they cannot base punitive-damage awards on harms to others. Thus, in that case, the punitive-damages award against Philip Morris for its deceptive marketing of cigarettes could be based only on the harms that individual plaintiff suffered, not on harms to other smokers. However, the Court qualified this holding by saying that juries may consider harm to third parties in assessing the "reprehensibility" of the defendant's conduct, which the Court says is the most important factor in determining the size of a punitive-damage award.

Thus, the Court says, in the same opinion, both that juries cannot base their punitive damages on harms suffered by third parties and that juries can consider harms to third parties in determining punitive damages. If that seems incoherent, it is because the Court did such a poor job of explaining this. Trial judges are likely to struggle for years with how to formulate jury instructions that simultaneously tell the jury to consider and not to consider harms to others besides the plaintiffs. Appellate courts are left with little guidance on when punitive-damage awards are allowed and when they are unconstitutional. How can a court of appeals possibly determine whether the punitive-damage award violates this command?

Finally, I believe that the increasing use of sarcasm and even ridicule in judicial opinions is undesirable. No justice in Supreme Court history has consistently written with the sarcasm of Justice Scalia. No doubt, this makes his opinions among the most entertaining to read. He has a great flair for language and does not mince words when he disagrees with a position. But I think that this sends exactly the wrong message to law students and attorneys about what type of discourse is appropriate in a formal legal setting and what is acceptable in speaking to one another.

Examples of this abound. In dissenting opinions, he describes the majority's approaches as "nothing short of ludicrous" and "beyond absurd," "entirely irrational" and not "pass[ing] the most gullible scrutiny." He has declared that a majority opinion was "nothing short of preposterous" and that it had "no foundation in American constitutional law and barely pretends to." He talks about how "one must grieve for the Constitution" because of a majority's approach. He calls the approaches taken in majority opinions "preposterous" and "ridiculous" and "so unsupported in reason and so absurd in application [as to be] unlikely to survive." He speaks of how a majority opinion "vandalizes . . . our people's tradition." And in a recent dissent, Scalia declared:

> Today's tale . . . is so transparently false that professing to believe it demeans this institution. But reaching a patently incorrect conclusion on the facts is a relatively benign judicial mischief; it affects, after all, only the case at hand. In its vain attempt to make the incredible plausible, however—or perhaps as an intended second goal—today's opinion distorts our Confrontation Clause jurisprudence and leaves it in a shambles. Instead of clarifying the law, the Court makes itself the obfuscator of last resort.

So what can be done to change how the Supreme Court communicates, and how much difference would it make? My suggestions for improving communication by the Supreme Court are implicit in the above criticisms. To be explicit:

1. The Court should offer brief reasons for denying certiorari. Some explanation is better than nothing. Perhaps it could even be a sentence: "Certiorari denied because of the lack of an adequate split among the lower courts," or "Certiorari denied because of perceived procedural problems in the case." I am not optimistic that the Court will ever do this, because it is additional work and because it assumes that there is a consensus among the justices who

denied certiorari. Yet, from the perspective of lawyers and parties who have lost what is often their final chance, some explanation would be tremendously helpful and appreciated.

2. All Supreme Court public proceedings should be broadcast. This includes oral arguments and the announcement of decisions and anything else done in open court.

3. The Court should announce a day in advance which cases will be coming down on the following day.

4. There should be a paragraph or two released along with decisions, summarizing the Court's decisions. These would not be authoritative and would have no precedential value. In this way, it would be the same as the syllabus now released, but with an additional, clearer paragraph or two.

5. The Court should spread out its release of decisions during the last weeks of the term. There is no reason decisions cannot come out over four or five days of those weeks rather than on a couple of days.

6. There should be presumptive word and page limits for Supreme Court opinions. The Court, like all courts, believes that the discipline of word and page limits leads to better briefs. The same is true for the Court.

There are thus many simple steps that can be taken to improve communication by the Court. And they all can be done by the Court on its own. But do the justices care? Will they be willing to consider changing practices that have long been followed? Can they look at these issues not just from their perspective but from those of the lawyers, judges, journalists, scholars, and public who read their opinions?

And if these changes are implemented, will they make a difference in the Court's decisions? They certainly would help people be better informed about the Court, but would they change what the Court does? I think so. Changing how opinions are written and communicated may, in some instances, cause a justice—and therefore the Court—to come to different conclusions. Over the long term, a society that much better understands the Supreme Court is more likely to produce one that better performs its constitutional duties.

Post-Argument Briefs. Arguing a case in the Supreme Court is an exhilarating, but also frustrating, experience, because there are so many questions and so little time to answer them. Often a lawyer will get a sentence or two out in response to a question and then get a question from a different justice about something else. In an argument in 2005, I received a question from Justice Stevens. Before I could answer, Justice Kennedy added something to the hypothetical and then Chief Justice Rehnquist added something to that. I got one sentence out in response to the Rehnquist hypothetical before Justice Scalia asked me a question about something else. In a more recent argument, in 2013, I was at one point asked three questions in a row by different justices before I could answer any of them. These are typical experiences for Supreme Court advocates.

The justices are well prepared and ask difficult questions, often seeing the case differently from how the lower courts or the lawyers perceived it. After the argument, I always wish for the chance to elaborate more or to answer with the benefit of reflection. The justices would benefit from more thoughtful and complete answers.

There is an easy solution: allow each side to file a short post-argument brief. It can be limited to ten pages, or even less. The purpose of oral argument is to allow the justices to ask the lawyers the questions that concern them the most. Permitting the lawyers to provide more complete answers to the most important questions, and with the benefit of some reflection, can only help the decision-making process.

Ethics and Recusals of Supreme Court Justices. Throughout history, one of the Supreme Court's greatest strengths and virtues has been the impeccable ethics of its justices. The Court rarely has been tainted by scandal. Even rumors of ethical transgressions by justices are exceedingly rare. When there were allegations of improprieties by Justice Abe Fortas, he quickly resigned from the bench.

Fortas had been a prominent Washington lawyer and was close to President Lyndon Johnson, who named him to the Supreme Court in 1965 to replace Arthur Goldberg after Johnson persuaded Goldberg to resign to become the UN ambassador. Three years later, when Earl Warren announced his retirement contingent on the confirmation of his successor, Johnson nominated Fortas to be chief justice, and Judge Homer Thornberry to take Fortas's place as associate justice.

During his confirmation hearings to be chief justice, Fortas was extensively questioned about having received $15,000 for nine speeches at American University. Fortas also was questioned about his close relationship with President Johnson. All of this occurred in 1968, not long before the presidential election. Senator Strom Thurmond led a successful filibuster, stressing that a lame-duck president should not be able to fill vacancies on the Supreme Court.

Fortas's nomination was withdrawn, and Earl Warren remained chief justice. Not long after, more serious ethical issues came to light. In 1966, while a justice, Fortas had accepted a $20,000 retainer from Wall Street financier Louis Wolfson and signed a contract that was to provide him $20,000 a year for the rest of his life.

Wolfson was under investigation for securities violations at the time. When he was indicted, Fortas returned the money. After being convicted, Wolfson asked Fortas to help secure a pardon from President Johnson, which Fortas refused to do. When all of this came to light, impeachment resolutions were prepared against Fortas. He resigned from the bench, apparently at the urging of Chief Justice Warren.

In recent years, there have been some issues concerning the ethics of Supreme Court justices. In 2004, the Supreme Court had on its docket an important case concerning a claim of executive privilege by Vice President Dick Cheney. While the case was pending, Justice Antonin Scalia went duck hunting with Cheney. There was a request for Scalia to recuse himself, which he refused.

More significantly, a few years later it was revealed that Justice Clarence Thomas had not disclosed his wife's income for a number of years, even though this is required by law. Justice Thomas said that this was inadvertent and a result of his not reading the forms correctly. But year after year, he had clearly represented on these forms that his wife had no income, when that was not at all the case. As professor James Sample noted, "On a repeated basis, over a period during which his spouse earned $686,589.00 in income from a conservative foundation that opposed the [Affordable Care Act] on both policy and legal grounds, where the federal disclosure form asks, under potential criminal penalty, for spousal income, Justice Thomas checked 'none.'"

Even allegations of improprieties have significant costs, because it is so important that justices be beyond reproach. Codes of judicial ethics require that judges avoid even the appearance of impropriety. Nowhere is that more important than on the most visible court in the country, the U.S. Supreme Court.

Several steps should be taken to help ensure that there is both the perception and the reality of a Court complying with the highest possible ethical standards. First, the ethical standards applied to lower federal court judges should be applied to Supreme Court justices. With the exception of a few laws, the laws regulating ethics that all other federal judges must follow are not applicable to the Supreme Court. This should be changed immediately. There is no justification for this omission.

Second, no longer should it be left to each justice to decide for himself or herself whether to participate or be recused in a case. If a party requests that a justice be disqualified, it is entirely up to that justice whether to do so. Following the motion for Justice Scalia to recuse himself in the Cheney case, Scalia refused to do so by declaring that he could be sufficiently fair and impartial.

It should be axiomatic that a justice should not be ruling on his or her own disqualification. A simple alternative procedure would be to choose three other justices at random to rule on any motion that a justice be recused. Of course, there is the danger that the justices will simply defer to one another, but it is reasonable to assume that the justices will take this responsibility seriously, and no matter what, it is better than the current approach to recusal.

Finally, if a justice is disqualified from a case, a procedure should be devised whereby a retired justice (if one or more are alive), chosen at random, can participate as a justice instead. For example, in her first year on the Supreme Court, Justice Elena Kagan was recused from about one-third of the cases on the Court's docket, because they were matters that had been handled in her office when she was the solicitor general of the United States. When a justice is ill, as William Rehnquist was for many cases in his last term, again there are only eight justices participating. This creates a real danger of a 4–4 split, which means the lower court's decision is affirmed by an evenly decided court. No one's interests are served by this. All of the time spent briefing and arguing the case is wasted. The law remains unsettled until the Supreme Court can find another case posing the issue.

In many states, including California, if a state supreme court justice is recused, an appeals court judge fills in. An easy solution for the U.S. Supreme Court would be to allow a retired Supreme Court justice to participate. At this moment, there are three retired justices—Sandra Day O'Connor, David Souter, and John Paul Stevens. Both O'Connor and Souter continue to actively serve as judges, regularly sitting by designation on federal courts of appeals. If a justice is disqualified, one of the retired justices should be chosen at random. This would also lessen the pressure on justices to participate even when a conflict of interest, or the appearance of one, should cause them to withdraw. Senator Patrick Leahy has introduced legislation to accomplish this, and it should be adopted.

Courts throughout the world have been plagued at times by ethical improprieties by their judges. Sometimes this has been true in state courts in the United States. But ethical concerns about Supreme Court justices have been rare. Now that such concerns have surfaced, steps must be taken to ensure adherence to the highest ethical standards in the most visible and important court in the country.

Conclusion

One reason that I part company with scholars who propose eliminating judicial review is that I believe that the Supreme Court can be significantly improved. As I look back at some of the terrible mistakes made by the Court, I realize that they were not inevitable. In virtually every case that I have criticized, there was a dissent. Those dissents could have been the majority opinions.

A mystique surrounds the Court, one that for too long has shielded it from the criticism and scrutiny it deserves. It is time to realize that the institution we have so long revered is flawed and that change is essential. There are many things that can be done to improve the Court and its processes. Some can be implemented immediately by the Court, while others can be prescribed by statute; one or two would require a constitutional amendment. Taken together, they would be the most significant changes in the Supreme Court and its operations since its inception. Reform is long overdue.

Conclusion: How Should We Think and Talk About the Supreme Court?

I n 2005, Salvadoran immigrant Francisco Castaneda, a legal resident of the United States, was detained by the U.S. Immigration and Customs Enforcement (ICE) authorities for possession of methamphetamine. Pursuant to an agreement between the U.S. government and California, Castaneda was held by the California Department of Corrections and Rehabilitation in San Diego. While in custody, he repeatedly sought treatment for a lesion on his penis that was growing, frequently bleeding, and emitting a discharge. It became increasingly painful, and a lump developed in his groin. A U.S. Public Health Service physician assistant and three outside specialists said that he needed to have a biopsy to see whether he had cancer. However, officials of the ICE and the Department of Corrections refused to allow him to have this procedure, which he was told was "elective." Castaneda was denied the biopsy and was treated with ibuprofen and given an additional ration of boxer shorts.

His symptoms grew worse and worse. He filed a grievance report, asking for the recommended biopsy and stating that he was "in a considerable amount of pain and . . . in desperate need of medical attention." Soon after, he filed a report saying that his lesion was emitting a foul odor, continued to leak pus, and had increased in size, pressing further on his penis and increasing his discomfort. He complained of increased swelling, bleeding from the foreskin, and difficulty in urination. Still, he was not allowed to get the recommended biopsy.

Several months later, a California Department of Corrections official wrote that Castaneda said that his "symptoms have worsened. States he feels a constant pinching pain, especially at night. States he constantly has blood and discharge on his shorts. . . . Also complains of a swollen rectum which he states makes bowel movements hard." Castaneda was prescribed laxatives. The following day, Castaneda complained that the lesion was growing, that he could not stand and urinate because the urine "sprays everywhere," and that the lesion continued to leak blood and pus, continually staining his sheets and underwear. The response was to once more increase Castaneda's weekly allotment of boxer shorts.

Finally, a year after the biopsy had been recommended, it was performed. The test revealed that Castaneda was suffering from squamous cell carcinoma of the penis. Castaneda's penis was amputated, leaving only a two-centimeter stump. The cancer had already metastasized to his lymph nodes and throughout his body. He died a year after his diagnosis. He was thirty-six years old.

Before he died, Castaneda brought a lawsuit against the officials of the Public Health Service who had refused to provide the recommended biopsy. The U.S. Supreme Court previously had ruled that deliberate indifference to the medical needs of a prisoner is cruel and unusual punishment in violation of the Eighth Amendment. A person who is incarcerated cannot go and see a doctor to get treatment. Such a person depends entirely on those detaining him to provide essential medical care. If anything exemplifies deliberate indifference to a prisoner's medical needs, it was the experience of Francisco Castaneda.

The defendants moved to dismiss the lawsuit, but both the federal district court and the federal court of appeals ruled against them and said that the litigation should go forward. The Supreme Court in 2010 unanimously reversed and ordered that the lawsuit be dismissed. The Court held that the suit could not go forward because a federal statute created immunity from liability for Public Health Service officers. Justice Sotomayor, writing for the Court, stated, "Our inquiry in this case begins and ends with the text of §233(a)." The Court held that since the statute creates absolute immunity for Public Health Service officers, there could be no claims against them.

How can it be that a statute can preclude a constitutional claim? Even though this was a unanimous decision, this can't be right as a matter of constitutional law. Congress, by statute, cannot negate a constitutional right or its vindication. As a matter of human decency, it can't be right that a person can experience what Castaneda went through and be left with no remedy.

As I read the Supreme Court's decision in *Hui v. Castaneda* and then taught the case, I wondered if the Supreme Court hadn't lost faith in the courts and the importance of their being available to provide remedies to individuals. In fact, I think that many of the cases discussed in this book, especially from the Roberts Court, reflect a loss of faith in the judicial process. Its decisions denying recovery to those injured by generic drugs, its restrictions on class actions and its favoring of arbitration, its dramatic expansion of immunity for governments and government officials—all give the strong impression that the Supreme Court no longer trusts the courts and has lost confidence in the importance of judicial remedies.

I begin this chapter with *Hui v. Castaneda* because I think that it helps to answer some of the criticisms that might be leveled against the thesis that I have advanced throughout this book: Have I been fair to the Court, or am I just complaining that it has not been liberal enough? Is it realistic to expect that the Court could have done better? Has the Court just been following the law, and is it really the law—the Constitution and statutes—that is to blame and not the Supreme Court?

Fair Criticisms?

From the outset, in writing this book, I have been concerned that it would be criticized as a liberal's whining that the Court's decisions have not been liberal enough. But my goal was not to write *The Liberal Case Against the Supreme Court;* it was to make a case against the Supreme

Court that those all across the political spectrum can accept. *Hui v. Castaneda* was a unanimous case, and it was written by a liberal justice; but my hope is that all can agree that the Court was wrong in denying any remedy to Francisco Castaneda.

I do not expect that many today, even staunch conservatives, would defend the Supreme Court's decisions about slavery in the nineteenth century, its upholding of "separate but equal" for fifty-eight years, its allowing restrictions on ineffectual speech during World War I, its permitting the evacuation and internment of Japanese Americans in World War II, or its decisions from the 1890s through 1936 striking down more than two hundred federal, state, and local economic regulations. These and other historical examples provide a strong case against the Supreme Court, even if conservatives may disagree with some of my more recent examples of what I regard as misguided Supreme Court decisions.

I imagine that someone could say that I have picked out the occasional failures but that overall the Supreme Court has been a success. After all, the country has functioned as a democracy with freedom for more than two hundred years. The Supreme Court and the federal judiciary deserve some of the credit for that. But they also must shoulder some of the blame, and often a lion's share of it, for the denials of equality and liberty that have occurred through American history. It is no defense of the Supreme Court to say that it could have done much worse. My central point is that it could and should have done so much better.

The many examples throughout this book show that we are not talking about an occasional, isolated mistake. I want the reader to look cumulatively at the Court's decisions concerning race, its rulings about civil liberties in times of crisis, its decisions striking down essential economic regulations, its failure to do all it could to bring about school desegregation and ensure effective counsel for everyone facing a prison sentence, its decisions interpreting federal statutes to protect business at the expense of consumers and employees, its closing of the courthouse doors to those injured by the government. These are not minor matters in society; they involve some of the most important questions that have confronted the

United States throughout its history. They are not small blips that mattered for a short time. The Court protected the rights of slave owners for the first seventy years of American history. The Court enforced "separate but equal" for fifty-eight years. The *Lochner* era lasted almost forty years.

Could the Court Have Done Better?

Another criticism I expect is that I am being unfair to the Court because it was not realistic to expect it to have done better. I imagine the argument would be that the Court is a relatively powerless institution. In the words of Alexander Hamilton, in *The Federalist*, no. 78, the Court lacks the power of the "purse or the sword" and relies on voluntary compliance from other branches of government. Some of the most prominent justices and scholars in history—such as Felix Frankfurter, Alexander Bickel, and Jesse Choper—have reasoned from this that the Court has limited political capital and that it must be very cautious in what it does. Those who take this view might respond to my examples by arguing that it is unrealistic to expect the Court to have done better, given its limited powers and its need to conserve its political capital.

Hui v. Castaneda is useful here, too. It would not have cost the Court any of its political capital to rule in favor of Francisco Castaneda. Allowing Castaneda's estate to sue the prison officials who denied him essential medical treatment would not have harmed the Court's institutional legitimacy in any way.

More generally, I do not share the premise that the Court's political capital is scarce or that this is an excuse for the Court's failure to perform its key constitutional duties throughout so much of American history. When *Bush v. Gore* was decided, I was often asked whether the ruling would undermine the Court's legitimacy. I immediately said no—the Court's legitimacy was the product of all that it had done over two centuries, and no single decision or even series of decisions would undermine it. I was right. According to Gallup polls, 65 percent of Americans expressed confidence in the Court as an institution in September 2000, three months before the decision, and 62 percent expressed confidence in June 2001, six months after it.

One explanation of this, of course, is that *Bush v. Gore* enhanced the Republicans' view of the Court and lessened the Democrats' confidence in the Court, so it evened out. Again, the Gallup polls provided some support for this, showing that approval of the Court among Republicans went from 60 percent in August 2000 to 70 percent after the decision in December, while approval among Democrats shrank from 70 percent in August to 42 percent in December.

More important, the Supreme Court's legitimacy is not fragile. The credibility of the Court is the product of all that it has done over the course of American history; it is the result of confidence in the Court's methods and overall decisions. It reflects popular understanding of the desirability of resolving disputed questions in the courts and under the Constitution, even though it means that everyone knows that, at times, they will be on the losing side.

Moreover, if the Court made the mistakes described throughout this book because it was trying to preserve its credibility, then it seriously miscalculated. These decisions ultimately tarnished the Court and its legitimacy far more than they enhanced its reputation. Nonetheless, despite all of its failures, the Court retains its high credibility. As Professor John Hart Ely observed, "The possibility of judicial emasculation by way of popular reaction against constitutional review by the courts has not in fact materialized in more than a century and a half of American experience."

The Court's credibility, in part, is likely a function of its operating without scandal and with procedures that are open and fair. I think, too, that its credibility is a function of people not sufficiently recognizing that the justices were making choices not dictated by the Constitution or the laws, and not holding them accountable for their decisions.

Could the Court realistically have done better? I accept that it likely could not have eliminated slavery in the early years of American history, but it did not need to so aggressively protect the rights of slave owners or invalidate the Missouri Compromise in *Dred Scott v. Sandford*. It did not need to uphold "separate but equal" in *Plessy v. Ferguson* and could have done so much more to advance racial equality in the twentieth century and now. It could have ruled in favor of speech during World War I, found Japanese evacuation and internment unconstitutional in World War II, and done much more to protect civil liberties after 9/11. The rulings during the forty years of the *Lochner* era, striking down so many laws, certainly cannot be explained as the Court's trying to preserve its political capital. Nor can the more recent rulings interpreting statutes to protect business or denying relief to those suing the government be seen as inevitable or necessary for protecting the Court's legitimacy. None of these decisions have enhanced the Court's reputation and credibility. It is quite justifiable to have expected the Court to do better in all of these areas.

Is It Just Following the Law?

A final criticism of my thesis might be that it really isn't the Court's fault—that it was just following the law and that the real blame should be directed at the provisions of the Constitution and the federal statutes, not the Supreme Court's interpretation of them.

When John Roberts appeared before the Senate Judiciary Committee at his confirmation hearings, he proclaimed, "Judges are like umpires. Umpires don't make the rules; they apply them. The role of an umpire and a judge is critical. They make sure everybody plays by the rules, but it is a limited role. Nobody ever went to a ball game to see an umpire." The power of this conservative rhetoric was also seen in Justice Sonia Sotomayor's subsequent confirmation hearings, where she repeatedly told the members of the Senate Judiciary Committee that judges must "apply, not make the law."

Each of these brilliant jurists gave a terribly misleading impression of judging on the Supreme Court. Unlike umpires, justices on the Supreme Court create the rules. Anything the Supreme Court decides makes the law. Speaking of justices as umpires ignores the tremendous discretion the Supreme Court, and often the lower courts, have in deciding the cases before them.

John Roberts and Sonia Sotomayor should be ashamed of themselves for giving the American people such a misleading impression of what justices do. When John Roberts wrote in *Parents Involved v. Seattle* that diversity in elementary and high schools is not a compelling government interest and that school systems cannot use race as a factor in assigning students to achieve racial diversity, he was not being an umpire in any sense of the word. Roberts was taking his conservative values and using them to make desegregation more difficult. We can argue over whether his view is desirable, but there is no dispute that it was his views and not anything in the Constitution that explains his opinion. When Sonia Sotomayor wrote the opinion denying Francisco Castaneda recovery for his constitutional claim, she was, in fact, *making* a legal rule—that a statutory immunity can preclude recovery for a constitutional claim—not *applying* one.

Justices have tremendous discretion, in part because the Constitution is written in such broad language. The justices ultimately get to decide what is "cruel and unusual punishment" or what "equal protection of the laws" requires or what a law "respecting" the establishment of religion looks like or what constitutes "liberty." The justices cannot say that they are just following the text of the Constitution and being umpires, because the text gives them so much latitude. Does Section 3 of the Defense of Marriage Act, which says that federal law requires that marriage be between a man and a woman, deny equal protection of the laws? Nothing in the text of the Constitution can answer that question. Is a prison sentence of fifty years to life for stealing $153 worth of videotapes cruel and unusual punishment? Nothing in the text of the Constitution can answer that question. The decisions, in these and so many areas, are very much a product of the justices and their values.

Also, even if none of this were so, justices have tremendous discretion, because balancing competing interests is a persistent feature of constitutional decision making. How should the president's interest in executive privilege and secrecy be balanced against the need for evidence at a criminal trial? How should a defendant's right to a fair trial be balanced against the freedom of the press? No constitutional rights are absolute, and the Court has said that even the most precious rights can be infringed on if a government action is necessary for achieving a compelling government interest. Even race discrimination by the government is allowed if this test is met. But there is no way for justices to decide what is "compelling" except by making a value choice.

In deciding whether colleges and universities have a compelling interest in affirmative action and in using race as one factor in admissions decisions, all nine justices agreed that the issue to be decided was whether diversity in the classroom is a compelling government interest. The answer cannot be found in the text or the original understanding of the Equal Protection Clause or any other source. The justices had to make a choice about the importance of diversity, and not surprisingly, in *Grutter v. Bollinger,* in 2003, they split 5–4, with the five most liberal members then on the Court (Stevens, O'Connor, Souter, Ginsburg, and Breyer) voting that affirmative action serves a compelling interest and the four most conservative justices (Rehnquist, Scalia, Kennedy, and Thomas) dissenting.

In the context of campaign finance, the justices have had to decide whether spending money in elections is speech, whether corporations should have the same speech rights as individuals, and whether restrictions on corporate election spending are justified to prevent corporate wealth from distorting the political process and to protect shareholders who do not want their money spent that way. None of these questions can be resolved based on the language of the First Amendment or its original meaning, even if somehow that could be known.

Constitutional law constantly asks, as does so much of law, what is reasonable. Under the Fourth Amendment, which prohibits unreasonable searches and arrests, courts routinely focus on whether the actions of po-lice officers are reasonable. For example, the issue in a recent case was whether it was "unreasonable" for the government to take DNA from any-one arrested for a serious crime to help investigate other, unsolved crimes. The Court, by a 5–4 vote, upheld this as constitutional, concluding that it was reasonable because the law enforcement gains outweighed the inva-sion of privacy. Under the Takings Clause of the Fifth Amendment, courts examine whether the government, in taking private property for public use, acts out of a reasonable belief that its action will benefit the public. What is reasonable requires a choice by the justice or judge; it can-not be determined based on the text of the Constitution or its original meaning. It is all about the judge's perception of reasonableness, which is a product of the judge's life experiences and views.

In other words, all justices—liberals and conservatives—are making value choices. What, then, does a justice base his or her decision on? I am most definitely not arguing that it is just a matter of justices deciding based on a whim or their personal preferences. Throughout American history, the Supreme Court has based its constitutional decisions on many sources: the Constitution's text, its framers' intent, the Constitu-tion's structure, the Court's prior decisions, society's traditions, and con-temporary social policy considerations. A conscientious judge interpreting the Constitution will look to all of these sources in deciding cases and in explaining the rationale for his or her conclusions.

Of course, the fact that many sources are considered helps to explain why the Supreme Court has enormous discretion in deciding cases. So often these sources point in conflicting directions, or in no direction at all, because they just don't address the matters that the Court needs to resolve. This is what constitutional decision making always has been and always will be about. The justices cannot hide their decisions behind the text of the Constitution; the decisions described throughout this book reflect value choices made by the justices. They should be blamed or praised for their choices.

The central question in constitutional cases is so often whether the

Court should defer to the government or overrule the government's choices.

In fact, any Supreme Court decision striking down a government action can be criticized on the grounds that it is anti-democratic and the Court should have deferred to the political process. Both liberals and conservatives do this. On June 25, 2013, the Supreme Court declared unconstitutional a key provision of the Voting Rights Act of 1965. The five most conservative justices—Roberts, Scalia, Thomas, Kennedy, and Alito—made up the majority. Justice Ginsburg's dissent argued that the Court should have deferred to Congress. She stressed that Congress had compiled a voluminous record providing a continued need for the requirement that jurisdictions with a history of race discrimination get preclearance before changing their election systems. She noted that the vote in the Senate was 98–0 and there were only thirty-three "no" votes in the House of Representatives to extend the challenged provision for another twenty-five years. She wrote, "It is well established that Congress' judgment regarding exercise of its power to enforce the Fourteenth and Fifteenth Amendments warrants substantial deference."

The next day, June 26, the Court declared unconstitutional Section 3 of the Defense of Marriage Act. This time the liberal justices were in the majority, joined by Justice Kennedy. Justice Scalia wrote a dissent strongly criticizing the majority for not deferring to Congress. He said that the majority's holding was "jaw-dropping. It is an assertion of judicial supremacy over the people's Representatives in Congress and the Executive." Scalia pointed to the overwhelming margin by which the Defense of Marriage Act had been passed and argued that the Court should have deferred to Congress.

Tellingly, the four most conservative justices would have deferred to Congress on the Defense of Marriage Act but not on the Voting Rights Act. The four most liberal justices would have deferred to Congress on the Voting Rights Act but not the Defense of Marriage Act. Only Justice Kennedy was in the majority in both cases and voted to strike down both laws.

Liberal and conservative justices alike defer to the legislature when they agree with it and are willing to overrule it when they disagree. Let's stop pretending it is any other way.

Each year, as I teach first-year law students, I have the strong sense that many, maybe even most, come to law school believing that the law exists external to what the courts say and that the role of the justice is to find it and mechanically apply it. I speak often to audiences of non-lawyers and hear this view of the law in the questions I receive. It is such an appealing notion, and one that lets the courts escape responsibility for their choices. But it is an illusion that has no relationship to reality.

Let's admit that this emperor has no clothes. The justices made a value choice to favor the corrections officials over Francisco Castaneda, just as justices made a value choice to favor slave owners, and the government when it interned the Japanese Americans, and businesses when they have struck down so much regulatory legislation.

If we see the Court in this way, we can begin to hold it accountable for its decisions. Then we can fully appreciate the powerful case against the Supreme Court for the choices it has made throughout history. And then, and only then, can we think about how to reform the Court and make tragic mistakes less likely.

No institution in society is more important than the Supreme Court in ensuring liberty and justice for all. It is an institution, though, that has failed too often in these tasks. It is time to get past the facade of the marble columns and the mystique of justices who appear in robes from beyond heavy curtains, and focus on how to change the Court and its processes to make it more likely to live up to its crucial constitutional responsibilities. Freedom and equality—the Constitution's greatest aspirations—will be threatened in the future, likely in ways that we cannot now imagine. We will need a Court, perhaps even desperately so, that does better than it has in the past.

Acknowledgments

This book was far harder to write than I could have imagined. Although I have been teaching and writing about constitutional law for more than three decades, writing this book forced me to think about the Supreme Court in a very different way. I realized that, especially in my teaching, I presented a generally favorable picture of the Supreme Court. I discovered that even in my own mind I had been making excuses for the Court. The challenge in writing this book was to try to stop doing that and look critically at the Court, throughout history and now, appreciating its successes and recognizing its failures.

As a result, writing the book took longer than I had planned. I am very grateful to Wendy Wolf, at Viking, for her patience in waiting for the manuscript and for her wonderful suggestions on an earlier draft. I also am so appreciative to my literary agent, Bonnie Nadell, for helping me to formulate the thesis for this book and for pushing me to get it done. I had wanted to work on a book with Bonnie for many years, and I hope that this is the first of many projects that we will do together.

My work on this book was tremendously aided by many talented research assistants at the University of California, Irvine School of Law: Francisco Balderrama, Facon Bekam, Hikmat Chehabi, Melissa Martorella, James Miller, Kathryn Riley, Philip Syers, and Tina Salvato.

As always, my wonderful assistant, Brandy Stewart, provided tremendous support and made it possible for me to juggle everything to get this book done.

No words can express my appreciation to a few very special people who took time from their own work to read this manuscript and give me invaluable suggestions. Joan Biskupic, Jeff Chemerinsky, Howard Gillman, and Jim Newton read the entire manuscript and offered me terrific suggestions on how to make it better. I tried to take all of their advice, but if there are instances where I didn't follow their suggestions, this book is the worse for it. They are all superb writers, whom I only can try to emulate, and their comments helped me enormously.

Finally, the thoughts and ideas of Catherine Fisk are reflected on every page of this book. We talked about every aspect of the manuscript, and whenever I was stuck, her guidance helped me move forward. She also believed that I could get this book done when I had serious doubts, and her confidence in me mattered more than words can say.

I have dedicated this book to my family—to Catherine and to Jeff, Kim, Adam, Alex, and Mara. They are truly the greatest joy in my very blessed life.

Notes

Introduction: Assessing the Supreme Court

1   **Carrie Buck was born:** The story of *Buck v. Bell*, on which this is based, is told in detail in Harry Bruinius, *Better for All the World: The Secret History of Forced Sterilization and America's Quest for Racial Purity* (New York: Vintage, 2007); and Paul A. Lombardo, *Three Generations, No Imbeciles: Eugenics, the Supreme Court, and* Buck v. Bell (Baltimore: Johns Hopkins Press, 2008).

2   **He began his "family history":** Lombardo, *Three Generations,* 134 (quoting deposition of Harry Laughlin, Transcript of Record at 41).

2   **"there is a look about it that is not quite normal":** Paul A. Lombardo, "Three Generations, No Imbeciles: New Light on *Buck v. Bell,*" 60 *New York University Law Review* 30, 60–61 (1985).

2   **Paul Lombardo found Carrie Buck:** Stephen J. Gould, "Carrie Buck's Daughter," 2 *Constitutional Commentary* 331, 336 (1985) (quoting a letter from Paul A. Lombardo, of the School of Law at the University of Virginia).

2   **Stephen Jay Gould tracked down her records:** Ibid.

3   **Carrie Buck's sister, Doris:** Paul Steven Miller, "Genetic Testing and the Future of Disability Insurance: Thinking About Discrimination in the Genetic Age," 35 *Journal of Law, Medicine and Ethics* 47, 48 (2007).

3   **Before World War II:** Victor W. Sidel, "The Social Responsibilities of Health Professionals: Lessons from Their Role in Nazi Germany," 276 *JAMA* 1679 (1996); Jeremiah A. Barondess, "Medicine Against Society: Lessons from the Third Reich," 276 *JAMA* 1657, 1657–60 (1996) (noting that the German Medical Association, in accordance with the German sterilization law of 1933, published a journal to guide physicians and special "eugenical courts" in determining which patients were appropriate subjects for sterilization).

3   **Buck's attorney, Irving Whitehead:** Lombardo, "Three Generations," 33, 38–39 (describing Whitehead and his role in the eugenics movement).

3   **His opinions in many areas:** For example, his opinion in *Abrams v. United States,* 250 U.S. 616, 624–31 (1919) (Holmes, J., dissenting), articulated the idea that the First Amendment is meant to create a marketplace of ideas.

4   **Holmes began his opinion:** *Buck v. Bell,* 274 U.S. 200, 205 (1927).

4   **"swamped with incompetence":** Ibid., 274 U.S. at 207.

4   **In some of the most offensive:** Ibid.

4   **more than twenty thousand forced sterilizations:** Edward J. Larson, "The Meaning of Human Gene Testing for Disability Rights," 70 *University of Cincinnati Law Review* 913, 916 (2002).

4   **Altogether, . . . "over 60,000 Americans":** Roberta Cepko, "Involuntary Sterilization of Mentally Disabled Women," 8 *Berkeley Women's Law Journal* 122, 123 (1993) (reporting that after *Buck,* twenty states embraced eugenic sterilization legislation, resulting in more than sixty thousand sterilizations of women prior to 1950).

4   **It is not that her case:** Although the briefs and oral argument transcript reflect that the key arguments were made, others dispute the quality of the representation. See John G. Browning, "Justice Red in Tooth and Claw: A Review of *Three Generations, No Imbeciles: Eugenics, the Supreme Court and* Buck v. Bell, by Paul A. Lombardo," 37 *Journal of Law, Medicine and Ethics* 517, 520 (2009) ("Buck's attorney, Irving Whitehead, failed to offer more than a token defense. This is not surprising. Whitehead was himself a eugenics advocate, a founding member of the Virginia Colony's board of directors, and a key supporter of the sterilization campaign being pushed by Dr. Albert Priddy, the Colony's superintendent").

4   **In fact, most lower courts:** Victoria Nourse, "*Buck v. Bell:* A Constitutional Tragedy from a Lost World," 39 *Pepperdine Law Review* 101, 102n8 (2011) ("Prior to 1922, only one of seven challenges upheld a sterilization law").

7   **Great Britain, for example:** Mark Tushnet, *Taking the Constitution Away from the Courts* (Princeton, N.J.: Princeton University Press, 2000), 163.

7   **In the Netherlands:** Ibid.

8   **Harvard law professor Laurence Tribe:** Laurence Tribe, *American Constitutional Law,* 3rd ed. (Mineola, N.Y.: Foundation Press, 2000), 10.

9   **Professor Thomas Grey:** Thomas Grey, "The Constitution as Scripture," 37 *Stanford Law Review* 1, 3 (1984).

10 **The Court's choice in 1857:** *Dred Scott v. Sandford,* 60 U.S. 393 (1857), discussed in chapter 1.

11 **The Court's choice in 2011:** *Connick v. Thompson,* 131 S. Ct. 1350 (2011), discussed in chapter 6.

13 *Bush v. Gore:* Bush v. Gore, 531 U.S. 98 (2000), discussed in chapter 7.

13 *Citizens United v. Federal Election Commission: Citizens United v. Federal Election Commission,* 558 U.S. 310 (2010), discussed in chapter 7.

13 *Shelby County, Alabama v. Holder:* Shelby County, Alabama v. Holder, 133 S. Ct. 2612 (2013), discussed in chapter 7.

15 **Soon after her sterilization:** Lombardo, "Three Generations," 60–61.

15 **the Court declared in** *Skinner v. Oklahoma:* Skinner v. Oklahoma, 316 U.S. 535 (1942).

15 **"We are dealing here":** Ibid., 316 U.S. at 541.

16 **Twenty-two states:** Lisa Powell, "Eugenics and Inequality," 20 *Yale Law and Policy Review* 481, 489 (2002).

16 **In July 1971:** *Stump v. Sparkman,* 435 U.S. 349 (1978).

17 **As Justice Potter Stewart said:** Ibid., 435 U.S. at 367 (Stewart, J., dissenting).

Chapter 1: Protecting Minorities

22 **Consider . . . a case from 1842:** *Prigg v. Pennsylvania,* 41 U.S. (16 Pet.) 539 (1852).

23 **Story was one of the most revered:** Melvin I. Urofsky, *The Supreme Court Justices: A Biographical Dictionary* (New York: Garland, 1994), 590.

23 Story said that the "object of this clause": *Prigg v. Pennsylvania,* 41 U.S. at 311.

23 the Fugitive Slave Clause "was so vital": Ibid.

23 "we have not the slightest hesitation": Ibid., 41 U.S. at 613.

24 *Dred Scott v. Sandford: Dred Scott v. Sandford,* 60 U.S. (19 How.) 393 (1856).

24 After Emerson died, his estate was administered by John Sandford: His name was actually Sanford, but it was misspelled by a clerk and the misspelling has remained in the name of the case.

25 Taney was the fifth chief justice: Clare Cushman, *The Supreme Court Justices: Illustrated Biographies, 1789–1995,* 2nd ed. (Washington, D.C.: Congressional Quarterly Books, Supreme Court Historical Society, 1995).

25 "a subordinate and inferior class of beings": *Dred Scott v. Sandford,* 60 U.S. 404–5.

25 The Court reviewed the laws: Ibid., 60 U.S. at 409.

25 The first was *Marbury v. Madison: Marbury v. Madison,* 5 U.S. (1 Cranch) 137 (1803).

26 "the act of Congress . . . is therefore void": *Dred Scott v. Sandford,* 60 U.S. at 451–52.

26 But on May 26, 1857: Gwenyth Swain, *Dred and Harriet Scott: A Family's Struggle for Freedom* (St. Paul, Minn.: Borealis Books, 2004).

27 Spielberg's recent movie: The movie is drawn from a brief description of these events in Doris Kearns Goodwin, *Team of Rivals* (New York: Simon & Schuster, 2005).

29 Soon after the Fourteenth Amendment: *Coleman v. Miller,* 307 U.S. 443, 448 (1939) (describing the history of the ratification of the Fourteenth Amendment).

29 Section 5 of the Reconstruction Act: 14 Stat. 429 (1867) ("[W]hen said State, by a vote of its legislature elected under said constitution, shall have adopted the amendment to the Constitution of the United States, proposed by the Thirty-ninth Congress, and known as article fourteen, and when said article shall have become a part of the Constitution of the United States, said State shall be declared entitled to representation in Congress").

30 the Slaughter-House Cases: Slaughter-House Cases (*Butchers' Benevolent Assn. of New Orleans v. Crescent City Live-Stock Landing & Slaughter-House Co.*), 83 U.S. (16 Wall.) 36 (1873).

31 "No questions so far reaching": Ibid., 83 U.S. at 67.

31 "[t]he most cursory glance at these articles": Ibid., 83 U.S. at 71.

32 Equal Protection Clause was meant to protect only blacks: Ibid., 83 U.S. at 81.

32 For example, in 1875: *Minor v. Happersett,* 88 U.S. 162 (1875).

33 Earlier justices had ruled: *Corfield v. Coryell,* 6 F. Cas. 546 (C.C.E.D. Pa. 1823).

33 This provision of the Fourteenth Amendment: *Adamson v. California,* 332 U.S. 46 (1947) (Black, J., dissenting).

33 "would constitute this court a perpetual censor": Slaughter-House Cases, 83 U.S. at 498.

33 " 'privileges and immunities' . . . are left to the State governments": Ibid.

33 Justice Stephen Johnson Field, in dissent: Ibid., 83 U.S. at 521 (Field, J., dissenting).

34 Professor Edward Corwin remarked: Edward Corwin, ed., *The Constitution of the United States of America* (Washington, D.C.: Legislative Reference Service, 1953) at 965.

34 only twice has the Court found anything to violate it: *Colgate v. Harvey,* 296 U.S. 404 (1935), relied on the Privileges or Immunities Clause to invalidate a state tax; it was overruled in *Madden v. Kentucky,* 309 U.S. 83 (1940). *Saenz v. Roe,* 526 U.S. 489 (1999),

used the Privileges or Immunities Clause to strike down a California law that limited welfare benefits for new residents to the level of those in the state that they moved from.

35 **The most important such case:** *Plessy v. Ferguson*, 163 U.S. 537 (1896).

35 **Although a northerner:** Ibid., 163 U.S. at 550–51.

36 **The Supreme Court rejected:** Ibid., 163 U.S. at 551.

36 **John Marshall Harlan was the sole dissenter:** Ibid., 163 U.S. at 559–60 (Harlan, J., dissenting).

36 **Justice Harlan concluded eloquently:** Ibid., 163 U.S. at 559.

36 **Harlan saw the obvious parallel:** Ibid., 163 U.S. at 560.

37 **Southern states, border states:** C. Vann Woodward, *The Strange Career of Jim Crow*, 3rd ed. (New York: Oxford University Press, 1974).

37 **In *Cumming v. Board of Education*:** *Cumming v. Board of Education*, 175 U.S. 128 (1899).

38 **In *Berea College v. Kentucky*:** *Berea College v. Kentucky*, 211 U.S. 45 (1908).

38 **In *Gong Lum v. Rice*:** *Gong Lum v. Rice*, 275 U.S. 78 (1927).

38 **The Court said that the law was settled:** Ibid., 275 U.S. at 87.

38 **In 1954, this changed:** *Brown v. Board of Education*, 347 U.S. 483 (1954).

38 **In October Term 1952:** For an excellent history of the litigation in *Brown,* see Richard Kluger, *Simple Justice* (New York: Random House, 1974).

39 **Justice William O. Douglas's autobiography:** William O. Douglas, *The Court Years: 1939–1975* (New York: Random House, 1980).

40 **In the words of Chief Justice John Marshall:** *McCulloch v. Maryland*, 17 U.S. (4 Wheat.) 316, 415 (1819).

40 **The cases were argued on October 13, 1953:** Richard Kluger provides a detailed description of what occurred in *Simple Justice* (New York: Random House, 1974) at 545–749.

42 ***Washington v. Davis,* in 1976:** *Washington v. Davis*, 426 U.S. 229 (1976).

42 **Justice Byron White, writing for the majority:** Ibid., 426 U.S. at 242.

42 **For example, in *Mobile v. Bolden*:** *Mobile v. Bolden*, 446 U.S. 55 (1980).

43 **"[O]nly if there is purposeful discrimination":** Ibid., 446 U.S. at 67.

43 **Similarly, in *McCleskey v. Kemp*:** *McCleskey v. Kemp*, 481 U.S. 279 (1987).

43 **A study conducted by . . . professor David Baldus:** David C. Baldus et al., "Comparative Review of Death Sentences: An Empirical Study of the Georgia Experience," 74 *Journal of Criminal Law and Criminology* 661 (1983).

44 **"must prove . . . discriminatory purpose":** *McCleskey v. Kemp*, 481 U.S. at 292.

44 **"would have to prove that the Georgia legislature":** Ibid., 481 U.S. at 298.

44 **punishments for crack cocaine:** Deleso Alford Washington, " 'Every Shut Eye, Ain't Sleep': Exploring the Impact of Crack Cocaine Sentencing and the Illusion of Reproductive Rights for Black Women from a Critical Race Feminist Perspective," 13 *American University Journal of Gender, Social Policy and the Law* 123, 134–36 (2005); Laura A. Wytsma, "Punishment for 'Just Us'—A Constitutional Analysis of the Crack Cocaine Sentencing Statutes," 3 *George Mason Independent Law Review* 473, 473–74, 490–91 (1995). For an excellent discussion of this and its racially discriminatory effects, see Michelle Alexander, *The New Jim Crow* (New York: New Press, 2010).

45 **Scholars such as professor Charles Lawrence:** Charles Lawrence, "The Id, the Ego, and Equal Protection: Reckoning with Unconscious Racism," 41 *Stanford Law Review* 317, 355 (1987).

45 **Professor Laurence Tribe explains:** Laurence Tribe, *American Constitutional Law*, 2nd ed. (Mineola, N.Y.: Foundation Press, 1988), 1516.

46 **"all racial classifications imposed by government":** *Adarand Constructors, Inc. v. Peña*, 515 U.S. 200, 227 (1995).

46 **Lempert forcefully explains:** Richard Lempert, "The Force of Irony: On the Morality of Affirmative Action and *United Steelworkers v. Weber*," 95 *Ethics* 86, 88–89 (1984).

47 **Lempert concludes, "A claim made":** Ibid.

47 **Professor John Hart Ely explained:** John Hart Ely, "The Constitutionality of Reverse Racial Discrimination," 41 *University of Chicago Law Review* 723, 735 (1974).

47 **The significance of the Court's failure:** *Parents Involved in Community Schools v. Seattle School District No. 1*, 555 U.S. 701 (2007).

49 **Justice Breyer concluded his dissent:** Ibid., 555 U.S. at 868 (Breyer, J., dissenting).

49 **In *J. A. Croson v. City of Richmond*:** *J. A. Croson v. City of Richmond*, 488 U.S. 469 (1989).

49 **In *Wygant v. Jackson Board of Education*:** *Wygant v. Jackson Board of Education*, 476 U.S. 267 (1986).

49 **In *Grutter v. Bollinger*:** *Grutter v. Bollinger*, 539 U.S. 306 (2003).

49 **In a companion case:** *Gratz v. Bollinger*, 539 U.S. 244 (2003).

49 **The Court returned to the issue:** *Fisher v. University of Texas at Austin*, 133 S. Ct. 2411 (2013).

50 **a "careful judiciary inquiry":** Ibid., 133 S. Ct. at 2420.

50 **"The reviewing Court must ultimately be satisfied":** Ibid.

Chapter 2: Enforcing the Constitution in Times of Crisis

54 **110,000 Japanese Americans:** William Manchester, *The Glory and the Dream* (Boston: Little, Brown, 1974), 299.

54 **under Executive Order 9066:** Ibid., 300.

55 **"Beginning at dawn on Monday":** Ibid., 300–301.

55 **The constitutionality of the evacuation:** *Korematsu v. United States*, 323 U.S. 214 (1944).

56 **Korematsu did everything he could think of:** Steven A. Chin, *When Justice Failed: The Fred Korematsu Story* (Houndmills, UK: Raintree, 1992).

56 **Justice Black stated:** *Korematsu v. United States*, 323 U.S. at 218–19.

57 **"hardships are part of war":** Ibid., 323 U.S. at 219.

57 **Korematsu is deeply objectionable:** Eugene Rostow, "The Japanese-American Cases: A Disaster," 54 *Yale Law Journal* 489 (1945).

57 **attorneys intentionally exaggerated the risk:** Peter H. Irons, *Justice Delayed: The Record of the Japanese American Internment Cases* (Middletown, Conn.: Wesleyan University Press, 1989).

57 **As Justice Frank Murphy lamented:** *Korematsu v. United States*, 323 U.S. at 235 (Murphy, J., dissenting).

57 **In England:** Ibid., 323 U.S. at 242n16.

58 **Korematsu's "crime would result":** Ibid., 323 U.S. at 243 (Jackson, J., dissenting).

58 **"This exclusion of 'all persons'":** Ibid., 323 U.S. at 242 (Murphy, J., dissenting).

58 **"I dissent, therefore":** Ibid.

59 **the Non-Detention Act:** 18 U.S.C. § 4001(a) (Non–Detention Act), which bars imprisonment or detention of a citizen "except pursuant to an Act of Congress."

59   **prominent jurists . . . have written books:** William Rehnquist, *All the Laws But One: Civil Liberties in War Time* (New York: Vintage, 2000); Richard Posner, *Not a Suicide Pact: The Constitution in a Time of National Emergency* (New York: Oxford University Press, 2006).

59   **"like a loaded weapon":** *Korematsu v. United States,* 323 U.S. at 245 (Jackson, J., dissenting).

59   **Whenever there has been a crisis:** Geoffrey Stone, *Perilous Times: Free Speech in Wartime* (New York: W. W. Norton, 2004).

61   **much opposition to the draft:** Ibid.

61   **the Espionage Act:** Pub. L. 65-24, 40 Stat. 217.

61   **"The postmaster at the time":** Thomas Healy, *The Great Dissent: How Oliver Wendell Holmes Changed His Mind and Changed the History of Free Speech in America* (New York: Metropolitan Books, 2013), 18.

61   **a law even more restrictive:** Sedition Act of 1918, Pub. L. 65-150, 40 Stat. 553.

62   **"a deduction from the basic American agreement":** Alexander Meiklejohn, *Free Speech and Its Relation to Self-Government* (New York: Harper Bros. Books, 1948), 27.

62   **"[s]elf-government can exist only insofar":** Alexander Meiklejohn, "The First Amendment Is an Absolute," 1961 *Supreme Court Review* 245, 255.

62   **"the central meaning of the First Amendment":** *New York Times v. Sullivan,* 376 U.S. 254, 273 (1964).

62   **Alien and Sedition Acts of 1798:** John C. Miller, *Crisis in Freedom: The Alien and Sedition Acts* (New York: Little, Brown, 1951).

63   **"Although the Sedition Act was never tested in this Court":** *New York Times v. Sullivan,* 376 U.S. at 276.

63   **In *Schenck v. United States*:** *Schenck v. United States,* 249 U.S. 47 (1919).

63   **As professor Thomas Healy pointed out:** Healy, *The Great Dissent,* 82.

64   **"Of course the document would not have been sent":** *Schenck v. United States,* 249 U.S. at 51.

64   **wartime circumstances made the situation different:** Ibid., 249 U.S. at 52.

64   **In some of the most famous words:** Ibid.

65   **A week after *Schenck*:** *Frohwerk v. United States,* 249 U.S. 204 (1919); *Debs v. United States,* 249 U.S. 211 (1919).

65   **"[f]or the most part . . . the articles were tame":** Healy, *The Great Dissent,* 84.

65   **"on the record it is impossible to say":** *Frohwerk v. United States,* 249 U.S. at 209.

66   **In *Debs v. United States*:** *Debs v. United States,* 249 U.S. at 211.

66   **Debs was a national political figure:** Healy, *The Great Dissent,* 86.

66   **Although he never got more than 6 percent:** Ibid.

66   **"you need to know that you are fit for something":** Ibid., 87–89.

66   **Holmes said that the speech was not protected:** *Debs v. United States,* 249 U.S. at 214–15.

66   **if its intent was "to oppose the war":** Ibid., 249 U.S. at 215.

67   **a group of Russian immigrants:** *Abrams v. United States,* 250 U.S. 616 (1919).

67   **Holmes invoked the powerful metaphor:** Ibid., 250 U.S. at 630 (Holmes, J., dissenting).

67   **Professor Healy observed:** Healy, *The Great Dissent,* 250.

67   **"Now nobody can suppose that the surreptitious publishing":** *Abrams v. United States,* 250 U.S. at 628 (Holmes, J., dissenting).

67 "never [had] seen any reason to doubt": Ibid., 250 U.S. at 627 (Holmes, J., dissenting).

67 But in a recent book: Thomas Healy, *The Great Dissent.*

68 the rise of McCarthyism: John Lewis Gaddis, *The United States and the Origins of the Cold War, 1941–1947* (New York: Columbia University Press, 1972).

68 Joseph McCarthy, a senator: Ellen Shrecker, *The Age of McCarthyism* (New York: Macmillan, 2007).

69 *Dennis v. United States: Dennis v. United States,* 341 U.S. 494 (1951).

69 Section 2 of the Smith Act: Act of June 28, 1940, 54 Stat. 670, 671.

69 Section 3 made it "unlawful": 54 Stat. at 671.

69 a formula articulated by . . . Learned Hand: *Dennis v. United States,* 341 U.S. at 510.

70 "Obviously, the words cannot mean": Ibid., 341 U.S. at 509.

70 those justices "were not confronted": Ibid., 341 U.S. at 506–7.

70 "[p]rimary responsibility for adjusting": Ibid., 341 U.S. at 525 (Frankfurter, J., concurring).

70 "[f]ree speech cases are not an exception": Ibid., 341 U.S. at 539.

71 Justice Black lamented: Ibid., 341 U.S. at 579 (Black, J., dissenting).

71 "[t]here must be some immediate injury": Ibid., 341 U.S. at 585 (Douglas, J., dissenting).

71 "How it can be said": Ibid., 341 U.S. at 588–89.

72 *Holder v. Humanitarian Law Project,* decided: *Holder v. Humanitarian Law Project,* 130 S. Ct. 2705 (2010).

72 Federal law prohibits: 18 U.S.C. § 2339B.

72 "Under the material-support statute": *Holder v. Humanitarian Law Project,* 130 S. Ct. at 2722.

73 He explained that prior cases: Ibid., 130 S. Ct. at 2737 (Breyer, J., dissenting).

73 In December 2005, the *New York Times:* James Risen and Eric Lichtblau, "Bush Lets U.S. Spy on Callers Without Courts," *New York Times,* December 16, 2005, A1.

74 *New York Times* reporter Eric Lichtblau: Eric Lichtblau, *Bush's Law: The Remaking of American Justice* (New York: Pantheon, 2008), 137.

74 "blood would be on their hands": Ibid., 208.

74 The law has long been clear: *Katz v. United States,* 389 U.S. 347 (1967).

74 The Foreign Intelligence Surveillance Act: Foreign Intelligence Surveillance Act (FISA), 50 U.S.C. §§ 1801–1885(c) (2012).

74 No challenge ever was heard: A federal district court declared the NSA surveillance unconstitutional: *American Civil Liberties Union v. National Security Agency,* 438 F. Supp.2d 754 (E.D. Mich. 2006). But the federal court of appeals reversed, in a 2–1 decision, for lack of standing: *American Civil Liberties Union v. National Security Agency,* 493 F.3d 644 (6th Cir. 2007). The Supreme Court then denied certiorari: 553 U.S. 1179 (2008).

74 Congress amended FISA: FISA Amendments Act of 2008, 122 Stat. 2436.

74 Upon the issuance of an order: 50 U.S.C. § 1881a(a).

75 On the day that the 2008 amendments were enacted: *Clapper v. Amnesty International USA,* 133 S. Ct. 1138, 1145–46 (2013) (describing the history of the litigation).

75 The Supreme Court, in an opinion by Justice Alito: Ibid., 133 S. Ct. at 1138.

75 "[I]t is speculative whether the Government": Ibid., 133 S. Ct. at 1149.

75 **"[a]llegations of a subjective 'chill' "**: Ibid., 133 S. Ct. at 1152.

76 **"The assumption that if respondents"**: Ibid., 133 S. Ct. at 1154.

76 **Justice Breyer, writing for the dissent**: Ibid., 133 S. Ct. at 1165 (Breyer, J., dissenting).

77 **166 prisoners at Guantánamo:** Dianne Feinstein and Dick Durbin, "How to Close Guantanamo," *Los Angeles Times,* August 13, 2013.

77 **José Padilla is an American citizen:** *Rumsfeld v. Padilla,* 542 U.S. 426, 430 (2004).

77 **Padilla says that during this time he was tortured:** *Padilla v. Yoo,* 678 F.3d 748 (9th Cir. 2012). (Padilla's suit describing his torture was dismissed by the federal court of appeals.)

78 **federal court in New York lacked the authority:** *Rumsfeld v. Padilla,* 542 U.S. 426 (2004).

78 **Justice Stevens wrote for the four dissenters:** Ibid., 542 U.S. at 455 (Stevens, J., dissenting).

79 **In a footnote near the end:** Ibid., 542 U.S. at 464n8 (Stevens, J., dissenting).

79 **Justice Scalia . . . was emphatic:** *Hamdi v. Rumsfeld,* 542 U.S. 507, 554 (2004) (Scalia, J., dissenting).

79 **The federal district court ruled in Padilla's favor:** *Padilla v. Hanft,* 389 F.Supp.2d 678 (D.S.C. 2005).

79 **the Fourth Circuit reversed:** *Padilla v. Hanft,* 423 F.3d 386 (4th Cir. 2005).

80 **In January 2006, the Supreme Court agreed:** *Padilla v. Hanft,* 542 U.S. 1062 (2006).

80 **Yaser Hamdi was captured:** *Hamdi v. Rumsfeld,* 542 U.S. at 507.

81 **On June 28, 2004, the Supreme Court held:** Ibid.

81 **The Non-Detention Act states:** 18 U.S.C. § 4001(a).

82 **Since January 2002:** Joseph Margulies, *Guantánamo and the Abuse of Presidential Power* (New York: Simon & Schuster, 2006).

82 **Senators Dianne Feinstein and Dick Durbin:** Dianne Feinstein and Dick Durbin, "How to Close Guantanamo," *Los Angeles Times* (Aug. 13, 2013).

83 ***Rasul v. Bush,* in 2004:** *Rasul v. Bush,* 542 U.S. 466 (2004).

83 **In March 2003, the United States Court of Appeals:** *Al-Odah v. Bush,* 321 F.3d 1134 (D.C. Cir. 2003).

83 **The court of appeals based this conclusion:** *Johnson v. Eisentrager,* 339 U.S. 763 (1950).

83 **The Supreme Court, in a 6–3 decision:** *Rasul v. Bush,* 542 U.S. 466 (2004).

84 **Immediately after the Court's decision:** Detainee Treatment Act of 2005, Tit. X, 119 Stat. 2739.

84 **In 2006, in *Hamdan v. Rumsfeld*:** *Hamdan v. Rumsfeld,* 548 U.S. 557 (2006).

84 **Congress then responded to *Hamdan*:** Military Commissions Act of 2006, 28 U.S.C. § 2241(e) (2007 Supp.)

84 **In *Boumediene v. Bush,* in 2008:** *Boumediene v. Bush,* 533 U.S. 733 (2008).

85 **"We hold that petitioners may invoke":** Ibid., 533 U.S. at 798.

85 **"Today the Court strikes down":** Ibid., 533 U.S. at 801 (Roberts, C. J., dissenting).

85 **"What competence does the Court have":** Ibid., 533 U.S. at 831 (Scalia, J., dissenting).

86 **For example, on June 11, 2012:** Erwin Chemerinsky, "Losing Interest," *National Law Journal,* June 25, 2012.

86 **In *Kiyemba v. Obama*:** *Kiyemba v. Obama,* 605 F.3d 1046 (D.C. Cir. 2010).

86 **In *Latif v. Obama*:** *Latif v. Obama,* 677 F.3d 1175 (D.C. Cir. 2012).

87   **D.C. Circuit judge David Tatel said:** Ibid., 677 F.3d at 1216 (Tatel, J., dissenting).

87   **The Supreme Court denied review:** *Latif v. Obama, cert. denied,* 132 S. Ct. 2741 (2012).

87   **"careless people" making messes:** Richard Brust, "The Guantanamo Quagmire," *ABA Journal,* October 5, 2012.

87   **"*Boumediene*'s airy suppositions":** *Latif v. Obama,* 677 F.3d at 1199.

88   **In February 2002, I argued:** *Coalition of Clergy, Lawyers, and Professors v. Bush,* 189 F.Supp.2d 1036 (C.D. Cal. 2002).

89   **This was precisely Justice Jackson's point:** *Korematsu v. United States,* 323 U.S. at 245 (Jackson, J., dissenting).

Chapter 3: Protecting Property and States' Rights

90   **the use of child labor:** Child Labor Public Education Project, "Child Labor in U.S. History," http://www.continuetolearn.uiowa.edu/laborctr/child_labor/about/us _history.html.

90   **By 1900, "children worked".** Ibid.

90   **two million children aged sixteen and under:** Russell Freedman, *Kids at Work: Lewis Hine and the Crusade against Child Labor* (Boston: Houghton Mifflin, 1994), 1–2.

91   **David Clark, publisher of the *Southern Textile Bulletin:*** Seymour Moskowitz, "Dickens Redux: How American Child Labor Law Became a Con Game," 10 *Whittier Journal of Child and Family Advocacy* 89, 112 (2010).

91   **In *Hammer v. Dagenhart,* in 1918:** *Hammer v. Dagenhart,* 247 U.S. 251 (1918).

92   **The Court said that regulating:** Ibid., 247 U.S. at 276.

92   **"The far reaching result":** Ibid.

92   **the Lottery Case:** *Champion v. Ames* (The Lottery Case), 188 U.S. 321 (1903).

93   **"[T]he possible abuse of a power":** Ibid., 188 U.S. at 363.

93   **the "pestilence of lotteries":** Ibid., 188 U.S. at 356.

94   **In 1941, the Supreme Court:** *United States v. Darby,* 312 U.S. 100 (1941).

94   **By the late nineteenth century:** Howard Gillman, *The Constitution Besieged: The Rise and Demise of the Lochner Era* (Durham, N.C.: Duke University Press, 1993); Morton Horwitz, *The Transformation of American Law, 1870–1960* (Cambridge, Mass.: Harvard University Press, 1992).

95   **The most famous case during this period:** *Lochner v. New York,* 198 U.S. 45 (1905).

96   **The Court in *Lochner* expressly declared:** Ibid., 198 U.S. at 53.

96   **In *Allgeyer v. Louisiana,* in 1897:** *Allgeyer v. Louisiana,* 165 U.S. 578 (1897).

96   **He quoted one study:** *Lochner v. New York,* 198 U.S. at 69 (Harlan, J., dissenting).

97   **The Court said, "Clean and wholesome bread":** Ibid., 198 U.S. at 57, 61.

97   **"There is no contention that bakers":** Ibid., 198 U.S. at 57.

97   **"It is impossible for us to shut our eyes":** Ibid., 198 U.S. at 64.

98   **With regard to laws protecting unions:** *Adair v. United States,* 208 U.S. 161 (1908); *Coppage v. Kansas,* 236 U.S. 1 (1915).

98   **In *Adair,* the Court said:** *Adair v. United States,* 208 U.S. at 174.

98   **The Court said that an individual:** *Coppage v. Kansas,* 236 U.S. at 19.

99   **In *Adkins v. Children's Hospital:*** *Adkins v. Children's Hospital,* 261 U.S. 525 (1923).

99   **Three years after *Lochner:*** *Muller v. Oregon,* 208 U.S. 412 (1908),

99   **In *Muller,* the Court upheld:** Ibid., 208 U.S. at 420.

99   **"women's physical structure":** Ibid., 208 U.S. at 421.

100 **"But the ancient inequality of the sexes":** *Adkins v. Children's Hospital*, 261 U.S. at 553.

100 **The Court reaffirmed *Adkins* in 1936:** *Morehead v. New York ex rel. Tipaldo*, 298 U.S. 587 (1936).

100 **Laws setting the maximum prices:** *Tyson & Brother v. Banton*, 273 U.S. 418 (1927) (maximum prices for theater tickets); *Ribnik v. McBride*, 277 U.S. 350 (1928) (maximum prices for employment agencies); *Williams v. Standard Oil Co.*, 278 U.S. 235 (1929) (maximum prices for gasoline).

100 **In *Weaver v. Palmer Bros. Co.*:** *Weaver v. Palmer Bros. Co.*, 270 U.S. 402 (1926).

101 **As Laurence Tribe remarked:** Laurence Tribe, *American Constitutional Law*, 2nd ed. (Mineola, N.Y.: Foundation Press, 1988), 578.

102 **"Court-packing plan":** For an excellent history of the Court-packing proposal, see Jeff Shesol, *Supreme Power: Franklin Roosevelt v. The Supreme Court* (New York: W. W. Norton, 2010).

102 **In *West Coast Hotel Co. v. Parrish*, in 1937:** *West Coast Hotel Co. v. Parrish*, 300 U.S. 379 (1937).

103 **"What is this freedom of contract?":** Ibid., 300 U.S. at 391.

103 **"There is an additional and compelling consideration":** Ibid., 300 U.S. at 399.

104 **it has long since repudiated:** *Lincoln Federal Labor Union v. Northwestern Iron & Metal Co.*, 335 U.S. 525 (1949).

104 **the "day is gone when the Court uses":** *Williamson v. Lee Optical*, 348 U.S. 483, 488 (1955).

105 **Dual federalism was the view:** Erwin Chemerinsky, *Empowering Government: Federalism for the 21st Century* (Palo Alto, Calif.: Stanford University Press, 2008).

105 **In *United States v. E.C. Knight Co.*:** *United States v. E.C. Knight Co.*, 156 U.S. 1 (1895).

105 **"Commerce succeeds to manufacture":** Ibid., 156 U.S. at 12.

106 **although the commerce power was the "strongest":** Ibid., 156 U.S. at 13.

106 **For example, in *Carter v. Carter Coal Co.*:** *Carter v. Carter Coal Co.*, 298 U.S. 238 (1936).

106 **"The employment of men":** Ibid., 298 U.S. at 303–4.

106 **"Every journey to a forbidden end":** Ibid., 298 U.S. at 295–96.

107 **Sick Chickens Case:** *A.L.A. Schechter Poultry Corp. v. United States*, 295 U.S. 495 (1935).

108 **The Court declared that enforcing:** Ibid., 295 U.S. at 548.

108 **In *Railroad Retirement Board v. Alton R. Co.*:** *Railroad Retirement Board v. Alton R. Co.*, 295 U.S. 330 (1935).

108 **the Shreveport Rate Cases:** *Houston, East and West Texas Railway Company v. United States*, 234 U.S. 342 (1914).

108 **"Congress in the exercise of its paramount power":** Ibid., 234 U.S. at 353.

108 **But in *Alton R.*:** *Railroad Retirement Board v. Alton R. Co.*, 295 U.S. at 368.

109 **Similarly, in 1936:** *United States v. Butler*, 297 U.S. 1 (1936).

110 **From 1937 until 1995:** Edward L. Rubin and Malcolm Feeley, "Federalism: Some Notes on a National Neurosis," 41 *UCLA Law Review* 903 (1994).

111 **In *United States v. Lopez*, in 1995:** *United States v. Lopez*, 514 U.S. 549 (1995).

111 **He was charged with violating:** 18 U.S.C. § 922(q)(2)(A).

112 **Five years later, in *United States v. Morrison*:** *United States v. Morrison*, 529 U.S. 598 (2000).

113 The case, *National Federation of Independent Business v. Sebelius*: *National Federation of Independent Business v. Sebelius*, 132 S. Ct. 2566 (2012).

114 **As Justice Ginsburg pointed out:** Ibid., 132 S. Ct. at 2610 (Ginsburg, J., concurring in part and dissenting in part).

115 **In *New York v. United States*, in 1992:** *New York v. United States*, 505 U.S. 144 (1992).

116 **The Court concluded that it was "clear":** Ibid., 505 U.S. at 188.

116 **The Court followed this decision in *Printz*:** *Printz v. United States*, 521 U.S. 898 (1997).

117 **"15,377 Americans were murdered with firearms":** Ibid., 521 U.S. at 940 (Stevens., J., dissenting).

119 **The overwhelming consensus:** Libertarian constitutional scholars continue to defend the *Lochner*-era decisions. David Bernstein, *Rehabilitating Lochner: Defending Individual Rights Against Progressive Reform* (Chicago: University of Chicago Press, 2012).

Chapter 4: What About the Warren Court?

120 **West Virginia Board of Education adopted a resolution:** Warren Sandmann, "*West Virginia State Board of Education v. Barnette*," in Richard A. Parker, ed., *Free Speech on Trial: Communication Perspectives on Landmark Supreme Court Decisions* (Tuscaloosa: University of Alabama Press, 2003), 100–115.

120 **The Barnette family:** "Recollections of *West Virginia State Board of Education v. Barnette*," 81 *St. John's Law Review* 79 (2007).

121 **The case came to the Supreme Court:** *West Virginia State Board of Education v. Barnette*, 319 U.S. 624 (1943).

121 **just three years earlier, in *Minersville*:** *Minersville School District v. Gobitis*, 310 U.S. 586 (1940).

121 **Nonetheless, in *West Virginia State Board of Education*:** *West Virginia State Board of Education v. Barnette*, 319 U.S. at 624.

121 **Justice Robert Jackson, writing for the Court:** Ibid., 319 U.S. at 633, 642.

122 **Warren, who had been a prosecutor:** For an excellent biography of Earl Warren, see Jim Newton, *Justice for All: Earl Warren and the Nation He Made* (New York: Riverhead Books, 2006).

122 **Hugo Black and William O. Douglas:** For an excellent description of Black and Douglas and the Court Warren was joining, see Noah Feldman, *Scorpions: The Battles and Triumphs of FDR's Great Supreme Court Justices* (New York: Grand Central Books, 2010).

122 **Eisenhower chose a Democrat:** For an excellent biography of William Brennan, see Seth Stern and Stephen Wermiel, *Justice Brennan: Liberal Champion* (Boston: Houghton Mifflin Harcourt, 2010).

122 **Richard Nixon ran for president:** Thomas M. Keck, *The Most Activist Supreme Court in History: The Road to Modern Judicial Conservatism* (Chicago: University of Chicago Press, 2004), 107–112 (quoting Richard Nixon: "I want men on the Supreme Court who are strict constructionists, men that interpret the law and don't try to make the law").

123 **Perhaps most important, in 1954:** *Brown v. Board of Education*, 347 U.S. 483 (1954).

123 **For example, in 1938:** *Missouri ex rel. Gaines v. Canada*, 305 U.S. 337 (1938).

123 **In *Sweatt v. Painter*, in 1950:** *Sweatt v. Painter*, 339 U.S. 629 (1950).

123 **"[W]e cannot find substantial equality":** Ibid., 339 U.S. at 633–34.

124   **during October Term 1952**: For an excellent, detailed description of the litigation in *Brown,* see Richard Kluger, *Simple Justice* (New York: Vintage, 1975).

124   **"In approaching this problem"**: *Brown v. Board of Education,* 347 U.S. at 492–93.

124   **"there are findings below"**: Ibid., 347 U.S. at 492.

125   **"Does segregation of children in public schools"**: Ibid., 347 U.S. at 493.

125   **Chief Justice Warren wrote**: Ibid., 347 U.S. at 494.

125   **a citation from psychology literature**: Ibid., 347 U.S. at 494n11.

125   **The Court ended its relatively short opinion**: Ibid., 347 U.S. at 495.

125   **"with all deliberate speed"**: *Brown v. Board of Education,* 349 U.S. at 294, 301 (1955).

125   **Richard Kluger eloquently**: Kluger, *Simple Justice,* 749.

126   **For example, in *Mayor and City Council***: *Mayor and City Council of Baltimore City v. Dawson,* 350 U.S. 877 (1955).

126   **The Court did the exact same thing**: *Holmes v. City of Atlanta,* 350 U.S. 879 (1955).

126   ***Browder v. Gayle,* in 1956**: *Browder v. Gayle,* 352 U.S. 903 (1956).

126   ***Turner v. City of Memphis,* in 1962**: *Turner v. City of Memphis,* 369 U.S. 350 (1962).

126   ***Johnson v. Virginia,* in 1963**: *Johnson v. Virginia,* 373 U.S. 61 (1963).

127   **Initially, when the first challenges reached**: *Colegrove v. Green,* 328 U.S. 549 (1946).

127   **However, in *Baker v. Carr***: *Baker v. Carr,* 369 U.S. 186 (1962).

127   **The first case to announce this principle**: *Gray v. Sanders,* 372 U.S. 368 (1963).

128   **"How then can one person"**: Ibid., 372 U.S. at 379.

128   **"The conception of political equality"**: Ibid., 372 U.S. at 381.

128   **In *Reynolds v. Sims,* in 1964**: *Reynolds v. Sims,* 377 U.S. 533 (1964).

128   **"Legislators represent people, not trees"**: Ibid., 377 U.S. at 562.

129   **Earl Warren said that of all the decisions**: Earl Warren, *The Memoirs of Earl Warren* (Garden City, N.Y.: Doubleday, 1977), 306.

129   **The Supreme Court in *Harper***: *Harper v. Virginia State Board of Elections,* 383 U.S. 663 (1966).

129   **"a State violates the Equal Protection Clause"**: Ibid., 383 U.S. at 666.

130   **a key provision of the Voting Rights Act**: *Shelby County, Alabama v. Holder,* 133 S. Ct. 2612 (2013), discussed in chapter 7.

131   **"The constitution was ordained and established"**: *Barron v. Mayor & City Council of Baltimore,* 32 U.S. (7 Pet.) 243, 247 (1833).

132   **States often did not provide counsel**: For example, in *Powell v. Alabama,* 287 U.S. 245 (1932), the defendants had been sentenced to death without representation of counsel.

132   **States punished individuals for invoking**: *Adamson v. California,* 332 U.S. 46 (1947) (upholding a state's allowing an inference of guilt to be drawn when a criminal defendant refuses to testify).

132   **Some states had official state churches**: Connecticut, for example, had an official state church until 1818, and Massachusetts until 1833. Until 1876, North Carolina allowed only Christians to hold public office. James H. Hutson, *Religion and the New Republic: Faith in the Founding of America* (New York: Rowman & Littlefield, 2000); Michael W. McConnell, "Establishment and Disestablishment at the Founding, Part I: Establishment of Religion," 44 *William and Mary Law Review* 5 (2006).

132   **In 1908, in *Twining v. New Jersey***: *Twining v. New Jersey,* 211 U.S. 78 (1908).

133   **it "is possible that some of the personal rights"**: Ibid., 211 U.S. at 99.

133   **In 1925, in *Gitlow v. New York***: *Gitlow v. New York,* 268 U.S. 652 (1925).

133   **Even more astounding, it was not until 1932**: *Powell v. Alabama,* 287 U.S. 45 (1932).

133 The Court held that in a capital case: Ibid., 287 U.S. at 67–68.

133 It was not for another thirty years: *Gideon v. Wainwright*, 372 U.S. 335 (1963).

134 In a criminal justice system: *Missouri v. Frye*, 131 S. Ct. 1399, 1407 (2012) ("Ninety-seven percent of federal convictions and ninety-four percent of state convictions are the result of guilty pleas").

135 "[R]eason and reflection require us": *Gideon v. Wainwright*, 372 U.S. at 344.

135 Quite important, though not without controversy: *Mapp v. Ohio*, 367 U.S. 643 (1961).

135 A half-century earlier: *Weeks v. United States*, 232 U.S. 382 (1914).

135 The Warren Court also applied to the states: *Benton v. Maryland*, 395 U.S. 784 (1969); *Malloy v. Hogan*, 378 U.S. 1 (1964).

136 Key provisions of the Sixth Amendment: *Klopfer v. North Carolina*, 386 U.S. 213 (1967); *Irvin v. Dowd*, 366 U.S. 717 (1961); *Pointer v. Texas*, 380 U.S. 400 (1965); *Washington v. Texas*, 388 U.S. 14 (1967).

136 states cannot impose cruel and unusual punishment: *Robinson v. California*, 370 U.S. 660 (1962).

136 Most famously, in *Miranda v. Arizona*: *Miranda v. Arizona*, 384 U.S. 436 (1966).

137 In *Dickerson v. United States*: *Dickerson v. United States*, 530 U.S. 428 (2000).

138 in the Boston public schools: National Center for Education Statistics, *Characteristics of the 100 Largest Public Elementary and Secondary Schools in the United States, 2012–13*, nces.ed.gov./pubs2011/2011301.pdf.

138 more is spent on the average white child's education: Preston C. Green III, Bruce D. Baker, and Joseph O. Oluwole, "Achieving Racial Equal Educational Opportunity through School Finance Litigation," 4 *Stanford Journal of Civil Rights & Civil Liberties*, 283, 298 (2008).

138 private elementary schools are: Gary Orfield, *Reviving the Goal of an Integrated Society: A 21st Century Challenge* (Los Angeles: The Civil Rights Project of UCLA, 2009), 9.

139 A year later, in *Brown II*: *Brown v. Board of Education*, 349 U.S. at 294, 301.

139 In 1958, in *Cooper v. Aaron*: *Cooper v. Aaron*, 358 U.S. 1 (1958).

139 It wasn't until 1964: *Griffin v. County School Bd. of Prince Edward County*, 377 U.S. 218, 229 (1964).

139 In the South in 1964: James T. Patterson, *Brown v. Board of Education: A Civil Rights Milestone and Its Troubled Legacy* (New York: Oxford University Press, 2001), 113.

139 In South Carolina, Alabama, and Mississippi: Ibid.

139 In North Carolina, only one-quarter: Ibid.

139 Similarly, in Virginia in 1964: Ibid.

139 It was not until seventeen years after *Brown*: *Swann v. Charlotte-Mecklenburg Board of Education*, 402 U.S. 1 (1971).

140 Stevens has argued, in a recent book: John Paul Stevens, *Five Chiefs* (New York: Little, Brown, 2011).

140 In *San Antonio Independent School District v. Rodriguez*: San Antonio Independent School District v. Rodriguez, 411 U.S. 1 (1973).

142 "Education, of course, is not among the rights": Ibid., 411 U.S. at 35.

142 Chief Justice Warren eloquently expressed: *Brown v. Board of Education*, 347 U.S. at 493.

143 *Milliken v. Bradley*, ensured: *Milliken v. Bradley*, 418 U.S. 717 (1974).

143 Duke professor Charles Clotfelter: Charles T. Clotfelter, *After Brown: The Rise and Retreat of School Desegregation* (Princeton, N.J.: Princeton University Press, 2004).

144 In *Board of Education of Oklahoma City Public Schools v. Dowell*: *Board of Education of Oklahoma City Public Schools v. Dowell*, 498 U.S. 237 (1991).

144 The Supreme Court's decision in *Parents Involved*: *Parents Involved in Community Schools v. Seattle School District No. 1*, 551 U.S. 701 (2007).

146 Breyer . . . attached an appendix: Ibid., 551 U.S. at 838 (Breyer, J., dissenting).

146 "savage inequalities": Jonathan Kozol, *Savage Inequalities* (New York: Crown, 2001).

147 As Senator Patrick Leahy remarked: 150 Cong. Rec. S11612-13 (2004) (statement of Senator Patrick Leahy).

147 The Bureau of Justice Statistics found: Caroline Wolf Harlow, *Defense Counsel in Criminal Cases, Bureau of Justice Statistics*, U.S. Department of Justice, Bureau of Justice Statistics, November 2000, http://bjs.gov/content/pub/pdf/dccc.pdf.

147 "Of defendants found guilty": Ibid., 1.

147 Radha Iyengar concluded: Radha Iyengar, *An Analysis of the Performance of Federal Indigent Defense Counsel*," NBER Working Paper No. 13187, National Bureau of Economic Research, June 2007, 3.

147 James M. Anderson and Paul Heaton: James M. Anderson and Paul Heaton, "How Much Difference Does the Lawyer Make? The Effect of Defense Counsel on Murder Case Outcomes," 122 *Yale Law Journal* 154 (2012).

148 compared with appointed counsel, public defenders: Ibid., 183–84.

148 If you can, hire your own: James C. Beck and Robert Shumsky, "A Comparison of Retained and Appointed Counsel in Cases of Capital Murder," 21 *Law & Human Behavior* 525 (1997) (finding a death sentence more likely to result when the defendant was represented by appointed counsel rather than privately retained counsel); Dean J. Champion, "Private Counsels and Public Defenders: A Look at Weak Cases, Prior Records and Leniency in Plea Bargaining," 17 *Journal of Criminal Justice* 253 (1989) (finding that defendants represented by privately retained counsel obtained better outcomes than defendants represented by public defenders). Not every study has found such differences. See Richard D. Hartley, Holly Ventura Miller, and Cassia Spohn, "Do You Get What You Pay For? Type of Counsel and Its Effect on Criminal Court Outcomes," 38 *Journal of Criminal Justice* 1063 (2010) (finding generally that public defenders and private attorneys have no direct effect on incarceration or sentence length); Pauline Houlden and Steven Balkin, "Costs and Quality of Indigent Defense: Ad Hoc vs. Coordinated Assignment of the Private Bar Within a Mixed System," 10 *Justice System Journal* 159, 170 (1985) (finding that the method of assigning attorneys to cases did not affect outcomes).

148 "We find that, in general": Anderson and Heaton, "How Much Difference," 188.

149 The American Bar Association's Standing Committee: ABA Standing Committee on Legal Aid and Indigent Defendants, *Gideon's Broken Promise: America's Continuing Quest for Equal Justice* (Chicago: American Bar Association, 2004), 38, http://www.americanbar.org/content/dam/aba/administrative/legal_aid _indigent_defendants/ls_sclaid_def_bp_right_to_counsel_in_criminal_proceedings .authcheckdam.pdf.

149 The ABA committee concluded: Ibid.

149 "inadequate financial support continues": National Right to Counsel Committee, *Justice Denied: America's Continuing Neglect of Our Constitutional Right to Counsel*, The Constitution Project (2009), 6-7, http://www.constitutionproject.org/pdf /139.pdf.

149 "the most visible sign of inadequate funding": Ibid., 7.

149 **Professor Douglas Vick explained:** Douglas W. Vick, "Poorhouse Justice: Under-funded Indigent Defense Services and Arbitrary Death Sentences," 43 *Buffalo Law Review* 329, 398 (1995).

150 **"the country's current fiscal crisis":** National Right to Counsel Committee, *Justice Denied,* 7.

150 **forty-two states cut funding:** See National Center for State Courts, *COSCA Budget Survey 2012* (2012), 9, http://www.ncsc.org/Information-and-Resources/Budget-Resource-Center/~/media/Files/PDF/Information%20and%20Resources/Budget%20Resource%20Center/COSCA_Budget_Survey_all_states_2012.ashx (listing these figures); see also Edmund G. Brown Jr., *2013-14 Governor's Budget Summary* (2013), http://www.dof.ca.gov/documents/FullBudgetSummary_web2013.pdf. Many states, though, had small or moderate increases in 2012, which followed significant cuts in the prior years. The most recent budget data shows that many states increased court funding last year. See National Center for State Courts, *Budgets & Funding,* http://www.ncsc.org/Information-and-Resources/Budget-Resource-Center/Budget_Funding.aspx.

150 **innocent people are convicted as a result:** National Right to Counsel Committee, *Justice Denied,* 6 ("Wrongful convictions also have occurred as a result of inadequate representation by defense lawyers").

151 **Nationally, five times more prisoners:** Dorothy E. Roberts, "The Social and Moral Cost of Mass Incarceration in African American Communities," 56 *Stanford Law Review* 1271, 1272 (2004).

151 **"[t]he individuals adversely affected by this crisis":** Vick, "Poorhouse Justice," 459.

152 **the "mercies of incompetent counsel":** *McMann v. Richardson,* 397 U.S. 759, 771 (1970).

152 **"to date, a federal forum has not been available":** Cara H. Drinan, "The Third Generation of Indigent Defense Litigation," 33 *New York University Review of Law & Social Change* 427, 467 (2009).

152 **But the Supreme Court, in *Strickland*:** *Strickland v. Washington,* 466 U.S. 668 (1984).

152 **"counsel was not functioning as the 'counsel'":** Ibid., 466 U.S. at 687.

152 **"counsel's deficient performance more likely than not":** Ibid., 466 U.S. at 693.

153 **"[I]t is often very difficult to tell whether":** Ibid., 466 U.S. at 710 (Marshall, J., dissenting).

153 **I can identify only two cases:** *Wiggins v. Smith,* 539 U.S. 510 (2003); *Rompilla v. Beard,* 545 U.S. 374 (2005).

153 **The Court's more recent decision:** *Cullen v. Pinholster,* 131 S. Ct. 1388 (2011).

154 **"[n]o constitutional right is celebrated so much":** Stephen B. Bright, "Turning Celebrated Principles into Reality," *Champion* (January–February 2003), 6.

Chapter 5: Employers, Employees, and Consumers

159 **On Wednesday, December 4, 2013:** *United States v. Apel,* 676 F.3d 1202 (9th Cir. 2012), *cert. granted,* 133 S. Ct. 2767 (2013).

159 **The justices emerged:** There are a number of excellent books describing the Roberts Court and profiling its members: Mark Tushnet, *In the Balance: Law and Politics on the Roberts Court* (New York: W. W. Norton, 2013); Marcia Coyle, *The Roberts Court: The Struggle for the Constitution* (New York: Simon & Schuster, 2013).

160 **Immediately to Roberts's right:** For an excellent biography of Justice Scalia, see Joan Biskupic, *American Original: The Life and Constitution of Supreme Court Justice Antonin Scalia* (New York: Sarah Crichton Books, 2010).

161 **allegations surfaced . . . Anita Hill:** For a discussion of the allegations and the hearings, see Jane Mayer and Jill Abramson, *Strange Justice: The Selling of Clarence Thomas* (Boston: Houghton Mifflin, 1994). A fascinating biography of Justice Thomas is Kevin Merida and Michael A. Fletcher, *Supreme Discomfort: The Divided Soul of Clarence Thomas* (New York: Doubleday, 2007).

161 **Establishment Clause of the First Amendment:** *Zelman v. Simmons-Harris*, 536 U.S. 639 (2002) (Thomas, J., concurring).

162 **children should have no First Amendment rights:** *Brown v. Entertainment Merchants*, 131 S. Ct. 2729 (2011) (Thomas J., dissenting).

162 **Congress should be very limited:** *United States v. Lopez*, 514 U.S. 549 (1995) (Thomas, J., concurring).

162 **ability of the United States to detain an American citizen:** *Hamdi v. Rumsfeld*, 542 U.S. 507, 554 (2004).

163 **allowing random drug testing:** *Board of Education of Independent School District No. 92 of Pottawatomie County v. Earls*, 536 U.S. 822 (2002).

163 **Ten Commandments monument:** *Van Orden v. Perry*, 545 U.S. 677 (2005).

163 **bestselling autobiography:** Sonia Sotomayor, *My Beloved World* (New York: Knopf, 2013).

165 **The first case was *Pliva*:** *Pliva, Inc. v. Mensing*, 131 S. Ct. 2567 (2011).

165 **In 1985, the label was modified:** Ibid., 131 S. Ct. at 2572.

165 **FDA ordered a black-box warning:** Ibid.

166 **failure-to-warn theory:** *Wyeth v. Levine*, 555 U.S. 555 (2009).

167 **Justice Stevens concluded the majority opinion:** Ibid., 555 U.S. at 581.

167 **The Court quoted the federal regulation:** *Pliva, Inc. v. Mensing*, 131 S. Ct. at 2575.

168 **"A Dear Doctor letter that contained substantial":** Ibid., 131 S. Ct. at 2576.

168 **"We recognize that from the perspective":** Ibid., 131 S. Ct. at 2581.

168 **"We acknowledge the unfortunate hand":** Ibid.

169 **As Justice Sotomayor objected:** Ibid., 131 S. Ct. at 2582 (Sotomayor, J., dissenting).

169 **"[t]he purpose of Congress is the ultimate touchstone":** *Medtronic, Inc. v. Lohr*, 518 U.S. 470, 485 (1996).

169 **"If Congress had intended to deprive injured parties":** *Pliva, Inc. v. Mensing*, 131 S. Ct. at 2592 (Sotomayor, J., dissenting).

169 **But the Court went even further:** *Mutual Pharmaceutical Co. v. Bartlett*, 133 S. Ct. 2466 (2013).

171 **She explained that "[a] manufacturer":** Ibid., 133 S. Ct. at 2491 (Sotomayor, J., dissenting).

171 **an "unwelcome choice" for a manufacturer:** Ibid.

172 **Roberts Court is the most pro-business Court:** Lee Epstein, Richard Posner, and William Landes, "How Business Fares in the Supreme Court," 97 *Minnesota Law Review* 1431 (2013).

173 **Vincent and Liza Concepcion purchased:** *AT&T Mobility LLC v. Concepcion*, 131 S. Ct. 1740 (2011).

173 **Yale law professor Judith Resnik:** Judith Resnik, "Failing Faith: Adjudicatory Procedure in Decline," 53 *University of Chicago Law Review* 494 (1986); Judith Resnik, "Managerial Judges," 96 *Harvard Law Review* 374 (1982).

174   The California Supreme Court said: *Discover Bank v. Superior Court,* 36 Cal.4th 148, 30 Cal.Rptr.3d 76, 113 P.3d 1100 (2005).

174   The Federal Arbitration Act is a law: Section 2 of the Federal Arbitration Act (FAA) makes agreements to arbitrate "valid, irrevocable, and enforceable, save upon such grounds as exist at law or in equity for the revocation of any contract." 9 U.S.C. § 2.

174   The Court stressed the efficiency benefits: *AT&T Mobility LLC v. Concepcion,* 131 S. Ct. at 1752.

175   Justice Breyer described the practical reality: Ibid., 131 S. Ct. at 1761 (Breyer, J., dissenting).

175   In *American Express v. Italian Colors Restaurant: American Express v. Italian Colors Restaurant,* 133 S. Ct. 2304 (2013).

176   "[t]here shall be no right or authority for any Claims": Ibid. 133 S. Ct. at 2308.

176   Scalia declared, "Truth to tell": Ibid., 133 S. Ct. at 2312.

176   long-standing principle under the Federal Arbitration Act: *Mitsubishi Motors Corp. v. Soler Chrysler-Plymouth, Inc.,* 473 U.S. 614, 637n19 (1985).

177   "Here is the nutshell version of this case": *American Express v. Italian Colors Restaurant,* 133 S. Ct. at 2313 (Kagan, J., dissenting).

177   Saint Clair Adams worked for a Circuit City store: *Circuit City Stores v. Adams,* 532 U.S. 105 (2001).

179   As Justice Stevens lamented: Ibid., 532 U.S. at 131–32 (Stevens, J., dissenting).

179   The Court's hostility toward class actions also was evident: *Wal-Mart Stores, Inc. v. Dukes,* 131 S. Ct. 2541 (2011).

180   First, the Court found the plaintiffs' statistical evidence: Ibid., 131 S. Ct. at 2555.

180   "may be attributable to only a small set": Ibid.

180   Second, the majority found the plaintiffs' expert witness: Ibid., 131 S. Ct. at 2554.

181   Scalia's majority opinion rejected the expert's entire testimony: Ibid.

185   In 1989, there was a series: Civil Rights Act of 1991, Pub. L. No. 102-166, 105 Stat. 1071, 1074 (codified at 42 U.S.C. § 2000e-2(k) (2006)).

185   An important victory for businesses over employees: *Ledbetter v. Goodyear Tire and Rubber Co., Inc.,* 550 U.S. 618 (2007).

186   By "the end of 1997, Ledbetter": Ibid., 550 U.S. at 643.

186   Justice Ginsburg, in her dissenting opinion: Ibid., 550 U.S. at 650n3 (Ginsburg, J., dissenting).

186   Obama signed the Lilly Ledbetter Fair Pay Act: Lilly Ledbetter Fair Pay Act of 2009, Pub. L. No. 111-2, 123 Stat. 5 (2009).

187   This is important, because women today: Marianne DelPo Kulow, "Beyond the Paycheck Fairness Act; Mandatory Wage Disclosure Law," 50 *Harvard Journal on Legislation,* 385, 386 (2013).

187   "African-American women earn only 62%": Jill C. Engle, "Promoting the General Welfare: Legal Reform in the United States to Lift Women and Children Out of Poverty," 16 *Journal of Gender, Race and Justice* 1, 8 (2013).

187   Surveys indicate that almost half of all working women: Heather Antecol and Deborah Cobb-Clark, "The Changing Nature of Employment-Related Sexual Harassment: Evidence from the U.S. Federal Government 1978–1994," 57 *Industrial and Labor Relations Review* 443 (2004); Louise F. Fitzgerald and Sandra L. Shulman, "Sexual Harassment: A Research Analysis and Agenda for the 1990s," 42 *Journal of Vocational Behavior* 5, 7 (1993).

187 **In 1986, the Supreme Court held:** *Meritor Savings Bank, FSB v. Vinson*, 477 U.S. 57, 64 (1986).

188 **In two cases in 1998:** *Burlington Indus., Inc. v. Ellerth*, 524 U.S. 742, 762 (1998); *Faragher v. City of Boca Raton*, 524 U.S. 775, 786–87 (1998).

188 **In 2013, the Supreme Court adopted:** *Vance v. Ball State University*, 133 S. Ct. 2434 (2013).

188 **Vance complained that Davis:** Ibid., 133 S. Ct. at 2439.

189 **Justice Alito, writing for the majority:** Ibid., 133 S. Ct. at 2433.

189 **As Justice Ginsburg noted in her dissent, the majority's opinion:** Ibid., 133 S. Ct. at 2455 (Ginsburg, J., dissenting.)

189 **"Trumpeting the virtues of simplicity and administrability":** Ibid., 133 S. Ct. at 2462 (Ginsburg, J., dissenting.)

190 **An important study was published in 2013:** Epstein, Posner, and Landes, "How Business Fares," 1431.

190 *New York Times* **reporter Adam Liptak wrote:** Adam Liptak, "Corporations Find a Friend in the Supreme Court," *New York Times*, May 4, 2013.

Chapter 6: Abuses of Government Power

192 **Thomas Lee Goldstein spent twenty-four years:** *Van de Kamp v. Goldstein*, 555 U.S. 335 (2009).

192 **As the federal court of appeals explained:** *Goldstein v. City of Long Beach*, 715 F.3d 750, 751 (9th Cir. 2013).

192 **"He became a murder suspect":** *Goldstein v. Superior Court*, 45 Cal.4th 218, 195 P.3d 588 (2008).

193 **"It is unlikely that Thompson was death-eligible":** *Goldstein v. City of Long Beach*, 715 F.3d at 762 (Reinhardt, J., concurring).

193 **"Despite a request to reverse Thompson's conviction":** Ibid., 715 F.3d at 715–16.

193 **In 1963, in** *Brady v. Maryland*: *Brady v. Maryland*, 373 U.S. 83 (1963).

193 **the Supreme Court held that prosecutors' offices:** *Giglio v. United States*, 405 U.S. 150 (1972).

195 **John Thompson was convicted and spent eighteen years:** *Connick v. Thompson*, 131 S. Ct. 1350 (2011).

196 **She wrote that throughout the trial, the prosecutor:** Ibid., 131 S. Ct. at 1370 (Ginsburg, J., dissenting).

197 **Long ago, in** *Marbury v. Madison*: *Marbury v. Madison*, 5 U.S. (Cranch) 137, 163 (1803).

197 **The Court said that "[t]he government":** Ibid.

199 **A six-hundred-page Senate report:** *Monroe v. Pape*, 365 U.S. 167, 174 (1961).

199 **"An Act to enforce the Provisions":** *Owens v. Okure*, 488 U.S. 235, 249n11 (1989).

200 **"[t]he very purpose of §1983":** *Mitchum v. Foster*, 407 U.S. 225, 242 (1972).

200 **As for federal officers, in 1971:** *Bivens v. Six Unknown Named Federal Agents*, 403 U.S. 388 (1971).

200 **Justice John Marshall Harlan, in an eloquent:** Ibid., 403 U.S. at 410.

201 **The Court has ruled over many decades:** Erwin Chemerinsky, *Federal Jurisdiction*, 6th ed. (New York: Wolters Kluwer, 2012), 548–85.

202 **It is this doctrine that explains:** *Stump v. Sparkman*, 435 U.S. 349 (1978).

203 **In** *Mireles v. Waco*, **a judge was upset:** *Mireles v. Waco*, 502 U.S. 9 (1991).

202 "judicial immunity is not overcome": Ibid., 502 U.S. at 11.

203 In *Imbler v. Pachtman*: *Imbler v. Pachtman*, 424 U.S. 409 (1976).

204 "harassment by unfounded litigation": Ibid., 424 U.S. at 423.

204 in *Bogan v. Scott-Harris*: *Bogan v. Scott-Harris*, 523 U.S. 44 (1998).

204 However, in *Briscoe v. LaHue*: *Briscoe v. LaHue*, 460 U.S. 325 (1983).

205 Thus, the Court concluded that allowing officers: Ibid., 460 U.S. at 343.

205 report on the Los Angeles Police Department: Erwin Chemerinsky, "The Rampart Scandal: Policing the Criminal Justice System: An Independent Analysis of the Los Angeles Police Department's Board of Inquiry Report on the Rampart Scandal," 34 *Loyola of Los Angeles Law Review* 545 (2001).

205 Javier Francisco Ovando: Erwin Chemerinsky, "The Role of Prosecutors in Dealing with Police Abuse: The Lessons of Los Angeles," 8 *Virginia Journal of Social Policy & the Law* 305, 306–7 (2001).

205 More than a hundred convictions were overturned: Michael Rowan, "Leaving No Stone Unturned: Using RICO as a Remedy for Police Misconduct," 31 *Florida State University Law Review* 231, 234 (2003).

206 Charles Rehberg, a certified public accountant: *Rehberg v. Paulk*, 132 S. Ct. 1497 (2012).

206 Rehberg challenged the sufficiency: Ibid., 132 S. Ct. at 1501.

207 "[W]e conclude that grand jury witnesses": Ibid., 132 S. Ct. at 1506.

207 "In the vast majority of cases involving a claim": Ibid., at 1506–7.

207 President Nixon was furious at him: *Nixon v. Fitzgerald*, 457 U.S. 731 (1982).

207 "unique status under the Constitution": Ibid., 457 U.S. at 750–51.

208 a subsequent case, involving President Bill Clinton: *Clinton v. Jones*, 520 U.S. 681 (1997).

208 Otherwise, what is left of the assurance: *Marbury v. Madison*, 5 U.S. at 163.

209 The test for qualified immunity was articulated: *Harlow v. Fitzgerald*, 457 U.S. 800 (1982).

209 The Court stated the legal test that still controls: Ibid., 457 U.S. at 818.

209 In 1995, Larry Hope was a prisoner: *Hope v. Pelzer*, 536 U.S. 730 (2002).

210 "the unnecessary and wanton infliction of pain": *Rhodes v. Chapman*, 452 U.S. 337, 346 (1981).

210 "the Eighth Amendment violation is obvious": *Hope v. Pelzer*, 536 U.S. at 737.

210 "This punitive treatment amounts to gratuitous infliction": Ibid.

211 The Court stressed that qualified immunity: Ibid., 536 U.S. at 740.

211 Thus, the key inquiry is whether: Ibid.

211 Savana Redding was a seventh-grade student: *Safford Unified School Dist. No. 1 v. Redding*, 557 U.S. 364 (2009).

212 In *Ashcroft v. al-Kidd*, in 2011: *Ashcroft v. al-Kidd*, 131 S. Ct. 2074 (2011).

213 "Is a warrant 'validly obtained'": Ibid., 131 S. Ct. at 2087 (Ginsburg, J., concurring in the judgment).

214 Second, Justice Scalia said: Ibid., 131 S. Ct. at 2083.

214 "A Government official's conduct violates": Ibid.

215 An illustration of this is found: *Padilla v. Yoo*, 678 F.3d 748 (9th Cir. 2012).

215 While being held as an enemy combatant: Jane Mayer, *The Dark Side: The Inside Story of How the War on Terror Turned Into a War on American Ideals* (New York: Random House, 2008) (describing torture and extreme interrogation techniques).

215 "extreme isolation; interrogation under threat of torture": *Padilla v. Yoo*, 678 F.3d at 752.

215 In fact, Yoo, now a law professor: John C. Yoo, *War by Other Means: An Insider's Account of the War on Terrorism* (New York: Grove/Atlantic, 2006).

215 "the Supreme Court had not, at the time of Yoo's tenure": *Padilla v. Yoo*, 678 F.3d at 759.

216 In fact, Judge Fisher's opinion recognizes this: Ibid., 678 F.3d at 763.

216 "Yoo is entitled to qualified immunity": Ibid., 678 F.3d at 763–64.

216 "We assume without deciding": Ibid., 678 F.3d at 768.

216 "severe physical pain": Ibid., 678 F.3d at 766–67.

218 In February 1958, James B. Stanley: *Stanley v. United States*, 483 U.S. 669 (1987).

218 He said that as a result of the LSD: Ibid., 483 U.S. at 671.

218 "This was the Government's first notification": Ibid., 483 U.S. at 672.

219 As Justice O'Connor forcefully argued: Ibid., 483 U.S. at 710 (O'Connor, J., concurring and dissenting).

219 the Eleventh Amendment is part of a larger constitutional principle: *Hans v. Louisiana*, 134 U.S. 1 (1890). Chemerinsky, *Federal Jurisdiction*, 421–96.

219 In *Florida Prepaid v. College Savings Bank*: *Florida Prepaid v. College Savings Bank*, 527 U.S. 627 (1999).

220 A year after *Florida Prepaid*: *Kimel v. Florida Board of Regents*, 528 U.S. 62 (2000).

221 A year later, in *Board of Trustees of University of Alabama*: *Board of Trustees of University of Alabama v. Garrett*, 531 U.S. 356 (2001).

221 In *Alden v. Maine*, in 1999, the Court held: *Alden v. Maine*, 527 U.S. 706 (1999).

222 "We hold that the powers delegated to Congress": Ibid., 527 U.S. at 712.

222 "The constitutional privilege of a State": Ibid., 527 U.S. at 754–55.

223 It has ruled that a local government: *Monell v. Department of Social Services*, 436 U.S. 658 (1978).

224 Another illustration of how difficult: *Board of Commissioners of Bryan County, Oklahoma v. Brown*, 530 U.S. 397 (1997).

224 Burns "used an 'arm bar' technique": Ibid., 530 U.S. at 400–401.

224 "a finding of culpability simply cannot depend": Ibid., 530 U.S. at 405.

225 On October 6, 1976, at approximately 2:00 a.m.: *City of Los Angeles v. Lyons*, 461 U.S. 95 (1983).

226 A survey in 1980 revealed: Erwin Chemerinsky, "The Story of *City of Los Angeles v. Lyons*," in Myriam Gilles and Risa Goluboff, eds., *Civil Rights Stories* (Minneapolis: West Publishing, 2007).

226 Gates responded that it was because of physiological differences: Quoted in James J. Fyfe, "The Los Angeles Chokehold Controversy," 19 *Criminal Law Bulletin* 61, 63–64 (1983).

227 "[a]bsent a sufficient likelihood that he will again be wronged": *City of Los Angeles v. Lyons*, 465 U.S. at 111.

227 two federal district courts ruled that women: *Jones v. Bowman*, 664 F.Supp. 433 (N.D. Ind. 1987); *John Does 1–100 v. Boyd*, 613 F.Supp. 1514 (D.Minn. 1985).

Chapter 7: Is the Roberts Court Really So Bad?

229 Edith Windsor and Thea Spyer: Ernest A. Young and Erin C. Blondell, "Federalism, Liberty, and Equality in *United States v. Windsor*," 2013 *Cato Supreme Court Review* 117, 121.

229 **After Canada changed its law:** *United States v. Windsor*, 133 S. Ct. 2675, 2682 (2013).

229 **In 2011, New York adopted:** Marriage Equality Act, 2011 N.Y. Laws 749 (codified at N.Y. Dom. Rel. Law Ann. §§ 10-a, 10-b, 13 (West 2013)).

229 **The Defense of Marriage Act:** Defense of Marriage Act (DOMA), 110 Stat. 2419.

229 **In 1993, the Hawaii Supreme Court:** *Baehr v. Lewin*, 74 Haw. 530, 852 P.2d 44 (1993).

230 **Section 2 of the act says:** Section 3 amends the Dictionary Act to say: "In determining the meaning of any Act of Congress, or of any ruling, regulation, or interpretation of the various administrative bureaus and agencies of the United States, the word 'marriage' means only a legal union between one man and one woman as husband and wife, and the word 'spouse' refers only to a person of the opposite sex who is a husband or a wife." 1 U.S.C. § 7.

230 **that did not occur until Massachusetts:** *Goodrich v. Mass. Dep't of Pub. Health*, 798 N.E.2d 941, 961 (Mass. 2003)

230 **"In determining the meaning of any Act of Congress":** 1 U.S.C. § 7

230 **There are more than a thousand federal laws:** *United States v. Windsor*, 133 S. Ct. at 2690.

231 **"DOMA seeks to injure the very class":** Ibid., 133 S. Ct. at 2694.

231 **Justice Kennedy quoted the House Report on DOMA:** Ibid., 133 S. Ct. at 2693.

231 **The Supreme Court had earlier held:** *Romer v. Evans*, 517 U.S. 620 (1996).

232 **Liberals, for example, are pleased with the Court's decision:** *National Federation of Independent Business v. Sebelius*, 132 S. Ct. 2566 (2012).

232 **Arizona's restrictive immigration law:** *Arizona v. United States*, 132 S. Ct. 2492 (2012).

232 **striking down the Medicaid provisions:** *National Federation of Independent Business v. Sebelius*, 132 S. Ct. 2566 (2012).

232 **key provisions of the Voting Rights Act of 1965:** *Shelby County, Alabama v. Holder*, 133 S. Ct. 2612 (2013).

232 **federal Partial Birth Abortion Ban Act:** *Gonzales v. Carhart*, 550 U.S. 124 (2007).

232 **its finding a Second Amendment right:** *District of Columbia v. Heller*, 554 U.S. 570 (2008).

234 **Court had no business deciding** *Bush v. Gore*: *Bush v. Gore*, 531 U.S. 98 (2000).

234 **Although the 2000 election was not so long ago:** For a detailed history of this litigation, see Jeffrey Toobin, *Too Close to Call: The Thirty-Six Day Battle to Decide the 2000 Election* (New York: Random House, 2001); Howard Gillman, *The Votes That Counted: How the Court Decided the 2000 Presidential Election* (Chicago: University of Chicago Press, 2000).

235 **A few days later, in** *Bush v. Palm Beach*: *Bush v. Palm Beach County Canvassing Bd.*, 531 U.S. 70 (2000).

236 **On Monday, December 11:** *Palm Beach County Canvassing Bd. v. Harris*, 772 So.2d 1273 (2236).

236 **Florida Supreme Court, by a 4–3 decision, reversed the trial court:** *Gore v. Harris*, 772 So.2d 1243 (2000).

236 **"[r]eceipt of a number of illegal votes":** Ibid., 772 So.2d at 1248.

236 **ordered "the Supervisor of Elections and the Canvassing Boards":** Ibid., 772 So.2d at 1262.

237 **U.S. Supreme Court . . . stayed the counting:** *Bush v. Gore*, 531 U.S. 1046 (2000).

237 **Justice Scalia wrote a short opinion:** Ibid., 531 U.S. at 1046 (Scalia, J., concurring).

238   On Tuesday, December 12: Ibid., 531 U.S. at 98.

238   "[w]hen the state legislature vests the right": Ibid., 531 U.S. at 104.

238   "In addition to these difficulties the actual process": Ibid., 531 U.S. at 109.

239   "Our consideration is limited to the present circumstances": Ibid.

239   "The Supreme Court of Florida has said": Ibid., 531 U.S. at 110.

240   Chief Justice Rehnquist wrote a separate opinion: Ibid., 531 U.S. at 111 (Rehnquist, C. J., concurring).

240   The chief justice concluded that the Florida Supreme Court: Ibid., 531 at 122.

241   "The endorsement of that position by the majority": Ibid., 531 U.S. at 128 (Stevens, J., dissenting).

241   "I fear that in order to bring this agonizingly long election process": Ibid., 531 U.S. at 158 (Breyer, J., dissenting.)

242   Vincent Bugliosi and Alan Dershowitz: Vincent Bugliosi, *The Betrayal of America: How the Supreme Court Undermined the Constitution and Chose Our President* (New York: Nation Books, 2001), 1; Alan M. Dershowitz, *Supreme Injustice: How the High Court Hijacked Election 2000* (New York: Oxford University Press, 2001), 5.

243   deciding a case that is not "ripe": Erwin Chemerinsky, *Federal Jurisdiction*, 6th ed. (New York: Wolters Kluwer, 2012), 119–29 (describing Supreme Court decisions creating ripeness requirement).

244   "Admittedly, the use of differing substandards": *Bush v. Gore*, 531 U.S. at 126 (Stevens, J., dissenting).

244   The political-question doctrine says: Chemerinsky, *Federal Jurisdiction*, 150.

245   More than two dozen lawsuits were brought: Ibid., 166.

245   The most famous articulation of the political-question doctrine: Alexander Bickel, *The Least Dangerous Branch* (New Haven: Yale University Press, 1962), 184.

247   The Supreme Court was quite explicit: *Bush v. Gore*, 531 U.S. at 111.

248   Justice Leander Shaw, in a concurring opinion: *Gore v. Harris*, 773 So.2d 524, 538-34 (Fla. 2000).

248   In *Murdock v. City of Memphis*: *Murdock v. City of Memphis*, 87 U.S. (20 Wall.) 590 (1875).

249   Hawaii designated two sets of electors: *Bush v. Gore*, 531 U.S. at 127 (Stevens, J., dissenting).

249   *Citizens United v. Federal Election Commission*: *Citizens United v. Federal Election Commission*, 558 U.S. 310 (2010).

249   a provision of the Bipartisan Campaign Finance Reform Act: The Bipartisan Campaign Reform Act of 2002, Pub.L. 107-155, 116 Stat. 81, enacted March 27, 2002, H. R. 2356).

249   In 1907, Congress adopted a law: Tillman Act of 1907, ch. 420, 34 Stat. 864 (1907).

250   "All contributions by corporations": President Theodore Roosevelt, Fifth Annual Message to Congress, 59th Cong., 1st Sess., in 40 Cong. Rec. § 96 (Dec. 5, 1905).

250   In 1946, this ban was extended: Labor Management Relations (Taft-Hartley) Act of 1947, Pub. L. No. 80-101, § 304, 61 Stat. 136, 159.

250   Congress amended federal election law in 1974: Federal Election Campaign Act Amendments of 1974, Pub. L. No. 93-443, 88 Stat. 1263.

250   In 2002, in the Bipartisan: 2 U.S.C. § 441b.

251   The Supreme Court . . . had upheld it in *McConnell*: *McConnell v. Federal Election Commission*, 540 U.S. 93 (2003).

251   state laws limiting corporate spending: *Austin v. Michigan Chamber of Commerce*, 494 U.S. 652 (1990).

252   "[p]olitical speech is indispensable to decisionmaking": *Citizens United v. Federal Election Commission*, 558 U.S. at 313.

252   "The censorship we now confront is vast": Ibid., 558 U.S. at 354.

253   "The Court has explained that disclosure": Ibid., 558 U.S. at 369.

253   First, the premise that spending money: *Buckley v. Valeo*, 424 U.S. 1 (1976).

253   Spending money is conduct: J. Skelly Wright, "Politics and the Constitution: Is Money Speech?" 85 *Yale Law Journal* 1001, 1019–20 (1976); J. Skelly Wright, "Money and the Pollution of Politics: Is the First Amendment an Obstacle to Political Equality?" 82 *Columbia Law Review* 609 (1982).

253   "Money is property; it is not speech": *Nixon v. Shrink Missouri Government PAC*, 528 U.S. 377, 398 (2000).

253   "In the context of election to public office": *Citizens United v. Federal Election Commission*, 558 U.S. at 394 (Stevens, J., dissenting).

254   important reasons for allowing restrictions of corporate expenditures: J. Fred Giertz and Dennis H. Sullivan, "Campaign Expenditures and Election Outcomes: A Critical Note," 32 *Public Choice* 157 (1977) (attempting to quantify the role of campaign expenditures in elections); Richard Briffault, "A Changing Supreme Court Considers Major Campaign Finance Questions: *Randall v. Sorrell* and *Wisconsin Right to Life v. FEC*," 5 *Election Law Journal* 74, 79 (2006) (discussing the effects of spending in elections).

254   the Court previously had allowed restrictions: *Austin v. Michigan Chamber of Commerce*, 494 U.S. at 673.

254   In 2012, the Supreme Court emphasized that unions: *Knox v. Service Employees Intern. Union 1000*, 132 S. Ct. 2277 (2012).

255   "At bottom, the Court's opinion is thus a rejection": *Citizens United v. Federal Election Commission*, 558 U.S. at 479 (Stevens, J., dissenting).

256   In fact, just four years earlier: *Garcetti v. Ceballos*, 547 U.S. 410 (2006).

256   "We hold that when public employees make statements": Ibid., 547 U.S. at 421.

256   Since Richard Nixon ran for president: Erwin Chemerinsky, *The Conservative Assault on the Constitution* (New York: Simon & Schuster, 2010) at 16.

257   It was not until 1978: *First National Bank of Boston v. Bellotti*, 435 U.S. 765 (1978).

257   The Supreme Court's decision in *Arizona*: *Arizona Free Enterprise Club's Freedom Club PAC v. Bennett*, 131 S. Ct. 2806 (2011).

258   As Justice Kagan noted in her dissent: Ibid., 131 S. Ct. at 2833 (Kagan, J., dissenting).

260   The Voting Rights Act of 1965: Voting Rights Act of 1965, 42 U.S.C. §§ 1973–1973aa-6; Dayna L. Cunningham, "Who Are to Be the Electors? A Reflection on the History of Voter Registration in the United States," 9 *Yale Law & Policy Review* 370, 373 (1991); Jennifer Denise Rogers, "Miller v. Johnson: The Supreme Court 'Remaps' Shaw v. Reno," 56 *Louisiana Law Review* 981, 985–93 (1996) (discussing importance of the Voting Rights Act of 1965).

261   Lawsuits were brought challenging the constitutionality: *Georgia v. United States*, 411 U.S. 526 (1973); *City of Rome v. United States*, 446 U.S. 156 (1980); *Lopez v. Monterey County*, 525 U.S. 266 (1999).

261   Most recently, the law was set to expire in 2007: Simon Lazarus, "Stripping the Gears of National Government," 106 *Northwestern University Law Review* 769, 823 (2012).

261 **it found that there were 650 instances:** Voting Rights Act: Evidence of Continued Need. Hearing before the Subcommittee on the Judiciary of the House of Representatives, 109th Congress, 34 (2006).

261 **President George W. Bush signed the extension:** Fannie Lou Hamer, Rosa Parks, and Coretta Scott King Voting Rights Act Reauthorization and Amendments Act of 2006, Pub. L. No. 109-246, 120 Stat. 577.

261 **In *Shelby County, Alabama v. Holder*:** Shelby County, Alabama v. Holder, 133 S. Ct. at 2612.

Chapter 8: The Question of Judicial Review

267 **I think here of *United States v. Nixon*:** United States v. Nixon, 418 U.S. 683 (1974).

267 **On June 17, 1972, a burglary occurred:** Carl Bernstein and Bob Woodward, *All the President's Men* (New York: Simon & Schuster, 1974) (telling the history of the Watergate break-in and the investigation of its cover-up); Fred Emery, *Watergate: The Corruption of American Politics and the Fall of Richard Nixon* (New York: Crown, 2012) (a detailed history of the events of Watergate).

268 **Cox subpoenaed tapes of White House conversations:** For an excellent history of these events, see Theodore White, *Breach of Faith: The Fall of Richard Nixon* (New York: Scribner, 1975).

269 **By coincidence, the House Judiciary Committee:** Impeachment of Richard Nixon, President of the United States, H.R. Rep. No. 93-1305 (1974).

269 **The opinion was written by Chief Justice Warren Burger:** *United States v. Nixon*, 418 U.S. at 683.

269 **"The President's counsel, as we have noted":** Ibid., 418 U.S. at 703.

270 **The Court acknowledged that the need for candor:** Ibid., 418 U.S. at 705.

270 **"the privilege can be said to derive":** Ibid., 418 U.S. at 705–6.

270 **"neither the doctrine of separation of powers":** Ibid., 418 U.S. at 706.

270 **"The impediment that an absolute":** Ibid., 418 U.S. at 707.

270 **allowing "the privilege to withhold evidence":** Ibid., 418 U.S. at 712.

270 **The tapes and transcripts showed that Nixon:** For a description of the events surrounding the revelation of the tapes, their content, and Nixon's resignation, see Bob Woodward and Carl Bernstein, *The Final Days* (New York: Simon & Schuster, 1975).

273 **They would "still be called upon to interpret":** James MacGregor Burns, *Packing the Court: The Rise of Judicial Power and the Coming Crisis of the Supreme Court* (New York: Penguin, 2009), 254.

273 **The power of judicial review was created:** *Marbury v. Madison*, 5 U.S. (1 Cranch) 137 (1803).

273 **"it is the province and duty of the judicial department":** Ibid., 5 U.S. at 177.

273 **The Netherlands, for example:** Mark Tushnet, *Taking the Constitution Away from the Courts* (Princeton: Princeton University Press, 1999), 163–64.

273 **Mark Tushnet in 1999 wrote a book:** Ibid.

274 **In a chapter titled "Against Judicial Review":** Ibid., 154.

274 **"[t]he effects of doing away with judicial review":** Ibid.

274 **He points out, "The examples of Great Britain":** Ibid., 163.

274 **He believes that the results of "popular constitutionalism":** Ibid., 183–86.

274 **Larry Kramer wrote a well-received book:** Larry Kramer, *The People Themselves: Popular Constitutionalism and Judicial Review* (New York: Oxford University Press, 2005).

275 "based on the fact that the Constitution never granted": Burns, *Packing the Court,* 254.

275 **an argument made in the nineteenth century:** James Bradley Thayer, "The Origin and Scope of the American Doctrine of Constitutional Law," 7 *Harvard Law Review* 129 (1893).

275 **contemporary academics who have called for an elimination:** Keith Whittington, *Constitutional Construction* (Cambridge, Mass.: Harvard University Press, 1999).

276 **This is the primary argument advanced:** *Marbury v. Madison,* 5 U.S. at 178.

276 **Chief Justice John Marshall explained:** Ibid.

276 **In a telling passage, Tushnet admits:** Tushnet, *Taking the Constitution Away,* 174.

277 **A lawsuit was initiated in 1990:** *Coleman v. Wilson,* 912 F.Supp. 1282, 1316 (E.D.Cal. 1995).

277 **The court found that mentally ill inmates:** Ibid.

277 **In 2007, a special master reported:** *Brown v. Plata,* 131 S. Ct. 1910, 1926 (2011).

277 **"the California prison medical care system is broken":** Ibid., 131 S. Ct. at 1927.

277 **"it is an uncontested fact that, on average":** Ibid.

277 **The three-judge court heard fourteen days:** *Coleman v. Schwarzenegger,* 922 F.Supp. 2d 822 (E.D.Ca. 2009).

278 **In 2011, the Supreme Court, in *Brown v. Plata*:** *Brown v. Plata,* 131 S. Ct. 1910 (2011).

278 **"Prisoners retain the essence of human dignity":** Ibid., 131 S. Ct. at 1928.

278 **On January 8, 2013, Governor Jerry Brown announced:** A Proclamation by the Governor of the State of California, January 8, 2013, http://gov.ca.gov/news.php?id= 17886.

278 **In April 2013, the three-judge court issued:** *Coleman v. Brown,* 922 F.Supp.2d 1004 (E.D.Cal. 2013).

278 **Rather than comply, Governor Brown again asked:** *Brown v. Plata,* 134 S. Ct. 436 (2013).

280 **California adopted a law:** *Saenz v. Roe,* 526 U.S. 429 (1999).

280 **In a case forty years earlier:** *Shapiro v. Thompson,* 394 U.S. 618 (1969).

280 **Such discrimination against out-of-staters occurs:** Erwin Chemerinsky, *Constitutional Law: Principles and Policies,* 4th ed. (New York: Wolters Kluwer, 2011), § 5.3 (describing law of the dormant commerce clause).

280 **a Michigan law that allowed in-state wineries:** *Granholm v. Heald,* 544 U.S. 460 (2005).

281 **Dean Kramer, for example, compares favorably:** Kramer, *The People Themselves,* 15–16.

281 **many states did not provide free attorneys:** *Gideon v. Wainwright,* 372 U.S. 335 (1963).

282 **in the vast majority of states, judges face:** Daniel Blynn, "Cy Pres Distributions: Ethics and Reform," 25 *Georgetown Journal of Legal Ethics* 435, 440 (2012) (thirty-nine states have elected judges); Paul Brace and Brent D. Boyea, "Judicial Selection Methods and Capital Punishment in the American States," in Matthew J. Streb ed., *Running for Judge: The Rising Political, Financial, and Legal Stakes of Judicial Elections* (New York: NYU Press, 2007), 186 (comparing review of capital cases with elected as opposed to unelected judges).

283 **Tushnet, for example, says that a populist:** Tushnet, *Taking the Constitution Away,* 190–91.

284 **"Populist constitutional law rests on the idea":** Ibid., 186.

284 **The Texas town that wanted student prayers:** *Santa Fe Indep. School Dist. v. Doe,* 530 U.S. 290 (2000) (declaring unconstitutional student-delivered prayers at high school football games).

285 **a famous book, published in 1991, by Professor Gerald Rosenberg:** Gerald Rosenberg, *The Hollow Hope: Can Courts Bring About Social Change?* (Chicago: University of Chicago Press, 1991).

285 ***Brown v. Board of Education* played a key role:** Harvard law professor Michael Klarman has argued that it was the backlash against *Brown* and desegregation that ultimately brought about change. Michael J. Klarman, "How *Brown* Changed Race Relations: The Backlash Thesis," 81 *Journal of American History* 81 (1994).

286 **In the Pentagon Papers case:** *New York Times v. United States*, 403 U.S. 713 (1971).

286 **A simple illustration of this:** *United States v. Lopez*, 514 U.S. 549 (1995).

288 **For example, in *The Hollow Hope*:** Rosenberg, *Hollow Hope*, 353–55.

288 **In 1973, when *Roe* was decided:** Mark A. Graber, "The Ghost of Abortion Past: Pre-*Roe* Abortion Law in Action," 1 *Virginia Journal of Social Policy & the Law* 309 (1994) (detailing pre-*Roe* abortion law); Paul Benjamin Linton, "*Roe v. Wade* and the History of Abortion Regulation," 15 *American Journal of Law & Medicine* 227 (1989).

288 **Linda Greenhouse and Reva Siegel have written:** Linda Greenhouse and Reva B. Siegel, "Before (and After) Roe v. Wade: New Questions About Backlash," 120 *Yale Law Journal* 2028 (2011).

289 **Alexander Bickel, in one of the most famous books:** Alexander Bickel, *The Least Dangerous Branch: The Supreme Court at the Bar of Politics* (New Haven, Conn.: Yale University Press, 1962), 16.

290 **Professor Jesse Choper noted:** Jesse Choper, *Judicial Review and the National Political Process* (Chicago: University of Chicago Press, 1980), 4; Jesse Choper, "The Supreme Court and the Political Branches: Democratic Theory and Practice," 122 *University of Pennsylvania Law Review* 810, 815 (1974) ("[T]he procedure of judicial review is in conflict with the fundamental principle of democracy—majority rule under conditions of political freedom").

290 **Similarly, the late professor John Hart Ely:** John Hart Ely, *Democracy and Distrust* (Cambridge, Mass.: Harvard University Press, 1980), 1.

290 **Professor Michael Perry also began his book:** Michael Perry, *The Constitution, the Courts, and Human Rights* (New Haven, Conn.: Yale University Press, 1982), 10.

290 **As historian Charles A. Beard remarked:** Erwin Chemerinsky, "Foreword: The Vanishing Constitution," 103 *Harvard Law Review* 43, 65 (1989) (quoting Charles A. Beard).

290 **James Madison and Alexander Hamilton led the fight:** Thomas I. Cronin, *Direct Democracy: The Politics of Initiative, Referendum, and Recall* (Lincoln, Neb.: iUniverse, 1999), 24–26.

291 **"The very purpose of a Bill of Rights":** *West Virginia State Board of Education v. Barnette*, 319 U.S. 624, 638 (1943).

292 **for stealing $153 worth of videotapes:** *Lockyer v. Andrade*, 583 U.S. 63 (2003).

292 **Ten Commandments monument:** *Van Orden v. Perry*, 545 U.S. 677 (2005).

Chapter 9: Changing the Court

294 **Tushnet said, "Looking at judicial review":** Mark Tushnet, *Taking the Constitution Away from the Courts* (Princeton, N.J.: Princeton University Press, 1999), 153.

295 **David Currie and Judge Frank Easterbrook:** David P. Currie, "The Most Insignificant Justice," 50 *University of Chicago Law Review* 460 (1983); Frank H. Easterbrook, "The Most Insignificant Justice: Further Evidence," 50 *University of Chicago Law Review* 481, 494–96 (1983).

295 **As Currie noted, "In constitutional cases":** Currie, "The Most Insignificant Justice," 468.

295 **Thus, "Duvall sat for twenty-five years":** Ibid.

295 **Currie notes that Justice John McKinley:** Ibid., 472.

295 **But such justices are not limited:** Albert P. Blaustein and Roy M. Mersky, *The First One Hundred Justices: Statistical Studies on the Supreme Court of the United States* (Mishawaka, Ind.: Olympic, 1978), 32–51. Based on a survey of academics, both Minton and Whittaker were ranked as "failures." The survey rated twelve justices "great" (J. Marshall, Story, Taney, Harlan I, Holmes, Hughes, Brandeis, Stone, Cardozo, Black, Frankfurter, and Warren); fifteen "near great" (W. Johnson, Curtis, Miller, Field, Bradley, Waite, E. White, Taft, Sutherland, Douglas, R. Jackson, W. Rutledge, Harlan II, Brennan, and Fortas); fifty-five "average"; six "below average" (T. Johnson, Moore, Trimble, Barbour, Woods, and H. Jackson); and eight "failure" (Van Devanter, McReynolds, Butler, Byrnes, Burton, Vinson, Minton, and Whittaker).

295 **a survey of academics put him and Whittaker:** Ibid.

297 **In one recent case about the privacy of text messages:** *City of Ontario v. Quon*, 560 U.S. 746 (2010).

298 **Social psychologists long have documented:** Ralph H. Turner, "Role Theory," in Jonathan H. Turner ed., *Handbook of Sociological Theory* (New York: Kluwer, 2001), 233, 233–34; B. J. Biddle, "Recent Development in Role Theory," 12 *Annual Review of Sociology* 67, 73–74 (1986) (describing "organizational" role theory). For a discussion of how role definition affects judicial behavior, see Jed Handelsman Shugerman, "The Twist of Long Terms: Judicial Elections, Role Fidelity, and American Tort Law," 98 *Georgetown Law Journal* 1349, 1401 (2010).

299 **The Alaska Constitution creates:** Alaska Const. art. IV, §§ 5–8; Kelly Taylor, "Silence at a Price? Judicial Questionnaires and the Independence of Alaska's Judiciary," 25 *Alaska Law Review* 303 (2008); Sosie M. Dosik, "Alaska's Merit Selection for Judges," 21 *Alaska Law Review* 305 (2004); Tillman J. Finley, "Judicial Selection in Alaska: Justifications and Proposed Courses of Reform," 20 *Alaska Law Review* 49 (June 2003).

299 **"The governor shall fill any vacancy":** Alaska Const. art. IV, § 5.

300 **United States Circuit Judge Nominating Commission:** Larry Berkson, Susan Carbon, and Alan Neff, "A Study of the U.S. Circuit Judge Nominating Commission," *Judicature* (September 1979), 104; Sheldon Goldman, *Picking Federal Judges: Lower Court Selection from Roosevelt through Reagan* (New Haven, Conn.: Yale University Press, 1997), 6.

301 **More generally, when Carter took office, in 1977:** Nancy Scherer, "Diversifying the Federal Bench," 105 *Northwestern University Law Review* 587, 589 (2011).

301 **Carter's merit-selection system made significant progress:** Ibid.

305 **This led Patricia Ireland:** David G. Savage, "Democrats Skeptical on Thomas Testimony," *Los Angeles Times*, September 12, 1991, A1, A18 (quoting Patricia Ireland of the National Organization for Women: "[Thomas] is apparently one of only two lawyers in the country who do not have an opinion on [*Roe*]. The other, of course, is David Souter").

305 **Thomas made this claim despite having written:** Clarence Thomas, "The Higher Law Background of the Privileges or Immunities Clause of the Fourteenth Amendment," 12 *Harvard Journal of Law & Public Policy* 63, 62n2 (1989); Erwin Chemerinsky, "October Tragedy," 65 *Southern California Law Review* 1497, 1501–2 (1992).

305   **Robert Post and Reva Siegel:** Robert Post and Reva Siegel, "Questioning Justice: Law and Politics in Judicial Confirmation Hearings," *Yale Law Journal* (The Pocket Part), January 2006, http://yalelawjournal.org/images/pdfs/27.pdf.

306   **Presidents, of course, have always considered:** Laurence H. Tribe, *God Save This Honorable Court: How the Choice of Supreme Court Justices Shapes Our History* (New York: Random House, 1985).

306   **During the nineteenth century, the Senate rejected:** Ibid., 20.

306   **Professor Grover Rees explains:** Grover Rees, "Questions for Supreme Court Nominees at Confirmation Hearings: Excluding the Constitution," 17 *Georgia Law Review* 913, 944 (1983).

308   **Professor Stephen Carter makes this argument:** Stephen Carter, "Essays on the Supreme Court Appointment Process: The Confirmation Mess," 101 *Harvard Law Review* 1185, 1198 (1988).

310   **Texas governor Rick Perry advocated:** Rick Perry, *Fed Up: Our Fight to Save America From Washington* (New York: Hachette, 2011).

310   **The idea is that each justice would be appointed:** Roger C. Cramton and Paul D. Carrington, *Reforming the Court: Term Limits for Supreme Court Justices* (Durham, N.C.: Carolina Academic Press, 2006).

310   **Supreme Court justices are serving ever longer:** Steven G. Calabresi and James Lindgren, "Term Limits for the Supreme Court: Life Tenure Reconsidered," 29 *Harvard Journal of Law and Public Policy* 769, 777–87 (2006).

312   **Paul Carrington and Roger Cramton:** Cramton and Carrington, *Reforming the Court,* 79.

313   **On Tuesday, December 12, 2000:** *Bush v. Gore,* 531 U.S. 98 (2000).

313   **A written opinion serves many functions:** Erwin Chemerinsky, "The Rhetoric of Constitutional Law," 100 *Michigan Law Review* 2008, 2010–22 (2002).

316   **a writ of certiorari on behalf of Morton Berger:** *State v. Berger,* 212 Ariz. 473, 134 P.3d 378 (2006).

316   **The Supreme Court, without explanation, denied review:** *Berger v. Horne,* 134 S. Ct. 626 (2014).

318   **What rationale is there for excluding cameras:** The primary advocate among academics against cameras in the Supreme Court has been professor Nancy Marder. See, e.g., Nancy Marder, "Sunday Dialogue: Putting the Justices on TV," *New York Times,* December 11, 2011, http://www.nytimes.com/2011/12/11/opinion/sunday/sunday-dialogue-putting-the-justices-on-tv.html?pagewanted=all&_r=0.

321   **October Term 2009 set the all-time record:** Adam Liptak, "Justices Are Long on Words, But Short on Guidance," *New York Times,* November 17, 2010.

322   **"Brown v. Board of Education, the towering 1954 decision":** Ibid.

322   **The decision in the Affordable Care Act case:** *National Federation of Independent Business v. Sebelius,* 132 S. Ct. 2566 (2012).

322   **In Crawford v. Washington:** *Crawford v. Washington,* 541 U.S. 36 (2004).

322   **Another example comes from the area of civil litigation:** *Philip Morris USA v. Williams,* 549 U.S. 346 (2007).

322   **For the third time in eleven years:** *State Farm v. Campbell,* 538 U.S. 408 (2003); *BMW of North America, Inc. v. Gore,* 517 U.S. 559 (1996).

323   **The Supreme Court, in a 5–4 decision:** *Philip Morris USA v. Williams,* 549 U.S. at 353.

323   **However, the Court qualified this holding:** Ibid., 549 U.S. at 355.

323 "nothing short of ludicrous": *Lee v. Weisman ex rel. Weisman*, 505 U.S. 577, 637, 638 (1992) (Scalia, J., dissenting).

324 "entirely irrational": *Austin v. Mich. Chamber of Commerce*, 494 U.S. 652, 685 (1990) (Scalia, J., dissenting).

324 not "pass[ing] the most gullible scrutiny": *Morgan v. Illinois*, 504 U.S. 719, 748 (1992) (Scalia, J., dissenting).

324 "nothing short of preposterous": *Romer v. Evans*, 517 U.S. 620, 652–53 (1996) (Scalia, J., dissenting).

324 "one must grieve for the Constitution": *Morrison v. Olson*, 487 U.S. 654, 726 (1988) (Scalia, J., dissenting).

324 "so unsupported in reason and so absurd in application": *Bd. of Educ. of Kiryas Joel Vill. Sch. Dist. v. Grumet*, 512 U.S. 687, 735 (1994) (Scalia, J., dissenting); *Grady v. Corbin*, 495 U.S. 508, 542, 543 (1990) (Scalia, J., dissenting).

324 "vandalizes . . . our people's tradition.": *J.E.B. v. Alabama ex rel. T.B.*, 511 U.S. 127, 163 (1994) (Scalia, J., dissenting).

324 "Today's tale . . . is so transparently false": *Michigan v. Bryant*, 131 S. Ct. 1143, 1168 (2011) (Scalia, J., dissenting).

327 During his confirmation hearings to be chief justice: Steven A. Drizin, "The Lee Arthur Hester Case and the Unfinished Business of the United States Supreme Court to Protect Juveniles During Police Interrogations," 6 *Northwestern Journal of Law & Social Policy* 358, 384–86 (2011) (describing events surrounding Fortas's resignation).

327 a claim of executive privilege by Vice President Dick Cheney: *Cheney v. United States District Court for the District of Columbia*, 542 U.S. 367 (2004).

327 There was a request for Scalia to recuse: *Cheney v. United States District Court for the District of Columbia*, 541 U.S. 913 (2004) (opinion of Scalia, J.).

328 Justice Clarence Thomas had not disclosed his wife's income: James Sample, "Supreme Court Recusal from Marbury to the Modern Day," 26 *Georgetown Journal of Legal Ethics* 95, 133–36 (2013).

328 As professor James Sample noted: Ibid., 132.

Conclusion: How Should We Talk and Think About the Supreme Court?

331 Salvadoran immigrant Francisco Castaneda: *Hui v. Castaneda*, 559 U.S. 799 (2010).

332 a California Department of Corrections official wrote: *Castaneda v. Hui*, 542 F.3d 682, 686 (9th Cir. 2008).

332 The U.S. Supreme Court previously had ruled: *Wilson v. Seiter*, 501 U.S. 294 (1991).

332 Justice Sotomayor, writing for the Court: *Hui v. Castaneda*, 559 U.S. at 805.

335 In the words of Alexander Hamilton: *The Federalist* 78 (Hamilton), in Robert Scigliano, ed., *The Federalist: A Commentary on the Constitution of the United States* (New York: Random House, 2001), 495.

335 Some of the most prominent justices and scholars: *Baker v. Carr*, 369 U.S. 186, 267 (Frankfurter, J., dissenting) ("The Court's authority—possessed of neither the purse nor the sword—ultimately rests on sustained public confidence in its moral sanction."); Alexander Bickel, *The Supreme Court and the Idea of Progress* (New Haven, Conn.: Yale University Press, 1970), 94–95; Jesse H. Choper, "The Scope of National Power Vis-à-vis the States: The Dispensability of Judicial Review," 86 *Yale Law Journal* 1552, 1580 (1977).

335 According to Gallup polls: Erwin Chemerinsky, "How Should We Think About Bush v. Gore?" 34 *Loyola University of Chicago Law Journal* 1, 3–4 (2002).

336 **approval of the Court among Republicans went from 60 percent:** Ibid.

336 **As Professor John Hart Ely observed:** John Hart Ely, *Democracy and Distrust* (Cambridge, Mass.: Harvard University Press, 1980), 47–48.

337 **When John Roberts appeared before the Senate Judiciary Committee:** Confirmation Hearing on the Nomination of John G. Roberts Jr. to Be Chief Justice of the United States: Hearing Before S. Comm. on the Judiciary, 109th Cong. 55 (2005) (statement of John G. Roberts).

337 **Justice Sonia Sotomayor's subsequent confirmation hearings:** "Sotomayor Pledges 'Fidelity to the Law,' CNNPolitics.com, July 13, 2009, http://www.cnn.com/2009 /POLITICS/07/13/sotomayor.hearing/index.html.

338 **When John Roberts wrote in *Parents Involved*:** *Parents Involved in Community Schools v. Seattle School District No. 1*, 555 U.S. 701 (2007).

339 **The justices had to make a choice:** *Grutter v. Bollinger*, 539 U.S. 306 (2003).

340 **"unreasonable" for the government to take DNA:** *Maryland v. King*, 133 S. Ct. 1958 (2013).

341 **On June 25, 2013:** *Shelby County, Alabama v. Holder*, 133 S. Ct. 2612 (2013), discussed in chapter 7.

341 **"It is well established that Congress' judgment":** Ibid., 133 S. Ct. at 2636 (Ginsburg, J., dissenting).

341 **The next day, June 26:** *United States v. Windsor*, 133 S. Ct. 2675 (2013), discussed in chapter 7.

341 **He said that the majority's holding was "jaw-dropping":** Ibid., 133 S. Ct. at 2698 (Scalia, J., dissenting).

Index